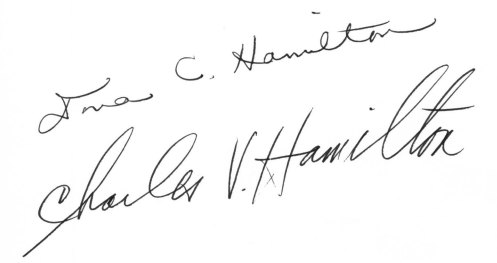

For C. Hamilton

Charles V. Hamilton

The Dual Agenda

The Dual Agenda

Power, Conflict, and Democracy Series

Robert Y. Shapiro, Editor

Power, Conflict, and Democracy:

American Politics Into the Twenty-first Century

This series focuses on how the will of the people and the public interest are promoted, encouraged, or thwarted. It aims to question not only the direction American politics will take as it enters the twenty-first century but also the direction American politics has already taken.

The series addresses the role of interest groups and social and political movements; openness in American politics; important developments in institutions such as the executive, legislative, and judicial branches at all levels of government as well as the bureaucracies thus created; the changing behavior of politicians and political parties; the role of public opinion; and the functioning of mass media. Because problems drive politics, the series also examines important policy issues in both domestic and foreign affairs.

The series welcomes all theoretical perspectives, methodologies, and types of evidence that answer important questions about trends in American politics.

Power, Conflict, and Democracy:

American Politics Into the Twenty-First Century

The Dual Agenda

Race and Social Welfare Policies of Civil Rights Organizations

Dona Cooper Hamilton and Charles V. Hamilton

Columbia University Press

New York

Columbia University Press
Publishers Since 1893
New York   Chichester, West Sussex

Copyright © 1997 Columbia University Press

Library of Congress Cataloging-in-Publication Data
Hamilton, Dona C.
The dual agenda : race and social welfare policies of civil rights organizations /
Dona Cooper Hamilton and Charles V. Hamilton.
       p.   cm. — (Power, conflict, and democracy)
   Includes bibliographical references (p.) and index.
   ISBN 0–231–10364–6 (cloth : acid-free paper). — ISBN 0–231–10365–4
   (paper)
     1. Afro-Americans—Civil rights—Societies, etc.—History—20th century.
   2. Afro-Americans—Government policy—History—20th century. 3. Civil
   rights workers—United States—Political activity—History—20th century.
   4. Public welfare—United States—History—20th century. 5. Lobbying—
   United States—History—20th century.   I. Hamilton, Charles V. II. Title.
   III. Series.
   E185.615.H277 1997
   323.1'196073—dc21   96–39536

♾

Casebound editions of Columbia University Press books are printed
on permanent and durable acid-free paper.

Printed in the United States of America

c 10 9 8 7 6 5 4 3 2 1
p 10 9 8 7 6 5 4 3 2 1

In loving memory of our daughter
Carol Louise Hamilton

CONTENTS

ACKNOWLEDGMENTS

Many individuals and institutions contributed to this project—conceptually, intellectually, financially—over the more than two decades of its development. We needed that help and are enormously grateful to all of them.

The late professor Russ Nixon of the Columbia University School of Social Work ("Full employment is the best income-maintenance program," he wisely counseled) was a lasting influence. Gladys Bing of the National Urban League library in New York City provided the first documents on that organization and the New Deal, which inaugurated Dona Hamilton's research for her doctoral dissertation (from which this larger study developed). From that point on, we gathered more than eight thousand pieces of archival materials covering six decades for this study.

Research libraries and their professional staffs were especially invaluable: Mary Wolfskill, Fred Bauman, and Mike Klein at the Library of Congress; Linda Hanson of the Lyndon Baines Johnson Library; Susan Voge of the Lehman College library; Susan McElrath of the Bethune Museum and Archives; the Columbia University School of Social Work library; Schomburg Library of New York; the Martin Luther King, Jr. Library and Archives; the State Historical Society of Wisconsin; and the Columbia University Oral History Collection.

Norman Hill of the A. Philip Randolph Institute gave us access to important materials on the Freedom Budget. Professor Judith Russell of Barnard College generously provided us her voluminous papers from the Nixon Archives. The scholarship of Professor Philip Thompson of Barnard College on race, politics, and public policy has informed our thinking on these issues. We appreciate Sen. Daniel P. Moynihan's permission to consult his papers at the Library of Congress.

We hardly could have amassed and kept track of these materials without the persistent research and other assistance of Austin Cooper, Kurt Dassel, Anthony Fletcher, Boyardo Gonzalez, and Debra McCoy. Hazel Sills expertly indexed thousands of documents early in the data-gathering stage. Aida Llabaly provided all-around secretarial help with her usual commitment and good humor.

We obviously benefited from research funds provided at critical times by the Research Foundation of the City University of New York, annual faculty research funds from Columbia University, and from a Lyndon Baines Johnson Library Foundation Moody Grant. At an early stage we were awarded a month-long stay as scholars-in-residence at the Rockefeller Foundation's Bellagio Study and Conference Center in Lake Como, Italy, giving us the opportunity to pull together our thoughts and concepts as we moved forward.

This brings us to the people who finally got their hands on our "first draft." Colleague and friend, Professor Robert Y. Shapiro of Columbia University was quite perceptive in making sure it was indeed only a first draft. His stern marginal comments without a doubt improved the original document immeasurably—draft after draft. Editor John Michel of the Columbia University Press gently and professionally convinced us that it was neither wise nor necessary to try to use each of the thousands of documents we collected. When he said "cut, cut, cut," we grimaced, and proceeded to do so. He and Bob Shapiro may not believe we are truly grateful for their tenacity and torture, but we assure them—now—we are. No author could have a better copyeditor than Roy Thomas, who probably had, we readily concede, the most daunting of tasks. Since we know what he was handed to work with, we fully appreciate his excellent professional skills and his meticulous "queries."

Several anonymous scholars read the drafts in progress and offered constructive critical comments that helped us think through and sharpen our organization and presentation, not to mention some dubious concepts we had assumed, inaccurately, to be self-evident.

All these sources were helpful, and we hasten to add, out of fairness to them, any harm done to the subject is our doing, not theirs.

ABBREVIATIONS

AAA	Agricultural Adjustment Administration
AARP	American Association of Retired Persons
ACLU	American Civil Liberties Union
ADA	Americans for Democratic Action
ADC	Aid to Dependent Children
AFDC	Aid to Families with Dependent Children
AFDC-UP	Aid to Families with Dependent Children—Unemployed Parent
AFL	American Federation of Labor
AMA	American Medical Association
AVC	American Veterans Committee
BLS	Bureau of Labor Statistics
BSCP	Brotherhood of Sleeping Car Porters
CAA	Community Action Agency
CBC	Congressional Black Caucus
CCC	Civilian Conservation Corps
CDF	Children's Defense Fund
CETA	Comprehensive Employment and Training Act
CIO	Committee for Industrial Organization / Congress of Industrial Organization
CORE	Congress of Racial Equality
CWA	Civil Works Administration
CWEP	Community Work Experience Program

EAC	Emergency Advisory Committee
FAP	Family Assistance Plan
FEPC	Fair Employment Practice Committee
FERA	Federal Emergency Relief Administration
FLSA	Fair Labor Standards Act
HEW	Department of Health, Education, and Welfare
HHS	Department of Health and Human Services
HUD	Department of Housing and Urban Development
ILGWU	International Ladies Garment Workers Union
JTPA	Job Training Partnership Act
MDTA	Manpower Development and Training Act
MOWM	March on Washington Movement
MTA	Metropolitan Transit Authority
NAACP	National Association for the Advancement of Colored People
NALC	Negro American Labor Council
NASW	National Association of Social Workers
NCNW	National Council of Negro Women
NEA	National Education Association
NETWORK	National Education Training Work
NGA	National Governors Association
NIRA	National Industrial Recovery Act
NLRA	National Labor Relations Act
NLRB	National Labor Relations Board
NMA	National Medical Association
NNC	National Negro Congress
NRA	National Recovery Administration
NUL	National Urban League
NWRO	National Welfare Rights Organization
NYA	National Youth Administration
OASDHI	Old Age, Survivors, Disability, and Health Insurance
OEM	Office of Emergency Management
OEO	Office of Economic Opportunity
OFF	Opportunities for Families
OMB	Office of Management and Budget
OPM	Office of Production Management
PBJI	Program for Better Jobs and Income

PCCR	President's Committee on Civil Rights
PIC	Private Industrial Councils
PPC	Poor People's Campaign
PSE	Public Service Employment
PUSH	People United to Serve Humanity (Operation PUSH)
PWA	Public Works Administration
SCLC	Southern Christian Leadership Conference
SNCC	Student Nonviolent Coordinating Committee
SSI	Supplemental Security Income
STFU	Southern Tenant Farmers' Union
TVA	Tennessee Valley Authority
USES	United States Employment Service
USOE	United States Office of Education
VISTA	Volunteers in Service to America
WIN	Work Incentive Program
WMC	War Manpower Commission
WPA	Works Progress Administration
YEDPA	Youth Employment Development Program Act
YOU	Youth Organizations United

The Dual Agenda

ONE

Introduction: A Warning Unheeded

On August 22, 1996, President Bill Clinton signed a welfare bill drastically changing the public assistance system that had been the law for sixty years. The new law no longer required the federal government to provide cash assistance to all eligible low-income mothers and children. Instead, the states would receive a stipulated lump sum (block grant) to run their own welfare and work programs, and they could determine largely how those capped funds would be spent. The federal law stipulated that the head of most welfare families work within two years or lose benefits. No family could receive aid for more than five years over a lifetime. Creating jobs for the needy would be a state responsibility.

In addition, the new law reduced a state's block grant by 5 percent if 25 percent of the state's welfare recipients do not work at least twenty hours a week. However, the law does not define the term *work*. The states will have to grapple with this problem. Restrictions were placed on unmarried welfare mothers under the age of eighteen: they had to attend school and live with an adult parent or guardian in order to receive assistance. A mother with a dependent child under age five is exempt from working if affordable child care is unavailable. States also could deny cash assistance, health care, and other social services to noncitizen, legal immigrant families. Further, federal benefits to low-income disabled children were to be reduced over a six-year period.

A strong supporter of Clinton's 1992 presidential bid and a civil rights activist in the 1960s, Rep. John Lewis (D, Ga.) called the new law "mean" and "downright lowdown."[1] Marian Wright Edelman, whose professional civil rights and child advocacy work dates back to the 1960s, condemned it as a "moment of shame."[2]

As the bill was being debated in the Senate in 1995, the magnitude of the proposals was not lost on many legislators. Sen. Daniel P. Moynihan (D, N.Y.) commented: "I fear we may be now commencing the end of the Social Security system. The one thing not wrong with welfare was the commitment of the federal government to help with provision of aid to dependent children. We are abandoning that commitment today."[3] And Sen. Paul Wellstone (D, Minn.) predicted that if the restrictions were passed, poor children would be the ones to suffer. He observed: "They do not have a lobbyist. They do not have the PACs [political action committees]. They are not the heavy hitters."[4]

We began this work aiming to document and explain the social welfare policy preferences of civil rights organizations over the last sixty years. What we discovered was that they had persistently warned of the dire consequences that would follow if the nation's serious racial and socioeconomic problems were ignored. The situation would worsen, and solutions would become increasingly costly and difficult. For the most part, that warning has gone unheeded.

Although civil rights groups have not been the "heavy hitters" in the unfolding decades-long debates, they have consistently tried to form liberal social welfare policies that would benefit not only blacks but all poor people.

The work of civil rights groups in fighting racial segregation and discrimination is well documented and widely known. This struggle—conducted in the courts, in Congress, in the executive branch, and through mass protest—has significantly reduced the vestiges of *legal* segregation and discrimination.

Much less is known, however, about the "social welfare agenda,"—the fight for social welfare policies to help the poor. The civil rights agenda attempts to overcome *race-specific* problems. Civil rights groups over the decades have been admonished to be more attentive to social welfare issues, to rise above a narrow focus on race and concentrate on helping all people, especially the poor. This cry came despite clear evidence that this was exactly what civil rights groups were doing and would continue to do. They always pursued a "dual agenda." But their efforts on the civil rights front overshadowed their work on the social welfare front precisely because civil rights has been such an important part of everything the groups have had to deal with.

Frequently, when they advocated policies, they were presumed to speak only for African-Americans. They were "civil rights" groups and consequently not expected to concern themselves with issues other than racial segregation and discrimination, and certainly not with economic issues that would benefit *all* poor people regardless of race and ethnicity.

Such was the case in 1937, when Walter White, executive secretary of the National Association for the Advancement of Colored People (NAACP), received this reply to his letter to Congressman Dow W. Harter (Ohio):

Dear Mr. White:

> This will acknowledge receipt of your letter of October 21st. The Record will disclose that I have always been in favor of anti-lynching legislation. I am hopeful that a satisfactory bill may be passed at the coming session.
>
> Very truly yours,

The next day (such was the efficiency of the U.S. mail in those days), White responded:

My dear Mr. Harter:

> Thank you for your good letter of October 25. However, my letter to you of October 21 was not about the anti-lynching bill but regarding the passage of a nondiscriminatory *wages and hours* bill at the next session of Congress. I am not surprised that you assumed that my communication had reference to the anti-lynching bill since that has been the subject of our correspondence for so long a time. *But you can see from my letter of the 21st that after all I can write about other matters* [emphasis added].
>
> Ever Sincerely,[5]

This 1937 exchange illustrates a persistent misperception of what civil rights groups have struggled for *on both fronts* during the past sixty years. Even when they called for social welfare policies that were not race-oriented, they were considered racially motivated or were simply ignored. Professor Theda Skocpol, for instance, writing in 1991, mischaracterized civil rights organizations and called for a greater focus on "universal" issues, concluding: "Civil rights groups tend to be preoccupied with defending affirmative action or pushing for measures targeted on the nonwhite poor."[6] The present volume will show the inaccuracy of this conclusion, not only in the 1980s and 1990s but in every decade beginning with the inception of the modern

American welfare state in the New Deal. Then and now, there have *always* been two agendas—civil rights *and* social welfare. Our study elaborates these efforts to pursue liberal social welfare policies.

Civil rights organizations have consistently emphasized three main points: (1) preference for a universal social welfare system that does not distinguish between social insurance and public assistance, (2) jobs for all in the regular labor market, and (3) federal hegemony over social welfare programs.

Regarding the first point, social welfare analysts and planners have debated the virtues of universal versus selective concepts of social welfare for years. They have argued that universalism is better than a selective concept of social welfare policy, for it does not separate society into contributors and recipients, and it recognizes that social welfare provisions play a large role in the economy and in manpower strategy. Policies are less likely to be punitive when they are not just for the poor; and no stigma is attached to receiving benefits, thus preserving human dignity. Such an approach is also seen as less costly to administer since a case need not be reviewed individually to establish eligibility.

Those favoring a selective social welfare policy have pointed out that universal allocations are expensive, for they may go to those who do not need them, and that selective benefits can be tailored to the needs of a specific population. Although civil rights organizations preferred universal programs, they feared that when resources could not provide benefits to all, the black population would lose out. To prevent this during the 1930s, they advocated that the poor "get first call on the benefits," which would require eligibility criteria based on need—means testing. In the 1940s and 1950s, when amendments to the Social Security Act were being considered, the organizations strongly favored universal social insurance programs. During the 1970s and 1980s, when public works programs were proposed, they supported universal programs but realized that these alone would be inadequate to overcome racial discrimination and segregation. The long-term unemployed would need special attention or "targeted" programs within universal programs. The issue of universalism versus selectivity persisted throughout the more than sixty years covered by this study.

The landmark 1935 Social Security Act created a two-tier social welfare system and therefore was not universal. Tier 1 encompassed social insurance: retirement and unemployment insurance, now popularly known as "Social Security" and "Unemployment Compensation." Tier 2 comprised public assistance for three categories of poor recipients: the elderly, the blind, and children from one-parent families. Tier 2 is now referred to as "welfare." Both tiers have changed over the years, but tier 1 continues to be preferred by the public for several reasons: its benefits are based on contributions by employees and employers and are considered a right. Tier 2, public assistance, is stigmatized because economic need must be proved to receive it. Public assistance grants are often regarded as undeserved and those dependent upon them are viewed as inferior. Tier 1 retirement insurance is indexed to the cost of living, and beneficiaries receive annual increments.[7] Most tier 2 grants can be increased only through legislation and thus have fallen far behind inflation. Since the passage of the Social Security Act, tier 2 programs have been politically vulnerable. Politicians have routinely attacked them and proposed various solutions to "the welfare problem" while they have supported tier 1, whose beneficiaries vote in much greater numbers than those in tier 2.

When the Social Security Act created this two-tier social welfare system, civil rights organizations rightly feared that tier 2 would become a social welfare trap in which many poor, especially blacks, would become permanently ensnared. While the bill was initially under debate, they urged the inclusion of *all* occupations under tier 1 coverage, but agricultural and household domestic workers—almost two-thirds of the black working population— were excluded. The organizations correctly predicted that this would lead to continued dependency and subordination because many blacks would be forced to rely on tier 2 assistance when they could not work.

The second main point of civil rights organizations—jobs in the regular labor market—was directly related to the two-tier social welfare system. "Regular" jobs would provide eligibility to tier 1 social insurance benefits, especially retirement pensions and unemployment compensation, and would offer opportunities for economic and social advancement.

The third point—federal hegemony in financing and in setting eligibility standards as well as implementing and monitoring programs—was preferred for three reasons:

1. When program administration and financing were left to state and local governments, especially in the early years, the black population was more likely to be excluded from benefits.

2. Society had become more mobile. Allowing each state to establish its own policies, especially residency requirements, would create a hodgepodge

and make it more difficult for people living in depressed areas to move across state lines in search of better jobs.

3. Without federal hegemony there was no way to redistribute resources to the poorer states.

Our data show that civil rights organizations never wavered in their commitment to a universal social welfare system, jobs in the regular labor market, and federal hegemony. These three policy preferences are the focus of our book. Our research has relied mainly on the archival materials of the civil rights organizations: congressional testimony, speeches, letters, memoranda, personal notes, and reports. During each period we concentrate on the national civil rights groups most prominently involved in advancing the social welfare agenda before national policymakers. During the New Deal, World War II, and immediately after, this meant only a few major groups: the NAACP, the National Urban League (NUL), the National Council of Negro Women (NCNW), the National Negro Congress (NNC), and A. Philip Randolph's Brotherhood of Sleeping Car Porters (BSCP).

As the African-American struggle accelerated, new leaders and groups emerged: the Leadership Conference on Civil Rights, Dr. Martin Luther King Jr.'s Southern Christian Leadership Conference (SCLC), a reenergized Congress of Racial Equality (CORE), the Student Nonviolent Coordinating Committee (SNCC), the A. Philip Randolph Institute, and Operation PUSH (People United to Serve Humanity). Beginning in the late 1960s, even more national groups appeared: the Congressional Black Caucus, George Wiley's National Welfare Rights Organization (NWRO), the Children's Defense Fund, and the Black Leadership Forum. (An organization prominent during the 1960s, the Black Panthers, is not covered here because it was not directly involved in lobbying at the national level.)

This book covers years of changing political and economic environments to which civil rights groups had to adapt. Until the 1960s, racial segregation and discrimination were legal in the United States. Segregationists were powerful forces in Congress. Even when liberal social welfare policies were passed, they often paid homage to this de jure condition. Civil rights groups recognized that without adequate safeguards blacks would not get their fair share of government programs. Therefore they advocated an antidiscriminatory clause in social welfare legislation. But they lacked the political muscle to accomplish this goal and had to reconcile the clear benefits of the social welfare policies with their abhorrence of the continued discrimination those programs did not address. Earlier, they had reluctantly supported policies that allowed the continuance of racial segregation and discrimination in allocation and administration of resources. But from the 1950s to 1964, they decided to no longer subordinate the civil rights agenda to the social welfare agenda, causing an intense debate over strategy within the liberal policy community (for example, aid to education, housing, and health care).

Given the loose labor market and budget problems in the latter 1990s, the prospects for achieving the social welfare agenda pushed by civil rights groups are dim indeed. But our book will show that civil rights organizations have been attentive to these issues, frequently proposing very detailed approaches to achieving an economically just society for all. They predicted as far back as the 1930s that the failure to deal adequately with these problems would only lead to greater problems. Unfortunately, they were not heeded then, and only the most supreme optimist would suggest that they will be listened to now.

TWO

Coping with the New Deal

The 1929 stock market crash caused a sharp drop in industrial production, putting millions out of work. Factories closed; families lost their homes; farmers were forced off their land. Over one million people roamed the country seeking work and begging for food. Private charities were overwhelmed with requests for basic necessities. The country was in a crisis, but Republican president Herbert Hoover was slow to respond, believing that the depression was a temporary phenomenon that would soon pass; but the economy continued to fail.

Losing faith in Hoover's leadership, the country elected Franklin D. Roosevelt president by a wide margin, and when he assumed the presidency, he acted quickly and decisively to alleviate the severe hardship experienced by the unemployed population. Between 1933 and 1935, the New Deal administration created temporary programs to stimulate the economy and provide emergency relief for the unemployed. In 1934 Roosevelt began to propose permanent social welfare reform legislation to provide social and economic security that would act as a buffer should another depression or recession occur.

The National Association for the Advancement of Colored People (NAACP) and the National Urban League (NUL) were organizations to which the black population turned for help during the crisis. At the onset of the Depression, these established and respected organizations had been advocates for Negroes for a number of years. The NAACP was founded in 1909 to pursue political, social, and civil rights through the judicial system.

The founders stressed the importance of the ballot and vowed to end discrimination and segregation of Negroes. To aid this struggle, NAACP chapters were formed throughout the country.[1]

The NUL was established in 1910 when three organizations, the National League for the Protection of Colored Women, the Committee for Improving the Industrial Conditions of Negroes in New York, and the Committee on Urban Conditions Among Negroes, consolidated to form the National League on Urban Conditions Among Negroes (shortened to its present name in 1920).[2] It believed that nothing was more important than employment: "Unsocial conditions were largely the result of uneconomic conditions—one the effect, the other the cause."[3] The NUL established affiliates in several cities with large Negro populations in order to promote its work at the national level and to provide needed local services.

Since most black workers were the last hired and the first fired, they experienced the consequences of the Great Depression earlier than other groups. White workers were rapidly replacing them in the menial jobs they had traditionally held. The NAACP noted that unemployment among Negroes was "approximately four times the Negro proportion of the population," and the organization broadened its program to include "militant and specific attacks upon the economic barriers in the path of the Negro." It promised that this new direction would not dilute its legal defense activities.[4] It would work for "jobs and justice."[5] Reflecting its motto, "Not Alms But Opportunity," the NUL had, since its founding, provided employment services, concentrating on expanding employment opportunities for blacks by persuading employers to hire them in nontraditional positions. Now its efforts were geared toward helping them find jobs of any kind.

Emphasis on Jobs: "Not Alms But Opportunity" / "Jobs and Justice"

When Franklin D. Roosevelt was elected president, the NUL and the NAACP anticipated better times. League officials had known his new Secretary of Labor, Frances Perkins, as a social reformer, and Roosevelt had been a liberal governor of New York. The NUL sent a special memorandum to the president on "Social Adjustment of Negroes in the United States" to inform him of the economic conditions faced by Negro workers.[6] The memo "was carefully analyzed for the president" by Perkins, who in acknowledging receipt of the "factual summary" assured the league that "as the Administration undertakes the problems of relief administration, of providing work opportunities, of raising basic wage levels, . . . we shall not forget the special problems of the more than 10 million people who belong to your race."[7] The NUL appreciated this response, proclaiming, "The spirit of the administration unquestionably is that of giving to all of the country's citizens, regardless of race, creed, or color, the full benefits of federal services calculated to restore confidence and prosperity."[8] An article in *Crisis*, the official organ of the NAACP, viewed the New Deal "as an unusual opportunity to get in on the ground floor . . . since the whole country is off to a new start. . . . Never before in the history of the country has . . . the majority of Americans, regardless of color or creed, been so nearly equal economically."[9] But their enthusiasm dampened as it became apparent that New Deal legislation and programs were not the panacea they had anticipated.

Throughout the 1930s, discrimination and segregation were always present. The bulk of the Negro population lived in segregated communities and attended segregated schools; and for most of them, regardless of skill and education, jobs were limited to menial labor with the lowest wages. With few states providing laws to prohibit such practices, racism was a constant factor and influenced the organizations' social welfare agenda. As the New Deal administration enacted legislation that established programs, it became clear to the NUL and the NAACP that, because of discrimination, certain policies were more helpful than others to Negroes. The organizations believed that it was crucial for black workers to be provided with jobs rather than relief, and this was the touchstone for their assessment of New Deal legislation and programs. Since the New Deal was never able to provide jobs for all those willing and able to work, the organizations found that in work programs where eligibility was based on attributed need (need for a job) rather than economic need, black workers were less likely to get jobs. In work-relief programs with selective eligibility based on income (means testing), they were more likely to be included. Consequently, the organizations, in spite of the stigma attached to means testing, preferred New Deal work-relief programs that gave the poor "first call on benefits."

The organizations favored complete federal administration of programs with regulations that limited autonomy at the state and local levels, because black workers were more likely to be treated fairly when federal guidelines were followed. They preferred programs with a white-collar component because this made it more likely that work would be allocated according to levels of skill. They strongly favored an enforceable nondiscriminatory clause in legislation to assure that black workers were not discriminated against. They preferred programs that did not have a racial quota because blacks were disproportionately out of work in relation to their numbers in the total population. Quotas resulted in the exclusion of too many black workers. They thought it was important for black professionals to be included in the administration of the programs in order to protect and interpret black interests. They also favored set wage rates without a geographic differential because this had a greater potential to improve the standard of living in the South.

One of the earliest acts of the New Deal administration was the National Industrial Recovery Act (NIRA) of 1933. It was an omnibus act designed to stimulate the private-sector economy, relieve economic distress, and resolve conflicts between labor and management. Title I of the NIRA created the National Recovery Administration (NRA), which began to establish industrial fair-practice codes with minimum wage rates and maximum hours of work in all industries. These were anti-inflationary efforts to control a wage-price spiral and to protect workers from exploitation by employers. The NRA proved to be controversial and unpopular for many reasons. Some believed that too much power was given to large industries, thus creating monopolies; others thought that it gave the federal government too much control over business and labor. Some critics regarded it as inflationary. In addition, it attempted to supervise too many small businesses, and this caused the code compliance machinery to become clogged. It was ruled unconstitutional in May 1935.[10] Many of its policies surfaced in subsequent New Deal reform legislation.

Initially, the NUL was enthusiastic about the NIRA. An editorial in *Opportunity*, its official organ, described it as "the most significant piece of legislation enacted since the Civil War." It placed the government "in absolute control of industry" and gave labor the right to collective bargaining without interference from employers.[11] But this enthusiasm waned as problems developed. The first problem Negroes encountered was the exclusion of domestic and agricultural workers from code coverage.[12] This meant that, for almost two-thirds of the Negro workforce, there was little hope of receiving any increase in wages or any improvement in working conditions.[13] In industries where codes were being established, industrialists submitted codes for Negro workers "which shamelessly provided in one manner or another for a differential wage rate of twenty to forty percent."[14] Some industries proposed geographic divisions whereby the "blackbelt" states would have the lowest wage scale. Because there appeared to be no agency or person who spoke against such unfair treatment of Negro workers, twenty-two organizations, including the NAACP and the NUL, formed the Joint Committee on National Recovery. The Joint Committee monitored the establishment of codes in all industries where there was a substantial number of Negro workers and submitted briefs against the establishment of geographic wage rates.[15]

Establishing the codes was a long, laborious process. In order to speed reemployment, Roosevelt issued the "Blue Eagle Agreement," which represented voluntary compliance with the principle of the codes until they were established in a specific industry.[16] This blanket code had a disastrous effect on Negro workers, especially in the South. There, "employers decided that if they had to pay the minimum wage . . . they would not pay it to Negroes."[17] As a result, the displacement of black workers by white workers increased.

This large-scale dismissal prompted a serious debate in the black community. It was argued by some prominent Negro leaders—for example, Robert R. Moton, president of Tuskegee Normal and Industrial Institute (now Tuskegee University)—that a racial differential wage rate would prevent the mass firing of Negroes.[18] It had been a long-standing custom for southern industries and many northern ones to pay blacks less than whites. The NAACP argued that the real problem was discrimination and that a differential wage rate based on race would only compound this problem.[19]

The association asked delegates of the American Federation of Labor (AFL), at their fifty-third annual convention, to go on record as opposed to codes with wage differentials based on race and geographic areas. It told William Green, president of the AFL, "These differentials are a grave menace not only to Negro labor but to white labor as well, for white labor can never be permanently free as long as workers of Negro and other races are discriminated against." Green telegrammed that the matter would "be given every consideration and attention at earliest possible date."[20] A racial differential wage rate was not officially sanctioned, but minimum wage rates were established according to geographic areas, which amounted to a differential wage rate based on race for Negro workers in the southeastern states.[21]

An NIRA policy that gave organized labor certain rights also caused difficulties for black workers. Section 7a of the NIRA gave workers the right to organize and bargain collectively without interference from employers. Organized labor was able to use section 7a to expand its membership and help workers take advantage of collective bargaining–particularly in the coal industry and needle trades.[22] The NAACP and the NUL had reservations about section 7a, but not because they were against the principle of collective bargaining; they could see the advantages of this. Their concerns stemmed from the discriminatory policies of local unions that prevented black workers from becoming part of the organized labor movement and thus unable to benefit from its expanded power.[23]

The NAACP pressured Green to "abolish segregation and discrimination in treatment of Negro workers" and warned the AFL that it could "never win security for white labor as long as it permits the exclusion of black labor."[24] Green did not think that discrimination within the labor movement would be a serious barrier to employment opportunities for Negroes, commenting that there was "no general discrimination against Negro workers; they are free to join most all organizations chartered by the American Federation of Labor."[25] The experiences of black workers provided evidence to the contrary. Numerous incidents of discrimination were reported to NUL affiliates.[26]

As labor gained more control over New Deal work projects, more Negroes were denied work because they were not allowed to join locals. Civil rights organizations regarded this as a violation of NRA codes. When the NAACP asked the AFL to "promptly correct these abuses," Green replied "that it was impossible to interfere in the internal affairs of affiliated national or international unions except upon their consent."[27] This was certainly a reversal of his earlier statement denying that AFL unions discriminated; but Green's admission that this was beyond his control meant no action would be taken to eliminate this practice. Section 7a policies ceased to be an issue when the Supreme Court ruled the NRA unconstitutional.[28]

Not only were Negro industrial workers having problems with New Deal social welfare policies; Negro farmers were too. The Agricultural Adjustment Act was passed in 1933 to help farmers experiencing mounting crop surpluses and depressed prices for farm products. Roosevelt was anxious to get the farm bill passed and preferred a decentralized administration, perhaps because he knew that the southern bloc of the Democratic Party would not support an agricultural program with federal control.[29] The act created the Agricultural Adjustment Administration (AAA) and gave local landowners considerable autonomy in the administration of the program. As a result, there were great variations in the treatment of tenant farmers and sharecroppers.

Many sharecroppers and tenant farmers were excluded or underpaid even though there were clear guidelines as to how benefits were to be allocated between tenant and owner. Intimidation made them reluctant to challenge the large landowners who controlled the program. An NAACP investigation substantiated reports of widespread exploitation and discrimination.[30] It presented its evidence to New Deal officials along with a proposal regarding cotton acreage reduction contracts that would make it more difficult for landowners to exploit poor farmers, but it was not adopted; nor did these officials make any effort to curtail discrimination and exploitation. The situation worsened when landowners began to evict tenant farmers and sharecroppers because the reduction in the amount of cotton grown, as well as the development of mechanized farming, had made them redundant.[31] The NAACP asked the New Deal administration to withhold payments from landowners and to provide relief to homeless farmers until these problems were resolved. It conducted a letter-writing campaign through its branches to pressure for this policy and requested the placement of Negro administrators in key positions to aid and protect tenant farmers and sharecroppers, all to no avail.[32]

The NAACP also strongly supported the Southern Tenant Farmers' Union (STFU), an integrated organization composed of sharecroppers and tenant farmers formed to fight unfair treatment under the AAA. It contributed money, provided legal aid, and urged its branches and other organizations to do the same.[33] But history has shown the inability of the NAACP and the STFU to influence AAA policies. The southern bloc of the Democratic Party (along with various acts of intimidation) proved too powerful a force against the STFU's protests. Throughout the 1930s the NAACP tried to get an antilynching bill passed which it thought would substantially reduce intimidation in the South, but it was not able to garner enough support in Congress.

Civil rights organizations were also attentive to two New Deal youth programs: the Civilian Conservation Corps (CCC) and the National Youth Administration (NYA). The CCC provided jobs to young men, who lived in segregated camps. The NYA gave work to young men and women who lived at home or away at college.

Established in March 1933, the CCC, a federal program administered by the Department of Interior, became one of the most enduring New Deal work-relief programs, lasting into the 1940s. Its major project was reforestation. The NUL and the NAACP were especially optimistic about the CCC because Interior Secretary Harold L. Ickes had been chairman of the board of the Chicago NAACP and was viewed as a friend who shared their concerns over job discrimination. The CCC provided young men not only with badly needed jobs ranging from unskilled to highly technical but also with job training and basic education. Although the CCC was not means tested, priority was given to young men from families receiving public assistance.[34] And the program's policies included a clause prohibiting discrimination.[35]

The organizations also recognized aspects of the CCC that were problematic for Negroes. Although it was a federal program, local social service agencies selected enrollees, and in some areas of the country young black men were not enrolled. Moreover, in spite of federal control, Negro enrollees were usually relegated to unskilled jobs. And since the War Department operated the camps, the segregation policy of the Armed Forces prevailed, which severely limited black enrollment and participation because there were so few black camps and Negroes were not sent out of state (white youths were moved interstate according to where they were needed for conservation work). All-black camps were difficult to establish since there was always strong opposition in the community where they were to be located.[36] A quota based on the percentage of Negroes in the population further circumscribed the participation of poor black youth.

Yet because the CCC was under federal control, the NUL and NAACP could contact federal officials and call their attention to inequities in the program. As a result, some Negroes were assigned to administrative positions, and some young black men were enrolled in areas where they had been excluded. Although most of the supervisory jobs, even in the all-black camps, were held by whites, by 1935 there were one hundred black educational advisers as well as some black physicians and chaplains attached to black camps across the country. But the NUL and the NAACP were not able to desegregate the camps.[37]

The NYA, established in 1935, helped young people to continue their education. It was transferred to the Federal Security Agency in 1940.[38] Broad NYA policies were set by the federal government but interpretation of the policies was left to the states, and responsibility for day-to-day operations was left to local sponsors. Most participants were classified as skilled, an indication that the selection process was biased toward the more skilled.[39] In spite of a great deal of autonomy at the local level, the participation of Negroes in the program was about in proportion to their numbers in the population although there were no racial quotas.[40]

Negro youth fared well in this program, and NUL affiliates reported excellent relationships with the NYA.[41] The St. Louis UL's 1939 Annual Report epitomized the feelings of the NUL: "The local administration of the NYA is the closest approach that we have in St. Louis to fulfilling the ideals of New Deal laws."[42] In other New Deal programs, the organizations had found local autonomy to be disadvantageous to Negroes, but this was not the case for the NYA. In addition, although the organizations had found that in programs that were not means tested, the participation of Negroes was limited, this did not seem to affect their participation in the NYA. The positive experience Negroes had in the NYA is attributable to Mary McLeod Bethune's involvement as Advisor for Negro Affairs. A prominent Negro leader, Bethune had a great deal of influence and was able to funnel thousands of dollars to black youth.[43]

But of course neither the CCC nor the NYA could help everyone. The two programs together provided jobs and income for less than one-third of all young people in the country who were unemployed.[44] This made it even more remarkable that the participation of Negroes in the NYA was about in proportion to their numbers in the population, and this supports the organizations' belief that the involvement of black administrators could ease racial discrimination considerably by increasing access to New Deal benefits.

With their strong preference for jobs, civil rights organizations were especially interested in the New Deal's work and work-relief programs. The Civil Works Administration (CWA) and the Public Works Administration (PWA) were work programs; the only eligibility requirement for these was the need for a job. The Federal Emergency Relief Administration (FERA) and the Works Progress Administration (WPA) were work-relief programs, for which eligibility was based on income.

As winter approached in 1933, Harry Hopkins, a social worker on the White House staff who developed New Deal work-relief policies, realized that neither the CCC, FERA, nor PWA were adequately meeting the needs of the vast number of unemployed. A significant portion of the population faced extreme hardship during the cold weather. To ease this problem, the

Civil Works Administration was established in November 1933 (lasting through March 1934) and was funded entirely by the federal government.[45] Since Hopkins was anxious to employ as many people as possible as quickly as possible, he developed CWA projects that were labor intensive, that could be started easily, and that did not require any large expenditure for equipment. All projects were done on public property. White-collar work was an important component, and teachers, artists, and writers were hired.[46]

There was a CWA employment quota for each state determined by a federal formula, and this worried the organizations, especially since the program was not means tested and preference would not be given to relief recipients (ultimately, about 50 percent of CWA workers were taken from relief rolls). Projects had to be approved by the federal government, but selection and supervision would be done at the local level.[47] This meant that the program was likely to discriminate against black workers. The NUL contacted Hopkins and other New Deal officials, appealing for "a fair share" of the four million jobs to be provided. Although the NUL was assured there would be no discrimination in the CWA, numerous complaints poured into the league's headquarters, indicating otherwise.[48] Still, the program's short duration made it difficult for the organizations to intervene.

The New York UL was one of the few affiliates that managed to help a sizable number of unemployed Negro women. It created a visiting homemaker service and sent two hundred women into homes where there was sickness. Indeed, there was more demand for this service than it could provide. This was particularly helpful to the New York league because the majority of its job applicants were domestic workers.[49]

Although the CWA quickly created many jobs, the general public was critical of it, perceiving it as a costly program that for the most part provided nonessential "make-work" jobs. There was also a belief that it interfered with private-sector employment. Since it had been created as a temporary program to relieve the suffering of the unemployed during the cold winter, Hopkins began to dismantle the CWA in the South and proceeded North as the weather improved. FERA continued unfinished CWA projects and dispensed relief.[50]

The Public Works Administration was established under Title II of the NIRA in 1933 and was initially administered by the Department of the Interior. One of the New Deal's longest-lasting programs, it was placed in the Federal Works Agency in 1939. Billions of dollars were allocated for large public works projects (roads, dams, bridges, public buildings, and low-cost housing) that would be totally financed and constructed by the federal government. This approach was intended as a "pump priming" device to stimulate industry through the purchase of materials and equipment and payment of wages.[51]

Like the CWA, PWA eligibility was based on attributed need: one only had to need a job. Wages were based on level of skill and prevailing rates in geographic zones.[52] Projects were contracted out to local contractors; organized labor had a great deal of control over hiring. Work on PWA projects was superior to work-relief jobs because, although it was a public works program, contracts with local employers made the jobs similar to private-sector employment. Work was full time, and the jobs were regarded as essential with no stigma attached to them whereas in work-relief projects, part-time jobs were provided in order to distribute the benefits to more needy people; and since it was a means-tested program, a stigma was attached to the jobs.

While the bill that would create the PWA was being considered in Congress, Sen. Robert Wagner (D, N.Y.), at the request of the NAACP, introduced an amendment that would prohibit discrimination on public works projects.[53] Although the NAACP vigorously campaigned for passage of the bill with Wagner's amendment, it was not included in the act.[54]

In spite of this, the organizations were enthusiastic about the PWA, especially with Ickes in control, and suggested that he appoint a special adviser to keep him informed on matters concerning Negroes. Ickes thought this was a good idea but feared that the appointment of a Negro to this position would cause problems with certain segments of the white community which needed to be placated. For this reason, he appointed Clark Foreman as Advisor on Negro Affairs. Foreman was a liberal white from Atlanta who had been involved in interracial affairs for a number of years in his work with the Southern Interracial Committee and the Rosenwald Fund.[55]

The NAACP and the NUL were incensed and insulted with this appointment. They regarded Foreman as a friend so their objections were not directed at him but at being represented by a white person. Roy Wilkins of the NAACP accused Ickes of paternalism and said:

> The age of paternalism in relation to the races is past so far as Negroes are concerned and they bitterly resent having a white man officially designated by the government to advise on their welfare. Only a Negro can know true conditions of Negro people and voice their hopes because it is only by living as a Negro in America that the several nuances of discrimination and

exploitation are truly discovered. . . . If the time has not come when Negroes of expert training and wide experience can interpret the problems of their race to the government then the millions of dollars spent for Negro education by the government and by the paternalists themselves is [*sic*] wasted."[56]

An editorial in *Opportunity* said:

It would be futile to deny that in this instance the great mass of Negroes North and South view the appointment of a white man as an interpreter of the needs and aspirations of the Negro with profound disappointment and chagrin. . . .

It would be difficult to conceive of the appointment of a Gentile to interpret the aspirations and needs of Jews or a capitalist to represent labor, or a Japanese to speak for the Chinese or a Fascist for the Soviets. So it seems inconsistent to say the least that in matters of great moment Negro leadership should be compelled to abdicate in deference to a conception of race relations that should have passed with slavery.[57]

Ickes remained firm in his choice of Foreman but appeased the organizations somewhat by appointing Robert Weaver as Foreman's assistant. Weaver was a young Negro economist who had recently earned a Ph.D. from Harvard and had been working for the Joint Committee as it monitored the NRA industrial codes. Later, when Foreman left the PWA, Weaver was appointed to his position and proved to be extremely helpful to black workers.

When projects first began, however, it was clear that many black workers, especially skilled tradesmen, were being excluded from PWA jobs.[58] Negro workers at the Boulder Dam construction site, hired only as unskilled laborers, were not allowed to live in Boulder City, a government-owned reservation, which meant that they had to live several miles away in poor housing.[59] In Kansas City the superintendent of the intercity viaduct project told the league that he had no intention of using a mixed racial crew, but might use Negroes to push wheelbarrows when concrete was being poured.[60] Only five Negroes had ever been employed on the Coulee Dam project. The Seattle UL executive secretary thought this might be related to the insistence on separate housing for blacks.[61]

John W. Davis, head of the Joint Committee, went south to investigate conditions at the Tennessee Valley Authority's site in 1935. His detailed "Report of the Chief Social and Economic Problems" was sent to Roosevelt as well as to the chairman of the TVA and several federal executives and legislators. In the report Davis noted "discrimination in the employment of

Negroes, especially skilled workers, most colored employees being placed in the lowest wage brackets. Promotions for Negroes were non-existent." With the exception of "a handful of domestics," Negro workers were found to be excluded from residences in "model villages constructed for dam workers with federal funds." In the TVA's training program, certain courses were given only to whites.[62]

Three years later, the situation had not improved. The NAACP gathered affidavits from Negro workers on the TVA project and from other Negroes living in the vicinity. With this information, NAACP board member Charles Houston testified before a joint congressional committee investigating the TVA. He informed the committee that "many Negro workers were doing the same work as white skilled workers although drawing about half the pay." He also charged that "Negroes were being intimidated and terrorized to prevent them from joining unions."[63] The NAACP filed a "formal written protest."[64]

Ickes had ordered "no discrimination against any person of color or religious affiliation" on PWA projects, but there was no way to enforce his order.[65] One of the problems was the lack of a precise definition of just what "no discrimination" meant, so that it could be written into PWA contracts. As PWA projects continued to discriminate, Ickes and Weaver turned to the PWA's Legal Division to help them write a more stringent clause to prevent discrimination. In 1934 the Legal Division ruled that "the PWA could take any administrative steps necessary to make the provision effective."[66]

Weaver proposed a plan that clearly defined the phrase "no discrimination" and used low-cost housing construction to test it. His plan required that a certain percentage of Negro skilled workers, based on the proportion of Negro skilled workers living in each of the cities involved, had to be hired on all public housing construction. If the total amount paid to skilled workers each month did not show that the set percentage had been paid to Negro skilled workers, this was prima facie evidence of discrimination on the part of the contractor. A year and a half after implementation of the plan, Weaver thought it was a "workable solution to a difficult problem."[67] The number of Negroes working on federal housing projects had increased substantially.[68] Nonetheless, his plan was never extended beyond the PWA's low-cost housing division. But Weaver's involvement in the administration of PWA illustrated yet again how helpful Negroes in policy-making positions were to the Negro population. His solution, an early form of affirmative action, enabled a number of skilled Negro tradesmen to obtain PWA jobs.

The Federal Emergency Relief Act, passed in 1933, provided the first direct federal grants to states for public assistance and created the Federal Emergency Relief Administration (FERA). Enacted as a temporary measure to care for emergency needs through work and relief until the economy improved, it ceased to exist when the Works Progress Administration was created in 1935.[69] As FERA's director, Harry Hopkins made an effort to raise relief standards in the states through federal regulations attached to grants. Work was provided to recipients according to the number of days needed for the recipient to meet basic needs by a wage rate set by the federal government; work was mostly manual labor, but the test of need was considerably relaxed in favor of white-collar and professional workers. When FERA was discontinued, many of the states reverted to poor law standards for general relief that had been the case before FERA.[70]

FERA had policies that the NUL and NAACP preferred: it provided work relief with a set wage rate; it had the potential to provide work for black professionals; federal regulations discouraged discrimination and raised relief standards; there was no racial quota; and eligibility was established by economic criteria. The feature that civil rights organizations did not like was local administration; although federal guidelines discouraged discrimination, there was no mechanism to prohibit it at the local level.

The private sector did not like the wage rates, and they were frequently violated. A great deal of pressure to rescind them altogether came from the southern states. Although the wage rates were set according to the prevailing wages in geographic zones, in the South the federal wage rate was above the average wage paid to many Negroes in the private sector. The NUL argued that one of the goals of the New Deal was to raise living standards for American workers and that FERA should not capitulate to the demands of private interests. When Hopkins rescinded the thirty cents per hour minimum wage in Georgia, the league commented, "At last the government has abandoned the high idealism which marked the inception of the New Deal and has yielded to those whose conception of decent living standards for Negro workers is little above that of lower animals."[71]

The NAACP also criticized Hopkins's decision, saying: "Now that the final decision as well as administration has been turned over to local administration we predict that wage slavery and death will be the lot of the Negroes." The administration had "surrendered not only a principle that seriously affects its recovery program but the very flesh, blood and bones of

millions of American citizens helpless in the toils of prejudice and exploitation." The NAACP "vigorously" urged reconsideration of the decision,
believing that intelligent Southerners would support such a move.[72]

Even with the low wage rate in the Southeast, Negro workers had difficulty getting any work relief at all in some areas. To illustrate this hardship,
the NAACP publicized a lengthy handwritten letter it had received from a
Negro man in Florida. He wrote:

> We have had no work since last season. A great many have been on federal
> relief. When they tell us to register for civil work hundreds done so. Then they
> give all the work to the whites except three days before thanksgiven when
> about 60 Negroes was put in the Flamingo Swamp to work in the mud. After
> Thanksgiven no other Negroes have had a single hour's job. Hundreds of
> whites work every day.[73]

Local Florida relief officials were more likely to give work relief to white
recipients and relief to black recipients because relief was less costly and, of
course, had even more stigma attached to it than did work relief. There were
other complaints about the denial of work relief from other areas in the
South.[74] Civil rights organizations complained about this practice to
Hopkins and urged him to take steps to remedy the situation. Local relief
officials responded that Negroes preferred relief to work. The NUL asked its
affiliates to gather "irrefutable evidence to disprove these charges finally and
completely."[75] The organizations firmly believed that work was infinitely
better than relief and were convinced that this was the prevailing view in the
Negro community.

As the difficulties that Negro workers experienced under New Deal programs mounted, the NUL thought some mechanism was needed to stay
informed about the various economic recovery programs and to help apply
for programs and benefits. This took the form of Emergency Advisory
Committees (EACs), voluntary groups at the local level engaged in activities
that would be coordinated by the national office. They would have an "unof-
ficial relationship" with the NUL. T. Arnold Hill, the NUL's secretary of
industrial relations and also, at that time, its acting executive secretary,[76]
thought the NUL as currently set up was not able to launch a major national
movement—thus the need for the EACs. The EACs allowed the league to
expand into areas where there were no affiliates and, therefore, to fill a gap.
It also gave the NUL more control at the local level than its official *Terms of
Affiliation* allowed. By the end of 1933, 196 EACS had been organized in

thirty-two states and the District of Columbia.[77] (The NUL had forty-two affiliates.)

Through the EACs the NUL was able to document numerous incidents of violations of the NRA's codes and policies in the work and work-relief programs and, in some cases, to correct the situation. For example, Negro workers on the Federal Barge Line in St. Louis complained that they were treated unfairly in terms of the minimum wage and maximum hours of work. Hill sent a telegram to Labor Secretary Perkins and the situation was changed.[78] When young Negro men were not allowed to enroll in the CCC in Georgia and Florida, "the Director of Reforestation telephoned the NUL for definite data and reported subsequently . . . that centers for enrollment of Negroes had been designated in these States and directors . . . in other Southern States had been instructed to enroll Negroes." Again, Hill had wired Perkins, whose assistant had responded by wire, "Am taking the matter up energetically at once."[79]

Many of the affiliates found the EACs helpful because they provided a vehicle for collecting data that documented unfair practices in the programs. The executive secretary of the Tampa league told Hill, "The value of the EAC is not so much in local protest and accomplishment as it is in reflecting to national administrators the extent to which regulations are distorted when applied to Negro clients."[80] In 1937, due to a shortage of staff, a tight budget, and perhaps a change in the direction of New Deal programs, the NUL could no longer coordinate the EACs and they gradually faded away.[81]

As FERA came under more and more criticism, Roosevelt began to view it as a political liability and declared, "The Federal Government must and shall quit this business of relief."[82] There was a general consensus among New Deal policymakers that public assistance for the able-bodied should be in the form of work relief, and this was the catalyst for the passage of the 1935 Emergency Appropriation Act. This act created the Works Progress Administration to serve as a coordinating agency for work-relief programs; it was also to undertake "small useful projects." These "small useful projects" continued to expand, and the WPA became a massive work-relief program with an emphasis on the superiority of work over "the dole."[83]

The WPA was a federal program: all projects had to be approved by the federal office and the president. Most projects were sponsored by local governments, were labor intensive, and required no large investments in equipment and machinery. Several policies protected private industry. The program's wages were higher than relief payments, but they were lower than those paid by private industry and were based on levels of skill and the degree of urbanization in the areas. No funds were appropriated for projects that would compete with the private sector or benefit private interests. As the economy showed signs of recovery, WPA policies became more restrictive. Failure to register with the U.S. Employment Service resulted in dismissal from a WPA job. A rule established in 1939 prohibited workers from remaining on WPA projects longer than eighteen months. Persons eligible for unemployment compensation were no longer eligible for WPA work relief after the Social Security Act was passed. Only one member of a family could work on WPA projects, and preference was given to heads of households. The WPA was transferred to the Federal Works Agency in 1940.[84]

Given their experiences with earlier New Deal programs, the NUL and NAACP viewed the WPA cautiously. A federal program with a strong emphasis on work and with federal agencies at local levels, which the organizations favored, it provided white-collar jobs, discrimination was forbidden, and there was no racial quota. But the organizations saw serious flaws in the program too. One was the plan to pay a lower wage for public works than that paid by the private sector. Another was the lack of assurance that jobs, skilled and unskilled, would be allocated on the basis of need without racial discrimination. There was no enforcement mechanism to prohibit discrimination, and although it was a federal program, local governments had considerable control over programs and it was likely that local customs would prevail. In addition, the amount of money appropriated for public works did not seem to be enough to provide jobs for all those who were eligible for WPA benefits. The NAACP urged its branches "to be on the alert in their communities to see that the allocation of projects and jobs is made without discrimination against colored people."[85]

The organizations were also concerned about those persons classified as "unemployable" who, with FERA phased out, would have to rely on local relief agencies rather than a federal program. In anticipation of the passage of the bill, state and local relief officials had considered a reduction in relief appropriations and personnel, and they concocted dire punishments for "slackers" who preferred relief to work.[86]

The organizations soon realized that their fears were well founded. Under the WPA, the country was divided into zones. Zone 4, the southeastern states where a majority of unskilled Negro workers were located, paid the lowest minimum wage for unskilled labor (sixty-five cents per day). In an *Oppor-*

tunity editorial, the dismayed NUL questioned "the wisdom of the administration of setting the seal of approval on the wages of wretchedness." Such wages would condemn "Negroes . . . to perpetual peonage and poverty; to disease and illiteracy and despair."[87]

The NAACP sent a telegram to Roosevelt in protest, urging a "rearrangement" of "relief wages which . . . will fall with unusual severity upon Negro workers." It warned that in the South where racial prejudices are "notorious," two-thirds of the Negro population would be routinely classified as unskilled laborers and thus subjected to the lowest wage.[88] A letter from a New Deal official acknowledging receipt of the telegram made no comment on its content.[89]

Although the WPA's wages for most Negro workers were low, many were able to make some gains through the program. The Lincoln (Nebraska) UL "placed every woman certified and most of the men."[90] The Atlanta league was able to assist Negro physicians in securing appointments in WPA programs. The Visiting Housekeepers Project initiated by the New York UL under the CWA had been so successful in creating jobs for women with domestic experience that it was put under the supervision of the WPA's Department of Women's Work and was used in a number of communities across the country. The affiliates succeeded in getting self-help projects funded which provided needed resources and services in Negro communities.[91] Negro professionals such as artists, actors, writers, and teachers worked in education and recreation programs in Negro communities. The league's 1938 Annual Report stated, "The NUL has with good results kept in constant touch with the various Federal recovery services in Washington to further the interest of the Negro . . . in WPA employment."[92]

In the South, large landowners were shutting down WPA projects when they needed seasonal labor. An NAACP protest to the WPA "nipped a plan to close down relief projects in order to increase the supply of seasonal cotton pickers at sub-standard wages."[93] Even though WPA wages in the southern states were quite low, and in spite of the stipulation that WPA wages could not exceed those paid by the private sector, the WPA minimum wage was sometimes higher than the private-sector wage paid to Negro laborers; and working conditions were better. Under such circumstances, laborers were reluctant to leave WPA jobs.

In industrial areas, organized labor's control of jobs on WPA projects limited Negro workers' access to them. The executive secretary of the St. Louis league thought that Negro skilled workers were losing ground. Before the NRA, Negroes had done at least half of the cement and concrete work in St. Louis even though "the union was operating at that time [and] no Negroes permitted to join." With the growth of the New Deal work programs and the increased power of labor, Negroes were excluded from such work.[94] They were not allowed to join the unions, yet when they sought employment they were not hired because they were not union members. This was a bitter, frustrating situation that the organizations were unable to change.

In the late 1930s, as the economy slowly expanded, largely due to the growth of the defense industry, the New Deal administration began to dismantle the WPA. As this occurred, requests for jobs along with requests for food, clothing, and housing increased at local league offices.[95] The private-sector economy was not absorbing black workers as quickly as it was white workers. The WPA had not been perfect, but the organizations thought that dismantling it was a serious mistake. The cutback in WPA jobs was the topic of a series of editorials in *Opportunity*. One editorial said, "Curtailment of WPA is a step backward; it is an opening invitation to all those who would make capital out of misery and despair."[96] Another editorial called for a substitute for the WPA. Private industry "returning to life may find a place for whites, but if it follows traditional methods, will be slow to open to Negroes except at the very lowest levels." Many skilled workers and those in white-collar occupations "have a dreary outlook for the immediate future."[97] Still another editorial expressed concern about the availability of regular employment for Negro workers. The writer realized that the WPA had high costs, but wondered whether in the end it was not worth the price in the preservation "of those human values of dignity and self-respect which employment—regular employment—gives to the man and woman who find no job in the private sector. . . . Relief is not enough."[98] The NAACP expressed a preference for employment too. "We want work, not relief," an editorial in *Crisis* contended, and called attention to the lack of employment opportunities in private industry.[99]

When the WPA was sharply curtailed in 1940, over eight million people were still unemployed.[100] The organizations strongly believed that some kind of permanent public works program was needed. They doubted if the private sector would ever be capable of absorbing all workers willing and able to work. Without a public works program, the organizations predicted that a large proportion of the Negro population would become permanently dependent on public assistance. They feared that this would place the Negro population in a tenuous position in a society with a strong work ethic; it would limit Negroes' ability to advance, to be viewed as responsible, contributing members of society. Their concerns were compounded with the establishment of the permanent programs created by New Deal reform legislation.

The Beginning of the American Welfare State: Arguing for Inclusion

Reform legislation that was of special interest to the NUL and NAACP was the Social Security Act and the National Labor Relations Act, both passed in 1935, and the Fair Labor Standards Act, passed in 1938. In enacting this legislation, the federal government assumed more responsibility for the poor, the elderly, and the unemployed and provided some measures to prevent exploitation of workers. This was the beginning of the American welfare state, but much of the black population was denied the protection that the new legislation provided.

With the constant presence of discrimination, the creation of permanent social welfare programs without any legal mechanism to prevent discrimination was troublesome for civil rights organizations. As each bill was debated, they tried, unsuccessfully, to add an antidiscriminatory amendment. In order to overcome the absence of protection against discrimination, they preferred federally administered programs because Negroes were more likely to be included. Because the organizations recognized the importance of the legislation to the entire country, they usually supported it even though it did not provide the antidiscriminatory protection they had sought; but they testified against the Social Security Act because too many Negro workers were excluded from social insurance coverage.

The landmark 1935 Social Security Act provided old age insurance, unemployment insurance, aid to the poor elderly and blind, aid to destitute children in one-parent families, services for "crippled children," and public health services. It created a two-tier social welfare system. Tier 1 (the preferred tier) provided social insurance; tier 2 provided public assistance. The act was amended in 1939 to include survivor's insurance under tier 1, with the belief that most children from one-parent households would eventually be covered by this policy.

Roosevelt's initial concern was to provide unemployment and old age insurance. The bill was drafted by his small Committee on Economic

Security and introduced by Senator Wagner and Congressman David Lewis (D, Md.).[101] Many issues were considered while the bill was under debate, including methods of financing, coverage, size of the grants, actuarial considerations, and administrative responsibility. There were also political decisions to be made: what policies to include or to omit in order to get the bill through Congress.[102]

The main concerns of the NUL and NAACP were identical to those of Roosevelt—old age and unemployment insurance. The organizations paid less attention to the public assistance portions of the bill. The three policy issues of greatest interest to them were administrative responsibility, coverage, and method of financing. They sought federal administration and universal coverage, and opposed geographic differentials. They also thought that all grants should be indexed to the cost of living and financed by means other than workers' contributions.[103]

The Committee on Economic Security had recommended universal coverage for old age and unemployment insurance, but when Treasury Secretary Henry Morgenthau testified before the House Ways and Means Committee, he mentioned the Treasury Department's concern about such broad coverage. The department thought it would be very difficult to collect payroll taxes from agricultural and domestic workers. The House committee took this opportunity to immediately exclude these workers from coverage under old age and unemployment insurance. This exclusion seemed more related to political considerations than to the difficulty of collecting contributions. The southern bloc of the Democratic Party opposed federal administration and was unlikely to support a bill that required farmers to contribute to agricultural workers' benefits.

When the NAACP learned of this exclusion, it wired Roosevelt and Morgenthau, asking Roosevelt to support universal coverage and urging Morgenthau to withdraw the recommendations that had prompted it. The NAACP argued that this would exclude "more than two million Negro wage earners normally gainfully employed in these occupations."[104] Roosevelt referred the telegram to the Economic Security Committee, which explained to the NAACP that universal coverage was "the position which has been taken by our committee."[105] Morgenthau told the association that he had been misunderstood, that he had not recommended the exclusion of agricultural and domestic workers but had simply suggested that "there might be great difficulty at the start of the program in collecting contributions from transient laborers, domestic servants, and agricultural workers." He reported that the Bureau of Internal Revenue was trying to find "a way by which collections from these sources might be made." He assured them that if that was not possible, "there [was] no proposal to exclude them from the benefits of the non-contributory system."[106]

During Senate hearings, Sen. Robert Byrd (D, Va.) attacked the federal administration policy in the bill. Southern farmers feared the measure might serve as a means for the federal government to interfere with the way in which they handled "the Negro question." After a few days of hearings before the Senate Finance Committee, it was obvious that the bill would not pass with so much federal control. The states were given administrative responsibility for public assistance programs with a matching state-federal funding scheme, and a state-federal administrative structure was devised for unemployment compensation. Old age insurance remained under total federal administration.[107] The organizations believed these changes made it even more important for them to pressure for the inclusion of agricultural and domestic workers under the first tier programs; there was more federal control.

The NUL and NAACP believed that funding for social insurance should come from general revenues, rather than the contributions of workers, because the majority of Negro workers had incomes at a subsistence level, making it difficult for them to contribute. It was futile for them to pressure for this policy because Roosevelt strongly opposed it. The president preferred workers' contributions because he thought this would make old age insurance different from relief. The benefit would be viewed as a right to those who contributed, and the program would seem self-supporting, thus making it harder for future legislators to dismantle. In addition, Roosevelt believed that the use of general revenue funds would put too much demand on the government's resources, already overwhelmed by the Depression. Further, the president hoped to give private industry an incentive for reducing unemployment by requiring it to make contributions to unemployment compensation.[108]

While the bill was being debated in Congress, the NAACP conferred with Abraham Epstein, executive secretary of the American Association for Old Age Security. Epstein had been an advocate for old age insurance for a number of years and had influenced the drafting of the bill. He thought the NAACP's concerns about the exclusion of agricultural and domestic workers were quite valid; it would "perpetuate inequality" by discriminating against Negroes, but he did not think "that anything could be done to change the situation." He told the association that his first interest was in social insurance, and he "did not see how we can solve the Negro problem through social insurance." Furthermore, these workers were still "entitled" to the "non-contributory old age pensions" and could receive it without making a contribution.[109] He advised the NAACP to wait until the bill was passed and then "negotiate" with federal administrators to pressure states where there were disparities in public assistance standards.[110]

The NAACP did not think that Epstein and Morgenthau, with their assurances about the inclusion of these workers under old age assistance, clearly understood its concerns. It believed that relegation of domestic and agricultural workers to the second tier was extremely unfair; a large proportion of the Negro *working* population would be denied the tier 1 benefits (unemployment and old age insurance) and forced to rely on the stigmatized tier 2 public assistance programs when unable to work.

The NAACP testified against the Wagner-Lewis Economic Security Act. Representing the association before the Senate Finance Committee, board member Charles Houston said the NAACP had been inclined to testify in favor of the bill, but the more it studied the bill the more it began to look "like a sieve with holes just big enough for the majority of Negroes to fall through."[111] He informed the committee that the exclusion of domestic and agricultural workers from old age and unemployment insurance meant the exclusion of at least 50 percent of Negro workers. Furthermore, he doubted if the southern states would implement the old age assistance program since a large proportion of Negroes would be eligible for benefits. For these reasons, he favored the inclusion of agricultural and domestic workers under the contributory system and a completely federal old age assistance program with guarantees against discrimination.[112]

Competing social security bills were introduced in the House: the Wagner-Lewis bill and a bill introduced by Ernest Lundeen (Farmer-Labor Party, Minnesota). The Wagner-Lewis bill went to the Ways and Means Committee, the Lundeen bill to the Labor Committee. Both bills were reported favorably out of committee, but the Lundeen bill was eventually rejected by Congress.

The Lundeen bill was referred to as the "workers' bill" and was considered quite radical. Based on the belief that unemployment "was a disease of the capitalist system," it proposed that the beneficiaries of this system should compensate the victims. The Lundeen proposal was a completely federal plan and was to be administered by a panel of workers. It provided universal coverage and included professionals, the self-employed, and those who had worked part-time because they were unable to find full-time jobs. It would pay benefits equal to the prevailing local wage, indexed to the cost of living, and funded by individual and corporate income taxes and inheritance and gift taxes.[113]

The NUL testified in favor of the Lundeen bill before the Labor Committee. Representing the league, Hill said he favored the bill because it included "farmers and domestics and personal service workers." He told the Labor Committee that shutting off benefits to workers in these occupations "would almost immediately exclude almost two-thirds of all Negro workers."[114] Hill also supported the bill because it would provide federal administration, pointing out that the experiences of Negroes with state governments had not been satisfactory. Other reasons for support were that benefits were indexed to the cost of living and were financed by taxes rather than workers' contributions, and that the bill provided protection to workers engaged in strikebreaking or to workers who refused to work at less than the average local or trade union wage. Hill thought it was especially important for agricultural workers to be covered because they would constitute a large part of the unemployed as agriculture became more mechanized. Overall, Hill believed that the poorest group should have "first call" on the act's benefits.[115] After the NUL's testimony, it asked its constituents to back congressmen who supported legislation combining features of the bill that it had mentioned.[116]

The NAACP liked the Lundeen bill too, noting that it was "being supported by all the liberal and radical groups, . . . it provides for workers, farmers and professionals without discrimination because of race, creed or color"; but it did not testify for the bill.[117] The bill was regarded as a Communist Party proposal to get the support of the working class. Conservative Republicans helped to get it out of the Labor Committee and added amendments, hoping this would make any social security legislation unacceptable to the majority of Congress. There were of course some genuine supporters of the Lundeen bill, like the NUL, but it was never given serious consideration.[118] The NUL's testimony in favor of a bill perceived to be associated with the Communist Party was a clear indication of how strongly it favored the bill's policies.

In spite of the NUL's disappointment over the exclusion of agricultural and domestic workers, once the Social Security Act was passed the affiliates conducted educational sessions to inform Negroes about the act and to help those who were eligible for benefits to apply.[119] New Deal historian William E. Leuchtenberg later said that the Social Security Act was landmark legislation, but it had many faults:

> In many respects, the law was an astonishingly inept and conservative piece of legislation. In no other welfare system in the world did the state shirk all responsibility for old age indigency and insist that funds be taken out of the current earnings of workers. By relying on regressive taxation and withdrawing vast sums to build up reserves, the act did untold economic mischief. The law denied coverage to numerous classes of workers, including those who needed security most: notably farm laborers and domestics. Sickness, in normal times the main cause of joblessness, was disregarded. The act not only failed to set up a national system of unemployment compensation but did not even provide adequate national standards.[120]

The NUL and NAACP would have agreed.

In 1937 the NAACP reviewed the two tiers created by the act. It did not think that old age assistance was adequate; recipients were not able "to maintain minimum fair living standards." It again lamented the exclusion of agricultural and domestic workers from unemployment compensation, saying, "the relief rolls are no substitute. Relief is a dole which robs a person of self-respect and initiative. Unemployment compensation is more like an insurance against hard times, and as insurance, may be accepted with self-respect and self-assurance." The NAACP thought the situation of these workers was even more precarious because of the "widespread action of southern boards arbitrarily removing Negro relief recipients off relief rolls and forcing them into the cotton fields with no guarantee as to hours, wages, or conditions of labor." Furthermore, the South was lobbying to broaden the definition of agricultural workers "so as to rob more Negroes of the benefits of unemployment compensation."[121]

The NAACP and NUL attempted to add agricultural and domestic workers to the social insurance programs whenever an amendment was under consideration. Since the act's passage, amendments to it have resulted in changes for which the organizations advocated. Seventeen years later, a 1952 amendment finally elevated domestic and agricultural workers to the first tier.

Another needed reform sought by liberal legislators was a mechanism for settling disputes between management and labor. There were a series of long strikes in industrial areas throughout the country which were not resolved by Roosevelt's National Labor Relations Board (NLRB) because employers frequently ignored its decisions. In 1934 Wagner introduced a "Labor Disputes" bill, hoping to eliminate this problem by giving the NLRB more power in the resolution of these disputes. One portion of the bill, which civil rights organizations found particularly objectionable, would legalize closed shops.[122]

Roy Wilkins described this section of the bill as "fraught with grave danger to Negro labor" because it "rigidly enforces and legalizes the closed shop. . . . Thousands of Negro workers, barred from membership in American labor unions," would be "absolutely shut out of employment." Wilkins proposed an amendment that would allow closed shops only when a labor organization did not restrict its membership on the basis of "race, creed or color."[123]

Wagner's original bill had allowed closed shops *if* the union had no such membership restrictions, but the AFL opposed this clause and it was eliminated.[124] The NAACP regarded closed shops as synonymous with "white shops" and carefully planned a strategy to prevent passage of the bill if it did not include Wilkins's amendment. Rather than testify at committee hearings, the association decided to wait until the bill reached the Senate floor and then have its antidiscrimination amendment introduced by a "friendly" senator, in the hope that this would catch the AFL off guard and prevent it from rallying strong support against the amendment.[125] Since correspondence from AFL officials repeatedly espoused egalitarian policies, it would be difficult for the AFL to publicly fight the amendment.[126] A letter from an NRA official informed Walter White that he had conferred with Green and other labor leaders and was told that they opposed an antidiscrimination amendment because it was unnecessary: "There would be no discrimination amongst any man for his color."[127] White responded that the NAACP "was taking the liberty of making this letter public in order that colored workers and the public at large may be informed."[128] The association thought it had ample evidence to prove that AFL affiliates had routinely discriminated against Negro workers. The NUL did not follow the NAACP's strategy. Hill testified before the Education and Labor Committee, saying that the league was in favor of the bill but felt compelled to register a "definite protest against the adoption of the Wagner bill in its present form" because it did not protect Negro workers from discrimination.[129]

Apparently, neither the NAACP nor the NUL was able to find a senator willing to introduce Wilkins's amendment. James Couzens (D, Mich.) told the NAACP that since he was not on the Education and Labor Committee, he did not think he was well enough informed about the bill to introduce an amendment.[130] Wagner told the NUL he was not willing to do so because he thought it would lessen the bill's chances of passing.[131] The introduction of the amendment ceased to be important when the bill, which did not have Roosevelt's initial support, failed to reach the Senate floor.

Wagner reintroduced the bill in 1935, and, again, the NUL and NAACP were ambivalent about it because the section that legalized closed shops remained unchanged. Lester Granger, an NUL staff member (and later executive secretary), explained the NUL's position in a press release: "The bill gives greatest protection to that part of labor least in need of it. . . . It protects the right of labor to organize, but does nothing to protect the rights of minority groups to enter organized labor bodies."[132]

Although the bill did not have Roosevelt's support until the very end, once it received his support it breezed through Congress. The National Labor Relations Act gave organized labor considerably more power. It gave labor the right to bargain collectively and prohibited employers from interfering in the establishment of unions in their plants. It legalized closed shops but gave no protection to workers who were excluded from membership in the unions involved.[133]

The NUL believed that the increased control that organized labor had over "regular jobs" made it imperative for Negro workers to become an integral part of the labor movement, and with this in mind it established Workers' Councils throughout the country. It hoped this new program would help convince Negro workers that it was to their advantage to become part of the organized labor movement whenever such an opportunity came along. The NUL believed it was more likely to accomplish the program's goals with all-black councils, but quickly pointed out that it was not setting up black unions. It believed that black and white workers must work together in labor organizations.[134]

Encouraging black workers to join unions was difficult because negative experiences with labor unions had made them bitter. Many regarded unions as their natural enemy and believed they had gained more from the employers who had hired them than they had from organized labor; they saw no advantage to joining a union.[135] In addition, some affiliates in cities with one major industry were reluctant to establish the councils. These affiliate boards thought such an activity was too controversial and might cause racial conflict.[136] They could also have feared alienating major contributors.

The executive secretary of the Akron UL even objected to the league's plan to hold a regional conference in Akron because the labor program would be discussed. He thought such a program would result in "muddying the waters for the few Negroes who work in local Rubber Companies." During recent labor disturbances, the Akron UL had been responsible for "keeping the Negro Rubber workers with the 'foot in the middle of the road'" and "no Negro had lost a job." He was convinced that if the Akron UL had promoted "the ideals of the National office . . . it is questionable if today any Negroes would be employed in Rubber."[137] In spite of all these difficulties, by 1938 the NUL had established seventy councils in twenty-one states.[138]

In order to pressure the AFL to remove "the color line in the labor movement," the NAACP picketed the 1934 AFL convention in San Francisco with the help of its San Francisco branch.[139] A telegram was sent to AFL president William Green, calling upon the AFL "to abolish segregation and discrimination in treatment of Negro workers." It warned the AFL that it could "never win security for white labor as long as it permits the exclusion of black labor from unions."[140] Responding, Green claimed that there was "no general discrimination against Negro workers; they [were] free to join most all organizations chartered by the AFL." He was disappointed because of "the lack of a general response on the part of Negro workers to become affiliated with organized labor."[141]

No one would have disputed Green's denial of AFL discrimination more than AFL member A. Philip Randolph, president of the Brotherhood of Sleeping Car Porters (BSCP). For years he had tried to persuade delegates to AFL conventions to pass a resolution that would exclude local unions that denied black workers membership. At the 1934 convention, perhaps with the aid of the NAACP pickets, Randolph finally persuaded the AFL to appoint a Committee of Five to at least investigate discrimination in its ranks.[142]

The Committee of Five was supposed to hold regional hearings in order to hear from a broad spectrum of workers, but it chose to hold all the meetings in Washington, D.C.[143] Reginald Johnson represented the NUL and Charles Houston the NAACP. After assuring the committee that the league understood the advantages of collective bargaining, Johnson thoroughly described the limiting effect that discrimination by local unions had had on employment opportunities for Negro tradesmen. He recommended the adoption of Randolph's resolution, pointing out that real penalties had to be brought against unions that refused to comply "with the spirit of organized labor and the pronouncement of the A F of L Council on the subject of international brotherhood."[144]

Houston illustrated two problems confronting Negro workers: "The express exclusion written into the constitutions and by-laws" of labor organizations, and "the exclusion and discrimination" they practiced "by subterfuge even where the constitution expressly prohibits the color bar." He insisted that "the record show that the hearing was incomplete" because no hearings were held in industrial centers with large Negro populations. He urged the committee to hold regional hearings because Negro workers "who had suffered the greatest discrimination" could not afford to come to Washington.[145]

The AFL's Committee of Five was expected to report on the hearings and make recommendations at the 1935 AFL convention in Atlantic City. In an effort to help persuade the convention to adopt Randolph's resolution, the NUL lobbied convention delegates and asked its affiliates to lobby local labor officials.[146] Before the convention, the Committee of Five's report to the AFL executive council had recommended adoption of Randolph's resolution, but the executive council failed even to mention it to the convention. Randolph tried to bring his resolution to the floor for a vote, but the Resolution Committee, with Green's support, engaged in parliamentary maneuvering that enabled them to evade the entire issue.[147] The AFL did not want to risk alienating any delegates; arguments between the industrial and craft unions had escalated, and the AFL was desperately trying to prevent a loss of membership to the industrial union movement.[148] It thought that presenting Randolph's resolution would compound its problems. As a result, discriminatory AFL affiliates felt no pressure to open membership to black workers.

The NUL and NAACP recognized the importance of industrial unions. They believed that many Negro workers were not union members because the AFL had made few efforts to organize workers in large-scale industries.

When John L. Lewis organized the Committee for Industrial Organization (CIO) shortly after the 1935 AFL convention, civil rights organizations urged those in mass industries to join.[149] The NAACP was more visible than the NUL in its support of the CIO. The NUL, in its continuing efforts to remove the barriers that prevented skilled Negro craftsmen from obtaining work and work-relief jobs in New Deal programs where AFL locals controlled hiring, instructed its Workers' Councils to appear neutral in the craft versus industrial unions dispute.[150] Although the CIO enrolled many more Negro workers than the AFL, both the NUL and NAACP remained skeptical about the CIO's egalitarian claims. They had heard the same from the AFL.[151]

The passage of the NLRA without the protection that the NAACP and NUL had sought for Negro workers was a serious blow. The organizations had made a concerted effort to help Negroes become an integral part of the labor movement but had made very few inroads. The Workers' Councils helped a little; some workers from these groups were successful in joining existing AFL locals, but a council was more likely to form an all-black union—something the NUL had not intended to happen.[152] Discrimination on the part of organized labor, especially the AFL, continued to be a major concern of the organizations.

The Fair Labor Standards Act of 1938 (also referred to as the Wages and Hours bill) was introduced in Congress by Hugo Black (D, Ala.) in 1937. The bill, which proposed the establishment of a minimum wage and maximum hours of work, went through a long skirmish in Congress before it passed because it had no strong backing from any group.[153] Even organized labor was initially against the bill because it proposed geographic wage rates. Once these were removed, labor backed it; but southern Democrats, who favored the geographic wage rates, united with conservative Republicans to prevent passage of the bill.

The NAACP and NUL supported the bill because they thought higher wages and regulated hours of work would improve living conditions in the South. Furthermore, the bill had a provision that would regulate child labor, which would be especially helpful in the South where Negro children toiled long hours in the cotton fields. The organizations' main concerns were the same ones they had had when the NRA codes were being established: the possibility of geographic wage rates and the exclusion of agricultural and domestic workers.[154]

The NAACP urged the AFL "to resist the inclusion . . . of geographic wage differentials." Green assured the association that it had always opposed this.[155] When the AFL wrote its own version of the bill and excluded agricultural workers, White asked it to reconsider this position, saying, "As you of course know, agricultural workers are today the most impoverished and exploited laborers in the United States." He urged Green to "insist on the inclusion of these workers who need the benefit of protective legislation more than any other single group."[156] The AFL did not respond to the NAACP's plea, and the NAACP did not dwell on this issue, perhaps because so many other occupational groups had been excluded. The act would cover only those workers engaged in the production of goods which involved interstate commerce (which was defined quite narrowly). The NAACP directed its attention to preventing the establishment of geographic wage rates.

When it appeared that regional wage rates were going to be established to make the bill more palatable to the South, the NAACP asked its members to contact their congressmen and insist that "any attempts to fix a sub-standard of wages and hours for Negro workers be resisted to the utmost."[157] It also sent out letters to several congressmen, asking them to oppose the differential wage rate.[158]

Those who argued for a differential wage rate in the South based their argument on the differences in the cost of living, maintaining that it was considerably lower in the South. The NAACP countered this by circulating statistics which revealed "no fundamental differences in standards of living." White said these findings were further substantiated by a 1935 WPA study and contended that the price of food and other consumer goods was actually higher in the South.[159] Another argument used to support regional wage differentials was the low cost of housing in the South. The NAACP argued that using housing costs was not a fair comparison because so much of the housing in the South, especially in Negro communities, was sub-standard.[160]

John W. Davis, then president of the controversial National Negro Congress (NNC), asked the NUL to join its national campaign to promote passage of the bill. NUL Executive Secretary Eugene Kinkle Jones told Davis that he thought "it would be a mistake for Negroes to press too strongly for passage of the Wages and Hours bill." The bill was "desirable, but inasmuch as the chief opposition to the bill has come from the South, the Southerners would take advantage of the wide appeal from Negroes to round up opposition based on racial animosities." Jones noted that the bill then had the support of labor, and he thought this support would probably be sufficient to get the bill passed. Visible support by Negroes might do more harm than good. Jones advised the NUL affiliates of the position of the national office: it was in favor of the bill; not campaigning for it was a matter of "strategy and technique–wisdom dictates caution."[161]

After an endorsement that argued against geographic wage differentials in an *Opportunity* editorial, the NUL did not openly support the bill.[162] But there was probably more involved than a political strategy; rejecting Davis's offer might also have been related to the NUL's reluctance to ally with the NNC. The NNC was regarded as a radical organization, and the NUL did not wish to attach its name to any of the NNC's endeavors.

The NNC evolved from the Joint Committee that was formed in 1933 to monitor the NRA's industrial codes. When the NRA was ruled unconstitutional, this seemed to eliminate the need for the Joint Committee. It struggled to survive by expanding its objectives and, by 1936, had become the National Negro Congress. For a time Randolph was president, Granger was a regional director, and Hill served on the national council, which included at least one member of the Communist Party.[163]

As the NNC expanded, there was concern that its broad agenda would duplicate the services of the NUL and NAACP. The NNC sought to appease these concerns with a statement preceding its list of objectives: It would not "usurp the work of existing organizations" but seek "to accomplish unity of action of existing organizations."[164] It seemed to be carving out the role of convener; it would bring other organizations and groups with common interests and concerns together. In this process, it alienated many of its constituents, including the NAACP.

The NNC infringed upon what the NAACP must have regarded as "sacred territory" when the NNC launched a fund-raising campaign to advocate for federal antilynching legislation. This caused a great deal of confusion among the NAACP's contributors since this had been a major effort of the association for many years. White complained to Davis that the NAACP had worked hard and incessantly for many years on this issue, and it seemed part of common sense to use "machinery now in existence" instead of creating additional machinery and dividing up "the already inadequate funds for the fight for anti-lynching legislation."[165] After this disagreement, the NAACP maintained a polite distance from the NNC.

Other prominent black leaders criticized the NNC too. In explaining why he chose not to stand for reelection as NNC president, Randolph, who had always been staunchly anti-Communist, described the NNC as "a miserable failure, so far as representing the sentiment of American Negro people is concerned."[166] It was criticized by black church leaders because it had not involved any religious leaders in its activities, although some churches had supported it. Church leaders accused the NNC of carrying "our race on an excursion of Sovietism and Atheism, using enough alloy of religion to decoy the race until they have our followers captured by this sinister strategy."[167] The NNC's standing in the black community thus mitigated against its ability to bring organizations together to work on common concerns and problems.

The NAACP did not agree with the NUL's strategy to remain silent while the Wages and Hours bill was being considered in Congress. But it did not join the NNC campaign—it continued to work alone. As the bill seemed on the verge of passing, White asked Charles Houston and Thurgood Marshall to consult with Robert Weaver and draft an amendment that would prohibit discrimination in contracts financed by federal funds.[168] The amendment, if drafted, was not included in the act.

The Fair Labor Standards Act (FLSA) was very weak because too many concessions had been made to diverse groups. It established a minimum wage of twenty-five cents an hour and a work week of forty-four hours, allowing two years to reach a minimum wage of forty cents per hour and a forty-hour week. Agricultural and domestic workers were among the many occupations excluded from coverage as were, under the child labor provisions, children employed in agriculture.[169]

Industry committees would make decisions about the wage rates. Regional differentials were prohibited, but administrators were "required to give consideration to such factors as freight rates, cost of living, cost of production and wages established for like or comparable work by collective labor agreements."[170] This meant that local employers might have a great deal of influence over the establishment of wage rates—something the NUL and NAACP regarded as detrimental to Negroes in the South.

There was speculation that black workers might be threatened with displacement by white workers, as had happened with the NRA's "Blue Eagle Agreement." An editorial in *Opportunity* warned Negro workers not to enter into any collusion with their employers and asked "the Negro press, the Negro church, and Negro social workers . . . to use every influence they can command to prevent Negro workers from participating in any effort to sabotage the Act." Reports in the press about widespread shutdowns of southern industries, throwing thousands of Negroes out of jobs, made Negro workers feel vulnerable. The editorial predicted that there would be some suffering due to loss of jobs, but that the gains "which must inevitably come to Negro workers will ultimately far outweigh the losses which now seem to impend." In the long run, and especially because the administrator of the act had been Industrial Commissioner of New York State and was known to the NUL, the league believed that the integrity of the act would be maintained.[171] Apparently the NAACP needed more assurance than this. It urged the appointment of "colored people to the national and administrative boards" as "the only effective guarantee against discrimination."[172]

When some black employers refused to pay the minimum wage to their employees, the NUL severely criticized them. These employers claimed that they were "trying to give Negroes an opportunity to work" and if they had to pay the minimum wage, they could not remain in business. In an editorial the NUL asked, "What price Negro business if it must rest on the privilege of exploiting Negro workers? And what can we say to those who advocate a lower wage for Negroes on the basis of race and color in Mississippi and Alabama, if we seek the same type of opportunities ourselves?"[173]

After a long argument about whether or not they would be classified as agricultural workers, tobacco workers ended up with FLSA coverage. The NAACP watched the tobacco industry closely as the date for the act to become effective approached. It called upon its branches in North Carolina and Virginia "to be on the alert for evidence of discrimination by employers who will attempt to supplant Negro workers with whites rather than pay the former the increased wage."[174] The NAACP also pressured for a study of the "relative costs of living" in various parts of the country, "particularly with respect to alleged differences between the North and the South." It thought this was important to Negro workers because the language in the act regarding regional differences and the minimum wage was too ambiguous.[175]

The passage of the FLSA completed Roosevelt's New Deal reform legislation agenda. This legislation established programs that, for the most part,
excluded blacks from coverage because the benefits were attached to an
employed status and to occupations in which few blacks were employed.
Consequently, the legislation did not improve the social and economic condition of most black workers. When the economy began to expand and New
Deal work and work-relief programs were gradually dismantled, the private
sector did not absorb black workers at the same rate that it absorbed white
workers. The dire predictions of the NUL and NAACP were coming to
fruition. Employment discrimination remained a barrier to jobs for blacks,
forcing many to rely on public assistance to survive. As these problems persisted, civil rights organizations turned their attention to the defense industry, which was recruiting white workers but refused to hire blacks.

THREE

Fighting for Fair and Full Employment

During World War II and the postwar period, civil rights organizations continued their efforts to help the black population gain employment, making the introduction of fair and full employment legislation of vital interest to them. A full employment policy was needed to assure that jobs were available, and a fair employment policy was needed to assure that black workers had equal access to work and would not be relegated to the lowest-paying and least desirable jobs, regardless of their level of skill. Fair and full employment were essential to the well-being of black Americans.

Temporary Fair Employment Practice Committee

In the late 1930s the nation's attention turned to the threat of war in Europe. Millions of workers remained unemployed, but with the development of the defense industry jobs were becoming more plentiful. Unfortunately, most black workers were not affected by this expansion of the economy because the defense industry refused to hire them. Jews and "hyphenated Americans" also had difficulty obtaining defense jobs.[1] The NAACP and NUL were appalled; the country was spending massive amounts of money on the defense industry, but Negroes were not included in any of the plans.[2] It was crucial for Negroes to participate in the country's defense efforts, not only because of their strong belief in democracy but also because exclusion could have serious social and economic repercussions for Negro Americans, who needed to be broadly seen as contributing, participating members of society. The NUL said:

It is important that Negroes be encouraged to participate freely and whole-heartedly in a national effort, for that sense of participation helps to build a feeling of pride and social responsibility necessary for the Negroes' continued advance within the American community.... It is our experience that public attitudes and procedures regarding the Negro that are developed during an emergency period are apt to remain as part of the community's established thinking long after the actual emergency has passed; thus any advances or losses experienced by Negroes at this time will directly affect the social and economic status of Negroes during the next several decades.[3]

Both organizations launched an all-out effort to help black workers gain employment in the defense industry and obtain training in government-sponsored vocational defense classes. But Negroes who applied for admission to training programs were not admitted. Instead, they were confronted with a vicious circle of logic: The rationale used to exclude them was that the jobs for which workers were being trained were not open to Negro workers; therefore the training was a waste of taxpayers' money. However, when they applied for jobs, the defense industries claimed they could not employ anyone who was not trained.[4]

To rectify this problem, the NUL brought several of its affiliate secretaries to Washington to meet with defense agency officials. To convince employers that Negro workers were capable of performing defense industry jobs, the NUL published a pamphlet ("Mr. Employer, I Can Run Your Machines"), distributing it "among employers and key persons interested in the use of Negro labor."[5]

The NAACP sent lists of industrial plants with government contracts to its branches and urged them "to visit the plants and confer with chambers of commerce and employment agencies in a concerted effort to secure employment of Negroes in the huge program." It also "issued a call to Negro workers to apply for jobs at all defense plants and to notify the N.A.A.C.P. if they were refused employment."[6] In spite of the desperate need for workers, the defense industry recruited whites from other areas and ignored local black workers who applied for jobs.

Civil rights organizations firmly believed that organized labor was contributing to the problem, that there was a "tacit collusion between labor and management."[7] "Labor unions, chiefly those affiliated with the American Federation of Labor, continued to prevent Negroes from being employed in war and private industry by the use of constitutional clauses and ritualistic practices which barred Negro workers from membership."[8] The NAACP warned the AFL's William Green that it would seek an amendment to the National Labor Relations Act that would deny the benefits of the act to discriminatory unions if such practices did not cease. It thought the AFL should be taking "the lead in breaking down barriers confronting black workers within its ranks." In contrast, the CIO was "making great strides towards integrating colored workers into its organized labor market." The only response the NAACP received from Green was a reaffirmation of the AFL's "former position toward organizing all workers into the AFL regardless of creed, color or nationality."[9]

During the Depression, the organizations had believed that the federal government should accept responsibility for prohibiting discrimination in programs financed with government money. Now, in federal contracts with private industry, they saw this situation replayed as one in which defense industries with government contracts should not be allowed to discriminate in programs using public funds.[10] Although a national defense law included provisions outlawing discrimination because of race, creed, or color, it contained the same limitations as had antidiscriminatory clauses in New Deal legislation: there was no enforcement mechanism.[11] Black Americans made up 10 percent of the population, yet only 3 percent had been admitted to defense training programs.[12] This was clearly discriminatory.

The defense agencies responded slowly. The Office of Production Management (OPM) asked industries with defense contracts to refrain from discrimination, and the United States Office of Education (USOE) issued a memorandum instructing state education offices to provide training facilities for Negroes that were "equal to those provided whites." These instructions had no effect on discrimination as defense industries continued to recruit workers from other areas.[13]

This provoked the OPM to send a stronger letter explaining that industries were expected to "utilize *all* available local labor before recruiting additional labor from outside of their local areas." The NAACP realized that OPM would have great difficulty enforcing this policy, but it nevertheless regarded the letter as significant because it was "the first official recognition by the government of the treatment of Negro workers."[14] The NUL thought the OPM had made "a breach" in the barriers which industrial management and organized labor had erected to exclude black workers, but the league feared that it would result in token compliance, "an insincere demonstration, . . . the conspicuous admission of a few Negroes to plants and training schools in order that it might be said, 'We have no policy of racial discrimination.'"[15]

In order to increase the pressure on Washington officials, the NAACP conducted a letter-writing campaign directed at Congress, the president, and the heads of defense agencies. Forty-six branches of the NAACP picketed plants in their areas with signs calling attention to discriminatory employment practices ("LET'S BLITZKRIEG THE COLOR-LINE" and "IT'S OUR COUNTRY TOO! WE WANT WORK").[16] Still there was no change in the defense industry's hiring practices.

The National Council of Negro Women (NCNW), founded in 1935 by Mary McLeod Bethune, became involved because it was concerned about the exclusion of Negro women and youth from defense industry jobs and training. When Bethune created NCNW, she envisioned it as a powerful coalition that would embody all the major national Negro women's organizations. She thought such an organization was needed to address economic, political, and social issues that affected Negro women and their families.[17] By the early 1940s it had at least twenty-nine affiliates (sororities and church, professional and civic organizations) and a small paid staff.[18] The main function of the national office was to keep its affiliates informed about current legislation under consideration and other social issues which they, in turn, were to disseminate at the local level. Based in Washington, D.C., the NCNW was a frequent participant in conferences and meetings on social welfare legislation arranged by various civic and lobby groups. Because of Bethune's close association with Eleanor Roosevelt around issues related to minorities, women, and children, she was believed to have considerable access to the White House; this heightened NCNW's prestige in the black community.

A. Philip Randolph, along with White, Hill, Granger, Bethune, and other national black leaders, had been conferring with the president and defense industry officials for several months "seeking the participation and integration of Negroes in national defense." Randolph decided that all the efforts of the organizations had been fruitless, that black leaders "were not going to get far; [and that] . . . some other technique of action" was needed. With this in mind, he formed a national March on Washington Committee which began to organize local committees. His idea "took root and spread like a prairie fire," quickly gaining the support and cooperation of Negro organizations throughout the country and taking the form of a massive March on Washington Movement (MOWM).[19]

MOWM threatened to march if the president did not issue an executive order prohibiting discrimination in "all government departments . . . and national defense jobs" and desegregating the armed forces.[20] When it appeared that MOWM was large enough to provide an impressive demonstration of power, Roosevelt was given the date on which a march on Washington would occur. The massive support MOWM had generated alarmed Washington officials; they feared racial conflict if so many Negroes descended upon the city to demonstrate.[21] Several meetings with MOWM leaders were held, as the president and other officials tried to stop the march.[22] During these negotiations, Roosevelt offered to establish a committee to investigate discrimination and to personally ask the heads of defense plants to give Negro workers "the same opportunity to work in defense plants as any other citizen," but the committee would accept nothing less than an executive order.[23] By this time the march had gained its own momentum; organizers were not sure they could call it off, even if they wanted to. Realizing that the march was inevitable unless MOWM's demands were met, the president issued Executive Order 8802 two days before the march was to occur. MOWM "postponed" the march rather than canceling it.[24] The postponement helped maintain MOWM as a useful leverage as the fight against discrimination and segregation continued.

Executive Order 8802 stated that there should be "no discrimination in the employment of workers in defense industries because of race, creed, color, or national origin," and it established the Fair Employment Practice Committee (FEPC) to enforce it by investigating complaints of discrimination and taking "appropriate action to redress grievances."[25] The order did not mention the second demand—the desegregation of the armed forces—but MOWM decided not to push this issue, perhaps because the black population was so ecstatic about getting even this much. The establishment of the FEPC was regarded as a great leap forward.

Although MOWM leaders had some input in the wording of Executive Order 8802, the NAACP was not satisfied with it because it once more gave considerable control to the states in determining the qualifications of individuals for hiring and training. This had been a perennial problem in New Deal work and work-relief programs, and the association feared this allowed a loophole for those who wished "to evade and abort the clear intention" of the president. It suggested the adoption of "drastic Federal rules" to establish general qualifications for all applicants.[26] When the United States Employment Service (USES) allowed its state and local offices to fill job orders specifying race, creed, color, or national origin unless state laws prohibited this, the NAACP argued that this was a violation of Executive Order 8802 since it allowed "44 states to fill orders for workers specifying only 'white,' 'gentile,' 'Protestant,' or 'native born.'"[27] The executive order did not include industries that had government contracts prior to its signing, and the NAACP objected to this too. It wanted the wording changed to "all contractors holding existing contracts and those thereafter to be affected, shall be bound by the non-discriminatory decree of President Roosevelt."[28]

No changes were made in the wording, but this did not deter the organizations. They warned their constituents that it was not going to be easy to use the order because there had been very little support from Congress or the president before MOWM, and even with the order it would "take all the vigilance of . . . such organizations as the Urban League and the NAACP" to detect "evasions and negations by men who had been nurtured too long in the noxious atmosphere of racial prejudice."[29]

The NAACP's first step was to gather data about employment and training opportunities for Negro workers. It asked its branches and the affiliates of the NUL to interview personnel managers at defense plants, officials in charge of training and apprenticeship programs, placement officers at state employment agencies, and union officers (especially those from unions that were known not to admit black workers). They were also asked to secure affidavits from Negro workers who were trained for certain jobs but denied employment. It reminded its branches and the NUL affiliates that Executive Order 8802 was "not popular with most employers and most trade unions. It takes courage, hard work, and alert intelligence to make an unpopular law or decree work."[30]

The NCNW "deplored the lack of integration of women in the defense program." It was its "understanding that WPA white collar workers were being laid off on the presumption that they [would] be absorbed in defense industries," but black women were not being so employed. It wanted these women admitted to defense industry training programs. Adamant about the inclusion of Negro youth, the NCNW resolved "to take whatever steps necessary" to assure that the "oncoming generation" received the benefits of federal, state, and city vocational training programs in order to improve economic conditions through better jobs and higher wages. It "hoped that the President's Executive Order [would] be effective."[31]

The FEPC did not appear to have high status or high priority within the administration. Composed of five members and a chair (all appointed by the president to serve on a part-time basis without compensation), and with no provision made for field staff, its jurisdiction was limited to industries under government contract and to government agencies concerned with vocational and training programs. It was to engage in informal negotiations, secure voluntary compliance with the executive order's nondiscriminatory principle, and hold hearings in areas where widespread discrimination had been reported. When discrimination was verified, the party involved was supposed to take the steps needed to comply with the executive order, but if the party refused to comply, there was very little that FEPC could do because it had no judicial enforcement power. It could only request the cancellation of a contract or a denial of manpower and materials or, ultimately, it could refer the case to the president for final disposition.[32] The reality was that defense contracts could not be voided because of discrimination, and this gave FEPC very limited leverage when its investigations validated charges of discrimination.[33]

Consistent with its belief that Negroes should be included in the administration of programs, the NAACP pressured the president to appoint a Negro to the FEPC and was pleased when Roosevelt appointed two: Attorney Earl B. Dickerson, a Chicago alderman and president of the Chicago UL, and Milton P. Webster, vice president of BSCP.[34] In addition, White had considerable influence with the executive secretary of FEPC, and with White's encouragement five Negroes were hired as staff members. The organizations also appreciated the numerous contacts that FEPC had with Robert Weaver, who was working in OPM's Labor Division and who shared the concerns of the NUL and NAACP. The FEPC's integrated staff frequently startled many who visited its office since this was certainly not the norm in Washington.[35]

The FEPC, however, was slow in responding to complaints. About three months after it began its work, the NAACP was able to cite only a few situations in which the FEPC had been helpful in gaining employment for Negro workers. The NAACP said, "These instances are but a drop in the bucket, but they may well be the beginning of a real foothold for Negro workers in defense industries."[36] Recognizing that the FEPC's limited power and small staff hindered its functioning, the association urged the president to increase staff as well as the committee's power by requiring fines or penalties for violations of the order.[37]

After the FEPC had been in operation about a year, the NUL was concerned because only three hearings had been held and the president had not canceled any defense contracts although "concrete evidence of discrimination against Negroes and Jews [had] been unearthed by the Committee." But the NUL could see positive aspects of the committee's work. The hearings had done an excellent job of focusing public attention on the problems of racial discrimination in employment. The fact that the government was using its influence and prestige to break down discrimination gave hope to Negro Americans. However, the NUL thought the FEPC had a "flagrant weakness" in its lack of power to enforce its own decisions and predicted that the FEPC would go down in history as nothing more than a goodwill gesture if compliance was not enforced by the government.[38]

State agencies persisted in barring Negroes from defense industry training programs, using the same rationale they had used before the executive order—training was a waste of money because black workers were not hired for these positions, even when trained. The NAACP continued to regard this as a violation of the order; it was unfair because it would keep black workers unskilled "by denying them the training provided by the tax money of all the people."[39] The NAACP encouraged and admonished Negro workers to fight for training that was provided or subsidized by the government because this was an unprecedented opportunity for them to improve their chances for employment during and after the war. An editorial in *Crisis* read:

> This is our chance to get training for thousands of our people. Of course we will have to fight to get them jobs, but it is easier to fight for a trained man than for an untrained one. Of course there will be a great depression after the war and millions will be unemployed, but here again the man with the training will have a shade better chance in the struggle. The lesson is: *Get training!*[40]

When the NAACP testified before a Senate subcommittee investigating manpower resources and the most advantageous way to use them, it contended that discrimination against Negro workers accounted for a large part of the manpower shortage. Prejudice against Negroes in the educational system had been transferred to the three major training programs: the union apprentice system, training by private industries, and defense training by the government. It testified that the apprentice system and training in private industry were controlled by craft unions that shut black workers out; government training programs had capitulated to local and regional prejudices, especially in the South. Even with the executive order, USES continued to make job referrals on the basis of race, which resulted in "wasteful underemployment." The bulk of Negro workers were "relegated to, and frozen in, the subordinate services," and this had "artificially induced manpower shortages. . . . Negro women were victims of 'double discrimination—race and sex" because industry had failed to give even "token employment" to them "at a time when white women [had] been widely integrated into the training and employment picture." The manpower shortage could be solved by "using to the fullest extent all available or potential labor without regard to race, color, or creed." One-tenth of the workforce was not being utilized.[41]

The FEPC compiled a long list of violators in the South and prepared to hold hearings in Birmingham. Although there was great opposition to this by the private sector and the government (because it was an election year), the FEPC prevailed. When the hearings were completed, some proponents of FEPC principles were not sure whether the hearings had helped or hindered efforts to eliminate discrimination. On the positive side, some industries had changed their hiring policies. On the negative side, the hearings had aroused the wrath of the southern Democrats; the white South felt that the sanctity of the southern way of life had been threatened.[42] "Black professors testified as experts, black workers accused white unions and employers of job discrimination, and black committee members occupied seats of authority, questioned white witnesses, and sometimes challenged them in a manner unfamiliar to the Deep South."[43] Since it was an election year and southern votes were essential, this placed the FEPC in jeopardy.

In order to placate the South, Roosevelt abolished OPM, the agency that the FEPC had relied heavily on for fieldwork, and transferred FEPC to the War Manpower Commission (WMC). The NUL and NAACP vigorously opposed this because it made the FEPC dependent for funding on Congress, instead of the president, and all of its cases would have to be referred to WMC for final determination.[44] The MOWM threatened a march.[45] The storm of protests forced Roosevelt to respond. In a public statement he said his intent was "to strengthen the Committee and revitalize Executive Order 8802." He thought the "friendly supervision" of the chairman of the WMC would "be of great assistance" to the FEPC.[46] The NAACP was convinced that the transfer made the FEPC politically vulnerable; the southern bloc of the Democratic Party would attempt to sabotage its activities. It noted that the U.S. Employment Service and Office of Education, which were under the WMC, were permitting discrimination at local levels by acquiescing to local norms. The president saw no need for the NAACP's concerns; the FEPC would remain under his control because he was the Chief Executive and the transfer would further the work of the FEPC.[47] The NAACP remained unconvinced. The FEPC had submitted several estimated budgets to Paul McNutt, head of the WMC, and nearly three months had elapsed without any action; moreover, the FEPC was currently operating without a budget. In addition, the WMC was trying to cut costs by combining several local FEPC offices with local WMC offices. The NAACP, NUL, and Dickerson believed this would result in further dilution of the FEPC's power.[48]

McNutt, who was a liberal and probably favored antidiscriminatory measures, attempted to control the FEPC because he wanted to protect the president from any political repercussions that might result from its activities. The committee negotiated with him for months to become more autonomous but gained very little.[49] The organizations' reservations were further validated when McNutt indefinitely postponed FEPC's scheduled hearings on the southern railway industry and the unions involved. The NAACP asked the president to overrule the cancellation because "it would rob FEPC of the last vestige of justification for its existence and . . . open the flood gates of discrimination." It would "not only reverse the healthy trend against discrimination, but [would] directly and dangerously affect successful prosecution of the law." It criticized the president for not giving "the militant support" he had given other agencies like the National Labor Relations Board and the Securities Exchange Board when they were under attack by "reactionary forces."[50] The NUL's board said the policies of the railway and the unions had "long been a disgraceful blot on the nation's employment record" and urged McNutt to reconsider the cancellation.[51]

The FEPC struggled to survive; it was in political limbo because it had so little support from the administration. As cases mounted, there was little it could do other than hold meetings. Government officials would not meet with the committee or return its calls. Many regarded it as a political mistake—a troublemaker that stirred up racial conflict—and it was under constant attack from southern legislators who pressured Roosevelt to abolish it. Secretary of State James F. Byrnes advised against this; he thought the FEPC served as a buffer, and without it appeals from black Americans would go directly to the White House. It seemed wiser to issue a new executive order and form a new committee. Executive Order 9346, issued on May 27, 1943, gave the new FEPC what it had denied the old committee: independent status in the Office of Emergency Management (OEM), field offices, and a half-million dollar budget.[52] Furthermore, the new order built on Executive Order 8802 by authorizing the committee to not only "take appropriate steps to redress grievances," as order 8802 had done, but also to "take appropriate steps to obtain elimination of . . . discrimination."[53]

Some of the committee members had resigned prior to Executive Order 9346 when it was clear they no longer had the president's support, but the two black Americans chose not to do so, regarding resignation as capitulating to the FEPC's opponents. When Roosevelt appointed the new committee, he chose not to reappoint Dickerson. The NUL thanked Roosevelt for "re-establishing the FEPC as a functioning body" and asked him to "retain those members of the old Committee who have served faithfully and whose resultant experience is of tremendous value to the Committee in discharging its continuing duties." It wished "to stress the importance of the leadership given by Earl B. Dickerson."[54] Dickerson, regarded by the administration as too combative, too hard to control, and therefore a political risk, was replaced by P. B. Young, an elderly, conservative southern black editor of the *Norfolk Journal and Guide*.[55] Webster, perhaps because he had the support of organized labor, was reappointed.

With its new independent status, the committee developed policies that expanded its jurisdiction over complaints to include all those with government contracts (private employers, unions, private educational institutions, and government agencies), not just those with contracts pertaining to the war effort. In addition, this included complaints against all employers and unions engaged in industries essential to the war effort, whether or not they had a contract.[56]

When the railroad hearings were finally held, FEPC found that the contract between the union and the railroads was "designed for no other purpose than to cut down the employment of Negroes as firemen and to increase the hiring of white persons in these positions." The railroads and unions refused to obey the FEPC order to end their discriminatory practices because they regarded the FEPC as "wholly without constitutional and legal jurisdiction and power to issue the directives." The employment of "Negroes

as firemen would have disastrous results which would antagonize the travel-
ing and shipping public." The issue dragged on until Roosevelt appointed a
North Carolina judge to "negotiate an understanding with the railroads and
the unions on the problem."[57] Although the judge found no illegality in the
FEPC's actions, a report was never issued. The whole episode was regarded
as damaging to the FEPC. In spite of its independent status and expanded
jurisdiction, it revealed how little power the FEPC actually had and encouraged contractors to ignore it.[58]

Nevertheless, the defense industry gradually began to hire black workers,
and by 1944 the NUL could state in its annual report that "the actual employment of Negro workers is no longer a serious problem in major industrial
centers." But the problem of the placement of skilled workers remained.
Whether the FEPC could be credited with expanding employment opportunities for black workers in the defense industry is debatable. A crucial shortage of labor certainly made employers more amenable to hiring black workers than they had been before the war. The country had full employment;
everyone able to work was needed in the war economy. Many historians view
this as the major reason for the employment of blacks, and not the FEPC's
activities. Still, the NAACP, NUL, and NCNW perceived the FEPC as a very
important agency for Negroes and believed that the experiences of black
workers during the war would have been quite different without it. The
FEPC's public hearings made the country more aware of discriminatory
employment practices. The agency was instrumental in helping skilled black
workers obtain jobs commensurate with their abilities and that traditionally
had not been available to them. While more successful in the North than in
the South, even in the South it had made some inroads. There blacks were
admitted to defense training classes (although many had to leave the area in
order to get defense jobs), and in some industries in the South blacks even
worked on integrated shifts.[59] The organizations doubted that these things
would have been accomplished without the FEPC's intervention. When
Randolph started a drive for a permanent FEPC, they supported him.

Efforts to Establish a Permanent FEPC

With the end of the war imminent, civil rights organizations worried about
what would happen to Negro workers during the reconversion from war to
peacetime production. Since they were the last hired and lacked seniority,
they would in fact be the first fired. A serious economic depression was

anticipated, making black workers a disproportionate number of the unemployed. The FEPC would be needed then just as it had been needed during
the war. With Randolph's leadership, a liberal interracial coalition of religious, civic, and labor leaders established the National Council for a
Permanent FEPC. Randolph was a cochairman along with the Reverend
Allan Knight Chalmers, a prominent white theologian.[60]

Lester B. Granger became ambivalent about the establishment of a permanent FEPC because "the present FEPC still [had] to prove its effectiveness." He believed that a careful study of "government responsibility and
function in the field of minority rights" was needed before a campaign for a
permanent FEPC was launched. If this was not done, the end result could be
"a decidedly unwise long-term policy."[61] After Granger expressed this opinion, the NUL became more attentive to race relations and job placement
through contacts with major "industrialists and business men."[62] Racial tensions were increasing, largely over competition for jobs and housing, and the
NUL believed that, as a social service agency and an organization concerned
with interracial cooperation, it was in a unique position to be effective in
helping persons of "different racial and cultural backgrounds learn to work
together."[63] It would become a national coordinating agency "used in behalf of interracial cooperation," a "troubleshooter."[64] A grant from the
Rosenwald Fund enabled it to develop a community relations program to
improve the relationship between Negroes and whites in areas where there
were large numbers of veterans seeking education and employment.[65]
Although it testified in favor of a bill to establish a permanent FEPC as well
as other legislation, the NUL became less active in the National Council and
less involved in pushing for the passage of social welfare legislation. (It may
have also feared that lobbying activities would jeopardize its tax status as an
organization eligible for tax-deductible charitable contributions.) The
NAACP and NCNW, however, remained active supporters of the National
Council.

As the National Council for a Permanent FEPC was preparing to introduce legislation establishing a permanent agency, amendments proposed by
Sen. Richard Russell (D, Ga.) to appropriations bills concerned with dismantling wartime agencies threatened the temporary FEPC itself. The
National Council therefore decided to table its current efforts until the
appropriations crisis was over and to concentrate on helping the temporary
FEPC survive.[66] The NAACP thought this was a wise move because it was

important to have "a clear distinction between FEPC's appropriations and bills . . . before Congress for the establishment of a permanent FEPC"; some congressmen and the general public were confusing the issues.[67]

In the appropriations debate, southern congressmen were vitriolic in their attempts to block funding for FEPC. They described it as an organization dominated by Negroes and controlled by Communists: its policies would end the free enterprise system, and its integrated staff threatened racial purity and Christianity; it was guilty of creating racial conflict.[68] In spite of these vicious attacks, and through the efforts of the NAACP, NUL, organized labor, and other organizations, the Russell amendments were defeated. FEPC received another half-million dollar budget, which enabled it to continue for at least another year.[69] Owing to illness, P. B. Young, Dickerson's replacement on the FEPC committee, resigned, and Charles H. Houston of the NAACP was appointed in his place.[70]

The National Council could now return its attention to seeking permanent FEPC legislation and to the formidable task of getting it through Congress. Expectations for its small staff were monumental: to encourage introduction of this legislation in Congress, monitor its progress, lobby, elicit favorable testimony, organize local pressure groups throughout the country, and do fund-raising. While the National Council's constant shortage of funds limited its effectiveness, it was nevertheless instrumental in arranging for three fair employment bills to be introduced in the House and one in the Senate.

The bills would establish a permanent FEPC with jurisdiction over all contractors performing services for the national government, all industries affecting interstate commerce, and all labor unions in any of the industries affected. Government contracts could be withheld from violators. Its enforcement powers would be the same as similar government agencies— FEPC orders would be enforceable through the courts. The agency would be responsible to Congress rather than the president and would require Senate confirmation of the president's nominees for committee members as well as undergo congressional scrutiny of its rules before becoming effective.[71]

The NAACP, NUL, and NCNW testified in favor of the legislation. Representing the NAACP, Walter White told the House committee that the temporary FEPC's accomplishments were "phenomenal," given the hostile attacks upon it, but it had "only scratched the outer surface." Negroes continued to face employment discrimination because of the policies of private-sector employers, craft unions, and the federal government. White believed that competition for jobs after the war could lead to racial hostilities without "remedial steps which will wipe out the causes of riots." He urged the committee to recommend "the enactment of legislation for a permanent, adequately staffed, adequately financed, and an adequately armed Fair Employment Practice Committee to the end that job justice be accorded to every man on the basis of his ability." One congressman, openly hostile to White's testimony, implied that a permanent FEPC would create racial discord rather than prevent it. White politely responded, "I think we perhaps disagree on what will promote unity and what will promote disunity."[72]

Representing the NUL, Reginald Johnson testified before the House committee. He said much had changed for the better as a result of the temporary FEPC's activities, but there were "still many individual instances of unfair labor practices that are based entirely on race, creed, color, and national origin. . . . It [was] the League's interest to stress the need for the enactment of this legislation and point out to the House Labor Committee certain factors it should consider in the enactment of fair employment legislation." It was essential for the legislation to incorporate "adequate safeguards . . . into the structure of USES" that will "not permit relapse into the diversified and discriminatory hiring practices this agency and its State affiliates followed prior to the establishment of the War Manpower Commission." Fair employment practices should apply to layoffs in order that "we will not again have social ghettos of racial unemployment and relief" when demobilization of the defense industry begins. In addition, "the eventual demobilization of our armed force . . . will return more than 1,000,000 Negroes who will be expecting to secure employment in accordance with their qualifications. We cannot afford to permit them to be denied employment opportunity because of race." The bill should also "provide more severe penalties for those unions that have membership policies that deny full membership and protection because of race." They should be denied the protection of the National Labor Relations Board and the National Mediation Board. Johnson ended his testimony by providing the committee with a long list of unions that were discriminatory.[73]

Representing the NCNW, Mary McLeod Bethune testified in favor of the Senate bill. She said, "The right to work is a right to live. The bill . . . is one of the most important reconversion bills, for, as we shift from war production to peace-time production, our minorities must not find themselves again handicapped by race, religion, color, or national origin." Bethune said the FEPC had demonstrated there was a need for a permanent "congressionally constituted agency with enforcement powers." She urged the Senate committee to report the bill out favorably.[74] Although the House Labor Committee completed its hearings with no testimony against the bills, it seemed unlikely that any would pass because of strong opposition from the South. Roosevelt, in the midst of an election campaign and in failing health, tried to avoid the issue. The need for a permanent FEPC was not included in the Democratic Party's platform although the Republican Party included it. Nine days before the election, the president finally made a public statement endorsing a permanent FEPC. After that, he was silent on the issue; he did not mention it in his State of the Union message to Congress and made no overt effort to encourage passage of the legislation under consideration.[75]

When the Senate committee approved its bill, the National Council for a Permanent FEPC regarded this as a "victory and a challenge"—a victory because it was "the first congressional recognition that discrimination in employment on grounds of race, color or creed should be the concern of government in the reconversion and postwar period," and a challenge because the House committee had decided to postpone final action on its bill until after the election.[76] The National Council asked its members to write to key senators, congratulating them "on the statesmanship they have shown in piloting this bill thru [sic] the Education and Labor Committee," and to "write their own Senators urging them to work for early and favorable action on the Senate floor." It asked supporters of the bills to "get promises" from candidates "for either House or Senate seats, *before election*, while they are campaigning for votes."[77]

After Roosevelt died in 1945, a few months after beginning his fourth term as president, Harry S Truman assumed the presidency and publicly supported the establishment of a permanent agency.[78] But in spite of his support, the bills for a permanent FEPC did not move forward. The Senate bill was still to be debated and the House bill was lodged in the Rules Committee when a rift over tactics developed between the temporary FEPC staff and the staff of the National Council for a Permanent FEPC. The National Council did not think the FEPC staff should be doing "legislative work," especially when it was not coordinating its efforts with the National Council. The FEPC staff wanted to concentrate on efforts to get the House bill to the floor because they believed it would be difficult to get the bill through the Senate, but more likely if the House had already passed it. The National Council's staff and the NAACP thought it best to concentrate on the Senate bill, soon to be debated, since there was sure to be a filibuster and strategies to end it needed to be developed. In addition, more testimony for the bill needed to be scheduled.[79] The prolonged fight for passage of legislation to establish a permanent FEPC probably contributed to further rifts between the National Council and its coalition of organizations. Leslie Perry, head of the NAACP's Washington Bureau, told White that the relations between the CIO and the National Council were strained and "near the breaking point," because the staff of the National Council decided to try to get the Senate bill called up without consulting the CIO. The CIO thought the National Council "was acting in a high-handed manner" and was not "giving it (the largest organized force behind the legislation) full recognition in the Council." Perry added that the National Negro Congress (NNC) had become involved and this might be "some indication of what is behind the dissension."[80]

White was deeply concerned about the rift and cautioned Perry not to become "embroiled in a political duel." It had become apparent at a recent meeting White had attended in New York that the "Left Wing is planning to take over the fight for FEPC. Any quarrel between the supporters of FEPC would play right into the hands of its enemies and sound its death knell." White referred to an article from *Manuscript: A Washington News Letter* (a small weekly mailed to subscribers) that described the conflict between the National Council and some of the coalition organizations. The NNC was supporting Vito Marcantonio (American Labor Party, New York) who, like the FEPC staff, preferred to bring the bill up in the House before it was debated in the Senate.

The article also discussed the rift between the CIO and the National Council for a Permanent FEPC. Some congressmen told the CIO that there was no political advantage in supporting a permanent FEPC. They cited an election in Pennsylvania to prove their point. "Every Democratic Congressman from Pennsylvania signed the petition for discharge of the Rules Committee" and "only two percent of the Negroes in Pennsylvania [had] supported these Congressmen." White disputed this view, believing that an event in Kansas City, Missouri, provided a more accurate picture; there, "7000 Negroes (and a sprinkling of whites) turned out in a driving rain to discuss FEPC and how to 'slaughter Slaughter who slaughtered the FEPC' in the Rules Committee." White admonished Perry not to "let ourselves be dragged into a dirty political fight" and told him he thought his "sense" of what was going on with the NNC was very accurate.[81]

The National Council received a boost when Truman supported legislation for a permanent FEPC in his "message to the Nation."[82] But the House bill remained in the Rules Committee without enough votes to bring it to the floor. The NAACP supported a House resolution to lower the number of signatures required to bring a bill up on a discharge petition, but the resolution did not pass.[83] In the meantime, after twenty-three days of filibuster in the Senate, the bill for a permanent FEPC was displaced by an appropriations bill.[84]

Perry thought that a "new political quid pro quo" was needed. "Moral suasion" seemed sufficient for the fight for an antilynching law, which "was essentially a moral issue [that] did not affect the pocket book of any group, nor did it affect any recognized vested interests"; but current legislation of interest to the NAACP "such as FEPC, Minimum Wage, Housing, Price Control, etc. [ran] counter to what large and powerful financial groups regard[ed] as 'their interest.'"[85] It was becoming increasingly more difficult to find liberal congressmen who were willing to sponsor antidiscriminatory amendments to social welfare legislation. Recently, even Sen. Robert Wagner (D, N.Y.), who had been so helpful to the NAACP during the New Deal administration, had refused to add an amendment to a housing bill. Perry proposed that the NAACP reexamine its policy not to endorse or support political candidates; endorsement would give the association more bargaining power. Short of that, he suggested the *NAACP Bulletin* should report on the voting records of congressmen "which . . . it supports for reelection." The *Bulletin* could periodically publish a "Roll of Honor" and a "Roll of Dis-Honor."[86]

There seemed no hope for passage of legislation for a permanent FEPC when, once again, the temporary FEPC found itself in serious trouble. The agency had "been unable to get an authoritative statement as to its jurisdiction and responsibility since V-J Day" (the end of the war).[87] The Appropriations Committee had drastically cut the FEPC's budget even though it had a long list of cases it hoped to clear up. A case of particular concern was the Capital Transit Company (Washington, D.C.). The FEPC had been negotiating with this company and the unions involved for at least two years over its refusal to hire Negroes as platform workers and motor-men. When the FEPC finally issued a directive, not only did Truman hold it up, he chose not to meet with committee members. Houston resigned in disgust and followed his resignation with a scathing letter to Truman letting him know exactly how he felt about the way he had handled the affair.[88]

Concerned about the fate of the FEPC, thirty black organizations met in Washington. They sent a telegram to the president urging him to restore the appropriation for the FEPC "and to resist any and all legislative trickery to kill or emasculate the present agency." They warned Congress that "the record and vote of this measure will be one of the chief determinants of our support in future elections." Neither this nor a letter-writing and telegram campaign conducted by the National Council for a Permanent FEPC had any effect.[89]

By mid-1946 all members of the FEPC had resigned. The National War Appropriations Act of 1946 had provided FEPC with only $250,000, which was to be used "for completely terminating the functions and duties of the Committee." The end of the war, followed by the wholesale cancellation of war contracts, had raised questions concerning the committee's jurisdiction over private industry as it reconverted to peacetime production. Truman issued an executive order continuing the FEPC's work under the duties and responsibilities of previous executive orders, but the substantially decreased appropriation left FEPC short of staff, forcing it to close most of its field offices. Further cuts made it necessary to put all employees on leave without pay, and active operation ceased on May 3, 1946. The FEPC's final report to Truman strongly supported the need for a permanent FEPC and emphasized that "executive authority [was] not enough to ensure compliance in the face of stubborn opposition." Only "legislative authority" would insure compliance when employers or unions have "refused after negotiation to abide by the National policy of non-discrimination."[90]

At the NAACP's annual conference in 1946, Clarence Mitchell, labor secretary of the NAACP, chronicled the history of the FEPC and its demise. The FEPC had experienced "five troubled years" fighting for its existence and had "been the victim of the most cynical political short-changing ever since it was established by President Roosevelt" in 1941. Its operations were always curtailed by a lack of funds, but it accomplished much "in spite of its supposed supporters rather than because of them." Mitchell continued:

Although the high priest of falsehood, Senator Bilbo, has accused FEPC of stirring up trouble, most of its settlements were accomplished peacefully. . . . Its successes would have been more numerous if the agency had enjoyed the support of important war agencies such as the War Department, the War Production Board, and the War Manpower Commission. All too frequently these agencies crippled the action of FEPC. . . . We are now back where we were at the beginning of the defense program. . . . It is now clear that neither in the White House nor in Congress was there a real intention to establish a strong permanent FEPC if it could possibly be avoided."[91]

Mitchell recommended that the NAACP continue its efforts to establish a permanent federal FEPC and, in addition, concentrate more effort on the establishment of state FEPCs that "are administered fairly and forcefully." Thousands "of colored men and women who for the first time in their lives drew a living wage when they worked in war plants" are now "jobless and without a real hope for work at their newly acquired skills." It was time to push for "fair and full employment."[92] One of the resolutions adopted at the NAACP's annual conferences in 1946 and 1947 was a renewal of its "support and demand for federal fair employment practice legislation with adequate powers" as well as the establishment of enforceable state FEPCs.[93]

The NAACP worried about the return of USES to state control, believing that federal control over this agency was absolutely necessary until enforceable fair employment practice laws at the state level were established. Since the federal government was to continue to pay the cost of operating these offices, the NAACP convened a meeting with the Secretary of Labor and USES officials and invited several other organizations, including the NUL, the CIO, the AFL, the American Jewish Congress, and the Japanese American Citizens League. A Latin American organization from the Southwest was unable to attend but sent a strong letter endorsing the purposes of the conference as outlined by the NAACP. This assembled group proposed that no state should receive federal money unless there were "policies and procedures for promoting the full utilization of minority groups in local employment and training programs serviced by the agency." This included the assignment of "adequate staff to see that policies designed to prevent discrimination are followed in local offices" and a policy whereby no office would accept discriminatory work orders. Furthermore, there should not be separate offices for blacks as there were in the South, and no employer should be able to use the offices to recruit workers in a discriminatory manner. The NAACP thought the first step should be the abolition of segregation

in the District of Columbia office. The Labor Department promised immediate integration of this office but would not make a commitment about
state offices.[94]

Shortly after this meeting, the Labor Department announced the integration of the District of Columbia's USES offices, as promised. Unfortunately, it continued to allow D.C. and state offices to accept discriminatory
job orders, and made a feeble response to the NAACP's concerns with a new
field instruction manual outlining USES policies regarding service to minority groups. USES offices were "to promote equitable employment opportunities for all applicants on the basis of their skills, abilities, and job qualifications" and "make definite and continuous effort with employers with whom
relationships are established, to the end that their hiring specifications be
based exclusively on job performance factors." Mitchell regarded the policies
in the manual as weak and proposed that the NAACP "study the legal aspects
of this question and make an effort to prevent the Department of Labor
from spending the $42,000,000 it will hand out to states unless adequate
safeguards are included."[95] The NAACP, also concerned about discrimination in federal agencies, began a concerted campaign to end it at its 1946
annual conference when it declared, "Wherever our flag flies over a Federal
establishment there also do we find job discrimination is in full force and
effect."[96] The association advocated an executive order to abolish discrimination in federal government agencies and gathered complaints and affidavits which it hoped would convince federal officials and the general public that this was needed. Its data showed that numerous Negro Americans
(including many honorably discharged veterans) had been denied employment in major government agencies. Several had scored very high on civil
service tests and were rejected "solely because of their race."[97] To correct this
situation Mitchell met with key government officials, and an executive order
drafted by the NAACP was circulated among "friendly" heads of departments who might be able to influence Truman. At White's urging, the
President's Committee on Civil Rights recommended the establishment of
an FEPC for federal employees. More than a year later, with no response to
this recommendation, White asked Truman to make a statement against the
discriminatory practices of federal agencies in his 1948 civil rights message
to Congress, and to issue a "strong" executive order. Although Truman's message promised to issue the order, he delayed in doing so. The NAACP's pressure for the executive order escalated with the support of the NUL, NCNW,

and CIO as well as some heads of government agencies.[98] The two-year campaign for an executive order was finally rewarded when, in 1948, Truman
issued Executive Order 9980, which forbade discrimination in federal agencies and established the Fair Employment Board.

The NAACP regarded the order as "a long step forward" by the federal
government that would keep the national fight for a permanent FEPC alive.
It believed the association's continuing activities to be essential in assuring
the Fair Employment Board's survival, and that the board should engage in
"positive action" to eliminate discrimination rather than merely to hold
hearings on individual cases. The NAACP's 1948 annual report noted the
progress that had been made by the various federal agencies, but problems
in the Post Office and the army remained unresolved. The NAACP was also
active in several states where FEP legislation was being considered.[99]

By 1949 the NAACP's Washington Bureau had evolved to the point where
it could maintain a close watch on all social welfare and civil rights legislation, keep its constituents informed, and encourage letter-writing campaigns. When legislation for a permanent FEPC was once again introduced
in the House and Senate, the NAACP immediately organized a letter-writing
campaign aimed at getting the bills out of committee.[100] Passage of FEPC
legislation (along with antilynching, anti-poll tax, and antisegregation
issues) became a top priority, but the FEPC bills languished in committees,
and in 1950, due to the "status of the legislation," the NAACP for the first
time in several years did not include a resolution dealing with FEPC.[101]

The Korean War prompted the NAACP to ask Truman to issue an executive order reestablishing the FEPC, this time with broader scope and
enforcement powers than the World War II order had provided. At the
NAACP's urging the Labor Department had removed racial designation categories from its application forms, and now the association sought to persuade it not to accept any discriminatory orders from defense plants.[102] By
1952 there was no permanent FEPC, but there were two bills under consideration in the Senate and White testified in favor of them. It was a familiar
story: Negro workers were again being barred from defense industry jobs by
the same companies that had barred them at the beginning of World War II.
Unemployment among black workers was almost twice that of whites in
1951. (The figures were quite low when compared with Depression figures
though: 5.9 percent versus 3.2 for whites in 1951, 5.7 versus 2.6 in 1952.) Once
again White spoke of the wastefulness of employment discrimination and

concluded that "fair employment undergirded by legislation is already long overdue. Whatever action we may take now should have been taken yester-day."[103] An NAACP Washington Bureau newsletter concerned with the 1952 election warned members to carefully question congressional candidates about their 1950 voting record for FEPC legislation since some were claim-ing that they had voted for it when in reality they had not.[104]

The efforts of the National Council for a Permanent FEPC and the orga-nizations that supported it did not result in a permanent federal FEPC, although many states passed FEPC laws with varying degrees of enforcement powers. The NAACP, NUL, and NCNW had advocated for *equal* employ-ment opportunities for Negroes. They had not sought any special consider-ation (such as affirmative action) for minority workers—just a chance to compete for jobs on an equal basis with other workers. The organizations' push to establish a permanent FEPC failed for several reasons. As had been the case during the New Deal administration, they could not overcome the powerful southern bloc of the Democratic Party and its coalition with con-servative Republicans. The National Council for a Permanent FEPC was not only limited by a lack of funds but also by the lengthy struggle to bring bills to the floors of the House and Senate. It was difficult to hold the support and attention of its coalition of organizations and the various minority popula-tions the bill would protect. According to historian Merl E. Reed, Catholics and Jews began to distance themselves from the movement as the Senate debates dragged on. Though both groups had experienced employment dis-crimination, Catholics resented "being lumped with colored people in America's thinking" and Jews pulled back "in the belief that their minority troubles were social, rather than economic, in origin." Neither group wanted statistics to be published "that indicated they had been helped by the FEPC."[105] This suggests that a "black stigma" was attached to FEPC and the National Council. Other groups, such as Jews and Catholics, may have felt uncomfortable as part of the coalition supporting the National Council and about being seen as having been helped by the FEPC because Negroes were very visible leaders in efforts to abolish employment discrimination.

The long and unsuccessful battle to pass this legislation certainly strained relationships among the organizations that supported it as they disagreed over tactics. The attempts of the "far left" to take over the National Council created additional friction among the coalition of organizations and caused some to distance themselves from it. Further, momentum to establish a permanent FEPC was hampered by the constant interruptions to help the temporary FEPC survive. Moreover, several other bills (e.g., federal aid to education, amendments to the Social Security Act, federal housing aid, the minimum wage, the extension of price controls, and full employment) also commanded time and attention from coalition organizations and limited the focus they could give to the FEPC issue. Still, the NAACP continued to regard prohibition of employment discrimination as a major priority. Title VII of the 1964 Civil Rights Act finally prohibited employment discrimination and provided the enforcement power the National Council for a Permanent FEPC had regarded as essential. Title VII has been crucial to the NAACP's continuing efforts to end employment discrimination through the judicial system.

Pushing for a Full Employment Policy

The same concerns for the FEPC prompted the organizations to support full employment legislation. They believed that without such legislation Negro Americans would experience very hard times as unemployment increased after the war. The defense industry was in the midst of reconversion and there were massive layoffs. But even after reconversion was accomplished, it seemed unlikely that the private sector would be able to absorb all persons willing and able to work. The organizations sensed that the government was not at all concerned about black workers since there was no longer a need to produce war materials. Government seemed "to throw over-board the war-impelled provisions for the housing and employment of the Negro population, both of which were tolerated as long as they were deemed essential to efficient direction of the war effort."[106]

Although the Department of Labor had developed plans to help key areas adjust to the reconversion, the organizations were dissatisfied with these because they were based on 1940 data and did not consider the population changes that had occurred since then. Thousands of Negroes had migrated to areas where defense jobs were available, and a reverse migration was highly unlikely, particularly when there were no jobs at the other end. Most of the black population would remain in the cities where they had been employed during the war, and the majority of returning black servicemen would probably choose to settle in industrial areas, expecting the same access to jobs that their white counterparts had. The competition for jobs could create a volatile situation.[107]

Civil rights organizations believed that the Full Employment Act of 1945, introduced by Sen. James E. Murray (D, Mont.), would ease the conflict. The act was quite strong and gave citizens a "right" to a job. It assigned the federal government the responsibility to provide jobs when the unemployed were unable to obtain private-sector employment.[108] The organizations strongly supported this policy because it would ensure that Negroes would not be dependent on public assistance when they were unable to find jobs. The NAACP sent a resolution endorsing the bill (S. 380) to its sponsors, urging "immediate enactment of the Full Employment Act of 1945" establishing "the fundamental right of every person in a democracy to have full-time remunerative employment in a useful occupation." The endorsement described the act as absolutely essential because, when the war ended, "there [was] a grave danger that reconversion from wartime production to peacetime production [would] result in great economic dislocation, leaving millions of returning soldiers and war workers without jobs."[109]

Knowing that the perennial problem of discrimination would not be solved by the bill, the NAACP considered pressing for an antidiscriminatory clause, which Perry had discussed with Bertram Gross, a member of Murray's staff. The preamble to the bill stated "that it is the right of 'all Americans' to be gainfully employed," and Gross thought that under "those circumstances, . . . no particular reference to racial groups . . . was necessary." Perry "heartily [agreed] with him inasmuch as the bill [would] probably have tough going at best. . . . Any provision . . . would be meaningless in so far as it confers any positive benefits on minority races." The bill would be "construed as a little FEPC," and this would lessen its chances for passage.[110]

White received a letter from Murray thanking him for the NAACP's endorsement and suggesting that the NAACP help shape public support "by printing informative literature for use by your local organizations and affiliated groups."[111] Murray and the House sponsor, George E. Outland (D, Calif.), also invited the NAACP to a full employment conference in Washington. The sponsors were bringing several national organizations together to discuss possibilities for a nationwide campaign for passage of the bill and deemed the NAACP's cooperation "vital" to this endeavor.[112] The conference brought together approximately thirty-five national labor, civic, religious, and professional organizations, with the NAACP the only black organization in attendance and represented by board member Judge William H. Hastie. Each organization formally endorsed the bill and informed the group of its plans to aid its passage. Hastie said, "The Negro has the most to lose if the objectives are not achieved. The fact must be brought home to minority groups that they will never be able to make progress unless there are adequate jobs for people." The NAACP planned to use its monthly "mailing list of over 500,000" to aid passage of the bill.[113]

Both the NAACP and NUL testified in favor of the bill. Julius A. Thomas, director of NUL's Industrial Relations Department, represented the league before a House committee. He testified that thousands of black workers were being laid off daily because of cutbacks in production, and that these workers "face the possibility of prolonged unemployment unless our economy can be made to work more efficiently." The experiences of Negro workers had shown that when jobs were scarce, it was difficult for them to work; and when jobs were plentiful, they were relegated to low-paying jobs that were below their level of skill. Those who had served in the armed forces had learned new skills and would "not be satisfied with the typical traditional porter and janitor job." Full employment legislation was needed to stabilize the economy.[114]

A copy of one NUL report, "Racial Aspects of Reconversion," sent to Truman before the testimony, was submitted as part of Thomas's testimony. The report pointed out that Negroes needed job security, but because of job discrimination, full employment would not completely eliminate their "job problems"; full and fair employment was necessary to improve the economic status among Negroes. The report urged passage of not only the full employment bill but the bills for a permanent FEPC as well as amendments to the Social Security Act to include agricultural and domestic workers under social insurance.[115]

Representing the NAACP before the Senate Banking and Currency Committee, White testified that a full employment program was of major interest to the NAACP because it was "so fundamental to the well-being and development of the Nation and every community in it." The NAACP was particularly pleased with "the right to work" policy. White's testimony was quite similar to the NUL's. He emphasized the new skills of black workers and servicemen, and he thought "it was understandable . . . that many Negro workers should anticipate with serious misgivings the possibility that the return to peacetime economy may deprive him [sic] of most of those newly acquired jobs in industry." The country would not solve the overall problem of reconversion unless it faced "squarely and dispassionately the precarious position of 13,000,000 Negroes in our society." Most had been employed in "strictly war production," in industries that would suffer the most severe postwar cutbacks. Furthermore, most of the returning Negro servicemen would not be satisfied with the jobs they had before the war. Because of these expectations and the competition for jobs that was bound to occur, many "prophets of gloom in the United States" were predicting postwar race riots. White thought that the only way to avoid this was with a full employment policy. The NAACP wanted "white Americans to have jobs because if they do they will not be tempted to gang up on Negroes who have employment." It wanted Negro workers "to have their full and fair share of jobs that are available so that they can live like decent human beings free from resentment because their color alone deprives them of employment."[116]

As a war correspondent for two years, White had talked to Negro troops who had expressed "grim pessimism" about what postwar America would be like. This pessimism could only be disproved by demonstrating through the passage of the full employment bill that "our announced aims were sincerely enunciated—that this is a war for freedom and democracy for all men." Although Perry had advised against advocating for a nondiscriminatory clause, White called for the passage of the bill with "safeguards added to prohibit discrimination on account of race, creed, color, or national origin in the administration of its benefits."[117]

White concluded his testimony by urging the passage of several other bills before Congress: the bill for a permanent FEPC; a bill to establish a national housing policy; bills to amend the Social Security Act to provide health insurance and to provide benefits, under the contributory portion, to agricultural and domestic workers; and bills to end lynching and the poll tax.[118] An NAACP press release publicized the testimony and informed its constituents of its reasons for endorsing the full employment bill.[119]

At the next meeting of the coalition campaigning for the bill, the NAACP was not the sole black organization: representatives of the NUL and NCNW also attended.[120] By this time, a coalition of "northern reactionaries and Dixie Democrats" had spearheaded strong opposition to the bill, so discussions centered on tactics to counteract this.[121] The bill had been reported favorably by a subcommittee but was in jeopardy before the whole Senate and Banking Committee. "Conservative committee members" objected to "the declaration that employment is a basic American right, which the government should guarantee" and demanded that this clause be removed. The

NAACP believed that if the opposition succeeded "in watering down and otherwise emasculating the Full Employment and Unemployment Bills it will mean that most of the reconversion and post war legislation ... such as FEPC, Social Security and the Housing Program, will be seriously imperiled." It urged all organizations to "write their senators to support the meaningful bills or amendments when it reaches the Floor of the Senate."[122]

The association wired several senators, soliciting their support for retaining the right-to-employment clause in the bill. It said "a policy ... to assure the existence at all times of sufficient employment opportunities to enable Americans to freely exercise this right is an important post war concept which should be codified into law."[123] It urged them "to oppose with vigor all amendments calculated to weaken" these policies.[124] However, as the NAACP had feared, the bills were watered down considerably as they moved through the House and Senate. Before it could distribute its pamphlet about the bill, the pamphlet had become obsolete because the House bill had already deleted the policy most important to the NAACP: the *right* to employment.[125]

At first the bill did not have strong support from labor, which feared that it would minimize its programs. However, massive layoffs during reconversion and the realization that the bill was popular among the rank and file influenced labor to support the bill. The CIO gave it a stronger endorsement than the AFL but reminded its members that the bill was not a cure-all but a supplement to union programs.[126]

The Employment Act of 1946 was passed without giving workers the "right" to a job. It merely promoted "maximum employment, production, and purchasing power" and required the president to give an annual economic report to Congress which would be referred to a joint committee. The powerful lobbying efforts of private industry, especially the National Association of Manufacturers, various Chambers of Commerce, the Committee for Constitutional Government, and the American Farm Bureau, all working to defeat the bill, were too strong for the bill to pass with a policy guaranteeing jobs for all. Private industry contended that the bill would kill initiative, that the government work programs to be created during recessionary periods would compete with private industry, and that its full employment policy would be inflationary.[127] The considerable resources available to the organizations opposing the bill, as compared to the coalition supporting the bill, gave them a distinct advantage in the battle.

The end of the war and the swift reconversion to peacetime production reduced the general public's fears about an immediate depression. Postwar demands for housing and consumer goods as well as aid to war-torn areas in the world resulted in a booming economy in the United States. Most of the population no longer regarded the bill as necessary.[128]

For black Americans, the passage of the act in its diluted form was a serious defeat and left the majority of the black population in a vulnerable condition. Most were not members of unions and therefore not privy to their benefits; there was no federal FEPC to protect blacks from discriminatory employment practices; and a large proportion lacked unemployment compensation coverage, a first-tier benefit under the Social Security Act and an important buffer during periods of economic recession. Fair and full employment policies would have surely made a significant difference in the quality of their lives; both were crucial to the availability of jobs for the Negro population.

FOUR

Pursuing Social Security

As with the struggle over fair and full employment, the civil rights organizations discovered that the difficult problems of pushing both their civil rights and social welfare agendas continued with concerns about social insurance, including health care, during the 1940s and early 1950s. Most states had no antisegregation or antidiscrimination laws, and the same issue of federal over state control remained, which they considered necessary if Negroes were to get a fair share of benefits. And the issue of selective versus universal social welfare policies was equally manifest as the organizations advocated for comprehensive universal social insurance programs.

Pursuing Universal Health Care

Enacting legislation to provide a comprehensive federal social security system with universal health care has proved to be a long and hitherto unsuccessful struggle. In 1934 a health care proposal was included in the first draft of the Social Security Act. Since Roosevelt was more interested in legislation that would provide old age and unemployment insurance, he thought it wise to table the health issue rather than place the entire act in jeopardy. However, some health care gains were made through Titles V and VI of the Social Security Act which established a preventive public health program, some child and maternity health care programs, and training programs for health care personnel. The president recognized that adequate health care was a serious problem in the country, and after the passage of the Social Security Act, he appointed an interdepartmental committee to coordinate health and welfare activities. In addition, a health conference, called by Roosevelt in 1938, resulted in a recommendation for a national health program. Sen. Robert Wagner (D, N.Y.) acted upon this recommendation by introducing a health bill in 1939 that vested federal administration in the Children's Bureau, the Public Health Service, and the Social Security Board, but it was not passed.[1]

The bill would have provided grants-in-aid to various programs established by the 1935 Social Security Act, and given the states considerable autonomy in developing plans. Grants would have been available for child and maternal health, general public health services and investigations, construction of hospitals and health centers, general purpose medical care, and insurance against loss of wages during periods of temporary disability. Anticipating strong opposition to the bill if it allowed too much federal control, Wagner assured the senators that "under no circumstances will the Federal Government undertake to furnish medical care. Administration . . . will be through the states, which will develop their own plans . . . with a view to supplementing, not displacing, the existing efforts of the professions, the localities, charitable organizations and the hospitals." Federal grants would have been made to states on a matching basis, and each state could have developed a plan supported by insurance contributions, general revenue, or both. A state could provide services only to the poor or also include "others more fortunately situated in the economic scale." To provide more federal funding to poor states in greatest need of medical care and health facilities, the bill authorized grants "on a variable matching basis, depending on the relative financial resources of the several states, and determined by the per capita income of their inhabitants." In this way, it was hoped that the bill would "raise the general level of health protection throughout the country, while reducing the existing wide variations among the States, especially between rural and urban areas." The bill would not "establish a system of health insurance, or require States to do so."[2]

The NAACP was very interested in this bill but thought it was "inadequate" because there were no "safeguards" to ensure "equitable distribution of funds in the states where Negroes and whites [were] forced to use separate hospitals, clinics and other health services." When it approached Wagner about this, he "felt that putting in provisions on the basis of need was sufficient"; he did not think it was necessary to have any protective clause for minorities in the bill. Walter White told him that attempting to protect minorities on the basis of need "would mean nothing in Mississippi." The South had a long history of providing separate and inferior facilities for

Negroes in spite of the great need of its black population, just as its system of segregation and discrimination was at least partly responsible for widespread poverty among southern blacks. Wagner advised the NAACP to "make a fight for a more air-tight provision" when the bill reached the floor.[3]

However, the NAACP chose to push for an amendment before the bill reached the floor. At its annual conference it resolved to carry on "an active and sustained fight through direct political action and public opinion to make available to all citizens the facilities of every hospital, medical school and health agency, to the end that identical services and health agencies be furnished to all citizens."[4] A press release solicited "interested persons" to write Senator Wagner and urge him to include amendments to "safeguard health services for colored people in the states having separate health services for each race." The bill, as drafted, did "not make any requirement upon the states which [maintained] separate health facilities for the two races." The association believed that if the bill was "passed in its present form, the states could accept health funds and spend them as they pleased without regard to the racial population of each state."[5] At its Southern Regional Conference, the NAACP's southern branches resolved that "state and federal funds for health work be allocated justly in proportion to the health needs of the Negro." They also supported the employment of "Negro doctors, dentists, nurses and social workers" on the staffs of public health bureaus and departments, and the establishment of "Negro advisory committees to be named by state and federal health agencies to assist with the Negro work."[6]

NAACP lawyer Thurgood Marshall helped prepare a statement for NAACP board chairman Dr. Louis T. Wright to present when he testified in favor of the bill before a Senate subcommittee. The testimony had to emphasize the need for amendments requiring the states to allocate federal funds in an equitable manner. Marshall advised Wright that the bill provided grants to states in four areas: maternal and child welfare, public health work and investigations, hospitals and health centers, and medical care and insurance for illness and loss of wages during periods of temporary illness. The areas would be funded separately, and it was important for Wright's testimony to indicate that the NAACP advocated an equitable distribution of funds in each.[7]

Wright testified in favor of the bill, presenting an amendment for each of the four sections of the bill, as advised by Marshall. The amendment considered to be the most important (carefully written by the NAACP after many consultations with its board members) required a state that maintained separate health facilities to distribute funds for "minority and racial groups" so that these monies were "not less than the proportionate need that each minority racial group in such states bears to the needs of the total population of that state."[8] Other amendments presented by Wright would prohibit discrimination in the salaries or wages paid to personnel, require all administrative reports from the states be made public, require a public hearing on all proposals before approval by the federal government, and require the appointment of federal and local advisory councils that were representative of minority groups.[9] The NAACP, through these amendments, hoped to establish more federal control over state and local health programs in order to reduce the effects of discrimination and segregation.

Although the NAACP adamantly opposed segregation, it did not regard integration of health facilities in the South as a realistic goal and felt forced to settle for separate but equal facilities. Such an approach clearly hinged on an equitable distribution of funds. Although it was widely known that facilities for blacks in the South were inferior to those for whites, the NAACP believed that firm evidence was needed to convince Congress that separate facilities in the southern states were unequal and that safeguards were needed. Since such data were not readily available to the NAACP, the association explored ways to obtain this information.[10] The NAACP learned that the Children's Bureau had some data on the amount the state of Mississippi was spending on Negro health, but the agency refused to release it. After some discussion the bureau agreed that it was not an "issue of right or wrong, but a matter of judgement."[11] It disheartened the NAACP that an agency advocating for children would not take political risks to help Negro children in the South obtain better health care.

The NAACP became hopeful that safeguards would be included when the Senate committee, while rewriting the bill, "adopted the general principal that there should be safeguards in the bill for the protection of minority rights."[12] However, this was only mentioned in a preliminary report and the NAACP thought it absolutely necessary that it be written into the bill. The association became even more hopeful that safeguards against discrimination would be included when the Senate passed the Federal Hospital Act with an amendment that prohibited discrimination "on account of race, creed or color and insured equitable distribution of the federal money appropriated . . . for hospitals in areas too poor to build and maintain hospitals." The NAACP urged speedy passage of the act by the House and reaffirmed its support of the Wagner bill if it included amendments against discrimination. The association regarded the Federal Hospital Act as important but noted that "it remedies but a small segment of the broad and basic needs of national health which can and will be adequately handled only by federal aid."[13] Wagner's bill was favorably reported out of the Committee on Education and Labor but went no further.

In 1943 an omnibus bill to amend the Social Security Act by establishing a comprehensive social insurance system was introduced in the Senate by Wagner and James E. Murray (D, Mont.) and in the House by John E. Dingell (D, Mich.). The Wagner-Murray-Dingell bill recognized the inadequacy of the current system and reflected concerns about problems that were bound to arise during the transition from war to peacetime production. It was believed that a sound comprehensive social security system could alleviate these problems.

The bill included a federal system of hospital and medical insurance. Medical care would be financed through the Social Security payroll tax—thus expanding the first tier under the Social Security Act. The bill did not provide health insurance to the unemployed indigent, which was left to the states and private charity, nor did it provide dental care. Hospitalization was time-limited and therefore would not cover long-term care or any catastrophic illness that required an extensive hospital stay.[14]

The NAACP's immediate concern was the absence of any means for protecting Negroes from discrimination in the programs the act would create, although Wagner had indicated that he had no objection to an antidiscrimination clause in the bill.[15] Leslie Perry, administrative assistant at the NAACP's Washington Bureau, recommended that the association endorse the principle of the bill without "giving unqualified endorsement to the bill itself." The social insurance features of the bill were "entirely satisfactory," but there were difficulties with Title IX, which dealt with medical, hospitalization, and related benefits, and gave the states considerable autonomy. It is well known, Perry noted, that "the Negro is, and will continue to be, vulnerable to prejudice and discrimination where employment and medical care is involved." Perry expected the bill to "undergo considerable modification" before reaching the Senate floor and even then anticipated a "knock-down and drag-out fight" over it because it was being "bitterly attacked by the American Medical Association and other groups."[16]

The NAACP's Advisory Committee regarded the bill's provisions as "so generally desirable that the Association should give its unqualified support even though it [did] not contain anti-discrimination clauses." The committee thought the NAACP "should not try to have an amendment offered if in so doing it would in anywise endanger favorable consideration of this measure."[17]

The National Medical Association (NMA), a professional organization of black physicians, supported the NAACP's endorsement and made an effort to counteract the AMA's criticisms of the bill. The AMA described the bill as socialistic and communistic and predicted that it would end private medical practice by placing all doctors under government control. The NMA pointed out that the bill allowed full freedom of choice for doctors to accept or refuse patients. It especially appreciated the policy of paying doctors from a federal fund. All too frequently, the resources of Negro patients dropped during an illness and they were unable to pay their doctors for medical care. The NMA recognized that there would be no financial gain for physicians whose patients were mostly wealthy, but physicians in poor rural and urban areas would probably make substantial financial gains.[18] In a press release, the NAACP urged "speedy and favorable action on the Social Insurance Act" and announced that it was working with "other progressive forces," including the AFL and the CIO, "to get better social security."[19] The bill, however, did not make it through Congress, perhaps because it was too comprehensive—in addition to the health programs, it proposed significant changes needed to create a comprehensive social security system.

In 1945 Truman supported the passage of health care legislation when he presented an Economic Bill of Rights to Congress which included the "right to adequate medical care and the opportunity to achieve and enjoy good health" as well as "the right to adequate protection from the economic fears of sickness." A few months later, he sent a message to Congress supporting a health care bill. He reminded Congress that the nation had been shocked to learn about the "wide-spread physical and mental incapacity" among "the young people of our nation" that had been revealed during routine Selective Service exams during World War II. Nearly 30 percent were found unfit for military service.[20]

Truman said there was a need for health care legislation that would attack five basic problems. The first problem was the unequal distribution of doctors and hospitals: rural areas were in great need of health facilities and services. The second difficulty was the lack of public health services as well as facilities for maternal and child care. Although public health services had made important contributions to national health, they were still inadequate. The third issue was the lack of medical research and professional education, especially in the areas of incurable diseases such as cancer and mental health. The fourth problem was related to the high cost of individual care; both poor and "normally self-supporting people" were unable to pay for health care when they needed it. And the fifth was the loss of earnings when sickness struck. Sickness not only brought doctor bills, it also cut off income.[21] Truman recommended that Congress adopt a comprehensive modern health program for the nation which would overcome the five basic problems he had delineated.[22]

When the Wagner-Murray-Dingell bill was rewritten to include the president's recommendations, it focused solely on health care and was introduced as the National Health Act of 1945. The act would "make available basic health services to all the people wherever they live and whatever their income."[23] It broadened the current federal grants-in-aid to the states for public health services and maternal and child health services; it provided grants-in-aid to nonprofit institutions engaged in research or professional education; it provided federal grants-in-aid to the states to meet the costs of medical care for needy persons. A prepaid medical care plan (payable to doctors, dentists, nurses, hospitals, or other medical agencies) would provide "ready access to medical care . . . by eliminating the financial barrier between the patient and doctor or hospital." Patients would have free choice of doctors, and doctors would be "guaranteed the right to accept or reject patients," while hospitals would be guaranteed freedom to manage their affairs. It gave most administrative control to the states.[24]

When Wagner presented the bill, he emphasized the freedom of choice policy, knowing that a major AMA criticism would be government control of health care. He also tried to reassure insurance companies, voluntary hospitals, trade unions, fraternal groups, and "any other groups" involved in providing medical care by explaining that the bill would allow the utilization of existing service organizations and encourage the creation of new ones. The surgeon general was to "decentralize the administration of the program to the extent possible," and state and local administration would be given preference.[25]

Dr. W. Montague Cobb, a Negro physician and board member representing the NAACP, testified before the Senate Committee on Education and Labor, emphasizing the relationship between poverty, discrimination, and poor health and raising objections because the bill did not prevent discrimination and separate facilities. But in the end, he strongly endorsed it.

Cobb said the NAACP was "most acutely aware of the need for the legislation in respect to that segment of the population which it primarily represents," but health was not a racial problem: "Poor health in any segment of the population is a hazard to the nation as a whole." Using 1940 census data, Cobb confirmed that "the plight of the Negro is worse than that of the white." For Negroes, life expectancy at birth was ten years lower than whites, and the mortality rate was 81 percent higher in rural areas and 95 percent higher in urban areas; nearly all diseases showing excess mortality in Negroes were preventable. Cobb conceded that 1943 statistics showed some improvement, but Negroes continued to lag behind whites, which indicated that they did "not share as rapidly or as fully in the application of medical advances." The statistics also indicated that the standard of living "associated with a rising income increased the health status of Negroes as measured by various indicia of illness."[26]

In light of these facts Cobb said, the NAACP had a "natural and vital interest in any measures which make for the improvement of the general health, particularly that of the economically poorly circumstanced." But the association did have some valid concerns. Since 79 percent of the black population lived in the South, programs had to be implemented in a way that would assure no discrimination in any locality. In the provisions for training, Negroes should "be integrated into the program at all levels, administrative as well as professional, without respect to the section of the country."

Moreover, unlike the AMA, the NAACP did not find that prepaid personal health service benefits would jeopardize the traditional free choice of "physician by patient, and patient by physician." Cobb pointed out that "the furor over free choice of physicians can have no meaning for millions of Negroes as well as millions of whites in poor circumstances, because down the years these people have been without any medical services whatever."

Cobb also attacked the concept of separate but equal facilities:

This was a myth and would prove to be again a myth should it be attempted. . . . We wish to declare emphatically for the elimination of the entire racial separation practice in the construction of any new facilities, and in the operation of all new plans for the distribution of medical care and for the integration of Negro professional personnel into all levels of the plan according to qualification. Recent experience with attempts to assure adequate professional personnel through the separate system of professional education [has] proved how sterile and ineffective is this plan. It has resulted in there being not only inadequate numbers of general practitioners (and nurses), but also of specialists in the respective fields.[27]

The NAACP was also concerned because the bill allowed the administration of the program by "private auspices, particularly state and local medical societies." It was "unequivocally and unalterably opposed to any arrangement of this kind." In many states and the District of Columbia, local medical societies had "consistently barred Negro physicians from membership, and the American Medical Association, through the technicality of not admitting to its membership physicians who are not members of their local societies, [had] extended the effect of racial discrimination."

After raising these objections, however, Cobb "heartily" endorsed the bill because "S. 1606, for the first time in history," overcame the economic barrier to medical services "for millions of American citizens who sorely need but cannot afford such care." He said the NAACP regarded the bill as "one of the most progressive and potentially beneficial pieces of legislation of recent years" and strongly urged its passage.[28] In addition, an endorsement resolution made at the NAACP's 1946 annual conference "particularly approved of the principle of grants-in-aid to the states based on their financial needs."[29] This resolution was based on the premise that the federal government would ensure an equitable distribution of funds.

The bill was rewritten and introduced as the National Health Insurance and Public Health Act in 1947. In a confidential letter, Murray informed Perry of the considerable changes that had been made in the bill: it would establish a system of local administration under statewide plans; each state would be allocated a definite amount of money from the National Health Insurance Fund and, in turn, would allocate funds to each local area according to the principles of allocation stated in the law; federal administration of the program would be by a five-person board from the Federal Security Agency, and administration within the state would be at the local level; unemployed needy persons would be covered if contributions to the national insurance fund were paid, on their behalf, by a public agency; financing for the national program had not been resolved but presumably employer and employee would each contribute no more than 6 percent of the employee's earnings to an insurance fund; and public health services would expand through federal grants-in-aid.[30]

Although this new draft did not meet all of the NAACP's policy preferences, the organization thought it was considerably better than the alternative bill introduced by Sen. Robert Taft (R, Ohio). In a memorandum Perry described this bill to Roy Wilkins as "the brain child of the American Medical Association, which automatically un-endears it to us." He doubted if either bill had "a ghost of a chance of being passed or receiving serious consideration by the Congress" anytime soon, but he was arranging testimony for the Wagner-Murray-Dingell bill.[31]

The Taft bill was very different from the Wagner-Murray-Dingell bill: it would not create a national health care system; it would grant federal aid to the states to provide medical care for low-income families and individuals but did not require a state to participate; it had no redistributive policies aimed at improving medical care in the poorer states; there were no standards to determine income levels at which eligibility for the program would be established; and dental care to poor children was to be provided on a sliding fee scale.

Albert W. Dent, president of Dillard University (a private black university in New Orleans), was on the board of the Committee for the Nation's Health. His testimony in favor of the Wagner-Murray-Dingell bill explained why it was better for the Negro population. Although Taft's bill contained an antidiscriminatory clause, Dent said it was "meaningless in a Federal bill giving grants-in-aid for State health programs." Enforcement of the clause was "a pious hope because it is a State-controlled program of medical aid for the indigent. . . . Southern states will not change their policy of discrimination simply because a Federal Bill says it should." In contrast, the Wagner-Murray-Dingell bill proposed a federal program with a decentralized administration that would guarantee national standards of medical service because the nondiscrimination clause would be enforced from the federal level. Taft's bill was "based on the repugnant principle of charity," whereas the Wagner-Murray-Dingell bill financed medical care "through minimum weekly deductions from the payroll in a similar manner to social security deductions." The Taft bill gave "virtual control of its administration to organized medicine," which would apply to federal administration as well as state and local boards and would "shut out Negro doctors from participation in

the many states where they are excluded from the county medical societies."
Dent concluded that just a comparison of the enforcement clauses of the
bills made the National Health Insurance and Public Health Act clearly "the
most beneficial to the Negro people." In addition, the bill had "many other
features which would prove vitally beneficial in contributing to the sound
health of our nation."[32]

Cobb again represented the NAACP when he testified for the National
Health Insurance and Public Health Act. Like Dent's, most of his testimony
attacked the Taft bill, stating that in the South where racial wage differentials
were "traditionally notorious," the usual presumption was that Negroes
required "less income than others for their total necessities." He feared that
this same erroneous premise would be applied to the health needs of
Negroes. Their needs "would be presumed less and they would get less of any
benefits provided."[33]

Furthermore, the Taft bill did not appear to offer the freedom of choice
of the Wagner-Murray-Dingell bill; "apparently, the 'low income' patient
could be made to secure his medical services from whom and under whatever plan a State would see fit to dictate." In addition, the low-income classification would require a "costly and unnecessary administrative organization . . . for the sole purpose of determining who qualified as 'needy' in the
varying standards of particular localities," and it would stigmatize those
receiving the care. The NAACP preferred universal coverage, finding the
"low income classification" in the Taft bill "nebulous, inadequate, discriminatory, wasteful, and atavistic. If enacted into law, no one could predict how
long its evil effects would halt real progress."[34]

Cobb contended that the administrative structure in the Taft bill allowed
too much control by state and county medical societies and by the AMA. He
reiterated part of his earlier testimony about the restrictive membership
policies of the AMA which made AMA membership contingent upon
membership in local medical societies. This was the case in seventeen states
and the District of Columbia. The AMA had never deviated from this policy in spite of the efforts of black physicians to change it. Exclusion from
local medical societies meant exclusion from public and private hospital
staffs. This was so not only in the South but in urban areas in the North and
the West. "Obviously," Cobb stated, "this markedly handicaps the Negro
physician both as to his training and the service he is able to render." The
Taft bill did "little else than preserve the existing systems" for paying for

medical services and made "a new demand upon the Federal treasury for a totally inadequate lump sum to provide medical care for the indigent." The testimony reaffirmed the NAACP's endorsement of the Wagner-Murray-Dingell bill, and it opposed the "limited and partisan approach" represented by the Taft bill.[35]

While the Wagner-Murray-Dingell bill was under consideration, numerous measures were introduced in Congress to limit its scope.[36] In the end, those in favor of the bill were not able to overcome the lobbying power of the AMA and other private-sector organizations, such as the National Association of Manufacturers. Neither bill passed. The health care issue was not seriously considered again until the introduction of legislation during the Johnson administration, culminating in the establishment of Medicare and Medicaid in 1965.

Expanding Social Security

No one knew quite what to expect when World War II ended, but everyone anticipated that the reconversion of the defense industry to peacetime production and the demobilization of the armed forces would cause high unemployment and perhaps another depression. It was feared that considerable social instability would occur as individuals and families attempted to cope with these changes. Some people would return to areas where they had lived before the war; some would remain in areas where there were better employment prospects; and others would roam around the country seeking employment. The omnibus Wagner-Murray-Dingell bill, introduced in 1943, reflected the belief that a comprehensive and universal social security system could prevent social instability after the war.

In addition to the federal health system discussed earlier, the major reforms in this bill would have made significant progress in the creation of the American welfare state envisioned by liberal social reformers in the areas of: disability insurance (including maternity insurance); the federalization and extension of unemployment insurance to provide dependents' allowances and the inclusion of domestic and agricultural workers; retroactive Social Security contributions for members of the armed forces; the expansion of old age and survivors insurance to include domestic and agricultural workers and the self-employed and an increase in benefits; a unified public assistance program through grants-in-aid to the states; and the creation of national public employment offices. This national social security system would encompass all the programs mentioned in the bill except the public assistance program. The social insurance programs would be financed by a payroll tax.[37]

The sponsors of the bill argued that, as a result of the war, labor had become much more mobile and that the current system allowing each of the states to establish different benefit amounts, different eligibility rules (including residency requirements), and different time limits for receiving unemployment compensation was no longer viable. The unemployed who moved to other states in search of work could lose unemployment benefits. Federal administration would meet the needs of a mobile labor force better than the current system. Civil rights organizations, of course, supported the bill and were especially pleased with the proposal to completely federalize unemployment insurance. They thought it should also include a national minimum benefit that was not based on past earnings. Under the current system, some states paid benefits that were less than that "paid to the destitute by the local public welfare departments."[38] But as discussed earlier, the sweeping changes to the social security system were eliminated when the omnibus Wagner-Murray-Dingell bill was reintroduced as a national health bill.

In 1945, on the tenth anniversary of the Social Security Act, Truman pointed out that "we still have a long way to go before we can truthfully say that our social security system furnishes the people of this country adequate protection."[39] While commemorating this anniversary, the Social Security Board made several proposals for amending the Social Security Act that were very similar to those in the first Wagner-Murray-Dingell bill, recommending "a comprehensive system of social insurance, covering all major risks to economic independence and all workers and their dependents."[40]

Congress responded to the Social Security Board's recommendations by introducing more specific bills, such as the Unemployment Compensation Act introduced in the Senate by Harvey M. Kilgore (D, W.Va.) but eventually defeated. The NAACP was particularly interested in this bill because it anticipated high unemployment among black workers. The bill proposed a federal supplement to state unemployment insurance benefits that would raise the minimum benefit to $25 per week for twenty-six weeks. When the Senate Finance Committee deleted this provision, the NAACP sent a night letter in protest.[41] The bill would also extend unemployment insurance to discharged federal workers with payments based on state rates where they had been employed. The NAACP opposed this proposal because, along with the absence of a federal supplement, this meant lower grants for employees in the South where the largest proportion of the Negro population resided.[42]

Also anticipating high unemployment among Negroes, the National Council of Negro Women (NCNW) asked its member organizations to support amendments to the bill that would extend unemployment compensation to *all* employees; increase benefit amounts, particularly for low-income workers; and provide benefits during periods of extended or permanent disability. It told its affiliates that it was important to support these amendments "because of our collective interest in job security of *all* the people in the post war period, and because of our particular interest in guaranteeing to *Negro* men and women the fullest protection in periods of unemployment."[43]

When Mary McLeod Bethune testified before the House Ways and Means Committee, she noted the NCNW's particular concern over the economic plight of Negro workers who, because of discrimination, were relegated to the lowest level of employment. Their need for insurance against economic instability was the greatest because they were more subjected to the hazards of unemployment and seasonal work than any other group. Their low wages made it impossible for them "to lay aside anything for a 'rainy day.'" The war had presented many opportunities for these workers to enter industrial and commercial fields where their jobs were covered by social insurance, but after the war they were compelled to return to occupations not covered by any insurance protection. There was a clear need for "a more inclusive and comprehensive program of social security [to] effectively meet the needs of millions of workers who have no private or public resources when their need of assistance is greatest."[44] The 1946 resolutions from the annual conferences of both the NAACP and NCNW recommended expansion of Social Security to include those workers who were not covered.[45]

In 1947, with agricultural and domestic workers still excluded from unemployment insurance, the NAACP became especially concerned about the plight of agricultural workers, who were being rapidly displaced by mechanization. Because farm workers had neither the benefits of minimum wage nor unemployment insurance, the NAACP thought they needed the same kind of protection that industrial workers had. It considered organizing farm laborers as a union to help them win legislative advantages accorded to organized labor. The NAACP was also worried about migratory farm workers and resolved to work for the passage of legislation that would "make adequate provision for the orderly recruitment, housing, health, and other requirements of farm workers." It opposed the "continued importation of foreign agricultural workers when large supplies of unused agricultural laborers are available."[46]

An amendment to the Social Security Act extending compulsory old age and survivors insurance coverage to domestic and agricultural workers (first tier) was introduced again in 1949. It also authorized optional coverage for employees of state and local governments and nonprofit organizations, and it increased benefits and the tax rate.[47] Representing the NAACP, Clarence Mitchell testified before the House Ways and Means Committee that the NAACP had "repeatedly gone on record . . . in favor of the inclusion of domestic and agricultural wage earners under the Social Security Act. . . . Throughout the country, our 1600 branches are eagerly watching Congress to see whether these workers are kept in the bill."[48]

One reason that they had been excluded from the 1935 act was because the Treasury Department had reservations about its ability to collect payroll taxes from them. In his testimony Mitchell mentioned this "administrative difficulty." This time, however, a stamp program had been proposed as a means of collecting the tax, and Mitchell thought this might prove feasible but, if not, "the mere existence of administrative problems, real or supposed, should not stand in the way of extending coverage to people who need it badly."[49]

Mitchell also spoke about workers who had left household employment during the war and obtained social insurance through other jobs, but who would lose coverage if they returned to domestic work because they had been unable to work long enough to become eligible for benefits. He believed that many would be "forced back into domestic employment" and that contributions to social security were "in vain for these people." Another problem he saw was the stipulation requiring forty quarters of employment with at least $50 per quarter earnings before a worker could be eligible for old age and survivors insurance. He feared that wages for domestics would be too low to meet this dollar requirement, particularly in the South where 44 percent of all domestics were employed. He thought it was ridiculous to "expect that individuals earning such meager wages would in any way be able to provide for security in their old age. . . . It [was] equally unfair to consign workers to relief rolls while we make every effort to protect workers in other occupations who receive more pay and labor under more favorable conditions."[50]

Mitchell also testified before the Senate Finance Committee that the NAACP advocated a "comprehensive program of social security for all" which would make "substantial improvements" but it would "still not measure up to need." Unemployment compensation rates needed to be increased, and it was important to federalize the unemployment insurance system. In addition, a comprehensive system was needed for "sickness insurance to provide cash benefits and necessary medical and hospital care for all."[51]

Based on the various stances it had taken on specific legislation, the NAACP prepared a voting record of each member of Congress which, along with a "comprehensive analysis of the issues involved," were published in the *NAACP Bulletin* as a guide for voters. Its branches were urged to work for congressional support of the proposals it had made at the hearings.[52]

The Social Security amendment was passed in 1950 without all the policies the NAACP had advocated, but the organization was quite pleased that domestic and agricultural workers were finally covered under the first tier—the contributory program for old age and survivors insurance. There was no federal mandate, however, for their inclusion in the unemployment compensation program (which remained a state-federal administrative structure).

Immediately, the NAACP sought to resolve problems it anticipated in enrolling these workers in the social insurance system, and prepared a pamphlet, *The New Social Security Benefits*, to explain "the new parts of the law." It defined "regular employment," explained cash wages versus in-kind income, and cautioned that only cash wages counted. It explained "quarters"; it explained that insurance was different from welfare, and therefore one did not have to be in need to enroll in the social insurance program. The pamphlet gave instructions on how one obtained a Social Security card, and the NAACP's branches were asked to help inform workers.[53]

There were special problems with domestic workers who were leery of applying for social insurance, and with employers who refused to participate in the program.[54] Many Negro domestics feared that compulsory coverage would cause some housewives to dismiss their domestic help or at least "get along with less servants."[55] In discussing the content of the pamphlet as it was being prepared, the NAACP considered it important for workers to understand that their contribution had to be matched by their employer because some workers were angry that they had to contribute. The NAACP thought these feelings would be resolved once workers understood the difference between this benefit and public assistance.[56]

A press release was also prepared to explain the law. This release encouraged some domestic workers in Texas to request help from the NAACP. A group of housewives had refused to withhold their domestics' share of the taxes or to pay their share because "they did not want to act as unpaid tax collectors for the Federal government."[57] The NAACP's Southwest Regional Office responded by providing legal aid to the domestic workers who were having these difficulties and by describing the incident in its newsletter to alert others who might be experiencing the problem.[58] The NAACP cautioned domestic and agricultural workers not to be taken in by arguments used by the Texas housewives and encouraged them to "take full advantage of this law."[59] NAACP branches tried to overcome the difficulties of some domestics with more than one employer through "competent advice."[60] The organization thought the problems would eventually be resolved and envisioned "a Social Security card in every kitchen" where a domestic worker was employed.[61]

In spite of concerns about the possibility of social instability as the nation adjusted to the end of the war and peacetime, very few of the recommendations made by the Social Security Board were ever considered. The legislators chose to proceed in a piecemeal fashion, leaving unresolved many social welfare issues of concern to civil rights organizations. The resolutions passed at the NAACP's annual conference in 1951 advocated a comprehensive social security system similar to the system proposed by the Social Security Board. The resolutions again emphasized the need for a federal unemployment insurance system to prevent loss of income when workers moved across state lines, and to prevent discrimination in areas where "Negroes have not yet won political influence in proportion to their numbers"; the need for a comprehensive system of government health insurance "along the lines of President Truman's recommendation"; and the extension of disability insurance to cover all of the permanently disabled rather than only those disabled in industrial accidents. The NAACP also pushed for an increase in the minimum wage to one dollar (it had just been raised to seventy-five cents) and the inclusion of agricultural and domestic workers under the 1938 Fair Labor Standards Act.[62]

Throughout the 1940s, as legislation was introduced to expand the social security system, civil rights organizations consistently supported comprehensive programs with universal coverage and federal administration, hoping to lessen the effects of segregation and discrimination. But except for the inclusion of agricultural and domestic workers under first-tier old age and survivor's insurance, they were not successful. Shortly after this, they adopted a different strategy to overcome the persistent exclusion of an enforceable antidiscriminatory clause in social welfare legislation: they refused to support legislation that did not prohibit discrimination and segregation. No longer would they compromise their civil rights agenda in order to advance their social welfare agenda.

FIVE

Opposing "Liberal" Policies: The 1950s

A Change in Strategy

At the monthly meeting of the NAACP's Board of Directors on January 3, 1949, the members took up a recommendation by the board's Committee on Legislation that stated: "The committee recommend(s) that the Association withhold active support from any federal legislation in the fields of housing, health or education which does not expressly forbid segregation."[1] This language provoked "considerable discussion" on the board. One member suggested the modification: "We will concentrate every possible effort to have anti-segregation amendments written into the laws that are enacted on housing, health and education." It was not advisable, he and two others argued, to "take the attitude that if we cannot have all, we won't take any." Others, however, disagreed. The chairman of the board, Arthur B. Springarn, reminded his colleagues that that point had been "carefully considered" by the members of the Legislation Committee, who felt nonetheless that "the Association should take a definite stand." Accepting the modified language "would be tantamount to saying that we were simply putting up a bold front." Another board member, Judge Hubert Delany, pointed out that the original recommendation should not be changed. "The Association has gone on record as fighting segregation and discrimination and we must maintain that policy."[2] The board voted to accept its committee's recommendation to "withhold active support."

This discussion, which signaled a major shift in strategy, was a harbinger of the debate that would ensue for the next decade within the NAACP and the liberal community. From this point on, the NAACP, at least, would not agree to subordinate its civil rights agenda to its social welfare agenda. The matter was settled in a way it had not been for years. As recently as six days before the December 1948 meeting of the Committee on Legislation, NAACP officials were still pondering how to treat the two agendas. Leslie Perry had sent a lengthy memorandum to Walter White responding to a request for an opinion on various pieces of proposed legislation concerning the FEPC, antilynching, the anti-poll tax, antifilibuster tactics, Jim Crow travel, and segregation in the armed services. At the end, regarding grants-in-aid bills such as federal aid to education and housing, he wrote: "We have got to make a decision . . . whether we can support *any* legislation in which Congress recognizes the segregated pattern."[3]

A brief look at the NAACP's positions only a few years earlier will give some indication as to how drastic a shift in strategy this truly was. Before 1949, in regard to proposed legislation, the NAACP had essentially accepted the "separate but equal" formulation of the *Plessy v. Ferguson* decision of 1896. (To be sure, the association was challenging this doctrine in the courts, but its *legislative* strategy was quite different.)

In 1945 Roger Baldwin of the American Civil Liberties Union (ACLU) telephoned the NAACP to inquire whether the NAACP "was going to support a federal aid to education bill which provides for segregated schools." Roy Wilkins took the call and reported the substance of the conversation to his colleagues: "We had a little rough and tumble argument from then on. . . . He raised the question of principle we would not support the bill unless it contains a provision that those states with segregated schools will not be eligible to receive a federal grant." Baldwin also suggested that if the NAACP did not contest segregation outright, perhaps it would insist that no state would be eligible for federal money which did not equitably distribute state funds for use between Negro and white schools. Wilkins recorded:

> I explained our position at length and pointed out that if either of these provisions was insisted upon the bill would not have a ghost of a chance of passing and that we felt pragmatically that it would be better to secure additional Federal funds than to stand upon the principle and that we felt our members and the colored population of the Southern states felt the same way about this.[4]

Two years later, in 1947, the NAACP was taking rather mild positions on such issues. The statement adopted by the organization at its annual meeting in January dealt with fifteen items on its legislative agenda. In addition to the antilynching issue, the anti-poll tax, and a civil rights bill for the District of Columbia, among others, it stipulated:

> —A bill for government assistance to a low-cost housing program, similar to the Wagner-Ellender-Taft bill introduced in the 79th Congress, *with proper safeguards* for the rights of minorities.
> —A bill to provide Federal aid to the states for education *with proper safeguards* for the rights of minority groups in states having separate school systems.[5]

Federal aid to education was an especially vexing issue for the organization, precisely because the question of principle was so important and the fact of need and inequitable racial treatment so blatant. Leslie Perry adroitly attempted to present this dilemma in his testimony before a Senate subcommittee in support of federal aid even though the bill before the committee would maintain segregated schools. At the same time, the NAACP suggested elaborate amendments to an educational-aid bill that it was hoped would guard against discriminatory distribution of funds. In a letter to Roy Wilkins enclosing his testimony, he pointed out that the NAACP was "unequivocally opposed to segregation," but the organization was pursuing that issue through the courts: "I said that because this question had been raised in connection with previous bills I want to state that we do not regard this legislation as a vehicle for eliminating segregation."[6] Perry's testimony highlighted the racial discrepancies in southern states' expenditures on education for black and white students as well as on teachers' salaries. He called for a particular remedy—fifty dollars per year per student as a floor. Neither was the NAACP sanguine that a mere nondiscrimination clause in the law was sufficient. Such a provision, "no matter how well intentioned the framers might be—is not self-executing." The proposed law required a state's educational authority to audit the expenditure of funds. This did not impress the NAACP as sufficient, either. Perry told the subcommittee: "The entire history of the administration of state educational funds, where separate schools are maintained for the races, justifies our worse fears. Most of these States have shown a settled determination to distribute funds in an unequal manner." Therefore, the NAACP official proposed an elaborate, almost tortuously detailed "administrative procedure . . . whereby an aggrieved citizen with a bona fide complaint might make formal representations where it is alleged that funds are not being equitably apportioned by a State."[7]

The NAACP was clearly aware of the need for a good education in the new developing economy and of the harm done to those denied such an education and thus ill-prepared to compete:

> With the advent of the mechanical cotton pickers millions of agricultural workers will be displaced. Those persons will have to leave the land and find occupations in industry. Such a transition will put them in direct job competition with existing urban workers and will require new skills and know-how. They will undoubtedly need more than a bare minimum education which would be of dubious adequacy for a well-rounded and successful life even in rural areas. What is occurring in cotton is but a harbinger of what is happening, or will happen, in many other occupations and industries.[8]

Following the January 3, 1949, shift in strategy, the NAACP also proceeded to be more forceful in its positions on housing legislation. Slum clearance, the provision of housing for families displaced by such clearance, employment on construction projects for new housing, and residential segregation and discrimination were all concerns of the NAACP in the late 1940s. A housing resolution adopted at the organization's annual conference in 1947 stated: "We further urge that all housing, built in whole or in part by public funds, by loans guaranteed by agencies of the government or tax exemption, be open to all without discrimination as to race, color or national origin."[9]

Meanwhile, the NAACP was pursuing legal action against racial covenants in real estate deeds which prohibited sale of property to Negroes. In 1948 the U.S. Supreme Court ruled that such restrictive covenants were *not* enforceable by the courts. Such enforcement would amount to "State action" violative of the "equal protection of the laws" clause within the meaning of the fourteenth amendment to the Constitution.[10] That year, taking note of this legal victory, the NAACP adopted different language on housing at its annual conference:

> In order that we may benefit fully from the Supreme Court decision forbidding judicial enforcement of restrictive covenants, our branches are instructed to support the right of every American citizen to choose his own home and to move freely throughout his community, *and to support only such legislation, federal and state, as forbids segregation.*[11]

Before then, the NAACP had been "urging" that housing not be segregated, or calling for support "only" for legislation that sought such a goal. Even after the Board of Directors made its January 3, 1949, shift, the organization still had not become as forceful as it would be later. One month after the board meeting, Leslie Perry, testifying before a Senate Committee stated: "We . . . urge the Congress to write into S. 712[12] specific provisions prohibiting FHA [Federal Housing Administration], or any government agencies engaged in underwriting, making direct loans or furnishing other aids to housing, from making race, color, creed, or national origin a reason for granting or withholding insurance loans or aid."[13] He also suggested an amendment that would "assure that there shall be no discrimination or segregation because of race, creed, color or national origin in the project area. Federal funds derived from the taxation of all of the people can no longer be used to subsidize the iniquitous practices of racial segregation and discrimination."[14]

The NAACP was pleased with and took notice of the support it received from the CIO on these particular matters. Perry commented that Leo Goodman of the CIO National Housing Committee had testified before a House committee in favor of the NAACP's positions on "first preference to persons displaced from the clearance areas and requiring in the land assembly program 'covenants against covenants' to the housing bill." Noting that a *New York Times* article had reported that these amendments were "framed in consultation with the White House," Perry pointed out that he had written Thurgood Marshall "about this" a few days before. Regarding the CIO's support, he wrote in a later memorandum: "This is the first dent we have made in these groups and I believe that a number of others will follow."[15]

The Housing Act of 1949 was signed on July 15, 1949, but the two amendments advocated by the NAACP were defeated. The organization immediately turned its attention to the low-rent housing projects to be developed with the financial assistance of federal funds. The law gave authority to local city housing authorities and governing bodies for planning, development, and management of those new projects. The NAACP alerted its branches in a letter: "If Negroes are to receive an equitable share of this housing, they will have to do it on the local level." Therefore, each local branch should "act *immediately* and persistently." The local branches should be alert to site-selection, "design in terms of physical attractiveness and livability," and "employment of racial minorities" in local housing authorities, in project management, and in the "skilled and unskilled construction labor force." The national NAACP office specifically advised: "See that policy of all federal, state and local housing agencies be directed toward non-discrimination and non-segregation in any housing facilities to be provided with the aid of public funds or powers."[16]

On the matter of nondiscrimination in employment in construction of local public housing projects, the NAACP referred to an older order from the 1930s requiring protection against such racial discrimination. This provision (discussed in chapter 2) required the percentage of wages paid to Negroes to coincide with the percentage "of Negro skilled and unskilled laborers employed in construction work in the locality of the project."[17]

In a follow-up memorandum to its branches, the national NAACP office emphasized again the importance of diligent action at the local level. And it pinpointed some potential problems that, indeed, would come to plague many inner-city black communities for the next several decades. The memorandum advised:

> With regard to the slum clearance program, the branch must be ever watchful that such program is not used principally as a vehicle for getting Negroes out of desirable sections of the city and relocated in run-down segregated sections. . . .
>
> Consideration should always be given to whether the relocation site selected for displaced families will result in overcrowding and creating new slum conditions.[18]

In both instances, these forebodings, foreseen by the NAACP, came to fruition. The association attempted to provide specific legislative protection against such occurrences, but it simply lacked the political power to succeed.

In the months following the NAACP Board of Directors's January 1949 decision, some board members were clearly ready to be even more assertive in regard to the new policy. To be sure, the January decision had initiated a clear change of strategy, but when the board met on May 9, 1949, there was the feeling that the organization should be even more forceful. At that meeting, after taking up a number of matters,[19] the issue of segregation in housing and education was raised once again. One board member felt the January resolution should be reaffirmed and conveyed to friendly senators Hubert Humphrey (D, Minn.), Paul Douglas (D, Ill.), and Wayne Morse (R, Ore.). But another member, Judge Hubert Delany, believed that while the resolution on housing was all right (he had strongly supported it in January), the language in regard to education was too mild. In fact, as the minutes of the meeting indicate, he felt it was a "mistake" to apply the same language to education. He argued that the January resolution stipulating that the NAACP would "withhold active support from federal legislation in the fields of housing, health or education which does not expressly forbid segregation" should be modified. Delany wanted even stronger language regarding education. He preferred that any bill that did not stipulate that funds should go only to schools which did *not* segregate or discriminate "shall be actively opposed by the Association."

This sentiment was voted unanimously, and with this change the organization moved from passive rejection to active opposition.[20] Indeed, this language found its way into resolutions adopted by the NAACP's fortieth annual convention in July 1949. "Active opposition" became the association's new guide to policy on liberal social welfare proposals that did not provide explicitly for ending segregation or withholding federal funds from segregated facilities. This was a sea change from only a few years earlier when "pragmatism" and other political realities had pushed the group into a quite different stance.

This now set the stage for a new era in which the NAACP would push for both its civil rights agenda and its social welfare agenda, without subordinating the former to the latter as it had pragmatically done so often in the past.

The Catalyst for Change

What brought about this shift in strategy? Certainly, the U.S. Supreme Court's 1948 decision rendering restrictive covenants judicially unenforceable was an important incentive—especially on the housing issue. This further illustrates how the civil rights movement combined varied approaches within a multifaceted political system to pursue its goals. Victories in one arena spurred action in another, opening up possibilities for new arguments and strategies. The movement was operating on several fronts in pursuit of its dual agenda.

There is no doubt, however, that an unanticipated boost came from a private blue-ribbon committee on civil rights appointed in 1947 by President Truman. In retrospect, the report, *To Secure These Rights*, issued by that committee was likely the single most important factor in convincing the NAACP (and some others) that the previous strategy of subordinating the civil rights agenda to the social welfare agenda should be abandoned.

The two years following the end of World War II saw increasing mob violence against Negroes, especially toward military veterans returning home to the South. Blacks were beaten and lynched, and the instigators were seldom if ever apprehended or prosecuted. The situation grew worse almost by the month. In the summer of 1946 the NAACP called together several prominent blacks and whites and formed a group called the National Emergency Committee Against Mob Violence. The group met with President Truman in September 1946 and urged him to take action. After hearing details of rising incidents of civil rights violations and rampant violence, Truman reportedly exclaimed: "My God, I had no idea it was as terrible as that. We've got to do something!"[21] The decision was made to appoint a prestigious committee of private citizens to study the deteriorating racial situation and to make recommendations to the president. This was designated the President's Committee on Civil Rights (PCCR). Truman selected fifteen persons for the blue-ribbon panel and gave them their charge in a meeting at the White House in January 1947, with the observation: "It's a big job: go to it!"

The composition of the PCCR was politically well crafted, for among its fifteen members could be found two southerners (male and female), two blacks (male and female), two Jews, two labor leaders, two Catholics, two Protestants, two college presidents (one southern, one northern), and two corporate executives (one serving as chairman). The youngest member, at age thirty-two, was Franklin D. Roosevelt, Jr., a lawyer whose important family connection could hardly be lost on the public or press.[22] There were no die-hard segregationists on the committee. It was a group of people with exceptionally strong reputations in their respective fields, and who could be expected to represent—for that era—what could best be described as moderate-enlightened views on civil rights. They selected as their executive secretary a highly regarded professor of government at Dartmouth College, Robert Carr, who had just completed a book on the Civil Rights Section of the Department of Justice.[23]

The announcement of the PCCR's formation received wide attention in the press and evoked great (if at times cautious) expectations in the civil rights community. The NAACP immediately set out to claim credit for the committee's existence. Walter White sent a letter to all branch officers asking for detailed information to present to the PCCR on lynching, police brutality, denial of the right to register and to vote, and discrimination in employment, housing, transportation, recreation, education, and health. "We need specific instances," he emphasized, "cases which have been called to the attention of your branch or of which you have direct knowledge and can supply the details." (His memorandum did not ask for suggested recommendations from the branches.) He reminded the branches of the NAACP's role in the establishment of the PCCR, noting that one member, Dr. Channing Tobias, was an NAACP board member:

> This committee was appointed as the result of a delegation organized by the NAACP conferring with the President on September 19, 1946 at which conference it was urged that the Federal Government protect the rights of minorities in America and take action to stop flagrant denials of civil rights.[24]

For the next several weeks reports came in from around the country, and top officials of the NAACP sent to White their own suggestions of what he should include in his forthcoming testimony before the PCCR. Leslie Perry advised White that "a group of us" had met with Alexander, Ernst, and Tobias (of the PCCR) before the first meeting of the full committee. It was "a very interesting and lively discussion on the scope of the Commission's authority, and legal theories for effective antilynching legislation."[25] Perry was impressed that "if the afore-mentioned members have their way," there might well be a very effective antilynching recommendation adopted by the PCCR. Therefore, he felt that the NAACP should put on hold any ideas it had of proposing new legislation. In fact, he suspected the NAACP's proposals might be weaker than those recommended by the PCCR. He wrote:

> I call this to your attention because I think it would be most unwise for the NAACP to go off on its own hook at this time and introduce an Anti-Lynching or Civil Rights Bill which shows presently all the evidence of being much weaker than that which the Commission may bring in. Congressional opponents of effective antilynching legislation would readily seize on our sponsorship of a weaker bill to defeat whatever the Commission recommends in the way of an overall measure.[26]

Other NAACP officers recommended specific subjects White should highlight: "the necessity of protecting the *share* of the federal aid which Negroes will receive by tacking onto the legislation a proviso that there should be no *discrimination* on account of race or color in the aid given" (emphasis added); legislation outlawing racial segregation in interstate travel; setting up a permanent FEPC; segregation in the armed forces; and restrictive covenants in real estate transactions.[27]

Essentially, the NAACP was not advocating anything more than it had been for several years. When Charles H. Houston (then back in private law practice but still quite involved consulting with the NAACP on its legal cases) testified before the PCCR, he explicitly stated that he thought it unwise to recommend withholding federal money from states, agencies, and others that practiced segregation. He described himself as a "state's rights man" and insisted that by tying grants-in-aid to desegregation this would likely cause the segregationists to reject the grant "and you would fail to give aid to the people who need it most." One scholar studying the work of the committee concluded: "The civil rights organizations, all of them interracial in character, stepped lightly about the segregation issue. The PCCR might have as well."[28]

The fact is, however, that the PCCR chose not to avoid the "segregation issue," to the delight of civil rights organizations. After intense debates within the group, the PCCR decided (by a seven to five vote) to include the following among its thirty-four other recommendations:

> The conditioning by Congress of all federal grants-in-aid and other forms of federal assistance to public or private agencies for any purpose on the absence of discrimination and segregation based on race, color, creed or national origin.[29]

From that point on, the civil rights movement would not be the same. The committee's report did not have the force of law, but it *was* a political-moral statement of such power and prestige that it could not be ignored or conveniently shunted aside. Civil rights organizations were elated. The PCCR had indeed gone much further than the established civil rights groups had dared to go, and in doing so many felt the committee had contributed to a new and evolving political environment that made the civil rights agenda more politically viable. That, at least, was the thinking of the NAACP (and some others) who responded to this catalyst in a way they felt left them no choice—even if they wanted one.[30]

Four months after the report was released, the dean of the graduate school at predominantly black Howard University in Washington, D.C., wrote to Walter White on this precise point, inquiring about the NAACP's current (1948) position on federal aid to education in light of the PCCR report. Noting that the NAACP previously had supported federal aid if blacks would be guaranteed a greater *share* of the funds, he now wondered if such a position was any longer tenable. He wrote:

> It has occurred to me that so much water has gone over the dam since, that now this agreement seems to be a compromise on too low a level. You will recall that . . . the President's Committee on Civil Rights . . . recommended that no federal moneys be paid any state that insisted upon segregation. This

pronouncement makes our present position rather questionable, I think. The question I raise is whether we can afford to compromise on anything less. . . .

The NAACP should not be guilty of the charge of being willing to compromise on so much less than two distinguished committees recommended.[31]

He concluded his letter optimistically: "We have the most favorable climate of public opinion on the question of civil rights that we have had since Reconstruction. Thus, I assume that an enlarged program and redoubled efforts are being made to strike while the iron is hot."[32]

He assumed correctly, although the NAACP did not formally adopt its new position until more than a year after the report. But when it did, this ushered in a period of conflict and debate within civil rights ranks and among liberals that would test exactly how diffuse and receptive this more "favorable climate" really was. To what extent was the politics of race, especially in Congress, affected by this new situation? The next several years—at least the decade of the 1950s—would see open antagonism among liberal friends on the wisdom of this shift in strategy.

Disagreement Among Friends

The NAACP proceeded to draft and support antisegregation amendments to all social welfare bills coming before Congress. At least two NAACP board members (A. Maceo Smith and Mary McLeod Bethune) argued against attaching such a provision to the housing bill. Mrs. Bethune also did so in her capacity as head of the National Council of Negro Women, which issued a widely circulated appeal calling for different strategies on the civil rights front.

The NCNW argued that segregation could be fought "through executive and judicial" action. "Didn't we win the U.S. Supreme Court decisions against racial restrictive covenants?" Therefore, it was not really necessary to encumber the housing bill with the burden of an antisegregation amendment. Surely the latter would be a kiss of death in the Congress. "Do we put our Eggs in one Basket?"[33]

Mrs. Bethune's fellow NAACP board member, A. Maceo Smith, fully agreed with her, calling her position "a real measure of statesmanship and political know-how."[34] Smith also counseled an approach that did not combine social welfare legislation and civil rights issues, hoping to put the latter into a separate bill "where the civil rights issue could be fought out strictly on its own merits."

The NAACP was clearly aware of the political delicacy of the issue of civil rights generally. Whenever an antisegregation amendment was submitted, Leslie Perry noted how some of their allies did not even want to use the word *race* in the amendment because this amounted "to waving a red flag."[35] Instead, it was suggested that more subtle language be used when calling for measures against segregation, such as "any provision contrary to law," or "unenforceable at law." Perry felt: "Of course, we will continue to use our old original language in future testimony before the Committee [in Congress]. If we can get these groups behind this less obvious language, it would be all to the good."[36]

As the sessions of Congress proceeded, and the NAACP persisted in its opposition to any public funds being spent in any way on segregated facilities, the debate heated up. Charles Abrams, state rent administrator for New York, was an NAACP friend who clearly disagreed with the shift in strategy on housing legislation. He felt that gains over *public* housing segregation could very likely be made through the courts, thus not requiring a "rider" to be attached to congressional legislation. He felt that conservative "real estate" lobbyists had always used such a "rider" to defeat badly needed measures for public housing. And the NAACP, hopefully, would "not again be put in the position of unwittingly supporting the lobby's game."[37]

Clarence Mitchell sent back a blistering reply that demonstrated the depths of tension on this issue: "We may as well face the fact that when reactionary elements try to kill legislation with civil rights measures they are stepping into a breach created because some liberals simply do not have the guts to make a good fight for this just principle."[38]

The NAACP was becoming pure and uncomplicated in its position. Its friendly adversaries were continuing to make various pragmatic, tactical, legal arguments to try to sway the organization. This is not to suggest that the NAACP had no allies. A. Philip Randolph strongly supported the organization, and telegraphed the chairman of the House Banking and Currency Committee: "We believe . . . that it is better to have no bill unless the proposed NAACP amendment is included. . . . It is time that responsible legislators recognized that American Negroes are sick and tired of being told to take a back seat and to wait whenever we insist on outlawing racial segregation from every program financed by federal funds."[39]

Clarence Mitchell lost no opportunity to remind liberals that it was not the amendment that killed liberal social legislation, but the failure of liberal legislators to mobilize their strength. Even when an antisegregation amendment was not attached to a liberal housing bill, the bill still failed to pass. Mitchell noted that the bill would have passed if all the senators who purportedly favored such legislation without the amendment had been present and supported it. But eleven senators were absent. The NAACP was not able to get a senator to take the lead and introduce the amendment. But Mitchell had carefully canvassed the legislators. Several indicated they would vote for the bill even with the amendment, and he thus reminded Sen. Paul Douglas: "If the eleven members absent on that day had been present, it is fair to conclude that at least four of them, Chavez, Green, Murray, and Pastore, would have supported the bill on final passage. The result, then, would have been 53 to 43 in favor of the bill."[40]

The battle continued throughout the 1950s over housing policy. The situation was no different with the volatile aid-to-education issue. But the education issue had a distinctive attribute about it. Both sides—proponents and opponents of the antisegregation amendment—used the Supreme Court's 1954 *Brown v. Board of Education* decision to support their respective arguments. From 1949 the NAACP had (as with the housing issue) *actively opposed* any federal aid to education that did not require the recipients (states, school districts, institutions) to cease practicing racial segregation. The organization had enlisted the support of Congressman Adam Clayton Powell, Jr. (D, N.Y.) in this effort. (The perennial amendment became known as the "Powell Amendment.")[41] Year after year, in the early 1950s, the NAACP announced "we stand pat on our position."[42] Then came the historic 1954 decision declaring school desegregation unconstitutional, and the NAACP had a new weapon to add to its arsenal—or so it thought. Now the highest court in the country was on its side.

"Are we asking too much," Clarence Mitchell stated before a Senate committee, "to ask that as a condition of receiving this assistance the whole country agree to abide by the highest court in the land?"[43] If Congress did not pass the antisegregation amendment, this meant "that one branch of the government—the legislative—will be helping certain states to defy another branch of the government—the presidency."[44]

Thurgood Marshall saw no conflict between asking for congressional action in line with court action. As he pointed out, "All the branches of government are obliged by oath to obey and follow the Constitution." In fact, in passing a law, "the Congress would be working in concert with the courts in support of the Constitution."[45]

But there *were* opponents who saw the Supreme Court's decision as introducing a new element into the debate. Clearly, some wanted to avoid a political struggle in Congress which they felt would, in all likelihood, end in defeat for both the civil rights amendment and the overall social welfare legislation. Why not, then, leave the civil rights issue to the courts, which were less vulnerable to electoral political pressures. In addition, the federal judiciary was moving in the right direction on the issue. Members of Congress had to be politically pragmatic; judges could stand on principle.

The National Education Association (NEA) took such a position, suggesting that the Powell Amendment would not accomplish what the courts in time would likely achieve. The courts recognized the need to move in a deliberate and orderly fashion. The Powell Amendment advocates "show no faith in the power of the federal courts to see that their decrees are carried out in an orderly fashion."[46] The NEA chided those who saw the issue as one of morality. Where was the morality when insisting on the amendment would "allow those who are opposed to any kind of federal aid for education to wrap themselves in the mantle of concern for equal rights for all citizens?"[47]

This view was shared by Arthur Goldberg, counselor to the AFL-CIO (the two unions merged in 1955), who later, along with Thurgood Marshall, would serve as an Associate Justice of the U.S. Supreme Court. Goldberg felt that an antisegregation amendment was not "required," now that the Supreme Court had spoken:

> Since, by these decisions, all public schools in the states must be operated on a non-segregated basis, it necessarily follows that public schools built with Federal aid constitutionally can only be operated on a non-segregated basis. . . . The Supreme Court has made it clear that the Courts will enforce the constitutional requirement of non-segregation without the necessity of any implementing legislation.[48]

Another powerful voice from an ally in organized labor came from the United Automobile Workers (UAW) in the CIO. Taking a different stance from Goldberg, and in light of the Supreme Court's ruling, UAW president Walter Reuther put the burden on President Eisenhower and Attorney General Herbert Brownell. Recognizing the need for both "adequate educa-

tional opportunities" and nonsegregated education, the UAW wanted to
know if the executive branch would now allocate funds to the appropriate
agencies only on condition "that they comply with the non-segregation decision of the United States Supreme Court."[49] If the president would so
declare, "then the anti-segregation rider is obviously unnecessary." But if the
administration maintained that it still lacked such authority, notwithstanding the Court's decision, then it was

> morally obligated to make this position known immediately. . . . In the
> absence of such a clarifying statement, the UAW will urge the enactment of
> legislation providing for specific safeguards against federal funds for educa-
> tion being used in violation of the Supreme Court decision.[50]

The fact is that the Department of Health, Education, and Welfare (HEW)
had already informed Clarence Mitchell that it would only withhold grants
where there was "a court determination that a particular state or school district in question was not proceeding to make such a prompt and reasonable
start toward good faith compliance with the pronouncement of the Supreme
Court."[51] It was equally clear that neither the president nor his White House
staff would act otherwise.[52]

As could be expected, the NAACP and Congressman Powell were deluged
with letters urging them to rethink their strategy in light of the Court's
action. One writer pleaded: "As a life-long and sincere friend of the Negro
people . . . I admire your stand—in principle," but there should be a distinction made between legislative action and judicial action. "Your cause has the
benefit of the Court's decision. The courts will be on your side in any legal
action you may take, from time to time. But in the legislative halls you are
dealing with another factor—public opinion."[53] In other words, there were
different political realities that had to be taken into account in choosing
social action strategies. These were hardly admonitions unfamiliar to the
NAACP activists. They had heard the same advice from the National Council
of Negro Women five years earlier, as well as from within their own ranks.

The NAACP still had its strong supporters. The Brotherhood of Sleeping
Car Porters felt that failure to enact the amendment would, in fact, "be aid-
ing unwittingly others who seek to circumvent the intent of the U.S.
Supreme Court's ruling."[54]

Support from the American Veterans Committee (AVC) went even far-
ther, reminding its members that as far back as 1946 it had gone on record
for such legislation: "AVC was ahead of all other organizations, including the

NAACP."[55] Phineas Indritz stated that he would even suggest that such a condition be attached "to general legislation of primary concern to the South, such as the farm price support bill." Neither was he impressed with the argument that counseled reliance on the courts. Such action was "always time consuming. . . . The whole strategy of the segregationists is to drag and drag." Relying "solely on courts and executive action . . . is to jump from the Queen Mary to a drifting straw in a heavy sea." It was the duty of every branch to protect basic liberties. "The courts are the last, not the first, resort."

When the Chicago NAACP branch asked the national office for advice on how to approach Sen. Paul Douglas, who disagreed with the NAACP on this issue, Wilkins responded: "Keep protest in good taste, but make it strong."[56] Wilkins had asked the Illinois branches to write to Douglas, inasmuch as the senator "has received less than five letters from Illinois . . . although he has received almost 100 letters from NAACP units in other states." In a short note to Clarence Mitchell, Wilkins elaborated: "I did not want to put in writing that *one* letter only had been received by Douglas (from Illinois), so I softened it by saying less than five."[57]

Political power was, of course, always at the core of the debates among the liberals on strategy. No one misunderstood the inability of the liberal forces to garner sufficient strength to get all they wanted through a Congress with numerous technical legislative obstacles and a filibuster requiring more than a simple majority vote to defeat. Thus it was no surprise when Sen. Gordon Allott (R, Colo.) bluntly reminded the NAACP of his political situation. He had been asked by the association to introduce the antisegregation amendment in the Senate committee. He responded that, to be sure, he would vote for it, but as a Republican and with the Republican administration opposed, he was not sure if he would take the lead and introduce it. There were some "practical matters" to be taken into account. He told the NAACP that in Colorado he "had not been supported by colored voters."[58]

Clearly, he would appreciate a little political reciprocity from those who, understandably, felt their cause constitutionally and morally justified. He was aware that the NAACP was nonpartisan, but a senator could hardly be. Such were the political realities.

A clear illustration of the intersection of politics and principle on this issue is presented by the wrenching correspondence between Congressman Stewart Udall (D, Ariz.) and Clarence Mitchell in the heat of the aid-to-education battle. Udall was, indeed, a liberal friend of the civil rights cause, and he grappled with finding a way to resolve the dilemma posed by the NAACP's persistent antisegregation amendment strategy. Believing that linking the two agendas—civil rights and social welfare—was politically unwise, he introduced instead a bill that he hoped would deal with the matter in a manner acceptable to civil rights organizations. Instead of denying funds to states that maintained segregation, why not take a positive approach and offer additional funds to those states that were trying to deal with the "impact" of the Supreme Court's desegregation ruling? States would be faced with enormous fiscal problems of reorganizing their previous dual school systems. Udall proposed up to $150 million for each of the next four fiscal years to help in the transition. This would show the states that in the federal government they had a friend "willing to assist in the task ahead." "Instead of self-righteous criticism, the rest of the country would hold out a helping hand. Instead of threats, we would use understanding. In place of compulsion, we would offer cooperation."[59] Of course, he hoped that the NAACP would see the wisdom of his proposal and join him in the compromise. In a long and revealing letter to Clarence Mitchell, he implored:

> I have come to a hard decision. . . . It is clear that there is no difference between us on principle. We part ways only on matters of judgment. . . . There is room for honest disagreement on this whole question. Perhaps our main differences arise from the fact that by habit we are schooled in the art of the possible, while principle is the central thing in your work—and rightly so. Sometimes in our desire to get half-a-loaf our principles hang on the brink (and sometimes go over) but generally we have found that a modest program is better than none.[60]

The NAACP was not bending. Mitchell wrote back:

> I regret exceedingly that we must face you as an opponent on this amendment. . . . I am convinced that if the liberal members of Congress and the many organizations that are in favor of Federal Aid for School Construction would devote their energies to supporting rather than opposing our amendment, the southern opposition would collapse and the bill would become law. . . . I have been impressed with your desire to find a way out of difficult situations in which the Congress is placed by the intransigence of some of the southern members. Nevertheless, I believe it is a terrible mistake for you to oppose our amendment.[61]

To Udall the matter was one of hard, calculating pragmatic politics. To the NAACP the problem was bigotry and "intransigence" of segregationists and conservatives plus the timidity of liberals to stand up to them and fight.

Long-standing liberal friends were unable to convince one another. The antisegregationist amendments repeatedly went down to defeat over the years, but so did most of the liberal proposals.

It was clear throughout the decade as these battles ensued that they were creating turmoil within the liberal ranks. Principle versus pragmatism. At one point following defeat of school aid, an NAACP board member severely chastised his own colleagues for their shift in strategy. "We have been made to look like political suckers and amateurs because passing the Amendment was exactly what the enemies of the NAACP and the enemies of the Federal aid for schools wanted."[62] In addition, he argued, the NAACP needs allies—liberals, the church, labor groups—and "most of the labor groups except the UAW deserted us," as did a number of "sound liberals" in the House and Senate. He noted how close the vote of the liberal group, Americans for Democratic Action (ADA), was for the Powell Amendment—150 to 140.[63] The tactic of the antisegregation amendment should be dropped, he urged. Court cases could be brought against segregated facilities, as could later congressional action against appropriations to segregated schools. At least the federal aid would begin to flow. And this strategy might well be preferable because "reactionaries who do not want Federal funds for education might well hesitate to vote to deprive their districts of such funds after they were getting the funds."[64] If the segregationists, in other words, were already receiving federal dollars, they would be more receptive to keeping this aid, and modifying their ways, rather than "get something they do not have as yet."

The shift in strategy on the dual agenda was bound to elicit sharp disagreements from those who simply did not want to burden the social welfare agenda with the civil rights agenda. As we have seen, the 1950s were not the first time this debate appeared, but it was certainly highlighted during those years. At times, disagreement became almost vitriolic, questioning not only judgment but integrity. After the 1956 defeat of the aid-to-education bill, the president of a black college in Mississippi sent a blistering telegram to Congressman Powell: "I guess you are happy today you have burned the bridge for every Negro child and white to get the education they need. You would do anything to reach a political end."[65] Powell forwarded the telegram to Clarence Mitchell, who answered the black Mississippian: "Apparently, you do not know that most of your state delegation in Congress was opposed to the Bill with or without the Powell Amendment. What kind of telegram have you sent to your own representative?"[66]

This debate in one form or another would continue until 1964 when Congress finally passed Title VI of the Civil Rights Act. That provision expressly prohibited federal funds from being allocated to any states, agencies, or facilities that practiced racial segregation—the goal recommended seventeen years earlier by the President's Committee on Civil Rights and pursued by the NAACP since 1949.

SIX

Confronting an Ally: Organized Labor

There is little question that on balance the major civil rights organizations since the New Deal saw the interests of their constituents as clearly identified with those of the working class. This did not mean eschewing attempts to have friendly relations with management and business leaders. But it did mean that on most issues affecting wage-earners and the unemployed, the black organizations often found themselves allied with the more liberal forces in the growing labor movement. As during the New Deal, however, the issue of racial segregation and discrimination within some unions made the alliance a delicate and fragile one. Civil rights organizations were sensitive to the fact that Negro workers, notably in the industrial, service, and agricultural sectors, faced racial problems that the larger workforce did not encounter. Recognizing this fact made the pursuit of a dual agenda especially important for civil rights leaders. Roy Wilkins was explicit on this point, even as he addressed the problems it presented for union leaders: "It must be understood that all organized bodies have their primary and secondary purposes. The primary purpose of the NAACP is to combat discrimination against Negroes. The primary purpose of labor organizations is to protect the wages, hours, and working conditions of its members. Civil rights activity for them is desirable but must be secondary. Inevitably these differences in emphasis will produce tensions in greater or less degree."[1]

The NAACP on Labor Legislation and Union Practices

The problems faced in the New Deal persisted into the 1950s. In a set of resolutions in 1949, the NAACP called for the repeal of the Taft-Hartley Law.

Passed in 1947 over President Truman's veto, the law outlawed closed shops, permitted union shops except in those states where state law forbade them, and put other onerous burdens on organized labor. But the NAACP also resolved that, if the law were repealed (it ultimately was not), it wanted a stipulation that the National Labor Relations Board should "deny certification as a collective bargaining agency to any union which practices racial or religious discrimination against any workers."[2] The NAACP endorsed pending bills for increasing the minimum wage, but it also stipulated that agricultural and seasonal workers as well as working children be protected. In addition, it called upon Congress to pass "a broad legislative program which will stimulate economic development in those areas of the country which lag behind the rest of the nation." Aid to small businesses and assistance to families seeking to relocate to areas where employment opportunities existed were also on the support list. Other programs were endorsed, including effective enforcement of rent controls and an enlarged program for useful public works "to give more employment." The NAACP reaffirmed "our traditional support of organized labor" and specifically mentioned support of the International Longshoremen's Union "to equalize wages in Hawaii compared with the mainland."

Noting that some unions were less progressive than others, the NAACP stated:

> We hail the support for many of our legislative aims which has been given by both the AFL and the CIO and we call on the Railroad Brotherhoods who have usually been on the wrong side of civil rights legislation to join the two main divisions of organized labor in support of such measures.[3]

On the minimum wage, the NAACP in 1955 testified in the House and Senate for an increase from 75 cents per hour to $1.25, and it wanted to make sure that this covered agricultural workers and others not then covered by the minimum wage law. Noting the wage differential between Negroes and whites, Clarence Mitchell indicated that domestic service jobs were not covered, pointing out that 15 per cent of employed Negro men and 65 percent of employed Negro women were in that labor sector.[4] President Eisenhower had proposed an increase to ninety cents. Mitchell was urged by one group, the Citizens Committee on the Fair Labor Standards Act, to "pitch" his testimony on agricultural workers "rather than on domestic help . . . and hotel workers."[5] However, he was not interested in so limiting his testimony. A few years earlier he had gone on record in support of a minimum wage for laundry and cleaning workers in Washington, D.C. (thirty dollars for each work week of more than twenty-four but not more than forty hours).[6]

The working conditions of migratory farm workers received extensive attention of the NAACP's labor secretary, Herbert Hill. In the late 1950s he investigated labor camps in upstate New York, revealing several serious violations of labor contract laws and health standards. New York growers would send agents south to hire seasonal workers to harvest crops for several weeks to three months on farms in New York State. Payroll records were virtually never kept ("Of forty labor camps inspected only three operators were found to be complying with [the] law."),[7] and through unscrupulous bookkeeping (such as undisclosed deductions for transportation, "rent," and food) workers frequently received only one or two dollars at the end of a week's work. Sanitary conditions in the camps were often "utterly unfit for use by human beings." After months of harvesting crops under such conditions, workers were "returned in open trucks" to their home states "virtually penniless." Hill informed Governor Harriman that this was nothing less than "a vicious system of economic exploitation." The NAACP called for forceful action from the state's labor and health bureaus to address these conditions.

Meanwhile, some railway labor organizations had long posed a major problem for the NAACP. (During World War II, the temporary FEPC found that the Southern Railroad and its union had refused to hire blacks as firemen, but nothing was done to stop that practice.) Several unions—the Brotherhood of Locomotive Firemen and Enginemen, the Brotherhood of Railroad Trainmen, the Brotherhood of Locomotive Engineers, the Order of Railway Conductors, and the Switchmen's Union of North America—had specific provisions in their constitutions barring Negro membership. Other railway unions had set up separate, subordinate "auxiliaries" for Negro workers, which isolated them from effective participation in collective bargaining negotiations. Such arrangements also severely limited the hiring of Negro applicants. And even when the specific union constitutional language was repealed, the de facto exclusionary practices continued. The unions could at times be remarkably unsubtle in their racial attitudes and motives. A resolution of the Brotherhood of Locomotive Firemen and Enginemen on "Subject: Colored Firemen" candidly noted:

> As is well known, the character, habits and general mental make-up of a negro are such as to, in practically all instances, disqualify him for a position of responsibility and trust. . . .

If the truth were told, it is probably not exaggerating the situation to state that the employment of negro locomotive firemen has been, at least, indirectly responsible for accidents, loss of life and injury.[8]

Some union officials counseled patience and caution in dealing with this delicate matter. They noted that some locals were indeed making progress, and that to push the race issue might set back such efforts. Certainly, the union urged, this matter should not be presented to the government for enforcement. If this should occur, then the union would have to defend itself, not on the grounds "that the negro is undesirable as an engineman by reason of his race or color, but because of his inability to read and understand orders and instructions and by reason of his general mental deficiency."

Then, incredibly, the union resolution concluded:

Undertaking to establish this claim might result in some sort of an examination or test applicable to all locomotive enginemen, which might tend (1) to disqualify some white men, and (2) establish the fitness of an occasional negro to act as engineer. In fact, the whole situation, obnoxious as it appears to us, is one that must be handled with the greatest degree of tact and diplomacy.[9]

In other words, hiring on merit alone might end up benefiting some blacks while actually hurting some whites!

The NAACP was well aware of these sentiments, but it was in no mood for polite conciliation on the issue. In testifying before Congress on amendments to the Railway Labor Act, a spokesman for the NAACP, attorney Joseph C. Waddy,[10] indeed supported the principle of the union shop and the dues checkoff, but predicated that support on the inclusion of a specific provision that would "compel the representative chosen by the majority to permit the minority workers to membership in the union or to otherwise participate in the collective bargaining process."[11]

As in other instances, some black unionists urged the NAACP not to push the race issue. They felt that the protection of a union shop (where workers had to join a union *after* being hired) and the dues checkoff were more important than antisegregation amendments. One Negro officer of the Hotel Restaurant Employees and Bartenders International Union warned the NAACP that insistence on an FEPC "rider would surely mean the death of this legislation" and pointed out that approximately 140,000 out of 1,800,000 railroad workers were Negroes who would be hurt by the NAACP's action. He promised that his union would continue to support the work of the NAACP, the United Negro College Fund, and the National Urban League in their "efforts . . . to improve the economic and political security of the Negro people . . . and to eliminate the Negro 'Ghetto.'" But he cautioned that the association's approach to the Railway Labor Act was ill-advised.[12]

Walter White replied that the NAACP reaffirmed its support of organized labor but respectfully disagreed, and he insisted that the amendment was simply setting "the minimum standard that all democratic unions should subscribe to." A discriminatory union, he added, "can do fearful damage to colored workers."[13]

The NAACP hailed the merger of the AFL and CIO in 1955 as a "step in the right direction." But it was realistic in recognizing that this step would present some problems for the unions, especially for the AFL "in race relations." The CIO had a good record on this score, but "many AFL unions bar Negroes from membership . . . and attempts to make them change their policies have usually been futile. . . . What is the AFL-CIO now going to do about its racially exclusive unions?"[14]

The answer to this question soon became apparent. Blatant discrimination in some unions continued unabated. Herbert Hill of the NAACP documented evidence of this in a lengthy report five years later. The practice was not limited to one section of the country "or to some few industries or union jurisdictions." The pattern of discrimination took four forms: clear exclusion; segregated locals; separate racial seniority lines; and exclusion of Negro workers from apprenticeship training programs.[15] Even after the merger, two international unions were admitted with "lily-white" racial clauses in their constitutions.

Hill's attacks were particularly pungent, sparing no punches, and drew the ire of many labor union supporters. Some felt he had not given enough consideration to the good work done by organized labor in race relations, or considered how difficult it was for the umbrella AFL-CIO to coerce essentially autonomous locals. When Hill leveled charges against the liberal International Ladies Garment Workers Union (ILGWU), the furor erupted with overtones of anti-Semitism. The ILGWU's top officials were primarily Jewish. Hill (himself a Jew) accused the union of being mainly concerned with a "public image" of progressivism and little more.

These bitter fights between the AFL-CIO and the NAACP continued into the early 1960s with both sides realizing that each was caught in a difficult leadership dilemma. Neither the AFL-CIO's top leadership nor that of the NAACP wanted to accuse the other of personal racial or religious animosity. But each recognized that they had constituencies to protect and, equally if not more important, organizations to maintain and develop. The AFL-CIO pleaded for understanding that it needed time to move some of its locals to a more enlightened racial view, especially in those areas and industries where race prejudice was traditionally deeply entrenched. It saw no usefulness in imposing harsh penalties that could result in splintering the labor movement. To be sure, there were discriminatory unions, but hopefully these could be brought around. On the other hand, the NAACP was keenly aware of the history of exclusion experienced by Negro workers, whose patience was beginning to be sorely tested. Many Negroes had in fact become alienated, even refusing to support unions in their organizing efforts precisely because Negroes saw no ultimate benefit for themselves. They were suspicious of the reconciliatory words—and limited concrete action—from top labor leaders, thus making the NCAAP's work all that much more difficult in trying to convince black workers to stick with the unions as a friendly ally. Indeed, as conditions of discrimination persisted, this would test the very credibility of the NAACP itself among some Negroes.[16]

This was hardly an advantageous position for either the union or civil rights leadership groups to be in. Finding themselves on opposite horns of the dual agenda dilemma, both had to walk the tightrope (one delicately balancing the need to maintain its support base, the other its need to effect alliances with liberals).

Argument and Discord in the "House of Labor": The Negro American Labor Council

This racial tension was clearly manifested *within* organized labor itself. As a civil rights group, the NAACP could be expected to push its nondiscrimination agenda first: its membership went beyond labor union workers. But the issue became even more heated when the recognized leader of black unionism, A. Philip Randolph, took up these charges of union racism and brought them into the highest councils of the AFL-CIO. Coming from Randolph, such charges could not be easily dismissed. After the 1955 AFO-CIO merger, Randolph was elected as one of only two Negroes on the union's top policy-making body, its Executive Council.[17] As head of the Brotherhood of Sleeping Car Porters, with impeccable union credentials and a record of union loyalty, Randolph was a union insider, a proven friend as well as a staunch fighter for civil rights. In the latter role he had never bitten his tongue on the racial causes for the lowly plight of black workers, and everyone knew this. Neither was his work as organizer of the March on Washington in 1941 that led to Executive Order 8802 overlooked. Therefore, in 1959, when he strongly challenged his own organization, the AFL-CIO, on the continued existence of segregated and discriminatory unions, this was far more potentially damaging than any such charges coming from the NAACP's Herbert Hill (notwithstanding the fact that there was no substantive difference between the accusations leveled against labor by both Hill and Randolph).

As a "union man," Randolph had always taken his fight for equality for Negro workers directly to the unions. He pushed hard for the expulsion from the AFL-CIO of those locals that excluded Negroes or practiced discrimination. The AFL-CIO refused to take such action. During a heated exchange in 1959 between George Meany, head of the AFL-CIO, and Randolph, Meany shouted: "Who appointed you as the guardian of the Negro members in America?"[18] No one had, obviously, but the AFL-CIO leadership soon found out that Randolph had considerable support from organized Negro groups, the liberal press, and prominent individuals around the country. They would not let the impugnment of Randolph's integrity go unchallenged.[19] Especially supportive were the members and leaders of the NAACP.

In fact, at the annual meetings of the NAACP in 1958 and 1959 a decision was made to form an organization of Negro workers—the Negro American Labor Council (NALC). Under Randolph's leadership, it established several chapters around the country. The NALC's purpose was clear and simple: to fight for the rights of Negro workers in general, and within organized labor in particular. Interestingly, anyone who wanted to be a member of the NALC had to join the NAACP as well.[20] Understandably, such a move did not initially sit well with the leadership of the AFL-CIO, but the issues raised by the NALC were nevertheless put on the agenda for extensive discussion at the union's 1961 Executive Council meeting.

Randolph prepared a lengthy memorandum for that session.[21] Citing meticulous studies on the conditions of Negro workers prepared by the NUL and NAACP, Randolph presented the rationale for the existence of the NALC.

First, he defended a "Negro" organization within the "House of Labor" as being just as acceptable as the existence of the United Hebrew Trades and the

Jewish Workmen's Circle, which spoke for Jewish workers. These were "outstanding example(s) of the principle of 'operation self-help' under the most trying circumstances." And he noted that other groups—Italians, Irish, Puerto Ricans—had followed the same path. In true dual agenda terms, he stated:

> This movement [the NALC] has come into existence in response to a basic need and demand for an organization committed to Negro labor's rights and civil rights to fill an existing vacuum in the Negro community, because of a roadblock of discrimination and segregation against Negro workers' advance toward job opportunities and equality in the House of Labor, industry and government.[22]

He assured his colleagues that the NALC was "pro-Negro . . . not anti-white . . . . not anti-AFL-CIO, but pro-free, democratic trade unionism." The NALC was a true illustration of "self-reliance." It was only natural that Negroes would take the lead in pursuing Negro rights. The same was true of other groups throughout the world—for example, the Jews, or the Irish in their fight against "the mighty British Empire for the freedom of Ireland." "Who," Randolph asked in his memorandum, "could be expected to struggle, sacrifice and suffer, and even die in order to break the dismal and deathlike ghettos of Warsaw and south-eastern European countries except Jews themselves who have dedicated their lives to the building of a home in Palestine?" Who then could be expected to raise the issue of expulsion of two railroad unions that barred Negroes, but Negroes themselves? "It is distressing," Randolph wrote, "to note how the Negro American Labor Council has been distorted, derided and decried by some labor leaders, for existing and behaving much in the same manner as other minority members."

Then, in a prelude to racial discussions that would be heard a few decades later over the issue of affirmative action, Randolph spoke to and defended his call of specifically electing or appointing Negroes to official union positions. Such action had been attacked by union officials as "segregation and discrimination 'in reverse.'" Merit should be the sole criteria. To this, Randolph responded in his memorandum:

> This racial policy, because of the color caste culture of the United States, exists in government, politics, industry, business, school systems, the church, sports and the theatre. Hence, the attitude of labor is merely a reflection of the prevailing racial mores of the country.

For Randolph, a color-blind policy was naive and unrealistic in a color-conscious society.

Likewise, he could see no objection to the AFL-CIO expelling unions that did not comport with the AFL-CIO's principles. Did not the Executive Council expel (rightly, in Randolph's view) Communist-dominated unions, as well as corruption-ridden unions? Therefore, expelling racist unions was no different. Indeed, how could "the AFL-CIO dislodge the forces of racism which have reached the stage of institutionalization over a period of almost one hundred years, without a painful, major operation or revolution which must and will shake the House of Labor?" Kicking out racists was in a class with expelling Communists and racketeers.

Neither would Randolph apologize for his strong criticisms of organized labor, nor accept the charge of being antiunion. He asserted: "It is well-nigh self-evident that without criticism there can be no truth. Without truth there can be no freedom. And without freedom life is not worth living."[23]

On its part, the AFL-CIO leadership was not going to accept such criticism from one of their own. A press release described the Executive Council's reaction: the AFL-CIO was one of the strongest advocates for civil rights; while there were "many imperfections and shortcomings" in some unions, efforts were being made to overcome these faults; Randolph should cooperate with these efforts, not be critical of them. In addition, to expel a union would remove the members of that union from "corrective influences from the parent body through education and persuasion."[24] The AFL-CIO was giving "diligent attention" to the discriminatory practices of some unions. Randolph had insisted that more Negro delegates be elected to attend AFL-CIO conventions, and that the head of the AFL-CIO's Department of Civil Rights should be a Negro. The Executive Council countered that the election of delegates was a democratic process, not one to be directed from "the top." And as far as the head of the union's civil rights department was concerned, there was always the "need for professional knowledge." Neither was the union going to be pressured into setting a specific deadline for achieving the goals sought by Randolph. Randolph had recommended that locals that discriminated be given six months to open their membership to Negro workers. Failure to do so should result in notice of suspension within thirty days. Then, if no action were taken in another thirty days, the local union would be expelled. In response the AFL-CIO stressed the view that if there was a "gap" between "organized labor and the Negro community," the responsibility for that situation lay with Randolph. Randolph had accused Meany of failing to place "the moral weight of his office" behind the issue of civil rights. The Executive Council reminded Randolph that Meany had received many awards from Negro groups (including one from the National Urban League in 1959), implying that some black organizations apparently disagreed with his assessment of Meany.

The NAACP immediately characterized the AFL-CIO's treatment of Randolph as "moral bankruptcy."[25] How ironic, the NAACP noted, that the person who spearheaded the response to Randolph was the president of the Brotherhood of Railway Clerks, a union that had maintained segregated locals in the North and South for over half a century. The cause for a "gap" between Negroes and unions was to be found in the failure of "Mr. Meany and the AFL-CIO Executive Council" to take the required action necessary to end union discriminatory practices.[26]

Randolph welcomed this support from the NAACP. But he was not interested in a prolonged internal debate within the House of Labor. He and some of his NALC colleagues simply found themselves caught in a dilemma. They advocated a strong civil rights agenda of course, but they were also devoted union leaders who supported organized labor's agenda for its working-class members. In theory, those two agendas were not (or should not have been) in conflict; in practice, they clearly were. How then to reconcile this real dissension? Randolph proposed two different meetings: a labor-racial summit conference between AFL-CIO leaders and Negro civil rights leaders;[27] and another meeting between Negro trade unionists and Meany, along with "some AFL-CIO Vice Presidents [of unions] with large Negro memberships."[28] Ever the statesman, Randolph's purpose was clear: he wanted to defuse the "crisis of confidence" that had developed over race and organized labor issues.

The first meeting would be with distinctive civil rights leaders "to establish a spirit of good faith between the two groups." He hoped to focus on issues of common concern, for example, and especially on voter registration in the South. But the overall discussion would address the "elimination of every form of race discrimination."

The second meeting would concentrate on issues of race and discrimination within the labor movement itself and would cover all the specific problems Randolph had raised: segregated locals; apprenticeship training; union leadership roles, and, of course, support for liberal policies affecting all working people. The olive branch was clearly extended. Randolph noted that a goal of the second meeting would be "to seek to make it clear to AFL-CIO leadership that criticism of and opposition to race bias in trade unions by Negro trade unionists do not represent or indicate opposition to the AFL-CIO or its leadership."[29]

Various meetings were held, and at the beginning of the decade of the 1960s it was evident that Randolph would make his peace with his fellow leaders in the AFL-CIO. More than any other black leader at the time, he was faced with the task of balancing the two agendas. He fervently believed that the overall socioeconomic welfare of Negroes was tied to progressive policies and legislation. He also believed that organized labor was one of the strongest of allies in achieving those goals. In a sense, his call for two separate meetings was an explicit attempt to fashion two distinct lines of communication that could exist without necessarily challenging the arguments and decisions of each sphere. There would be a civil rights summit and action; there would simultaneously be a union-focused summit and action. In Randolph, the two fused. More than any other black leader at the time, he was *organizationally* in both camps at the same time. This obviously complicated his roles—other civil rights leaders did not have such explicit *dual* loyalties—but if handled adroitly, his position could be advantageous for achieving goals in both arenas.

As he obviously knew (being the experienced and wise tactician that he was), there would be those, especially in his own NALC ranks, who would need careful nurturing. At times, he was patient with and sympathetic toward those in the NALC who were more inclined to challenge the AFL-CIO on a number of issues. But he also had his limits. One such instance surfaced in 1962 when NALC's New York chapter issued a periodic newsletter,[30] one issue of which contained two articles: "Steel Workers Sold Out"; and "All African Trade Union Federation." Randolph lost no time in widely circulating a detailed eight-page memorandum strongly repudiating the two articles. "Both articles disturb and distress me."[31]

The "Steel Workers" article took exception to a contract recently negotiated between the United Steelworkers Union and the big steel companies, charging that the contract was a "sell-out." Randolph defended the union and strongly reprimanded the newsletter: "It is not the purpose and aim of NALC to presume to set itself up in judgment of the internal problems of AFL-CIO trade unions unless race bias is involved." The United Steelworkers Union was fully capable of negotiating in the interests of its members. In addition, he noted that there were NALC officers involved in negotiating the contract. Such attacks could only "cause both Negro and white members of the union to turn against our [NALC] movement." Randolph reiterated that "the job of NALC is not the appraisal of the value of trade union contracts; its primary interest is to fight racial discrimination in trade unions, industry and government, a major undertaking."[32]

Anyway, he doubted whether any member of the newsletter's editorial board had read the contract. And even if one of them had, the process of contract negotiation was so complex that it took "patient study and careful examination" to offer an informed judgment. But Randolph's main point was that this subject was outside NALC's domain.

The "All African Trade Union" article had described a meeting in Morocco to develop an approach to organizing African workers. There were countries ("formerly colonial masters") at the conference that attempted to "sabotage" the effort. A major participant in this disruptive scheme, the article asserted, was Irving Brown, the AFL-CIO's European representative. He wanted to "wreck this Federation." The article also implicated the African trade unionist, Tom Mboya, in the effort "to destroy the unity of the African workers."

Randolph was adamant in defending Brown and Mboya. The charge, "with an ideological slant of a distinct Moscow-oriented interpretation and evaluation," was damaging to the AFL-CIO. It spread suspicion among Africans toward the "integrity and loyalty" of the AFL-CIO. If such charges were allowed to go unanswered, this could lead to "the ideological polarization of the AFL-CIO and NALC which can constitute a kiss of death to our [NALC] movement." Randolph wanted to make it clear that he suspected the article to have been motivated by pro-Communist influences. He emphasized, as he had done many times before, that the "NALC . . . is unalterably opposed to Communists, communism, Fascism and racism." He would take steps to "disestablish" NALC before he would see it taken over by such forces and "abandon its anti-communist position."

Clearly, Randolph was chagrined:

> Thus, this Newsletter places the NALC between the devil and the deep sea. Obviously the leadership of AFL-CIO and ICFTU [International Conference of Free Trade Unions] cannot view with a friendly feeling any effort to torpedo a major phase of its international program. Nor can the leadership of NALC in good conscience sit in the high councils of the AFL-CIO and help formulate an African program and then oppose it and slander its leaders such as this Newsletter has done.[33]

Randolph then proposed that publication of the newsletter be discontinued; that all persons responsible for writing the articles "be disassociated from any official roles in NALC while the matter was being decided"; and that he serve as editor-in-chief of a new monthly newsletter.

Finally, Randolph felt compelled to restate the NALC's goals: It was definitely not a labor union but rather an organization working to eliminate "race bias" in trade unions, industry, and government. It did not propose or negotiate labor contracts or engage in activities that were properly within the sphere of duly elected unions. Equally important:

> It is not a civil rights movement. It is a black laborers' rights movement. It does not initiate civil rights struggles, but it will cooperate with the established civil rights movements, such as the NAACP, CORE, National Urban League, Southern Christian Leadership Conference, and other established civil rights movements.[34]

He concluded his statement on a political note: NALC was "non-partisan . . . *not non-political*" (emphasis added). It had clear political goals, which certainly placed him and the NALC on the far left of the political spectrum. NALC was committed to the formation of an American Labor Party, "but only if sponsored and backed by bona fide trade unions." The NALC was "also committed by convention action to government ownership and control of the railroads and public utilities."[35] These two political positions were hardly policies to be endorsed by the established civil rights groups, but Randolph was not asking them to do so. At the moment, he was engaged with charting a dual agenda course for his organization and his leadership. The decade of the 1960s was the time when that course for all the groups—civil rights, labor, religious, liberal—would be profoundly affected. The approach to the dual agenda was entering a new period.

SEVEN

Cautious Optimism: The 1960s

At the start of the 1960s the country was clearly on the threshold of a new burst of activity in race relations and the politics of race. Supreme Court decisions overturning legal segregation in various realms were accumulating. Mass direct action ignited by a bus boycott in Montgomery, Alabama (1955–56) had led to many other such actions going into the new decade. Black college students in North Carolina in February 1960 attracted the attention and involvement of thousands around the country with their sit-in protests against segregated public accommodations. Already, beginning in 1957, Congress had at last begun to respond to mounting pressure with the passage of civil rights laws (the first since 1875) aimed mainly at ending the denial of voting rights (1957 and 1960).

Established civil rights organizations, nationally and through their local branches and affiliates, were in the thick of this burgeoning activity, initiating and responding to new developments. Sensing that the country was on the cusp of a new day of liberal activism, they quickly sought to take advantage of this changing environment. Now would be the opportune time to renew efforts on both the civil rights and social welfare fronts. In addition, the new Democratic administrations of Presidents John F. Kennedy (1961–1963) and Lyndon B. Johnson (1963–1969), backed by more liberal congressional majorities, promised to be more responsive to racial justice and the economic needs of the poor.

Even with the obviously important civil rights laws being enacted, civil rights groups always understood that such victories were insufficient to alleviate dire socioeconomic problems that stretched over decades of neglect or parsimony. Thus, they decided to be even more forceful in pushing for their social welfare agenda, stepping up demands for a full employment economy, for federal hegemony over the states in social welfare program development and implementation, and for a social insurance system that minimized the impact of a two-tier structure of social provision. And they took care to indicate how demands from the social welfare agenda would relate to and support efforts being made in regard to the civil rights agenda.

In 1984 former congressman Parren Mitchell (D, Md.) mischaracterized those demands when he observed: "We made a serious mistake during the 1960s. We should have meshed in our agenda the demands of civil rights and economic parity at the same time. One is meaningless without the other."[1]

The fact is that the major civil rights groups *did* "mesh" the two agendas of civil rights and economics. Beginning in the early 1960s, virtually every major plan of action and policy statement included concern for both a fight against segregation and discrimination on the one hand, and, on the other, for effective programs to deal with socioeconomic problems for *all* Americans, not just for blacks. This chapter discusses three developments in the 1960s aimed at outlining what civil rights organizations believed should constitute the basic components of a liberal social welfare agenda. These were (1) the 1963 March on Washington, (2) a controversial new proposal by the National Urban League, and (3) the Johnson administration's response to these and other initiatives concerning the socioeconomic circumstances of black Americans.

A March for Jobs and Freedom

In the early 1960s the civil rights movement was becoming increasingly characterized by mounting direct action protests. Centering mainly, but not exclusively, in the South and often organized by such groups as CORE (e.g., "Freedom Rides" to desegregate interstate travel), the newly formed Student Nonviolent Coordinating Committee (SNCC), and Martin Luther King, Jr.'s Southern Christian Leadership Conference (SCLC), the demonstrations attracted national and international attention. Heroic efforts to overcome overt racist practices were chronicled daily in the media. Sit-ins, boycotts, and voter-registration campaigns were launched. Arrests, beatings, and bombings of black protesters by private white citizens and local officials were common. People began to talk of a "civil rights revolution."

In December 1962, long-time civil rights activist Bayard Rustin met with A. Philip Randolph. Agreeing that an effort should be made to provide more national focus and coordination to accelerating events, they decided that a national march on Washington should be organized. Always the advocate of focusing the plight of blacks on underlying economic causes, Rustin drafted a three-page memorandum calling for a two-day mass "action program" in the nation's capital in June 1963. What was needed, he believed, was full employment and effective measures to counter "structural unemployment." The memo stated:

> Integration in the fields of education, housing, transportation and public accommodations will be of limited extent and duration so long as fundamental economic inequality along racial lines persists. . . . An economically disprivileged people is not able to utilize institutions and facilities geared to middle-class incomes in an inflated economy. They cannot afford to patronize the better restaurants, integrated or not. . . . Clearly there is no need for Negroes to demand jobs that do not exist. Nor do Negroes seek to displace white workers as both are being displaced by machines. Negroes seek instead, *as an integral part of their own struggle as a people*, the creation of more jobs for all Americans.[2]

Randolph liked the idea but noted that it concentrated mainly on economic demands. While this was certainly a part of Randolph's long-standing commitment, he suggested that the agenda should include more explicit reference to civil rights demands. Rustin readily accepted this modification and suggested the name—a March for Jobs and Freedom.

Thus emerged the combination of the two agendas that would burst full-blown onto the national scene in August 1963. (The initial projected June date proved too soon to pull off such a massive undertaking.) From that point on for the next three decades (Parren Mitchell's observation notwithstanding), the dual agenda of the civil rights organizations would, indeed, be "meshed."

Randolph, still planning a two-day affair, decided to enlist the cooperation of the NAACP, CORE, NUL, SCLC, and SNCC. The projected dates would be June 13–14. Randolph's invitation suggested that "lobbying with the members of the House and Senate be carried on by a select group of Negro youth who will stress the plight of minority teenagers and the need for Congressional action to bring about constructive relief."[3] He hoped that the major civil rights groups would sign on as sponsors and send "a contribution, as soon as convenient." Reminiscent of his efforts twenty years earlier in planning a march on Washington, Randolph stressed that he wanted the financing of this endeavor to come primarily from Negroes: "The finances for the March will come from various Negro groups and any liberal or labor groups that may be sympathetic, but we will rely upon Negro forces as a main source of the money to finance the March and Mobilization."[4]

All the major groups signed on, but not without some grumbling from a few who were less than enthusiastic about such expensive mass action protests. Under the circumstances, given the heightened climate of mass activity, they had no choice but to participate. (At that precise time, King and SCLC were dramatically engaged in leading civil rights protests in Birmingham, Alabama, that were attracting worldwide attention. The Washington march, it was hoped, would direct attention to the seat of national decision-making power.) CORE enthusiastically endorsed the plan, with James Farmer promising that "CORE . . . will make a contribution as soon as possible. . . . This contribution will not be as large as we would like for it to be due to our own financial situation, but we will do our best."[5]

Recounting the event a few years later, Rustin noted that by June 1963, on the heels of the Birmingham protests, President Kennedy had introduced a civil rights bill and that "the urgency of that bill obscured the basic reason for the March." The purpose of the march, according to Rustin, "was to raise the economic question." He became reconciled to the reality of "civil rights" (segregation, the denial of voting rights, employment discrimination) being the dominant concern over economic issues, however, and eventually concluded that it probably did not take "anything from the March. I think it may, in fact, have helped it."[6]

Throughout the spring and summer of 1963, plans were developed, the original idea of a two-day event became changed to a one-day affair, and an August 28 date was set. Under the day-to-day direction of Rustin as Randolph's deputy,[7] elaborate plans were laid to bring at least two hundred thousand people to Washington. Many unions and religious groups participated.[8]

The "Official Call" for the march was issued on July 12, 1963, and was signed by James Farmer (CORE), Martin Luther King, Jr. (SCLC), John Lewis (SNCC), A. Philip Randolph (NALC), Roy Wilkins (NAACP), and Whitney Young (NUL). And to attest to the conscious decision to combine the two agendas of civil rights and economics, an organizing manual cited these two major categories under the heading "What are the demands of the March?"

I. The Civil Rights demands include:

Passage by the Congress of effective and meaningful civil rights legislation in the present session, without filibuster. Immediate desegregation of the nation's schools.

An end to police brutality directed against citizens using their constitutional right of peaceful demonstration.

II. The Job demands include:

A massive Federal Public Works Program to provide jobs for all the unemployed, and Federal legislation to promote an expanding economy.

A Federal Fair Employment Practices Act to bar job discrimination by Federal, State, and Municipal governments, and by private employers, contractors, employment agencies and trade unions.

Broadening of the Fair Labor Standards Act to include the uncovered areas of employment where Negroes and other minorities work at slave wages; and the establishment of a national minimum wage of not less than $2.00 per hour.[9]

The manual stressed that the march was to be nonpartisan, and that no funds would be accepted from political parties. Noting that participation was invited "from only the established civil rights organizations, from major religious and fraternal groups, and from labor unions," officials of the march "expressly reject(ed) the aid or participation of totalitarian or subversive groups of all persuasions." This was intended to send a message to those who were prone to accuse the civil rights movement of being influenced by Communists, a familiar charge leveled especially by southern segregationists and by some congressmen at that time.

A special appeal was made to get unemployed people to participate: "It will serve no purpose to hold a March for Jobs and Freedom if unemployed people are not able to come and add their voices and presence to the demonstration." All placards to be used in the march were to be provided by the march's National Office, thus assuring coherence of theme and guarding against possible embarrassing messages.[10]

In the several weeks before the march, Randolph made presentations emphasizing the dual agenda. Testifying before a House committee, he stated: "Economic and civil rights are inseparable."[11] Regarding the right to a decent livelihood, he noted:

All civil rights are built on this. It is not enough to outlaw discrimination in housing unless the Negro earns sufficient income to pay the rent or to buy the land. . . . The rising tide of discontent in both our northern cities and our southern cities is related to the number of adults without jobs and youth without futures. It is no accident that the greatest outburst in the civil rights struggle to date has taken place in an industrial city plagued with unemployment.[12]

Nonetheless, consistent with his long-standing self-described socialist views, he concluded:

> Yet so long as we are trying to share more equally in jobs of which there are not enough to go around, we have not tackled a major problem. We cannot have fair employment until we have full employment. Nor will we have full employment until we have fair employment. National planning for jobs for all Americans is an urgent need of the hour. Government must take leadership in investment policies, tax policies, public works policies.[13]

The historic March on Washington for Jobs and Freedom occurred on August 28, 1963. An official estimation was that 250,000 people had attended from all over the country. They came in the morning, and they were gone by nightfall. Martin Luther King's "I Have A Dream" speech is the oratorical legacy of that day, but there were many other significant aspects about the event. Contrary to the fears of some, there was no disorder or violence. It was a peaceful demonstration, up to that time the largest of its kind in the country's history. In his speech, echoing Randolph, Walter Reuther of the United Automobile Workers called for full employment *and* fair employment. Randolph himself spoke most directly to the dual agenda:

> But this civil rights revolution is not confined to the Negro nor is it confined to civil rights, for our white allies know that they cannot be free while we are not and we know that we have no future in a society in which six million black and white people are unemployed and millions more live in poverty. Nor is the goal of our civil rights revolution merely the passage of civil rights legislation. . . . We want integrated public schools but that means we also want federal aid to education—all forms of education. . . . Look for the enemies of Medicare, of higher minimum wages, of social security, of federal aid to education and there you will find the enemy of the Negro—the coalition of Dixiecrats and reactionary Republicans that seeks to dominate the Congress.[14]

All the speeches struck the right note of continued commitment to the struggle, the moral cause involved, and the importance of interracial coalitions. There was a good blend of history, vision, and optimism. It was Randolph, however, bred as he was in the two camps of organized labor and civil rights, who focused the mind on the dual nature of the struggle. In so doing, he sounded a warning of the political struggles that lay ahead. He had seen, as many others had, how difficult it was to mount an attack on both fronts at the same time. He was not sanguine about the outcomes, but he was prescient about the nature of the battles to come. The two agendas—jobs *and* freedom—were certainly linked, inevitably so. But he understood that, as so often in the past, the politics of the dual agenda would make that linkage a difficult one to pursue.

At the end of the march, the leaders met with President Kennedy at the White House. Initially, Kennedy had been wary of the march, fearing it could not be a mass, peaceful affair, and that it could possibly anger many in Congress. If that happened, the civil rights bill (introduced in June) would be jeopardized. After being convinced that the march would not be canceled, he and his advisers tried to influence its focus—toward the Congress, not on the administration. Therefore, pleased and impressed by the march's tone and decorum, when Kennedy met with the civil rights leaders he congratulated them for an apparently unprecedented turnout. He also focused attention on the difficult political problem of getting the civil rights bill through Congress. There was, as far as is known, no discussion in that White House meeting of the economic, social welfare issues on the march's agenda. But it *was* a march for "jobs" and freedom.

The National Urban League's "Domestic Marshall Plan"

Even before the historic march on Washington, the NUL's new head, Whitney M. Young, Jr., had made a controversial proposal that would come to influence much of the discussion of civil rights and social welfare policies into the 1990s. Picked from his post as dean of the Atlanta University School of Social Work, Young became the fourth executive director of the NUL in October 1961. A former urban league head in St. Paul, Minnesota, Young was well received in urban league and corporate circles. At thirty-eight he was experienced and ready for national leadership. Precisely what this new leadership portended became evident in a short time.

At the 1963 national conference of the NUL, Young called for a "special effort" to help Negroes, denied for so many years. He believed that in order for Negroes to take advantage of the new opportunities being slowly opened to them, they needed "special" attention from the public and private sectors in the form of programs specifically targeted to increase their educational and job skills. He compared this approach to America's foreign aid Marshall

Plan after World War II. This was necessary, he reasoned, to close the gap of deprivation between blacks and whites caused by decades of denial. He frequently talked of "correcting historical abuses."[15]

Young was definitely taking the NUL into a more active stance on social welfare policies. Commenting on Young's 1963 speech, three historians concluded: "The Urban League is still regarded as the most conservative of the civil rights groups. But the fact is that it may now be classed as a protest organization."[16]

In fact, under Young, the league felt it needed to be more assertive in presenting itself to the new Kennedy administration. In preparing for a meeting of top NUL executives with the president in 1962, the league outlined a proposed relationship. Recognizing that the administration was expanding into areas "in which the Urban League has had special concern and competence" (i.e., manpower training and development, youth employment opportunities, urban affairs and housing, and welfare services), the league optimistically proposed a role for itself: "The National Urban League now places at the disposal of the government its full resources and facilities throughout the nation, to serve as a vehicle for advancing government programs and services in these four areas in which the Urban League has similar interest."[17] The league then proposed that the various federal agencies meet with local urban league representatives to develop a working relationship. For the first time in the history of the civil rights movement, out of these meetings came a close institutional relationship between the national government and a major civil rights organization. As historian Nancy Weiss has noted: "The meetings gave the league the opportunity to establish personal as well as institutional relationships with those people at the federal agencies who had the greatest potential for influence over the economic and social welfare of black Americans."[18]

By 1963 Whitney Young had crystallized his thinking to the point where he was convinced that nothing less than a "crash program" was needed to overcome devastating socioeconomic problems facing Negroes. He proposed a set of general ideas, not a specific legislative agenda. In speeches and in his book, *To Be Equal*, he suggested that "the best schools and the best teachers" be placed in Negro communities, and that jobs be provided preferentially to Negroes "where two equally qualified people apply" and especially if a company had never before hired Negroes. Without question, he was calling for "preferential" treatment, although he tried to suggest otherwise. He argued: "The nation should not be misled by sloganeers of dubious motivation who conjure up fright phantoms by waving trigger phrases such as 'preferential treatment,' 'reverse discrimination,' 'indemnification,' and 'reparation' before unsuspecting, unthinking, and uninformed Americans."[19]

Whatever his response to the "slogans," he was surely raising an issue that some perceived as a wide departure from traditional civil rights and social welfare demands. Young attempted to show that if anything less than such a special, crash program was launched, there would be dire socioeconomic consequences. Achievements made on the civil rights agenda would be almost worthless.

Years later, in the 1980s and 1990s, conservatives would lament the deterioration of social conditions—crime, drugs, broken families—in the black communities. As several of the civil rights leaders before him, Young, in the 1960s, warned of these possibilities. Restricted racial ghettos were breeding grounds "spewing forth human wreckage and the major portion of criminal offenders."[20]

Neither was he willing to place complete responsibility on white Americans: "Negro citizens must exert themselves energetically in constructive efforts to carry their full share of responsibilities and to participate in a meaningful way in every phase of community life. It is not enough to man the machinery of protest."[21] It was the responsibility of Negro parents to attend PTA meetings, to take their children to libraries, to attend community meetings. Finally, he hoped that the country would see his ideas as a call for "an investment rather than a give-away program." This was an investment that would "pay-off—just as the Marshall Plan paid off in a prosperous Western Europe of strong and friendly allies; just as the G.I. Bill paid off in better-educated Americans, a revitalized housing industry, etc."[22] Such ideas from a more "radical" source would have been dismissed out of hand. But Whitney Young of the National Urban League in the early 1960s was not such a source. The NUL, in fact, was frequently referred to as the more "moderate-to-conservative group in the general spectrum of organizations speaking for a minority."[23] But Young signaled a new role for the organization.

To further indicate the decidedly new stance of the NUL, Young sent a memorandum in 1963 to all league affiliates mildly complaining of the lack of NUL recognition in the burgeoning civil rights protests. He did not expect the affiliates to initiate boycotts "or even to actively participate in such direct action activities as picketing." But he did believe it was necessary for the league to be involved in order to show the organization's relevance to the "resolution of some of these crisis situations." He candidly admitted that only a few years earlier "the power structure might have taken a dim view" of such NUL involvement. Now, however, he was convinced that increased presence of the NUL was the only way the organization could be of value "to that same power structure."[24] Young was clearly proposing a more policy-oriented and social-activist role than that of his immediate predecessor, Lester Granger. But times were changing. Throughout the 1950s Granger and most of the NUL Board had been wary about testifying before Congress on "social issues."[25] (As we have seen, this hesitancy was itself a change from the activities of the league during the New Deal.) Such changes over time reflected the constant and understandable efforts of the various organizations to adapt to new, evolving circumstances. They continuously debated within their ranks the most appropriate leadership styles and roles to fit changing times.

Young also felt that the NUL should not support the establishment of new biracial committees springing up around the country. He saw no need for such new groups, reminding the local affiliates: "This has been our traditional organizational structure and we [the NUL] should, therefore, be utilized for this purpose."[26] Clearly, Young was sensitive to the need to make sure the NUL did not get swept aside by the rising tide of civil rights activism in the 1960s. The NUL's shift was commensurate to that of the NAACP in 1949 when (as described in chapter 5) the NAACP decided to attach the "Powell Amendment" to liberal legislation.

There would be, however, strong critics of Young's views, and more than a few were liberals who had counted themselves as longtime allies of the civil rights struggle. Indeed, as the Powell Amendment of the 1950s had split liberal ranks, now Young's call for a "special effort" would have similar consequences in the 1960s and for decades to come. There was a major difference between the two debates, however. While the one over the Powell Amendment could be (and was) resolved with the passage of Title VI of the Civil Rights Act of 1964 (prohibiting the allocation of funds to segregated facilities), the issue of "special efforts" did not lend itself to such a neat conclusion. Young later suggested "a strict timetable" to go along with his plan, recognizing that this would be a good way to monitor efforts and convince people of the seriousness of the programs. He explained:

The Domestic Marshall Plan must include a strict timetable by which progress in these areas can be measured. The man in the ghetto no longer believes promises of better housing or more jobs. He has been lied to so often that he now will believe results, and nothing less. If we embarked upon a five year program to end slum conditions, for example, people could see visible signs of change after the first year, and they would believe that the nation really means to end slums and they would know that they too will have decent housing in a measurable and short period of time. Only such a timetable will convince the ghetto population that conditions are changing and riots can only retard advances.[27]

But this argument did not persuade the liberal critics who preferred to focus on what they considered to be the essentially undemocratic elements of the plan. It violated the "American philosophical creed," Daniel Bell wrote, that emphasized individual rights, not group rights based on "birth alone." He accepted the notion that special subsidies for the poor, "especially in nursery-school and elementary education," were legitimate, but he could not accept a plan that would end up discriminating "against others." He concluded: "But when one asks for special quotas or preferences, particularly in the cases of schools or jobs where places are limited, such a request serves to discriminate against others. And this is a much more difficult question, morally and practically, to solve."[28]

The managing editor of *Christian Century*, Kyle Haselden, by no means a racial bigot, also took issue with Whitney Young. In fact, he saw very dangerous racist signs in the proposal:

Compensation for Negroes is a subtle but pernicious form of racism. It requires that men be dealt with by society on the basis of race and color rather than on the basis of their humanity. It would therefore as a public policy legalize, deepen, and perpetuate the abominable racial cleavage which has ostracized and crippled the American Negro.[29]

It is not fair, Haselden argued, to penalize those whites for the sins of their forefathers. "It leaves with the descendants of the exploiters a guilt they cannot cancel and with the descendants of the exploited a debt they cannot collect." In addition, he maintained, racial preference would leave a stigma on the Negro that "will inevitably destroy in him the initiative and enterprise required of a minority people in a highly competitive society. Slavery corrupts ambition and self-reliance; so, too, does patronizing social status."[30]

These arguments—pro and con—would be made many times over the next three decades and find their way into court opinions, speeches, professional journals, editorials, and political commentaries centered around affirmative action policies. The 1990s (see chapter 12) would once again see these identical issues hotly rehashed.

Still, Whitney Young did have supporters among civil rights leaders who understood the basic sentiments he was trying to express.[31] A. Philip Randolph, always the advocate of dealing with these problems in the context of a broad approach to economic deprivation of *all* persons, continued to link fair employment with full employment. The problems were interrelated. But he understood that racial discrimination still persisted as a particular problem for Negroes, and he reiterated the point made in his 1963 March on Washington speech: Jobs were disappearing for all workers, "even for the hitherto privileged white workers." Nonetheless, he felt compelled to support the central argument Young was making: "While basically, Negro workers can only move forward when the great American working class is moving forward, Negro labor needs and is entitled to special and preferential treatment, in the form of preparation in training and education to enable it effectively to move forward."[32]

In the midst of this debate, the progressive League for Industrial Democracy was in the process of preparing a pamphlet on the *Economics of Equality*. It circulated a draft to its Publications Committee forewarning that the issue of "preferential treatment" or "reverse discrimination" was "a complex question which needs to be approached in moral, political, and economic terms." The purpose of the pamphlet was "to make available to civil rights activists a brief analysis of the Negro's economic plight, and to suggest in the context of the national economy the programmatic directions in which solutions may be found." Apparently unaware of the history of the social welfare agenda of civil rights groups dating back to the New Deal, the draft contained the following conventional wisdom, as if this needed to be made clear to those groups:

> Civil rights is taking on a broader definition. Reconstruction taught us the lesson that there can be no civil rights—no social or political equality—without economic security. Increasingly, therefore, the civil rights struggle will find itself concerned with economic criticism, social welfare and public planning.[33]

The draft document also made an assumption about the demands for civil rights and for social welfare programs. Consistent with prevailing social democratic thinking at the time, it assumed that in a society where jobs were plentiful and housing readily available, there would be no need to raise the civil rights issue. Such demands, it concluded, occur in a closed society. "The call for 'preferential treatment' would not arise in a full-employment economy. 'Benign Quotas' would not be demanded if there were no shortage of decent low-income housing."[34] The document indicated that the pamphlet "would probably be nearer A. Philip Randolph's preferential treatment for the poor, the unemployed, the aged, etc." The fact is, as we have seen, Randolph was more sophisticated and more racially sensitive than this analysis would suggest.

Such an analysis failed to understand the distinctive nature of the two agendas. Randolph never made that mistake. The civil rights agenda had always been concerned with *racial discrimination*. Even in times of high (or "full") employment, such as during World War II, discrimination still existed—discrimination in promotions, and even in racially based training programs. That jobs were plentiful would not necessarily mean the absence of such discriminatory practices. Many on the political left failed to grasp this point and, therefore, failed to understand the need for civil rights groups to continue to fight for *both* agendas.

This lack of understanding constitutes one of the major analytical differences between some civil rights leaders and many of their perennial liberal allies. Invariably, the different analyses focus on the relative importance of past and current discrimination in dealing with socioeconomic problems. The liberal allies sought to minimize the impact of discrimination and to focus substantially on universal social welfare programs for all the needy. The civil rights groups, as we have seen, were quite willing to emphasize such programs, but not at the expense of recognizing both the legacy and persistence of racism.

For this reason, it is clear why civil rights leaders were pleased with the language of President Lyndon Johnson in a commencement speech at Howard University in June 1965. The president spoke directly to the need to go beyond merely lifting racial barriers:

> You do not take a person who, for years, has been hobbled by chains and liberate him, bring him up to the starting line of a race and then say, "You are free to compete with all the others," and still justly believe that you have been completely fair.
>
> Thus it is not enough just to open the gates of opportunity. All our citizens must have the ability to walk through those gates.

This is the next and the more profound stage of the battle for civil rights. We seek not just legal equity but human ability, not just equality as a right and a theory, but equality as a fact and equality as a result.[35]

Four years later, Whitney Young stated that he had had several discussions with President Johnson in formulating the president's thinking on poverty issues. "I'd say a lot of our ideas really constituted some of the same concepts of the Marshall Plan."[36]

It is true that the language and sentiments were quite similar. But it is also possible that the president and his advisers were not prepared for the ideological and political fallout that was sure to come. What seemed like a reasonable, fair, and even moderate statement would not be taken as such in the policy and political circles that had the responsibility for fashioning concrete programs to implement this "next and . . . more profound stage" of the dual agenda.

A Report on "The Negro Family" and a White House Conference

Widely praised by all major civil rights groups, President Johnson's speech at Howard University was but one of many highlights in a year of front-page events in the field of civil rights and race relations: the dramatic march from Selma, Alabama, to Montgomery to protest the denial of voting rights in the South; President Johnson's inspiring nationally televised speech in which he introduced a new voting rights bill and adopted the refrain of the movement, "We Shall Overcome"; the passage of the Voting Rights Act in August; the riots in the Watts section of Los Angeles the same month; and the eagerly anticipated White House Conference in November.

The Howard University speech was the first time a president had addressed the problems of black Americans by focusing primarily on *socioeconomic* issues. From this point on, there would be specific recognition of something the civil rights leaders had known and been grappling with all along—that there were two agendas: civil rights *and* social welfare.

Another significant development occurred in 1965. Assistant Secretary of Labor Daniel Patrick Moynihan presented a report on the Negro family that cited census data documenting various alarming developments indicating that the family structure of Negroes was seriously deteriorating—namely, that out-of-wedlock births were increasing; teenage pregnancies were on the rise; single-parent households were becoming more numerous; and young black males were experiencing consistently high unemployment rates which made it unlikely that they could support their families, thus leading to desertion and family breakup. Further, school dropout rates among blacks were on the increase, and AFDC rolls for blacks were surging. All this was occurring, Moynihan noted, while *overall* employment rates for "non-whites" were, in fact, slowly rising. He emphasized that these devastating conditions had had their genesis in the history of slavery and were exacerbated by subsequent segregation and discrimination. What this meant to him was that a serious pathological condition had developed in the black ghettos which made it very difficult for those citizens to even begin to take advantage of the welcome opportunities currently being opened up by victories on the civil rights front. This pathology was now self-perpetuating. Citing an earlier analysis and warning of Negro family dysfunction by the black sociologist E. Franklin Frazier, Moynihan lamented the failure to heed Frazier's scholarship. Now matters had grown much worse. He concluded:

> At the heart of the deterioration of the fabric of Negro society is the deterioration of the Negro family. . . . It is the fundamental source of the weakness of the Negro community at the present time. . . . The family structure of lower class Negroes is highly unstable, and in many urban centers is approaching complete breakdown.[37]

Moynihan also cited studies and writings by other contemporary black scholars and activists such as Bayard Rustin, Kenneth Clark, Daniel Thompson, Whitney Young, and Dorothy Height as well as a 1950 article in the *Journal of Negro Education* and numerous other academic studies documenting over time the conditions to which he was calling attention. Disturbed by these obvious trends, he wanted to alert the administration.

Although Moynihan's report was initially intended to be a limited-circulation in-house document, the fact of its existence as well as fragmented observations from different sources were leaked to the media. For several months, it was difficult even for some members of Congress to get a copy of the formal report. Sociologists Lee Rainwater and William L. Yancey soon provided an account of the report and the controversy that had swirled around it for almost a year.[38] The print media, picking up the more sensational aspects of the report, which dealt with illegitimacy rates and ghetto pathology, in many instances left readers with an impression that matters were so bad that either virtually no government programs would do any good or that Negroes had to change their own moral attitudes and destructive behavior first. Moynihan's reference to historical causes stemming from slavery, segregation, and discrimination was of little importance in such a volatile situation. By the time the report became readily available to the public in late summer of 1965, the damage caused by limited release, careless reading, quick and incomplete summaries was already done.

In the meantime, Moynihan served as one of the two principal drafters of President Johnson's Howard University speech (the other being Richard Goodwin). The potentially incendiary statistics and references to illegitimacy and pathology made up only a minor part of the speech, but Johnson did endorse the proposition that conditions were so intolerable "that we have to act." What would be that immediate action? He announced a White House Conference for the fall that would include "scholars, and experts, and outstanding Negro leaders—men and women of both races—and officials of government at every level." The theme would be "To Fulfill These Rights."[39] The object would be to develop specific policies that would help American Negroes experience the rights which they were finally about to secure. In other words, the society was on the threshold of providing *civil rights* through recently (and soon to be) enacted legislation against de jure segregation and discrimination. Now the focus would be more on the social welfare agenda, to make sure that Negroes were actually in a position to take advantage of their newly won opportunities.

There can be little doubt that the thrust of that speech emanated from sentiments expressed in Moynihan's *Negro Family* report. As the speech explained, the "case for national action" was to be manifested first in the call for a conference, with a need to understand more fully the scope of the problems as well as to search for "other answers."

Attention in the civil rights community now turned to preparing for the conference. But in the interim, a firestorm of resentment against the still only partially available report developed. Seen by some activists as "blaming the victim" and putting the burden for improvement on Negroes themselves, the report came under strong attack from some civil rights leaders and mild rebuke from others.

Martin Luther King, Jr., viewed the report both positively and negatively. In a speech he expressed the hope that the report would lead to greater awareness of the enormity of the problem and to forceful action. But he also expressed a fear that "the danger will be that the problems will be attributed to innate Negro weaknesses and used to justify neglect and rationalize oppression."[40]

James Farmer of CORE was more condemnatory. Reading the report as putting blame "on the pathological condition of the Negro family and community," Farmer accused Moynihan of "a massive academic cop-out for the white conscience." As with others, he exonerated Moynihan and his colleagues of any racist intent, "but the fact that it may be used as such makes their innocence inexcusable."[41]

Whitney Young, pleased that the report had cited paragraphs from his book, To Be Equal, dealing with the tragic plight of the Negro male and the possible criminal consequences, reminded his audiences: "The Urban League movement, of course, has long been trying to focus public opinion on this question."[42]

Bayard Rustin was understandably pleased that at least Moynihan "was trying . . . to insist on the social and economic dimension of the race issue."[43] His main complaint was that the report offered no specific policy proposals and that the "data were presented in a form guaranteed to promote confusion." Rustin observed that the report was generally seen as a comprehensive analysis of the economic status and causes of deterioration in Negro families, when it was in fact not such a document; therefore it failed, he concluded, to focus on the positive aspects, such as the work civil rights organizations had been trying to do in dealing with the problems.

Robert L. Carter of the NAACP could "not understand the great shock that people were expressing over the report. . . . It's an old story and not a startling discovery and not new."[44] Carter's observation of nothing "new" was very likely part of the frustration and anger expressed by some civil rights leaders. Years later, analyses of these and other responses to the report suggest that civil rights leaders made a serious mistake in failing to heed the report. Some analysts have concluded that their harsh reaction created a mood among scholars and liberal activists which led them to avoid the clear realities the report was highlighting. "The vitriolic criticism . . . helped create an atmosphere that discouraged many social scientists from researching certain aspects of lower-class black life."[45] One author pinpointed "the ire of the civil rights community and of black scholars in particular" to the report that made the issues of "drug use, delinquency, and out-of-wedlock childbearing among blacks . . . taboo subjects for liberal social scientists until the early 1980s."[46] Such widely accepted assessments need further examination.

What really lay behind the negative reaction of civil rights leaders? While it was generally recognized that Moynihan agreed with their emphasis on a serious jobs program as at least one major part of the long-term solution, their frustration and anger probably stemmed from two sources. First, civil rights leaders obviously knew of the persistent and growing problems spotlighted in the report. They had been fighting segregation and discrimination on both the social and economic fronts for decades expressly to avoid these inevitable consequences of continued subjection—precisely the consequences they had envisioned when the NUL and NAACP were raising warning flags against exclusion from New Deal programs, against job discrimination, against restricted housing policies and practices, against poor schools, and against abominable health care. They resented the fact that these very predictable consequences were only now finally being discovered as "new," and that officials, oblivious until alerted by one of their own, now claimed to be shocked and astonished. Earlier warnings and truths apparently did not matter, and the seriousness of decades of neglect was not made manifest until it became recognized by white decision-makers as their own revelation. It took a Moynihan to point out and legitimize the complaints and failures of the past! The fact that Moynihan relied heavily on the earlier scholarship of Frazier and other black scholars—as if such work was unknown to civil rights workers—doubtless aggravated the resentment.

The second source of frustration and anger very likely lay in the explosive nature of the problems raised: illegitimacy, teenage pregnancies, promiscuous immoral behavior—in a word, SEX. Without question, the civil rights groups were keenly sensitive to these problems. But they were also aware of the potentially damaging aspect of such issues. The Moynihan report definitely talked about Negro sexual behavior. Black leaders had dealt with these issues in more polite or subdued terms. Perhaps they had been too subtle, but they knew that *any* evidence concerning out-of-wedlock births and similar matters, *no matter what the cause*, could give their adversaries ammunition against them. Although the report did state that there were many segments of Negro society not afflicted with such conditions, civil rights leaders understood that a general perception could otherwise develop. *All* blacks would be tarred with the broad brush of irresponsibility and degradation. Such a result was all too familiar to black Americans from long-standing and bitter experience. The weaknesses of those on the bottom would be ascribed to the entire race by an American public already prone to see blacks in a monolithic way. In fact, the NUL and NAACP, in their efforts to avoid the establishment of a two-tier social security system in the 1930s, had feared just such a perception if a majority of the black population was relegated to the second tier.

In this connection, it was the NAACP's Robert Carter who pointed to the crucial question. Since there was really nothing new or shocking in the report, he wanted to know what officials were actually going to *do* about these troubling conditions: "The real costs of doing what must be done in order to improve the structure of the Negro family are great. You're going to have to step on a lot of people's toes and a lot of changes are going to have to be made. My question is, is the Administration really prepared to do these things?"[47]

The short-term answer to Carter was "yes." The long-term outlook, however, was another matter, and certainly it was the long-term prospect that concerned Carter and many others. But for now President Johnson had said he would call a White House Conference for the fall to chart a course for dealing with these disturbing problems, and this he did.

Whatever the outcome, it was clear that this would be an important event. Its significance stemmed from its historic nature and subject matter: the first such meeting sponsored by a president of the United States which guaranteed maximum attention on the *social welfare agenda* of the civil rights movement. This was truly an opportune time for civil rights organizations to make the social welfare case they had been trumpeting for years, and to renew their commitment to both agendas. It was critical, therefore, to try to influence the agenda of the two-day event. Several preparatory meetings were held, and in August 1965 President Johnson met with Whitney Young and A. Philip Randolph. Lee White of the White House staff sent Johnson a memo of "talking points" for this advance session and advised that, given the universal approval of the Howard University speech,

> —focus on family structure in the Negro community, on the psychology of instilling strong desires to secure education and training, and on the recognition of how Negroes have really lived totally apart from the white culture and social world, should be good subjects for exploration. . . . There should

be considerable emphasis on economic opportunities through even stronger training and education programs. . . .

—The remarkable achievements of 1965 [which had included important legislation on voting rights, housing, education, the Medicare "break-through," and Head Start]. . . . These programs are now on the books and the Negro community should be encouraged to take full advantage of them—something that the Urban League is already doing.[48]

But August also brought an intervening, traumatic event: a major five-day riot, ignited by the arrest and beating of a black motorist by police, broke out in the black residential Watts section of Los Angeles. This explosion of outrage dominated the news for weeks. Rainwater and Yancey reported that the Moynihan report virtually became the official explanation for the causes of the rioting, as interpreted by the media, which once again focused attention on the still-hard-to-come-by report and further put civil rights leaders on notice that they should not let that document drive the agenda of the November conference.

Several civil rights leaders submitted lengthy memoranda to the conference planners setting forth suggestions of emphasis and topics for the conference. In every instance, the recommendation for job-creation programs was prominent on the lists. Likewise, the suggestions emphasized that such programs need not or should not be aimed only at helping blacks but rather should benefit all the poor. There was no attempt to hide the fact that such a serious approach would require a large expenditure of funds.[49] Meanwhile, it was decided that this fall conference of approximately two hundred people should be followed in the spring by a larger conference of a few thousand.

The November meeting set out to formulate policy proposals to be considered by participants at the subsequent meeting. In each of the work sessions, the discussions were wide-ranging, lively, and reasonably predictable. Summaries of each panel's deliberations were made, with a preliminary report attached. The session on the family stressed the need for a full employment policy, with public works as one possible source for jobs, but one participant stated that this did not mean "the WPA angle, because it has so many unpleasant connotations."[50] In addition to the obvious importance of jobs as a source of family income, the psychological factor was raised in terms of "effective Male [Role] Models."

> The question of a male model for children in low-income Negro families was raised repeatedly. . . . Whether or not the model must be resident in the

home . . . there was no dissent from the proposition that boys—and girls too—need to have before them the examples of competent, responsible, achieving men. . . . The way to achieve male models is to provide jobs for men so they are members of the community. Let youngsters see men naturally fill-ing jobs that command respect.[51]

Neither was it necessary that these "role models" be "men of outstanding eminence." In situations where children never saw their parents—certainly not the men—going to work, just the fact alone of their fathers being able to go out to do "everyday jobs" and earn an honest living could have a salutary effect on the children.

A session on health and welfare, chaired by Whitney Young, stressed the need for federal grants-in-aid to be funneled to a "regional planning system" instead of to individual states. Obviously motivated by the old concern regarding how some southern states treated Negro public assistance recipi-ents, the following recommendation favoring greater federal hegemony was made: "Abolish the several categories of public assistance, and the locally determined means test and residency requirements for receiving public assistance. Establish need, as determined by a *Federal* eligibility scale, as the sole criteria for receipt of assistance."[52]

The panel frequently spoke of vigilance in monitoring antidiscriminatory delivery of social services. The experiences of decades could not easily be erased from the minds of many who had witnessed blatant racial disparities in providing health and welfare services. Such experiences had clearly made it difficult to "delink" the civil rights and social welfare agendas. This diffi-culty led to continued discussions of universally applicable social welfare problems and racism in the same dialogue, the end of de jure segregation and discrimination, notwithstanding.

Attention was also given to the ongoing racial and economic plight of rural Negroes. Government policies to assist agriculture had not given "due consideration for the special needs and difficulties of sharecroppers, tenant farmers, and small farmers." And while many white farm families in the South had been able to supplement their incomes through additional employment in new manufacturing plants then locating in rural areas, racial discrimination continued to deny such opportunities to blacks.

But new times meant new costs, which almost certainly meant more taxes. The conferees, therefore, wary about how these additional tax burdens might be distributed, advised:

Since many of the actions advocated . . . involve large expenditures of federal funds, it is important in the drafting of such legislation that special care be taken not to rely on taxes that have a regressive quality. Otherwise, workers just above the poverty line will be paying for many of the programs established for those just below the poverty line.[53]

No one knew this better than the government officials who would receive the reports of this conference and would have the responsibility of presenting them to delegates attending the larger conference in the spring. And, unlike the November conference, the follow-up conference in June 1966 *was* more controlled by government officials and businessmen. A council of thirty people prepared a 104-page document summarizing the November conference which was to serve as the basis for discussions at the June meeting. Four broad topics were listed: economic security and welfare; education; housing; and administration of justice. Twelve discussion sessions of two hundred delegates each were organized, but each section discussed all four topics. Conspicuously absent from the agenda was any reference to the Moynihan report. In fact, even the November panel's preliminary report on the family had not been conveyed to the council.

With a gathering of more than two thousand people from all walks of life, the June conference was far more diffuse than the previous one. Several discussion sessions were sparsely attended, with many delegates choosing instead to mill around in informal groups and talk to friends. There was a conventionlike atmosphere. There would be no official, binding votes taken on resolutions. Rather the council planned to distill the various comments (from literally hundreds who spoke) into a final report to the president. In such a situation, thoughtful policy deliberations were impossible or not even attempted. A serious set of actionable recommendations from such a large, unstructured gathering could hardly be expected. Young, Rustin, Wilkins, King, and Floyd McKissick (representing CORE) attended, but their participation was minimal. SNCC decided not to attend.[54]

The council submitted its recommendations to the president several weeks later. There was no recommendation for a massive expenditure of funds, but the suggestion of guaranteeing a job to those unable to find one was there, as was the proposal to provide an adequate income for those on public assistance. Counseling services for youth and "disadvantaged workers" also received endorsement. The council emphasized the importance of getting the private sector as well as the state and local governments more involved in economic development programs for the poor. Overall the final report fell short of the grandiose proposals of the November meeting, and some concluded that it certainly did not live up to the high expectations generated by the Howard University speech a year earlier. But that heady period of exhilaration was over.

If the June 1966 conference was a letdown for the civil rights groups, at least they had, in the previous November meeting, gone on record with their best effort at defining what *they* believed to be the basic components of a meaningful social welfare agenda. Moreover, by the summer of 1966, the civil rights movement was taking new directions, even as the Johnson administration was turning its attention more and more to the war in Vietnam. When council members met with the president to deliver their final recommendations, Johnson spent four minutes talking about civil rights and fifty-six minutes on Vietnam.[55] Clearly, everyone had put the Howard University speech, the Moynihan report, and the frenetic activities of the conferences behind them. The Urban League and the NAACP would return to focusing their labors on implementing the 1964 civil rights and 1965 voting rights laws, and tending to various aspects of the war on poverty and Great Society programs, while dealing with the civil rights bureaucracies in the administration. SNCC and CORE, with their increasing call for Black Power, had already begun to transform themselves into more nationalist-oriented groups. Both organizations would change leadership and within a few years either die out (SNCC) or become an entirely different organization (CORE). Martin Luther King's SCLC was gearing up for a first major sojourn in the North with a move into Chicago that summer. The purpose was to launch an open housing campaign with protest marches, demonstrations, and community organizing.

The November conference did make it clear, however, that while the various organizations may have had quite different styles (and perhaps even different intermediate goals) for the civil rights agenda— through direct action protest, voter registration drives, lobbying Congress, instigating litigation, or working with the business community—there was nevertheless at least widespread agreement on the basic components of the social welfare agenda. Those features could be summed up in the belief that large financial resources needed to be committed over the next several years and aimed especially at creating real public-sector jobs in the tier-1 category. Such funds did not necessarily have to be earmarked for blacks only—in fact, hardly so.

Equally important was the need for long-term planning, preferably through a federal government program, but with greater private-sector involvement and accountability. These proposals might have been, as we shall see, quite expensive and expansive in scope, but no one could question the fact that the civil rights organizations were prepared to put a detailed social welfare agenda on the table, an agenda that all the established civil rights groups (and many prominent liberals not affiliated with any activist group) signed on to.

When such an agenda was finally put forward, its name was, appropriately, "A 'Freedom Budget' for All Americans."

EIGHT

Pursuing a Liberal Social Welfare Agenda

In the long struggle against segregation and discrimination, it was always understood by civil rights proponents that the complaints raised and the remedies sought had to be as specific as possible. No less was required in pursuing the social welfare agenda. As useful as inspirational speeches and broad policy statements were, they were of minimal value unless translated into more detailed language that could form the basis for specific legislative deliberations.

This chapter focuses on three activities of civil rights organizations geared toward accomplishing different aspects of that effort. The first was to present a specific document offering concrete numbers and analyses in regard to the general policies sought: the "Freedom Budget," introduced in 1966, laid out precisely what civil rights organizations had in mind when they advocated a liberal social welfare agenda. The second encompassed specific responses of civil rights organizations to the various social welfare bills and legislation proposed throughout the decade. If they could not get a favorable reception for their top-priority Freedom Budget, civil rights leaders knew they had to be prepared to engage those policies that national lawmakers were in fact willing to consider and to enact. In this sense, leaders continued the practice, going back to the New Deal, of testifying before Congress, seeking to form alliances, and hoping to extract the most liberal results possible. The third activity was an effort to translate the tactic of mass direct protest action, so effective in the civil rights struggle, to the pursuit of their social welfare agenda. Over the years there had been local mass protests, but the SCLC's

1968 "Campaign for Poor People" was the first time in the history of the civil rights movement that a mass protest would be conducted in Washington, D.C., and aimed at Congress and national agencies in order to achieve social welfare goals. Equally important, unlike the 1963 March on Washington, this action was intended to be more than a one- or two-day affair.

The Freedom Budget

At the November 1965 White House Conference, A. Philip Randolph promised: "In the near future, I shall call upon the leaders of the Freedom Movement to meet together with economists and social scientists in order to work out a specific and documented 'freedom budget.' I shall submit these recommendations to the President."[1]

He called on black and white experts to draft such a document under the auspices of the recently established A. Philip Randolph Institute. (Founded in 1965 by Randolph and Bayard Rustin, the Institute concentrated on issues of racial equality and economic justice, conducting workshops, issuing reports, and working closely with organized labor.) After several months and many drafts, the document was completed in the summer of 1966, approximately one month after the second White House Conference. Randolph circulated copies to all civil rights leaders and to many other individuals and organizations for their endorsement, being careful to note that he was not soliciting agreement on all the fine points, numbers, and projections contained in the analyses. "We have all had experience enough in such matters to know that unanimous agreement on all points, among those endorsing such a far-reaching endeavor, requires months if not years to achieve."[2] Such a process would dilute the substance and impact of the document. He assured recipients that "your endorsement would mean only that you are in general sympathy with the broad lines of direction of the Freedom Budget, and with the imperative necessity that the Freedom Budget be introduced into the nationwide discussion of the problems with which it deals."[3] What he wanted was the backing of all who advocated an effective war against poverty, including those in the civil rights, labor, liberal, and religious forces that represented "the coalition of conscience" displayed at the 1963 March on Washington.

A press conference was held on October 26, 1966, in Harlem to announce the release of the eighty-four-page document. While relatively short for the task it sought to achieve, the Freedom Budget contained many charts and innumerable economic statistics. Randolph had successfully attained the wide array of endorsements he had wanted (a total of 207). These consisted of all the major civil rights organizations, including CORE and SNCC (newly chaired by Stokely Carmichael). These latter two groups were important because of their burgeoning black nationalist moves. Signers included academics, religious leaders, labor leaders, and even a few entertainers. Many people doubtless signed the document out of respect for the venerable Randolph and not because they necessarily agreed with every item in it.

The basic objectives outlined in the Freedom Budget were: to achieve full employment as soon as possible (meaning an unemployment rate preferably no higher than 2 percent by 1968); to provide a guaranteed annual income for those who could not or should not work, especially single-female heads of households with children; to wipe out slum housing; to provide adequate health care; to clear up the nation's polluted water and air; and to rebuild the country's deteriorating transportation systems, projects that would also provide a source of employment. All these were to be achieved while concentrating on sustaining full production and high economic growth.

The document projected an "economic growth dividend" to come from full employment and maximized production. To be sure, there would be enormous federal expenditures, but these would be regained by more personal and corporate tax returns from a growing economy. In addition, figures were presented to show that the federal budget expenditures would not be a drain on the overall gross national product. Critical to the analysis was the thesis that initial increased public expenditures (combined with private investment) would contribute to maximizing production and purchasing power which would, in turn, create a *dividend* from economic growth. This dividend would be more than sufficient to sustain the financial needs projected by the Freedom Budget, without the need for more direct taxes to pay for the programs.

Anticipating that a main issue would be one of economic feasibility, the document frequently raised the question: "Can we afford" to do this? With projected numbers based on particular assumptions of annual growth (around 5 percent), the document concluded:

> When the outlays for national defense, space technology, and all international, are excluded from the proposed Federal Budget, the "Freedom Budget" proposals for all domestic programs in the Federal Budget would *average annually* only about 18.5 billion dollars higher, and over the ten years

aggregate only about 185 billion dollars higher, than if Federal Budget outlays for these domestic programs remained stationary at their 1965 size of 37.7 billion. This 185 billion dollars would be only about *one-thirteenth* of the "economic growth dividend."[4]

The Freedom Budget did not purport to "distort our traditional concepts of a 'mixed economy.'" It envisioned a lead role for the public federal budget but also proposed a commensurately important part to be played by the private, profit-making sector. What was needed was a "planned program" that would emphasize full employment and guaranteed annual incomes for those who could not be employed. It also concluded: "The battle should now be resumed for a nationwide system of health insurance."

To be sure, inflation was a concern. Noting recent volatile periods of recession, price increases, and fluctuation in price stability, the document concluded that, given the already high level of significant profit earnings, "selective price inflation" had resulted from unjustifiable business decisions to raise prices. Some price increases had come about because certain industries were eager to "get while the getting was good." If necessary, "tax policy and other measures" should be used to restrain such industries from unwarranted price increases.[5]

To the chagrin of some liberals, the Freedom Budget did not address the debate over the cost of the Vietnam War. Rather it adopted a guns *and* butter approach, emphasizing, of course, that the latter should never be sacrificed for the former. This, however, did not satisfy some liberal critics.[6]

Certainly, there would be a meticulous examination of the Freedom Budget's data and assumptions, as well as agreements and disagreements over its philosophy and statistical analyses. The important point is that, for the first time in the history of the civil rights movement, a comprehensive and specific *economic* proposal had been put before the country, a proposal initiated by the movement itself. The Freedom Budget represented the civil rights movement's general consensus on basic goals and principles—if not on every projection and statistic. Here was a statement of specific priorities that all the major civil rights organizations could endorse, one that explicitly recognized and combined the movement's two agendas. In a section entitled: "The Role of the American Negro in the 'Freedom Budget'," it stated:

> The only reason why the Negro will benefit relatively more than others from the liquidation of excess unemployment and poverty is not because he is a Negro, but rather because he is at the bottom of the heap. . . .

> There is an absolute analogy between the crusade for civil rights and lib-
> erties and the crusade which the "Freedom Budget" represents. This is
> because the "Freedom Budget" would achieve the freedom from economic
> want and oppression which is the necessary complement to freedom from
> political and civil oppression. And just as the progress thus far made on the
> front of civil rights and liberties has immeasurably strengthened the entire
> American political democracy, so will the "Freedom Budget" strengthen
> immeasurably our entire economic and social fabric.[7]

A few weeks before the document's official release, Rustin called the
White House in an effort to get a meeting with President Johnson. He
wanted the president to receive a delegation that would present the Freedom
Budget to him. Mindful of the upcoming 1966 midterm congressional elections, Rustin hoped to have the meeting before Congress adjourned but was
amenable to any time on the president's schedule. A White House aide
passed the request on to a top official in a memorandum that outlined
Rustin's arguments for holding such a meeting:

> He [Rustin] said that it would be most helpful if the President were to do this
> as it would serve to solidify "sensible" civil rights groups, labor organizations
> and religious organizations around a concrete proposal.
>
> Also, he said that Randolph had always gone out of his way to support the
> President. In the presentation, as Bayard saw it, the group would indicate that
> this report emerged from the White House Conference.[8]

The White House aide wanted to have the administration's economic advisers review the document, and "if we can defer giving Bayard an answer until
after the Congress adjourns, I think we will be in a better position to judge
the pros and cons."[9]

The document received wide coverage, and every civil rights leader was
asked about it by reporters. Roy Wilkins promised, "We'll use every method
possible to translate the proposal into reality,"[10] and noted that extended
lobbying efforts in Congress would be conducted by the umbrella group he
chaired, the Leadership Conference on Civil Rights. Whitney Young, recall-
ing that only "a few years ago" he had called for a "Domestic Marshall Plan,"
declared that the Freedom Budget, "with specific cost estimates," was based
on a similar principle and was a " 'blueprint' for what must be done to eliminate poverty."[11] Martin Luther King, Jr., suggested that he might organize
national demonstrations in support of the Freedom Budget.[12] Importantly,
a SNCC representative unequivocally supported the document:

Anything that deals with the question of poverty has something to do with the day-to-day lives of the poor in Loundes County [Alabama]. The Freedom Budget is something that they can begin to look at and use because the present poverty program is so inadequate. What is started here today can be meaningful if the people who are poor get behind the budget and say not, "Please give us a handout," but make it impossible for the country to function if it does not put the Freedom Budget into action.[13]

Asked if his party should support the Freedom Budget, Henry Winston, national chairman of the Communist Party, responded: "I say without hesitation, Yes. We should do it in the same way that everyone has from Stokely Carmichael [SNCC] to Roy Wilkins [NAACP] who have endorsed it. . . . It is basic to the strengthening of Negro-white solidarity."[14]

Predictably, press reaction to the Freedom Budget was mixed. The *St. Louis Post-Dispatch* editorialized that "no doubt economy-minded citizens will reject out of hand the proposed $185,000,000,000 'freedom budget for all Americans,' but we think there is a good deal to be said for the plan." Hoping that Americans would study it and not be misled "by false slogans," the editorial concluded: "A good many people may find, perhaps to their surprise, that it makes sense."[15] The *Washington Post* felt that the Freedom Budget "breaks no new ground," and asserted that the budget—by proposing the notion that poverty could be "substantially alleviated" by "sharply increasing" public assistance to the aged, disabled, and dependent children, and by enacting a negative income tax—could lead to "creating a permanent class of able-bodied dependents." The *Post*'s editors concluded that what was needed was to give hope to able-bodied recipients that they will gain "education, skills and incentives" which will permit them to become self-supporting. "Unfortunately few of the problems encountered in getting at the roots of poverty are touched on in the Freedom Budget."[16]

One columnist noted what he called a "remarkable" thing about "the Randolph proposals":

They are not directed solely or even primarily toward improving the lot of disadvantaged Negroes. This country has millions more white than Negro poor people, and the Randolph plan is intended to help them all.
    In fact, this lengthy document spends very little time talking about Negroes as such.[17]

In this sense, at least, Randolph, Rustin, and their colleagues had made their point. The Freedom Budget was not strictly a part of the civil rights agenda, but it *was* a showcase for the universalistic social welfare agenda of the civil rights movement. Still, getting the document to be seriously considered by even the most liberal legislators in that most liberal of times was a formidable task.

In May 1967 Dr. Arthur C. Logan, a prominent black physician and chairman of the Anti-Poverty Committee of the United Neighborhood Houses in New York City, testified on the "war on poverty" programs before a Senate subcommittee. (Randolph and Rustin had testified earlier in January when they presented the Freedom Budget proposals.) Sen. Joseph S. Clark (D, Pa.) was chairman, and senators Edward Kennedy (D, Mass.) and Jacob Javits (R, N.Y.) were members. These long-standing liberal northern senators were unquestionably supportive of civil rights and progressive legislation and had often urged more money for antipoverty programs. After some discussion with the senators on various aspects of the antipoverty efforts, Dr. Logan felt compelled to make another point. He believed the current antipoverty programs dealt with "remediation of the effects of poverty." This would not be sufficient. The following exchange took place:

> DR. LOGAN: If this is an antipoverty program, I think its goal must properly be the eradication of poverty and I think this is a very reasonable goal, as you have pointed out in many of your public pronouncements, and I would urge not for you, sir, for either of you gentlemen [Clark or Javits], but probably for some of your colleagues, that a careful reading of volumes like the freedom budget would be of very great value in terms of thinking on the part of our legislators toward really the eradication of poverty.
>
> SENATOR CLARK: Let me say, Dr. Logan, that I have had a look at the budget and I think in the best of all possible worlds, it would be a wonderful thing, but as a matter of pragmatic politics, it seems to me utterly unrealistic. . . . I don't want to prolong the argument, but we do, after all, live in a democracy and in the end Senator Javits and I have to represent our constituents and I don't think our constituents are anywhere near ready for that budget.[18]

The harsh facts of political life could not have been made clearer. At that point, the Freedom Budget was considered by some sympathetic and influential senators as politically non grata.

The brief period from 1963 through 1967 was arguably the most liberal period for the achievement of civil rights *and* social welfare legislation in America's history, but there was apparently still not sufficient political support in the country to generate sustained attention to the most explicit statement to date of the social welfare agenda by civil rights organizations. Yet these organizations could not be accused of having failed to raise the critical economic issues as they saw them—a charge inaccurately made years later by too many observers of the history of the civil rights struggle.

The Great Society and War on Poverty

Senator Clark had bluntly stated that, even in those liberal times, Americans were not ready for the sweeping socioeconomic changes envisioned by the supremely idealistic proposals put forth by civil rights groups. But there did seem to be some willingness to consider new efforts in the social welfare arena, and civil rights groups were vigorously involved in these debates.

The 1960s would see substantial efforts to reform the public assistance welfare system and to enact important new health care and aid-to-education laws as well as antipoverty legislation. Amendments to the public assistance and child welfare provisions of the Social Security Act were passed in 1962.[19] The NUL was attentive to the particulars of this new bill as it proceeded through the legislative process. The original proposal submitted to Congress by the Kennedy administration had been described by the NUL as "a sound, constructive one, designed for both immediate and long-term improvements."[20] Its important purpose was to begin to think of ways to help people get off welfare and even to avoid becoming welfare recipients in the first place. This called for social service counseling, job training, and other services. States were to be allowed to conduct their own experiments with welfare reform, and the proposal authorized community work and training programs for adults in the AFDC program. Importantly, it extended the AFDC program to unemployed and disabled parents, and stipulated that when recipients worked, the expenses of such employment should be considered as part of the calculation in inculcating an incentive to accept employment. Where welfare payments were made to persons deemed unable to manage the money, "restrictive" payments could be made to other parties on behalf of the welfare family. Sensitive to the clamor of some localities to set stringent residency requirements for welfare eligibility,[21] the Kennedy proposal set an outside limit of one year; a state that abolished residency requirements altogether would be rewarded with increased federal financial aid.

What the NUL liked about the various provisions of this proposal was the emphasis on social services to help rehabilitate welfare recipients and prepare them to become self-dependent. But there were problems with the bill as it emerged in altered form from the House Ways and Means Committee. The NUL lost no time in spotting those problems. Among these, the restrictive payment provision was enlarged to include "protective payments," namely, vouchers (which could be made out to landlords, grocers, or others), when it was determined by the state that the adult recipient was not using the funds in the best interest of the child. The NUL did not like this revision, stating: "This provision could be broadly interpreted and widely abused to deny the individual rights that have always been basic principles of the Social Security Act, and although federal funds are involved, the federal government will have no control."[22] Further, the NUL was unhappy over certain significant *omissions* in the revised version. Not included in the bill were direct federal aid to schools of social work and a national program of fellowships (as a former dean of social work, Whitney Young would hardly have overlooked this deletion); also left out were the incentive to liberalize residency requirements and the authority for state welfare departments to purchase services from nonprofit private agencies. Moreover, the NUL noted that the matching formula for aid to the elderly poor, blind, and disabled had been increased two and a half times over that authorized for needy children and their parents, a disparity that, unfortunately, favored certain persons in this tier 2 program over others—namely, dependent children.

The new law as finally passed emphasized the desirability of work for recipients but also stipulated that where adult recipients worked, their pay should not be less than the minimum rate established by state law and not less than the prevailing rate for similar work performed by those not on welfare. When a person was assigned to a work project (which work, incidentally, could not displace regularly employed public or private employees), expenses incurred in going to work had to be considered, and the recipient who refused to work for good cause could not be penalized. (As we shall see in chapters 11 and 12, these provisions proved to be a far cry from what would develop in "welfare reform" regarding "workfare," especially in the 1990s.) Importantly, the new law did provide for federal financial aid to those states that chose to give assistance to a second parent living with the family in cases where that parent was unemployed or incapacitated—creating the category of AFDC-UP. (This was first done in a temporary measure passed in 1961.) However, if an unemployed parent refused work training without good cause, aid could be denied.

If a child was placed, under court order, in foster care in a voluntary child-care institution, the law provided federal financial aid for such care. In this instance, the NUL's concern was met. Likewise, federal funds were earmarked for child care in public and private facilities licensed or approved by the state. These funds had to be matched by the state, and priority was to be given to low-income persons and in situations where day-care needs were the greatest. Regarding the NUL's major concern about "vouchers," the new law stipulated that such payments could indeed be made as long as there were clear safeguards for the recipient's rights.

The 89th Congress (1965–1967) produced the most prolific output of liberal legislation since the early days of the New Deal, passing an astonishing 181 bills of the 200 requested by the Johnson administration.[23] These included the Economic Opportunity Act (for the "war on poverty"); health care for the elderly and poor (Medicare and Medicaid, respectively); aid to elementary and secondary education, with formulas for distributing additional money to poorer school districts; support for the arts and humanities; environmental protection laws; model cities funds for community development; rent supplement support for poor tenants; and aid to urban mass transit systems.

The major civil rights groups welcomed all these measures even as they stepped up the pressure on the social welfare front. Financed through social security contributions, Medicare for the elderly was passed in 1965, expanding the first tier of the social welfare system. Three years earlier at its May 1962 Executive Committee meeting, the NUL had passed a resolution strongly endorsing the proposal.[24] In 1963 the NUL agreed to sign a petition to Congress circulated by the National Association of Social Workers, which called for "the inclusion within the contributory social insurance system of hospital, nursing home, diagnostic and home care benefits which would be available to persons over 65 years of age as a matter of right without regard to personal or family resources."[25] (The final bill, however, included a separate Medicaid provision for those persons not a part of the tier 1 social insurance program, which, oddly, allowed the poor to enjoy benefits denied Medicare beneficiaries.)

The NAACP was also on record in 1965 "strongly" endorsing Medicare. Dr. W. Montague Cobb, chair of the NAACP's National Health Committee, testified before the Senate Finance Committee that due to "astronomically" rising medical costs, persons over sixty-five "are in most need of financial assistance. . . . The most effective and logical way to provide this assistance would be through the Social Security System."[26] Reminiscent of his testimony over twenty years earlier on the subject, he told the committee that the argument of opponents that such a plan was "socialized medicine" was "pure nonsense" because the Medicare bill provided for payments to private physicians and respected "private insurance plans."[27]

The Urban League was interested in pushing other amendments to the Social Security Act. Regarding public assistance, the NUL's board adopted a resolution in 1965 "consolidating all categories of relief, including general assistance, into one program of assistance for which the only permitted eligibility requirement would be need." And there should be a "floor" for public assistance "below which no state could go and receive federal aid, assuring a decent level of living for those in need."[28]

The Great Society was launched, and the major civil rights organizations were in the thick of developments as effectively as they knew how to be. By early 1967, practical-minded policymakers, setting their sites much lower than the $185 billion social welfare agenda encapsulated in the Freedom Budget, sought to improve the legislative program embodied in the Economic Opportunity Act of 1964.

President Johnson met with a group of civil rights leaders on February 13, 1967. (Interestingly, neither Rustin, Randolph, nor Martin Luther King were present.) Only Roy Wilkins, Whitney Young, and Dorothy Height as leaders of major civil rights groups and signatories of the Freedom Budget were at the meeting.[29] Nevertheless, this was the first real opportunity to discuss that document (released four months earlier) with the nation's top civil rights leaders, albeit in the absence of its strongest sponsors.

The discussion, however, focused mainly on the civil rights agenda, which the White House apparently felt was a more fruitful way to engage these civil rights leaders. The president wanted to submit a bill that essentially covered what he had proposed the year before—namely, fair housing, nondiscriminatory federal and state jury selection requirements, laws against interference with civil rights activities, extension of the Civil Rights Commission, and giving the Equal Employment Opportunity Commission the ability to issue cease and desist orders. The president "pointed out that substantial efforts [will] be made [this year] to kill many of the most important Great Society programs, including Model Cities, Teachers Corps and Rent

Supplements."[30] He called upon the civil rights groups to help round up congressional support for those programs.

Although social welfare programs *were* mentioned, there was no explicit reference to the recently released Freedom Budget. Indeed, at two instances during the meeting, specific reference was made rather to the harmful effect of demanding too much. The president "pointed out that many of the friends and beneficiaries of his most important programs were continually attempting to offer bigger and better programs and in the process often crippled the Administration's programs." While not naming the Freedom Budget specifically, he singled out an "Older Americans" organization for criticism. Johnson had been asking for a 20 percent increase in Social Security benefits; the senior citizens group was insisting on 40 percent. Johnson concluded that such an unreasonable demand would likely play into the hands of the Republicans, who supported only an 8 percent increase. He felt this was bad politics on the part of the liberals. Likewise, Vice President Humphrey cautioned against "unrealistic" proposals ("He urged complete support for the Administration's programs and not for unrealistic proposals which we can't get"). This was a clear signal to Freedom Budget proponents that that document would not be on the table for serious discussion.

The programs embodied in the "war on poverty" legislation were all that could be expected. Although the Economic Opportunity Act had passed in 1964, its genesis lay in the last years of the Kennedy administration.[31] Notwithstanding the new access of civil rights leaders to the White House, there is little evidence that they were instrumental in drafting the initial antipoverty proposals. One person, Adam Yarmolinsky, who was active in that process while on loan from his job as assistant to the secretary of defense, noted: "Of all the principle people in the civil rights business, none of them were involved in this business."[32] It was also evident that there was a conscious attempt *not* to cast the "war on poverty" as a "Negro program," but rather as one related to all the poor. Yarmolinsky said:

> During the late winter, spring and early summer of 1964, we were concerned with explaining to the Congress and the public that the poverty program was in no sense a help-the-blacks program, and not only were we saying this, but we didn't think it was. We felt it would do very little for the blacks. We said, "Most poor people are not black, most black people are not poor"—was one of the slogans that we kept writing into speeches. . . . By '65, '66, OEO was if not a black, a very dark gray agency, and when we were putting it together it

hadn't the faintest gray tinge to it. If anything, color it Appalachian if you were going to color it anything at all. . . . As near as I can tell in '64, the '63 motivation was not a reaction to the need to keep the black vote or the poor vote, whatever that is. It was a very different concern.[33]

Enactment of the legislation took only five months from the time of its introduction to Congress. The Economic Opportunity Act of 1964 set up an independent agency—Office of Economic Opportunity (OEO)—and established a Job Corps along with a Neighborhood Youth Program, a domestic peace corps (Volunteers in Service to America—VISTA), and a Work-Study Program for college students. Secretary of Labor Willard Wirtz had argued for a bill that would put heavier emphasis on jobs, but to no avail.[34] An important Title II provided for the creation of local community action agencies (CAAs) that would formulate proposals to deal with services to the poor. Funds would come from the OEO. These local CAAs would include "maximum feasible participation" of persons in the "targeted" areas. Such agencies could be set up by local governments or private organizations.[35]

In a sense the law created a structure and mechanism for dealing with poverty. Specific programs beyond what were already in existence were to come from the various local communities. Except for a governor's veto power over particular proposals (which the OEO director ultimately could override), there was no role in this structure for the states. And even city and other local governments conceivably could be bypassed, a problem that created political headaches in some places as the programs were initiated.

The law appropriated $500 million plus an additional $462.5 million from existing programs to initiate the "war on poverty." Importantly, however, appropriations were to be approved on an annual basis, so that the OEO would have to go to Congress each year for its funds. Thus, while Congress had little input in originating and drafting the program, it would have continuing "oversight" in its operation.

The major civil rights groups stood squarely behind the legislation and became involved in programs around the country. For the next several years, into the 1970s, through congressional testimony, speeches, conferences, and correspondence, civil rights organizations made known their preferences and complaints. It is also important to recall the context. The 1960s were years of dramatic and traumatic events. The civil rights movement was reaching a crescendo with mass marches, boycotts, and direct action protests throughout the country. Debates over tactics were played out constantly in the media, at local rallies and meetings, on college campuses, and even in the churches. Malcolm X of the Nation of Islam became a controversial headline figure, calling for a brand of black nationalism that was strongly opposed by the established civil rights organizations. But it was also clear that this nationalist call was finding more than a few sympathetic listeners in the black ghettos, frustrated and angered by the slow pace of change. Riots in northern cities became annual occurrences, occasioned often by confrontations with the police. The devastating assassinations of President John Kennedy, of civil rights activists in the South and black worshippers in their churches, of Martin Luther King, Jr., and Robert Kennedy gave the period an urgent, traumatic, destabilizing character captured nightly on television. The emergence of "Black Power" as an assertion of a revived sense of group nationalism, especially in SNCC and CORE, further complicated relations within the reasonably consensual group that had mounted the 1963 March on Washington. Toward the end of the decade, new groups would emerge, mainly locally or regionally based, that were much more distrustful of and impatient with conventional modes of political participation (voting and polite lobbying) and more willing to challenge the nonviolence philosophy of the established leaders.

In the midst of this turbulence, civil rights leaders had to maneuver between a constituency needing and expecting more than ever before and a policy-making system unprepared to go the full lengths that they felt was necessary.[36] Headlines and news stories such as "Rights Coalition—Fractious, Fragmented" were not uncommon. "The frustration and criticism," one reporter concluded, "come not from the promise of the Great Society but from performance, and from the feeling that, at present, there is a recession in the national marketplace of human rights."[37]

In such circumstances, the target of the civil rights groups' social welfare agenda centered on the implementation and enhancement of "war on poverty" and Great Society programs. Testifying on OEO's programs, civil rights organizations basically focused on three concerns. First, they welcomed the national government's increased role in social welfare and constantly appealed for larger appropriations across the board for antipoverty programs. Wary of prejudicial state and local political influence (as during the New Deal), they argued against increasing efforts to dismantle the OEO and assign its programs to established departments and agencies of the national bureaucracy; they thought the OEO should remain independent and directly accountable to the president. Second, they strongly supported local participation in decision-making for community action programs and rejected congressional attempts to earmark funds, which only restricted the latitude for devising local, innovative service programs. Third, as always, they emphasized job-creation programs that would actually put more people to work.

Reminding the Senate of his "Domestic Marshall Plan," Whitney Young suggested that the "scale on which the war on poverty is being conducted is far too limited to do much more than act as a palliative."[38] "Two billion dollars per annum is not enough to do the job. Fifty billion dollars would be more like it." The NUL presented a 100-page report of a survey by its affiliates of poverty programs around the country, which covered 1,253 antipoverty programs in seventy-nine cities. As could be expected, the programs ranged in effectiveness from excellent to poor. Admittedly, poor results stemmed from poor administration and political infighting, but equally as often from lack of adequate funds. The report made recommendations for improvement.

While an increase in antipoverty appropriations seemed unlikely, civil rights groups calculated that at least they might be able to fend off cuts in funding, a threat frequently proposed by congressional opponents of the programs. Even this was not assured. In March 1966 Joseph Califano sent President Johnson a memorandum on a scheduled meeting the president was to have with civil rights and labor leaders. (This was an "off-the-record" meeting which each attender agreed not to publicize.) Califano listed some items to be discussed, and added: "[Whitney] Young recommended that, among other things, you assure the group that you will fight any cutbacks in funds for the War on Poverty in a forcible way." Johnson made a handwritten note in the margin beside the statement: "NO."[39]

Another concern related to the controversial "maximum feasible participation" provision in Title II for community action programs. This part of OEO's structure appealed to civil rights groups because it potentially could provide new civic experiences for poor people in local communities by involving them on CAA boards and in helping to run the programs, and, above all, by establishing direct links to the federal government.

But it soon became evident that there was no consensus on what was meant by "maximum feasible participation." In various localities over the years conflicts erupted over methods of selecting local CAA leaders and the proportion of poor that should be included. Established local elected political leaders (mayors, council members, county officials, and so on) were often charged with attempting to maintain control, and these issues were frequently fought out in the open and received extensive media coverage. In some areas, long-existing voluntary health and welfare agencies—better staffed, and with better-trained (and usually white) professionals—became the targets of criticism, usually on the grounds that they did not truly understand the poverty problems of the ghettos. When such professionals and local business leaders were on CAA boards, they were often accused of using their influence and skills to overpower the less educated and less adept representatives of the poor. These conflicts spotlighted some of the most visible and volatile bones of contention throughout the years of struggle over community action programs. These constant and conspicuous local battles (with their various charges—and frequent investigations—of embezzlement, fraud, nepotism, cronyism, personal power rivalries, and mismanagement) fed the public's growing image of a floundering "poverty program" that wasted money and simply led to political squabbling to control the federal dollars coming into the community. Yet civil rights groups persisted in their efforts to make the programs work.

Without question, results were mixed. In some areas, civil rights groups became very involved, but not in others. The NUL particularly was effective in some places, owing in no small part to its professional staff and its experience in delivering social services. White House officials recognized this and at times encouraged grants that had the imprimatur of the NUL. For example, Youth Organizations United (YOU), a program dealing with youth gangs, had come under congressional attack for misuse of funds. Joseph Califano sent a memo to President Johnson:

> After various foundations and the Urban Coalition [a national organization of business leaders] became interested in YOU, HEW and OEO suggested that it might be possible to fund some of the activities of YOU if the grant were made to a reputable organization like the Urban League or the Urban Coalition which would supervise and assume full responsibility for the activities of YOU.... While the Urban League could not provide complete protection against Congressional attacks on the Federal agencies for supporting YOU, Bert [Harding, an OEO official] believes the program is a sound one and it is far easier to defend a grant under which the Urban League accepts complete responsibility for the expenditure of Federal funds.[40]

Thus, civil rights groups were becoming inevitably embroiled in the politics of the antipoverty programs on the local and national levels.

Other issues were raised about the management of the antipoverty programs, especially in dealing with interracial and interethnic rivalries. Although initial drafters of the 1964 legislation hoped to avoid labeling the programs as especially being aimed at blacks, this clearly became an issue in the minds of some groups. The National Confederation of American Ethnic Groups sent a blistering letter to the White House in 1965. After the OEO had rejected a proposal from that organization (which represented several ethnic groups),[41] the organization came forward with a new, reduced proposal, but let the White House know in no uncertain terms that it considered the antipoverty operation to be pro-black and anti–poor white. If this scaled-down proposal was also rejected, "[the rejection] would strengthen those who claim antipoverty funds are available *only to the colored poor*—not also the white poor, as affirmed by the President."[42] The confederation insisted that the administration, specifically the president, make it clear to the OEO that other groups in addition to blacks were to be given equal opportunity to participate in the programs by receiving grants. Furthermore, the letter continued,

> The President has gone on record time and again, publicly and otherwise, favoring equal opportunity, and bigger and better jobs for Negroes. The Civil Service Commission and the State Department have even lowered examination requirements for colored applicants. Our groups point out that no such official concern has been shown U.S. ethnic groups, who continue to be treated as the "forgotten man" by those who declare themselves champions of the Civil Rights cause.
>
> This double-standard is causing widespread concern and resentment among our ethnic population. It is considered unfair that the ethnic groups should be penalized for their good behavior and forbearance.[43]

This letter presaged ethnic-racial discord that would become full blown a few years later in civil rights and social welfare debates around the country. Latent intergroup tensions were slowly emerging. However, as long as the civil rights agenda dealt with issues of de jure segregation of blacks, these ethnic feelings were not manifested, precisely because other groups were not generally victims of *legal* segregation. But now, in the 1960s, with attention focused on the social welfare agenda, some ethnic groups were not prepared to be quiescent. They wanted their piece of the action. The irony, of course, is that both civil rights leaders and Washington officials, in articulating the comprehensive programs aimed at the poor, always talked in universalistic, nonracial, nonethnic terms. But in the competitive rush to get grants from a federal treasury that was, at best, very limited when measured against the need, it was inevitable that there would be winners and losers.

The third major area of civil rights concern in regard to the antipoverty programs always returned to the subject of jobs for everyone able to work.[44] The fact that it was black leaders emphasizing the dire need of blacks obscured the actual universalistic nature and intent of the appeal, but employment for *all* those able to work remained the consistent priority. To be sure, there were other interests, but *no* testimony, speeches, or major writings left out the fundamental need for job-creation as a basic component of the "war on poverty."

Wilfred Ussery, the national leader of CORE and a strong supporter of Black Power, called congressional attention in 1967 to training for "New Careers," a plan developed by some liberal social scientists. There were jobs, he urged, that poor people, black and white, could readily perform "with a minimal amount of education"—as teacher aides in classrooms, as home helpers and foster grandparents, as health care aides.[45] More attention should be paid to these possibilities for expanding the labor market. (A "New Careers" provision was enacted as part of the amendments to the Economic Opportunity Act of 1967.) Several times he emphasized the prospect of unity between poor whites and poor blacks: "If black and white people cannot move collectively on a program such as New Careers with all its vast potential, perhaps it shall never move collectively on anything else again."[46]

Ussery called for a class-oriented political alliance of poor whites with poor blacks, hardly a new cry in American history. But coming from an outspoken advocate of Black Power, it struck some as strange and perhaps unbelievable. Without question, his interpretation of Black Power—and the need to coalesce with poor white power—was not the understanding of that concept held by a large segment of the society, which saw black nationalist sentiments as antiwhite and "separatist."

But the less strident or non-Black Power voices of the civil rights movement had been making the same points for decades on the need for interracial cooperation, with little success, which was not lost on Ussery and some of his Black Power colleagues in CORE and SNCC. In fact, a careful examination of the *social welfare* proposals of all the major civil rights leaders and activists reveals a remarkable similarity of interests and recommendations.

Civil rights groups surely differed in style, tactics, organizational structure, and even constituency bases, but their views were quite compatible with regard to the "war on poverty" programs, the Great Society programs, public assistance, and, above all, the importance of a full-employment economy.

On public assistance, the NUL was very disturbed by congressional moves in 1967 to pass harsh legislation affecting welfare recipients. The NUL objected to a proposal that would prohibit any state from receiving additional federal funds if the proportion of children "on relief" increased after 1967. While a plan to require states to offer birth-control information to welfare recipients was "acceptable," the NUL wanted to make sure that persons who did not voluntarily seek such information would not be punished. Likewise, the organization was wary about a proposal to "determine the paternity of children and then force fathers to support them." This "could lead to timely litigation during which innocent children may suffer."[47]

The proposed bill had some "desirable and exceedingly important features"—specifically, an increase in federal financing for social services such as family counseling, day care, family planning, foster care, special funds to cover costs associated with work and training, training for social workers, and a "provision for an incentive exemption of earned income."[48] But other provisions were "regressive and punitive," such as the freeze on the percentage of children for whom welfare support would be available, and the requirement that all unemployed adults on welfare engage in work or training "without regard to the impact of such work and training on family life, the availability of jobs at the end of the training period, or even an insistence upon receipt of established minimum wages." The NUL saw the bill as representing a "get tough" attitude "reminiscent of medieval poor laws and the alms house." Young reiterated the view that "it will serve no useful purpose to force people into training programs for jobs that do not exist and, in the process[, require] mothers to forsake the home."

The 1967 amendments, approved and passed by both House and Senate on December 15, 1967, required every state to participate in a work-training or work-incentive program for AFDC recipients that was to be administered by the Department of Labor. The states were to decide which recipients should be required to engage in training, but persons under sixteen or those in school or ill or incapacitated were exempt. State employment offices were to establish work projects with public service jobs for those who, after training, could not find work in the private sector. Those refusing to work or undertake training would lose their welfare benefits. Day-care centers were to be established, and the federal government would provide 80 percent of the funds for the work-training and day-care programs. Federal matching funds, however, would be available only for the children of unemployed fathers, not for unemployed mothers. There was indeed a limit placed on the amount of federal assistance for AFDC in each state; the "freeze" criterion was based on the percentage of children on AFDC (because of an absent parent) as of January 1, 1968. After that date, if the proportion of AFDC children under eighteen in the state rose above the established percentage, no additional federal funds to support the program would be forthcoming. (This provision, though it was never implemented—and was in fact repealed in 1969—would be raised again and strongly pushed by congressional Republicans in 1995–96.) Another provision required family planning services be made available to all AFDC recipients on a voluntary basis, and earmarked 6 percent of all maternal and child health appropriations for this purpose.

Although clearly not pleased with the direction of the social welfare agenda in the hands of unsympathetic forces in Congress, few people in the civil rights community believed that more could have been achieved, given the growing antagonism to more liberal legislation. Nevertheless, a newly formed group (founded in 1966), the National Welfare Rights Organization (NWRO), headed by former CORE leader George Wiley, went on the attack against restrictive welfare proposals. Testifying before Congress, Wiley insisted that the increase in AFDC rolls resulted mainly from a *good* thing— namely, that NWRO was alerting more people of their eligibility under existing laws to receive assistance. Many persons otherwise eligible had not applied for help because they were not aware "of their rights to public assistance." Therefore, "the increases in the welfare roles should be lauded, not scorned."[49] As reflected in the hearings of the Senate Finance Committee, many members of Congress, with a very different view of such outreach efforts, were alarmed at the growing welfare rolls and attributed this to family break-up and illegitimacy. Not true, Wiley argued. Rather, in addition to the good work of the NWRO, which encouraged more people to apply, this increase reflected population movement from southern states "where welfare policies are particularly restrictive and punitive to northern states where welfare relief is more accessible." (This argument was exactly what infuriated some critics of welfare who complained that some poor people shopped around for states paying higher welfare benefits.) Moreover, NWRO opposed requiring mothers of young children to find work outside the home. As Wiley put it: "For the government to try to force them into the job market when there are not enough jobs for the men in the ghetto, is to add insult to absurdity."

The plight of poor working women had already been pointed up in testimony from leaders in other organizations at previous hearings on the various "war on poverty" and Great Society programs. Dorothy Height of NCNW indicated that many of the programs provided crucial jobs for poor women, such as day-care sponsors or working in Head Start projects or in the Job Corps, thus giving them "occupational skills [they] can market for a fair wage."[50]

But as civil rights organizations continued to press for more financial support for antipoverty programs, it was clear that they faced an uphill battle. Soon, another organization, Citizens' Crusade Against Poverty, took up the fight. Walter Reuther was chair, and among others who served as vice-chairs were Dorothy Height, Martin Luther King, Jr., A. Philip Randolph, Bayard Rustin, and Whitney Young. In February 1968 the group issued a statement condemning proposed cuts in many of the programs: "No one can argue about the need for more jobs for the poor. . . . Our anti-poverty dilemma seems to be a question of limited priorities and choices."[51] If the administration was serious about fighting poverty, why could it not find money from farm subsidies ($2.8 billion annually) where "the wealthiest 10 percent received nearly 75 percent of the benefits; space research and technology ($4.8 billion); atomic energy research ($2.5 billion); $223 million to develop a supersonic aircraft for private commercial uses; tax loopholes for certain favored taxpayers; capital gains; oil and mineral depletion allowances." The president and Congress, the statement continued, should "figure out how to *stop* favoring a special class of wealthy citizens and *stop* cutting government spending at the expense of the poor."[52]

The statement reached the White House and President Johnson by way of the OEO. Noting the names of the vice chairs on the letterhead, Johnson penned a note to Califano telling him to call Walter Reuther, Robert Benjamin, I. W. Abel, Hector Garcia, Dorothy Height, Edgar Kaiser, Ralph McGill, Philip Randolph, Roy Wilkins, and Whitney Young—"and tell them to cut this stuff out."[53]

At the end of the month, on March 31, 1968, racked by rising unrest over the Vietnam War and growing domestic social problems, Lyndon Johnson announced he would not seek or accept the nomination of his party for reelection that coming November. Four days after that dramatic announcement, Martin Luther King, Jr., was assassinated in Memphis, Tennessee. The political atmosphere began to pall. Some antipoverty programs would continue. There would be continued protest and lobbying for increased appropriations and support from the federal government. But few could misread the changing environment—the zenith years of major new liberal social welfare legislation were over.

SCLC's Campaign for Poor People

Those who knew and worked with Martin Luther King, Jr., knew his strengths and shortcomings as a leader. When it came to detailed policy proposals, testifying before congressional committees, and buttonholing and lobbying wavering members of Congress, these activities were best handled by the NAACP, NUL, NCNW, Randolph, Rustin, and others. King's style and talents lay in his ability to address and organize masses for direct action protests. King was a southern Baptist preacher who had been thrust into the forefront of the civil rights movement in 1956 as leader of the historic Montgomery, Alabama, bus boycott. Several other black ministers led subsequent protests throughout the South and frequently called on King to aid their local causes. In 1957 he moved to Atlanta, Georgia, to share the pulpit of his father's Ebeneezer Baptist Church as copastor. In short order, recognizing the need to develop an organization that would build on the efforts of the various minister-led groups springing up, he and his colleagues formed the Southern Christian Leadership Conference (SCLC), headquartered in Atlanta. King was chosen as president, and affiliates were established first throughout the South, then in several northern cities. Introduced at the 1963 March on Washington by Randolph as "the moral leader of our nation," King was made by and helped to shape the civil rights movement at a critical juncture in its century-long struggle. He and SCLC joined the chorus of other civil rights leaders calling for greater commitment to the "war on poverty."

By 1967 King was also beginning to question the ultimate utility of resolutions and speeches, and congressional testimony. As useful and necessary as these were, they apparently were having little effect with decision-makers in Washington. He and some friends began to talk about a more direct way to dramatize the plight of the poor. Attorney Marian Wright, an NAACP Legal Defense Fund lawyer, called King's attention to the fact that in Mississippi, where she worked, federal policies subsidized large farm owners not to grow crops.[54] This meant that poor farm workers were out of jobs and frequently kicked off the land. One U.S. senator, James O. Eastland (D, Miss.), received $200,000 per year from farm subsidies *not* to grow crops on his land.[55]

It was proposed that SCLC launch a mass, direct-action protest demonstration in the nation's capital. The idea grew in favor with King, for this tactic had worked well in exposing the evils of legal segregation. The approach this time would also be to bring thousands of poor people to Washington, but not for just another one-day March on Washington as before. This time they would be prepared to stay—to instigate sit-ins at Congress, to tie up traffic, to disrupt the daily routine of the government and, if necessary, the city. In King's mind the goal would be simple—that is, a campaign for "jobs and income." The campaign would offer a good example of nonviolent protest, a clear alternative to the destructive violence of riots. King's plan did not immediately garner enthusiastic support from all his staff or SCLC board members, who had doubts about its tactics and substance. Such a protest might lead to greater frustration and riots. A simple "jobs and income" slogan was not specific enough. The successful outcome of a sustained project such as this could not be assured and would tax the organization's financial resources, already feeling the pinch of reduced donations because of King's public anti-Vietnam War stance. Some old friends, especially Bayard Rustin, strongly disagreed with the proposed campaign. He felt that the likelihood of failure to achieve sufficient results was too great, and that the political backlash could be horrendous.

However, King persisted. He clearly wanted to mount this protest campaign. It would be a test not only of his philosophy of nonviolence but also of his leadership. Plans for what came to be called the Poor People's Campaign (PPC) proceeded.

Again, against the advice of some of his staff, King agreed during this intense planning period to accept an invitation to go to Memphis to help a group of black sanitation workers who were on strike in that city. The issues involved economic-labor problems as well as charges of racial discrimination. He went to Memphis, participated in a march that turned violent, became embroiled in local internecine leadership struggles, and, upon leaving, became even more concerned about the consequences of such events for his nonviolent philosophy and leadership. This could hamper recruitment of support for the Poor People's Campaign, both in terms of actual participation and funds. Striving to salvage the situation, King returned to Memphis for another, hopefully peaceful, protest march, this time with his own staff to be more in control of the logistics and participants.

With the Poor People's Campaign projected to begin in late April 1968, King arrived back in Memphis on April 3, spoke to a mass meeting, and, the following evening, while standing on the balcony of his motel room, was shot and killed by James Earl Ray.

Once again, the nation was stunned. There appeared to be no end to the violence of that decade. (Only two months later, Sen. Robert F. Kennedy would be assassinated in Los Angeles while campaigning for the Democratic Party's nomination for the presidency.)

SCLC quickly chose a new leader, the Reverend Ralph D. Abernathy, who had been with King from the first days in Montgomery twelve years earlier. There was general agreement that the Poor People's Campaign should be pushed even harder, if only as a fitting memorial to King. The staff renewed its efforts and developed a more detailed strategy. This now included lobbying governmental agencies and Congress as the first phase, followed by marches and a call for a national boycott of selected economic targets around the country—all tactics that had worked in varying degrees in pursuing the civil rights agenda. The protesters would come from across the country and camp on a site in downtown Washington, building tents and makeshift plywood shanties for accommodations. The protesters would be poor people, the unemployed, sharecroppers, welfare recipients—black, white, Latinos, American Indians. Demonstrations would be held, depending upon official responses to the demands, and if necessary, the protesters would go to jail. They would stay in the city and at the campsite—called Resurrection City—until their demands were satisfied.[56]

Other civil rights groups would be hard pressed not to support the campaign, given the traumatic environment of King's death and the riots following it. Even if the tactic was questionable, certainly the goals—jobs and income—were laudable. The NAACP's Clarence Mitchell, along with others, was invited by Abernathy to a planning session. Abernathy's telegram stated:

Assassination of Martin King must not interrupt the central task of bringing basic economic and social freedom to all Americans. Administration likely to rest on passage of civil rights law as appropriate and sufficient response. New momentum must be launched to deal with the central issues of power for the dispossessed, jobs, income, and housing.[57]

Mitchell agreed to attend, but he admonished that he "wish[ed] to make it clear that there is not a scintilla of evidence to support the statement that 'administration is likely to rest on passage of civil rights law.' . . . I hope the conference will address itself to the practical question of getting votes in Congress."[58]

The White House received a copy of Mitchell's reply, and a staff member forwarded it to President Johnson in a memorandum that noted: "Clarence is 'militantly' for the President and increasingly disillusioned with his associates who urge new programs but are unwilling to concentrate on passage of proposed programs."[59]

Not surprisingly, the "Declaration" issued by the PPC resembled in many ways the basic principles previously articulated in the Freedom Budget and many other pronouncements. The emphasis was on jobs, a full employment economy, a guaranteed annual income for those unable to work, use of unused public lands for the poor ("a modernized Homestead Act"). The SCLC gave these demands a title: "A Bill of Economic and Social Rights."

As planned, before the thousands began assembling in Washington, SCLC organized small delegations to present their demands to various cabinet officials and congressional leaders.[60] Occurring over a three-day period, these sessions consisted of representatives from the major civil rights groups, who constituted the "Committee of 100" as the decision-making body of the PPC. They presented Washington officials with a list of "demands" for action and gave them ten days in which to respond. The plan was to receive the responses and evaluate them in time for the arrival of the first mass contingent of protesters, due on May 12, 1968. If, as was anticipated, all or some of the responses, either from the executive or legislative branch, were unacceptable or incomplete, then the next phase of the campaign would be implemented—protest demonstrations, further lobbying, possible sit-ins. It was understood that these activities could lead to arrests. In some cases, the demands spoke to existing bills pending before Congress, which is what the NAACP wanted to emphasize.

Some sessions covered the inadequacy of some existing laws. For instance, the Department of Labor was told: "You know as well as we do that MDTA [the Manpower Development and Training Act] is not training people for *real* jobs at *living* wages."[61]

On the issue of jobs, there was a clear difference between the PPC's preference for government "as the employer of *first* resort" and the view held by most government officials (and, incidentally, accepted by the NAACP) of the government as the employer of "last resort." The latter approach meant that all efforts to find or create private-sector jobs should be exhausted before attention was focused on government-created jobs of the kind associated with the New Deal's work projects.

Responses to the PPC's many demands came in within the ten-day period. Government officials certainly had no intention at least of insulting or further aggravating the protesters by denying them the courtesy of prompt replies, even if the substance of those replies was not entirely satisfactory. (This fact was itself a far cry from decades of previous experience by civil rights groups with decision-makers in Washington, a further indication of the new liberal environment in which they were operating.) Few, however, in Washington—whether protesters or policymakers—harbored any notions that the hundreds of demands could in fact be met to the PPC's full satisfaction. Reports of each session were prepared and the responses circulated and discussed at mass meetings on the campsite.

Mindful that Labor Secretary Wirtz had been one of the strongest advocates for a "war on poverty" that put priority on creating jobs for the poor, the PPC was disappointed with Labor's response to its demands. Protest leaders felt that the reply, "in time-honored tradition, [cited] past, inadequate and irrelevant accomplishments while ignoring this, our most important demand—immediate jobs for the poor." Protesters wanted the secretary of labor to testify before Congress in support of an emergency public service jobs program (which the PPC called "the first priority of the poor"), something he had refused to do shortly before because the White House had decided not to commit on such an undertaking.[62]

The protesters met with greater success in their contacts with OEO officials than with anyone else—not surprising, inasmuch as OEO was the one governmental agency set up explicitly and exclusively to serve the poor. This is why civil rights groups did not want it dismantled and its responsibilities assigned to other departments with their own multitude of interests to sat-

isfy. There was agreement to make guidelines for participating in local programs clearer, and OEO agreed to rely heavily on the PPC and other representatives of the poor in formulating antipoverty policies and programs.
Such concessions obviously pleased the protesters: "OEO is positive. . . . The
campaign is essentially victorious in its battle with OEO and should use it as
an ally in confronting other agencies and organizations."[63] The fact was
probably not lost on many observers, however, that this agency was
undoubtedly the least financially and politically able of all the agencies in
terms of its power to affect the lives of the poor in a major way. Nonetheless,
the PPC was grateful for whatever signs of unqualified support it could get
from official sources.

PPC leaders issued a "Critical Action Bulletin" to supporters across the
country, calling for support "NOW" for the bills pending in Congress: a
housing bill to provide six million new and rehabilitated housing units for
low- and moderate-income families over the next ten years; a "guaranteed
jobs bill" (which was "still in the hearing stage"); a bill to extend protection
of the 1935 National Labor Relations Act to farm workers to help them organize; an agriculture appropriations measure with amendments to provide
funds to "combat hunger."[64] This was the kind of action the NAACP wanted
and believed should be the primary focus of the PPC. It was specific, and it
dealt with the immediate political realities of rounding up votes on measures
then under consideration.

After weeks of intense protest and lobbying, the PPC had to face another
reality: its permit to camp on the site near the Washington Monument was
running out. They vowed to remain. But on June 24, 1968, authorities came
in and dismantled Resurrection City. Refusing to leave, Ralph Abernathy was
jailed for nineteen days.

Upon his release a rally was held that promised to continue the campaign
for poor people around the country. The protesters began to leave
Washington, but not before a long list of "Our Gains So Far" was issued.
Some thirty specific achievements were enumerated, including food programs by August 1 in one thousand of the nation's neediest counties; expansion of the school lunch program; more money for food stamps and for the
food commodities program; passage of the Civil Rights Act of 1968 against
housing discrimination; agreement by the Department of Labor to create
one hundred thousand new jobs by December ("six months ahead of the
earlier schedule"); the hiring of 1,300 poor people in thirty-three state

employment agencies; higher quality neighborhood health programs by HEW; agreement of the Justice Department to enforce rules against using "green card" farm workers (foreign workers in this country on temporary work permits) as strikebreakers; and an Interior Department agreement "to develop community control in Indian programs."[65]

To be sure, there were gains, but no one was prepared to suggest that the Poor People's Campaign had come anywhere near its major goals of a decent-paying job for all who wanted to work, or an acceptable guaranteed annual income for those who could not or should not work. To keep the campaign visible and viable, the SCLC called a national boycott of selected industries and commercial establishments.[66] This effort quietly died out.

The decade was coming to a close. Civil rights groups had formulated general and specific social welfare proposals, and had engaged in lobbying and mass direct action. If there was more the groups could have done, it surely did not occur to them. Would they have achieved more if they had worked harder for the $185 billion Freedom Budget? This hardly seems likely. Did they push hard enough for their central goal of "jobs?" There is no evidence that they could have argued more forcefully before the congressional committees, or with the White House, or in their speeches and writings. Did they fail to appeal to other groups to join in a liberal political alliance that would benefit not just blacks but everyone in the coalition? This is not supported by the strong evidence which indicates very conscious efforts to the contrary. What about the development of the so-called black-separatist groups, especially SNCC and CORE, that were perceived as bringing racially divisive issues into the civil rights movement by championing Black Power? Even if these groups were relatively large and growing—though they were just the opposite, relatively small and declining, especially beginning in 1966—they also joined in support of the important features of the social welfare agenda. They more than superficially supported the Freedom Budget and, as noted earlier, CORE insisted on demonstrating that there was no incompatibility between its call for Black Power and the necessity of blacks and whites to join in mutually beneficial political coalitions. Given the violence and rhetoric and trauma of those times, however, it is not surprising that such calls were either unheard or misperceived.

One lesson from the Poor People's Campaign became clear. However useful mass protest action could be—and might continue to be—in pursuing blatant targets of segregation and discrimination on the civil rights agenda, such tactics had to be recalculated when dealing with many of the problems placed on the social welfare agenda. Ending de jure segregated public accommodations in the South was not the same as negotiating for hundreds of millions of dollars from the federal budget for new jobs and needed social programs. Some observers have suggested that the issues of socioeconomic subjugation are more subtle and are thus more difficult to deal with than blatant conditions of legal segregation. Perhaps, but there was surely nothing subtle about Mississippi shanties and hungry, poorly clothed children. There was nothing subtle about clusters of men standing in unemployment lines or waiting in a line of five hundred men at a company posting a notice of ten job openings.

The problem was hardly one of subtlety of the issues but rather a lack of capacity to solve them. The civil rights agenda achieved very important gains into the mid-1960s precisely because the processes—mass action, electoral mobilization, litigation that raised serious constitutional questions—came together with sufficient political power and the will of decision-makers to move effectively. But the elements of process, power, and political will did not coalesce effectively behind the social welfare agenda. Other interests— economic and political—emerged to thwart that necessary combination. Other claims were being made on federal resources—especially the war in Vietnam and fears of inflationary pressures from domestic spending. Nor was there a solid ideological consensus on how best to deal with the problems that clearly existed, and that, if left insufficiently addressed, promised to grow worse.

NINE

Welfare Reform and Full Employment: The 1970s

An important change in the political climate occurred in 1968 when Democrats lost the presidency to Republican Richard M. Nixon. Whatever Lyndon Johnson's shortcomings were, no one believed that Nixon would be a better friend to civil rights leaders on either aspect of the dual agenda. Those leaders had no expectation that they would enjoy comparable access to a Nixon White House as they had had under Johnson.

Notwithstanding the occupancy of the presidency, civil rights organizations consistently maintained the three goals of their social welfare agenda: a universal social welfare system, jobs in the regular workforce, and federal hegemony over social programs. Of major concern during the 1970s were three reform proposals: the Family Assistance Plan, the Program for Better Jobs and Income (neither passed), and the Full Employment and Balanced Growth Act of 1978.

A full employment policy continued to represent an ideal welfare reform plan for civil rights organizations because it would be universal and provide jobs with no public assistance stigma attached to them. The organizations adamantly opposed a mandatory work policy in welfare reform legislation because it assumed that recipients preferred welfare over work. They argued that this policy was unnecessary; recipients preferred to work and would do so if jobs were available. What was needed was not welfare reform but a full employment policy.

The Family Assistance Plan

When the Social Security Act was amended in 1939 to include survivors insurance, it was thought that Aid to Dependent Children, established by the act, would "wither away" as poor widows and their children, toward which ADC had been targeted, became eligible for social insurance. But welfare rolls continued to rise, and by 1968 the number of families receiving AFDC was increasing at what many regarded as an alarming rate.[1] It was predicted that the rolls would rise another 50 to 60 percent within the next five years.[2] There was no way to cap the cost of the program because all families that met eligibility criteria were entitled to benefits.

The 1935 Social Security Act gave administrative responsibility for Aid to Dependent Children (ADC) to the states. The standards the states established for ADC were mostly derived from their existing state public assistance programs. Prior to passage of the act, all but six states had provided mothers' pensions to "worthy" mothers and their children. ("Worthy" meant that the mother was a widow or her husband severely disabled; the voluntary agencies cautioned against giving aid to deserted mothers, warning that this would encourage further desertions.) An unmarried mother had even greater difficulty getting assistance.[3] With such eligibility measures, no one had predicted that, by the 1960s, a considerable number of families headed by unmarried or deserted mothers would be assisted by AFDC.

Although the majority of AFDC recipients were white, blacks were over-represented in proportion to their numbers in the population. The public began to perceive AFDC recipients as mostly African-American families with children born out of wedlock and deserted by their fathers. This is exactly what the NUL and NAACP had warned would happen when the Social Security Act established a two-tier social welfare system. The tendency to generalize and to assume that the majority of blacks were "on welfare" meant that the entire race was affected by the stigma attached to welfare dependency. AFDC was criticized as a program that condoned immorality, encouraged desertion by the father, promoted dependency, and fanned racial animosity.

Welfare reform had been an issue during the tumultuous 1968 presidential campaign, and Nixon, running on a "law and order" platform, attacked the present system without specifying how he planned to change it. In his acceptance speech as presidential nominee of the Republican Party, he received a roar of approval when he told the audience:

I say it's time to quit pouring billions of dollars into programs that have failed. . . . Let us increase the wealth of America so that we can provide more generously for the aged, for the needy and for all those who cannot help themselves.

But for those who are able to help themselves, *what we need are not more millions on welfare rolls, but more millions on payrolls.*[4]

Most black Americans did not vote for Nixon, preferring the Democratic candidate, Hubert Humphrey, a civil rights supporter for decades and vice president under Lyndon Johnson. (Humphrey in fact received 85 percent of the black vote.) Nixon had no record in support of civil rights and during his campaign made no effort to appeal to black voters. He opposed issues championed by the civil rights organizations, such as open housing and school busing, and courted whites who were against many of the gains blacks had made during the 1960s civil rights movement.

Whitney Young congratulated Nixon on his election victory but warned him that he would have to work hard to gain the confidence of blacks. He assured him that the NUL was "ready to help him become president not of some Americans, but of all people."[5] Apparently, Nixon appreciated this and immediately began to establish lines of communication with black leaders. But because of his policies on civil rights, the "honeymoon" between Nixon and civil rights leaders was short-lived. In his autobiography, Roy Wilkins writes that he soon became very critical of Nixon because he stalled on integration by opposing busing in a way that "beclouded the issue" and split "the country just when the civil rights laws needed backing from the White House." Wilkins had hoped that Nixon would "try to be president of all the people," but instead "he allied himself with the worst enemies of black children."[6]

H. R. Haldeman's diary reveals Nixon's negative views about blacks as he discussed welfare reform, an issue high on his domestic agenda, with Haldeman and John Ehrlichman, chief members of the White House staff. Nixon said, "The *whole* problem is really the blacks. The key is to devise a system that recognizes this while not appearing to. Problem with overall welfare plan is that it forces poor whites into same position as blacks. . . . We have to get rid of the veil of hypocrisy and guilt and face reality." Nixon elaborated, "There has never in history been an adequate black nation, and they are the only race of which this is true. . . . Africa is hopeless, the worst is Liberia, which we built."[7]

When the task force appointed by Nixon to draft the bill began to exchange ideas about welfare reform, a consensus emerged that reform required more than incremental change, as had been done over the years with amendments to the Social Security Act; the welfare system needed a complete overhaul. Most agreed that it should be in the form of an income strategy; the services strategy of the "war on poverty" had failed. The idea of a negative income tax had been floating around for a number of years; in fact, it had been proposed to Johnson as a means of eradicating poverty, but this was in the midst of the Vietnam War and he had rejected it as too expensive.[8] Nonetheless, he did authorize a longitudinal study of its effect on work incentives.[9] Though the results of this study would not be available for a number of years, the negative income tax—conceived by conservative economists Milton Friedman and George Stigler as a permanent device for eliminating poverty through the graduated income tax—offered an appealing option to the Nixon administration. Friedman and Stigler believed the fluctuation of the earnings of low-income workers from year to year contributed to the incidence of poverty and that a negative income tax would help to resolve this problem by providing income to the working poor and to those not working.[10]

After much deliberation, much political maneuvering among the White House staff and cabinet members, and several drafts, the welfare reform bill emerged as a guaranteed annual income plan with elements of a negative income tax to provide work incentives. But Nixon preferred not to label it as a negative income tax or even as a guaranteed income plan because he thought this would be "poison" and the bill would never pass.[11] The bill was much more liberal than most of Nixon's cabinet and White House staff had anticipated, largely because the task force directed to write the bill was comprised of many "holdovers" from the Johnson administration (one of whom, James Lyday, had first suggested the negative income tax to Johnson).[12]

Because of a lack of consensus within the administration, more than eight months passed before the bill was introduced in Congress. Nixon, who had been elected on a fairly conservative platform, amazed the nation by proposing a national, permanent program that would considerably expand the federal government's responsibility for dependent persons and the working poor—the Family Assistance Plan (FAP). This represented a radical change from the policies of the current welfare system.

But once FAP was introduced, it was doomed from the beginning, for there did not appear to be any group that strongly supported it. Labor opposed it, fearing it would weaken union bargaining power; labor preferred a higher minimum wage and a full employment program with the government as "employer of last resort."[13] The southern states, which had much to gain from a significant increase in federal money, were, nevertheless, against it because they thought it would undermine their power structure and considerably reduce the availability of cheap labor.[14] Liberal Democrats opposed it, perhaps for purely partisan reasons. Civil rights organizations supported the bill at first, but harsh and punitive policies added in later amendments caused them eventually to testify against it. After several modifications, the Family Assistance Plan passed the House but not the Senate.

The heart of the plan was a federal guaranteed income, based on family size and income, for all poor families—even the working poor. It would supplant AFDC but require state supplements in states where the current AFDC grant was more than the proposed federal guaranteed income. Without the state supplement, families in at least thirty-four states would be worse off. The bill eliminated the incentive for a father to leave the home by including two-parent families. AFDC-UP, created in 1961, had given states the option of providing grants to families with unemployed fathers in the home, but in spite of the widely accepted belief that denying AFDC benefits to two-parent families contributed to the breakup of families, twenty-five states had chosen not to implement AFDC-UP. The plan would have the greatest impact in the southern states where AFDC grants were extremely low. In some of these states, the proposed amount that recipients could receive would be tripled. This would be extremely helpful to a large segment of the black population and to southern poor whites.

A special allocation provided job training and day care. The able-bodied were required to enroll in a state-run job training program, and those who failed to participate would be denied benefits (mothers of children under the age of six were exempted). Work-incentive policies allowed poor working families to keep a certain percentage of their earned income. In addition, the federal government would assume responsibility for three adult categories (the aged, the blind, and the disabled) that were currently the responsibility of the states. Originally, FAP was to be administered by the Social Security Administration, although it would operate separately from Old Age, Survivors, Disability, and Health Insurance (OASDHI); but by the time the bill went to Congress, federal administration had become a state option. While it was thought to be costly, the program was expected to become less so as more recipients became gainfully employed. It was a progressive plan that would be less demeaning than the existing welfare system and it would include the working poor.

The administration had assumed that liberals would support the Family Assistance Plan and was surprised when one of FAP's earliest and most vocal critics was the National Welfare Rights Organization (NWRO).[15] While the FAP bill was being developed, NWRO presented its own guaranteed annual income plan before a congressional subcommittee of the Joint Economic Committee. George Wiley told the subcommittee that "the basic need of poor people *is* money" and outlined a plan that would provide a grant at the "low-income poverty line" with a cost-of-living adjustment. Wiley's plan took heed of welfare rights by proposing that eligibility be established through a "declarative affidavit such as used by the Federal Income Tax System" and with a "built-in grievance system." The plan also allowed poor working families to keep part of their earnings. The NWRO opposed a negative income tax because it thought the work incentives in it "set the minimum income for those totally dependent on government support at too low a level."[16]

Wiley had hoped that the NWRO would serve in an advisory capacity as the welfare reform bill was being written since he wanted its version, with a "Guaranteed Adequate Income," to be considered.[17] To publicize its views, the NWRO held a national welfare rights rally in Washington where members lobbied Congress as well as Robert Finch, secretary of Health, Education, and Welfare (HEW). At the same time, the organization asked its supporters, Friends of NWRO, to live on a welfare budget for a week and contribute the difference in food costs to the welfare rights movement.[18]

Soon Wiley became disappointed and frustrated in his contacts with the Nixon administration and accused it of ignoring NWRO. Moynihan, Assistant for Urban Affairs, later wrote that this was, "strictly speaking, false. NWRO had been consulted; its officers had been to the White House; George Wiley was frequently in touch."[19] However, at least one person in the White House, Vice President Spiro Agnew, worried about the political implications of these contacts. Agnew sent Nixon a news clipping of an article in the *Washington Star* indicating that the administration was considering using NWRO, "a militant welfare organization, to be the Administration's broker in dealing with disadvantaged slum dwellers." Agnew said his personal experiences with NWRO had made him feel strongly that "this Administration would not like to be identified with it in

any way, and certainly not to the extent of a $100,000 a year grant." A pen-
ciled note on the memo asked Finch to "please talk to V.P."[20] According to
Haldeman's diary, Nixon frequently brooded over the administration's
problems in communicating with blacks. Nixon concluded that it was really
not possible, "except with Uncle Toms, and we should work on them and
forget militants."[21]

Nixon announced his new domestic program in a nationwide television
address, and upon its introduction in the House the FAP bill went to that
body's Ways and Means Committee. The NAACP, NUL, and NCNW all gave
testimony that supported the basic idea of a federal guaranteed annual
income but added reservations about many of the policies in FAP—especially its mandatory work requirement. These organizations did not think
this proposal was necessary; recipients would work if jobs were available. But
the NWRO had opposed the bill from the beginning, and its most serious
criticism concerned the amount of the proposed federal grant. And because
it was the most vocal against the FAP, the NWRO's message had the greatest
impact. To Congress, this meant that welfare recipients were more concerned about a larger grant than they were about jobs. As the bill was
amended, work incentives became more stringent.

During Wiley's first testimony before the House Ways and Means
Committee, he agreed the welfare system needed drastic change but was disturbed that each time welfare reform had been attempted, the public's primary concern always focused on the increase in the welfare rolls. He pointed
out that in 1962 experts had considered social services necessary to rehabilitate poor people and get them off welfare, but in spite of these services, the
rolls kept rising. In 1967 the "same experts" thought work and training were
the answer and the Work Incentive Program (WIN)[22] was created; yet "still
the rolls kept rising." Now, Wiley said, "the President is talking the same talk
about how to get people off of welfare. NWRO thinks it is time someone told
this Committee the truth about why the welfare rolls are growing." They
were growing because "millions of Americans" who had been denied adequate education, employment, and equal opportunities were "now beginning to turn to welfare as a basic source of support." NWRO believed that
"welfare should not be viewed as a problem . . . but rather as a solution."
Welfare was a way to "invest in human beings."[23]

There were several changes that NWRO believed to be paramount if the
bill was really going to help the poor. Foremost, the amount of the federal

grant was inadequate and needed to be raised. Also, NWRO distrusted the proposal for state supplements and wanted "clear and specific provisions" for federal enforcement as a part of the federal/state relationship along with explicit due process guarantees.[24] Moreover, NWRO vehemently opposed forcing mothers with school-age children to work. This policy came "perilously close to compelling involuntary servitude itself in violation of the 13th Amendment." NWRO thought the mother herself was in the best position to determine what effect taking a job would have on her young child. She had legal responsibility for the child, but "the actual control" was being taken away from her ("Such a split between responsibility and control is bad enough in most situations but in the family relationship it is intolerable"). Furthermore, considering a mandatory work requirement for mothers was "a matter of critical concern" when adequate jobs for men were not available. The NWRO wondered how jobs would be provided since FAP did not include any commitment to job development. It believed that adequate jobs should be guaranteed for all men able to work and for all mothers who "freely decide" to do so.[25]

The NAACP, NUL, and NCNW all testified in favor of the bill but with reservations that supported NWRO's objections to its policies. All agreed that the grant was too low. All were against forcing mothers to work. And all believed that most men would work if jobs were made available. Each organization also raised specific concerns. The NAACP's main concern was the proposed state administration of the program, especially in the South. In the absence of complete federal control, Clarence Mitchell, who testified for the NAACP, thought there should be an "automatic trigger under which the Federal Government would act if a State did not fulfill its duty toward its citizens." The NAACP thought this to be necessary because of its own experiences in trying to change situations in states where federal mandates were not adhered to and which had proved to be an extremely time-consuming and sometimes futile process.[26]

Young, representing the NUL and the National Association of Social Workers (NASW), of which he was then president, favored helping welfare recipients gain employment, but he was concerned because the plan proposed mandatory work without assuring that work would be available and in keeping with the recipients' interests and aptitudes. The NUL wanted "assurances" that they would "not be exploited, that a violin player [would] not be sent out to do domestic work." It recommended initiating government work and training programs that would provide protection and pay at least the minimum wage.

Young countered the criticism that FAP was too expensive by arguing that it should be seen "as an investment rather than an expenditure." He believed that concern over welfare "chiselers and deadbeats" was overblown, that society had "a strange way of making it appear that the only people that get help from the Government are welfare clients." But welfare clients were no more corrupted by government aid than other recipients. He contended that when corporations are helped, they call it defense contracts; or it's a " 'subsidy' when it goes to farmers not to grow things," and "research grants" when it goes to universities. "It is only 'welfare' when it goes to the poor." The costs of "social disintegration" had to be weighed against the cost of helping people "realize their full potential as taxpayers and as citizens."[27]

A few days later, a representative of the National Council of Negro Women (NCNW) testified. The organization was concerned that the federal benefit was below the poverty line; without more generous work incentives, the working poor would remain poor. Like the NAACP, it distrusted state administration and thought all training programs should be supervised by the federal government to assure that welfare recipients were not exploited.[28] The NCNW favored universal coverage and recommended "an end to the categorizing of the poor." It thought a welfare reform bill should include all poor because childless couples and individuals needed assistance too.[29]

Rep. John Conyers (D, Mich.) reinforced the views of civil rights organizations when he testified for an alternative bill, the National Income Program Act of 1969, which did not include a work requirement. He said mandatory work would be counterproductive. He had recently addressed the NWRO convention where members told him they needed job-training programs that led to jobs. A number of them "had gone through federal and local programs that didn't lead them anywhere, and they really wanted to get off welfare." They had asked him to make this point to the House Ways and Means Committee. The vast majority were willing to work if employment and child care were available.[30]

Wiley's charisma gave him easy access to the press, and his ongoing, relentless attack on FAP disturbed the White House. When he predicted that FAP would "promote civil disorder by forcing poor people into the streets to supplement their food grant," Nixon told Ehrlichman and Moynihan, "This should be knocked down."[31] Moynihan advised Nixon not to "dignify it" with a response; instead the administration should push the fact that its pro-posals would be doing "greatly more for those people on welfare who have been the worst off."[32] Moynihan thought "the basic fact of Wiley's situation [was] that FAP would put him out of business." His political base and con-tinued existence were dependent on the black poor. "There is nothing per-sonal about all of this. It is straight unionism," Moynihan said.[33]

After several months and with only slight changes, the Ways and Means Committee finally sent the bill to the floor of the House. The Democrats were accused of dragging their feet because they did not want Nixon to get credit for such liberal legislation. There was speculation that Wilbur Mills, chair of the Ways and Means Committee, had abruptly changed his tactics and reported the bill out because he believed that the plan would backfire once the public realized how expensive it was.[34] Forty-two states would have to supplement the federal grant to keep their grant from falling below the current level. Wealthier states would realize only a 10 percent savings and poorer states would have to reimburse the federal government by at least 50 percent of what they had been spending on welfare. Furthermore, the size of the federal grant for the adult categories, including the elderly poor, the blind, and disabled, had been increased.

Hoping to ward off an amendment for a smaller grant, the NWRO adopted a slogan, "$5500 or Fight!" which meant, according to Wiley, that "they would take to the streets for their demands, politically organizing against Russell Long, Wilbur Mills and other reactionary forces in their home districts, and protesting at public appearances of Mr. Finch and Mr. Moynihan."[35] The NWRO said $5,500 was the amount the Bureau of Labor Statistics (BLS) had stated as necessary for a family of four to live at a mini-mum level of health and decency. FAP would provide $1,600 plus $800 in food stamps.[36] The bill was passed by the House without any substantial changes.

The Senate Finance Committee then turned its attention to the bill. In his testimony before this committee, Young once again endorsed the basic con-cepts of the FAP but thought changes were still needed, especially its man-power policies. He accused the committee of getting bogged down in work-incentive formulas and being stymied by its attempts to devise a plan to assure that a welfare grant would never be larger than the income of the low-est paid worker. This was difficult because the grant was based on family size while wages were not. Young said he did not think there should be a cardinal rule that a person on welfare should not receive more than a person who was working; the basic criteria by which people were assisted ought to be need. The work-incentive policies reflected an assumption that people sought welfare over work, and this had created an entangled structure as they attempted to deal with manpower, child care, and income maintenance.[37]

Members of the committee agreed that the bill was getting away from the concept of separating income maintenance from social services. Young said this was one of NUL's greatest concerns. He proposed *universal* benefits: child care, manpower, and other provisions all had merit but they did not belong in the same bill. The country needed a manpower bill. The major goal should be full employment, whether the concern was welfare or not. Child care was crucial; it was absolutely necessary in a country where 40 percent of the women worked, but it should not be attached to welfare because it affected more than welfare recipients. The complex structure involved different levels of government, which would burden applicants and increase administrative costs since establishing eligibility required three different agencies reviewing applications case by case.[38]

When a vote in the Senate was imminent, NWRO lobbied even more forcefully against FAP and asked affiliates to visit senators in their home offices and to send people to Washington for hearings. Wiley was determined that NWRO members would testify in spite of the refusal of Senator Long, the "reactionary baron of the Senate Finance Committee," to hear them. If the Finance Committee refused to hear them, they would ask other interested senators to listen to their testimony. Wiley outlined the changes that were needed in the bill: to eliminate the forced work requirement, to avoid cuts in the welfare grants, and to restore and expand rights of welfare recipients.[39]

The Nixon administration was not pleased over the civil rights organizations' lack of support. Difficulties with the NAACP surfaced when Bishop Stephen G. Spottswood, chair of the NAACP's board, severely criticized Nixon's civil rights record during a speech at the association's annual convention. Leonard Garment, a White House staff member, defended the president and accused Spottswood of misstating and misrepresenting the administration's record "so as to present it in a highly distorting light."[40]

Spottswood replied, "I believe the charge that the overall stance of the administration has been anti-Negro is sustained by the record." The administration had failed in its "equal employment activity" and in its support of voting rights in the South. Spottswood reminded Garment that the NAACP had "long ago approved" the FAP but "still had reservations on certain aspects."[41]

Moynihan felt Nixon had every right to be bitter about Spottswood's comments and said, "The N.A.A.C.P. denunciation (unless Wilkins disowns it . . .) means in effect the political failure of all you have tried to do for the blacks and the poor. We have not overcome the distrust which you acknowledged early in the administration." Moynihan advised Nixon to "continue to do what you think to be right with respect to racial equality"; after all, had not Wilkins said that "no President in history had come near to proposing anything like the Family Assistance Plan, a proposal that would transform the lives of exactly those Southern blacks of whom Spottswood spoke?"[42]

More difficulties with the civil rights organizations developed following Moynihan's comments during an appearance on the *Today Show*. After his appearance, he sent a memorandum to Nixon explaining that the *Today Show* "had a full week of black 'leaders' denouncing us" and that he was pleased to get a "brief moment to reply." Nixon penciled "a good job" on the memo, perhaps not realizing that Moynihan's statements had angered and insulted the NUL. In response to a question about support for FAP, Moynihan had told the television audience, "The Urban League has a long respected tradition of social work. But you know, I'm afraid social workers are against this program because they fear it might put social workers out of work." When questioned further, he said, "People who make a living—and I'm afraid you could make a good living—giving advice to the poor somehow are frightened by the idea of giving them money and letting them run their own lives. That's what this bill is all about."[43]

Young was incensed. He said the NUL, NAACP, and NASW were on record as supporting the bill although they had reservations about it. "But the suggestion that social workers were against and greatly disapproved the reform of our welfare program because it might jeopardize their jobs is, to me, irresponsible." Young thought Moynihan was too intelligent to be that ill-informed so his comments had to be considered "malicious and political."[44] Moynihan wrote to Young assuring him that he had been misquoted and adding that he was sorry that Young was not going to join the administration.[45] (It was rumored that Nixon had offered Young a position on his staff.)

Representing the NAACP and the Leadership Conference on Civil Rights (of which he was then chair), Clarence Mitchell once again confirmed support for FAP but with reservations. The NAACP, perhaps alluding to NWRO, recognized that there were "some organizations that did not agree with the President's plan," but it backed it "as a step in the right direction and urged the adoption of amendments that would improve the overall bill."[46] The House committee's proposal for a public service jobs program was "essential"; training welfare recipients without simultaneously creating new job opportunities would be "meaningless." Even during periods of full employment there were persons who had great difficulty finding or holding jobs in the private sector; therefore, a "careful program of matching individuals to jobs in the public sector or in non-profit organizations would have untold value in our country." In addition, the NAACP supported an amendment by Sen. Abraham Ribicoff (D, Conn.) that would require pretests to evaluate major reform efforts before implementing them nationwide. The NAACP thought this would be helpful because there were too many uncertainties regarding the FAP's effect. The federal government had to be ready to operate programs if states were reluctant to accept responsibility.[47]

Changes made by the Finance Committee made FAP even more unacceptable to the civil rights organizations and NWRO. Due to the committee's belief that nonworking families should never get more than the working poor and due to its inability to design work incentives that would achieve this, two-parent households with an unemployed parent (AFDC-UP) were eliminated from coverage. To counter the objections to this exclusion, the bill would "grandfather in" those families currently covered by AFDC-UP, but future two-parent families in need would not be eligible. Other policies that the organizations had criticized in previous testimony remained unchanged: the federal income floor was below the poverty line, and the required amount of the state supplement was unclear. Mothers of school age children were required to work as a condition of the grant, but there was no guarantee that jobs would pay at least the minimum wage. There were inadequate provisions to protect the rights of welfare recipients.[48]

The NUL testified a third time when, with the help of Sen. Eugene McCarthy (D, Minn.), the NWRO itself held hearings in Washington. Jeweldean Jones Londa, the league's associate director of social welfare, represented the NUL and stated that in earlier testimony the NUL had "generally favored welfare reform legislation with reservations." However, since that time, proposed changes had lessened the potential effectiveness of the legislation. As a result, the NUL had compiled six minimum requirements which had to be met if it were to endorse the bill: (1) full financing and administration by the federal government, necessary because of "discrepancies and variations in the public assistance policies and financial bases of the various States"; (2) a minimum floor above the poverty line, and the elimination of food stamps in order to "preserve the dignity of the individual," because stamps were demeaning; (3) the removal of the compulsory work requirement for mothers because it was not necessary; (4) universal provisions for the "working poor," which would include households with unemployed fathers; (5) the use of a "simple affidavit" for all categories; and (6) the preservation of all rights held under current public assistance laws.[49]

Shortly after the NWRO's hearings, the Finance Committee turned the bill down, and it was speculated that the hearings had contributed to its demise. The hearings, chaired by Wiley dressed in a dashiki, and the media's depiction of militant welfare mothers demanding a larger grant and raging against the FAP because they were opposed to working, may have increased opposition to the bill. One NWRO member declared, "We only want the kind of jobs that will pay $10,000 or $20,000. . . . We aren't ready to do anybody's laundry or baby sitting except for ourselves." The audience clapped. Another member said she had heard Senator Long say that "as long as he can't get his laundry done he's going to put welfare recipients to work. . . . Those days are gone forever. . . . Senator Long should get his wife or mother to do his shirts." At a previous committee meeting, Ribicoff had proposed that welfare recipients clean city streets. The NWRO's testifier said, "He should get his wife and mother to pick up trash too." More applause. The hearings angered conservative senators who were against FAP and convinced many nonconservatives, who had been undecided, to vote against it.[50] Attempts to get a more liberal version of the bill on the floor of the Senate were unsuccessful, and the ninety-first Congress ended without acting on FAP.[51]

Also, not long after the NWRO's hearings, a new black organization, the Congressional Black Caucus (CBC), introduced the NWRO's bill, the Adequate Income Act. The CBC was formed by African-American members of Congress in 1971 with the goal of promoting the general welfare of black Americans nationwide through legislation.[52] This organization represented a crucial and important change for the civil rights groups because it provided a liaison with Congressional members who not only clearly and openly shared their aspirations and goals but were able and willing to introduce legislation with policies they preferred. The introduction of NWRO's bill illustrated this.

Congressman Charles B. Rangel (D, N.Y.) introduced the bill as the administration was trying to reach a compromise with the Senate. The bill proposed a minimum income that was one thousand dollars above NWRO's earlier demand of "$5,500 or Fight" and was to be derived from a federal grant, wages, or a combination of both. (This higher amount was based on a Bureau of Labor Statistics study showing how much a family of four actually needed to maintain even a low standard of living.)[53] But the bill never received enough support to be considered by the House.

By this time, according to Haldeman's diary, Nixon no longer supported the bill. He wanted to be sure that FAP was killed by the Democrats "and that we make a big play for it, but don't let it pass, can't afford it."[54] Shortly before FAP went back to the Finance Committee, Nixon directed his staff to adopt the term "workfare" when referring to FAP saying, "Regardless of objections of the more liberal minded members of the fold . . . henceforth all Administration spokesmen (including our people in Congress) *will use the term*."[55] (Nixon's motives in doing this are unclear. He had used this term in his acceptance speech when he was nominated for president by the Republican Party but had not insisted on its use until this time. Moynihan disliked the term and referred to it as "boob-bait.")[56]

In the next congressional session, another version of FAP (H.R. 1, Title IV) was reported out of the Ways and Means Committee and was passed by the House. The NWRO conceded that some of the "onerous provisions" had been removed. In the new version, two-parent families were once again covered. The amount of earnings a family could keep was increased. The committee had also agreed to include a program of public service employment. The NWRO viewed these changes "as a major concession," but other policies made it "the most oppressive measure yet proposed by an administration which [had] in the past callously and systematically disregarded the needs of impoverished children and their families." It was predicated on "the racist premise that people are poor and need assistance because of their personal failures or anti-social behavior." It was controlling and coercive with a "cumbersome administrative structure" that was "deliberately antagonistic to individual rights and unresponsive to human needs."[57]

It would allow employers to pay FAP workers 75 percent of the minimum wage. The NWRO noted that the states would not be required to supplement federal payments up to even their current AFDC level, and FAP families would be ineligible for food stamps. Many families, especially in urban areas in the North and West, would be worse off than they presently were under AFDC, and further, there was no cost-of-living adjustment.

The "forced work" provision had become "more repressive and punitive." Those able to work would be referred to Opportunities for Families (OFF), a separate program that would be run by the Department of Labor through state employment offices. The NWRO was particularly distressed because the bill now required mothers with children over three years of age to work with no assurance of adequate child care facilities. Recipients would have no control over where they would be required to work or the kind of work they would have to do. The legal rights of welfare recipients would be further eroded because rulings made by hearing examiners could not be appealed to the courts.[58]

Vernon E. Jordan, Jr. (who became executive director of the NUL after Whitney Young's tragic death in 1971) testified and supported NWRO's assessment of FAP; the NUL was in "total opposition to H.R. 1." It found "the family welfare provisions . . . more damaging to the best interests of the poor and the black than the present bankrupt welfare system they are designed to support." It was an "instrument of control and coercion with respect to employment, child rearing, family relationships, health care, drug use and other behavioral patterns." It empowered the secretary of HEW to make important decisions for recipients by determining who is able to work, the type and location of the required job or training program, child care arrangements, as well as any other supportive services needed. There were no incentives for the states to supplement the inadequate federal grant.[59]

Although the NUL, NAACP, and NCNW had supported work opportunities to help welfare recipients become gainfully employed, OFF manpower policies had become too punitive to be supported. The organizations wanted a *universal* manpower policy that would lead to jobs that paid a decent wage with opportunities for advancement—which OFF would clearly not provide. The organizations were not unhappy when the bill was defeated.

However, one portion that survived was a policy the civil rights groups had advocated during the 1930s. The Social Security Act was amended to establish a Supplemental Security Income (SSI), a federal program for the poor elderly, blind, and disabled. SSI considerably expanded federal responsibility for dependent persons by providing a federal guaranteed income with a cost-of-living adjustment.[60] Prior to this amendment, these categorical programs were administered by the states, a policy the NAACP and NUL had opposed while the Social Security Act was under debate. The NAACP very much favored this amendment but was concerned about the amount of the federal grant, which was quite low and would require state supplements if the current amount that recipients of public assistance were receiving from many of the states was to be maintained. The NAACP "went on record urging states to continue the provision and the maintenance of current grant levels."[61]

There are various interpretations concerning the defeat of FAP. According to the Nixon administration, the Democrats killed it because they did not want Nixon to get credit for such progressive social welfare legislation. The liberal Democrats blamed the conservative Republicans for tinkering with FAP until its policies became too punitive and regressive to accept. Others believed the civil rights organizations were at least partly responsible because they allowed the NWRO to lead the debate and it alienated potential supporters.

The NWRO's cause was weakened by its failure to emphasize the critical issue of jobs. The focus on the amount of the federal grant went against the grain of society's strong work ethic. A demand for jobs would have dispelled many of the myths and assumptions about welfare dependency. In addition, such an approach would have exposed the hypocrisy involved in developing a mandatory work policy for welfare recipients when it was clear that jobs were not available for all of them. If a demand for jobs had been the central theme, the public might have become more aware of the civil rights organizations' contention that the real source of the "welfare problem" was high unemployment. Civil rights groups consistently pointed out that the mandatory work provision was unnecessary because welfare recipients wanted to work, but legislators remained unconvinced.

Many advocates for the poor view the defeat of FAP as a lost opportunity, a squandered chance to make a fundamental change in the social welfare system by assigning responsibility for all poor families, working and nonworking, to the federal government. They argue that the grant was admittedly too low but would have increased, just as Social Security benefits had done. Perhaps the bill might have passed if, early on, it had received the full support of all the groups that normally support liberal legislation. But this is pure speculation; there is no way of knowing if such a progressive proposal (as the early version of the FAP was) would have survived the strong opposition from conservative groups.

Assumptions about the poor, which drove legislators to insist on very punitive work incentives, resulted in a plan that no longer met the goals of the original draft—to bring the working and nonworking poor out of poverty. The final version of FAP, H.R. 1, proposed a special minimum wage for recipients that was considerably less than the national minimum and which would have been tantamount to a differential wage rate for a large proportion of the African-American population (something the NUL and NAACP had fought against during the 1930s). It would have created a bureaucratic structure that would have increased administrative costs since establishing eligibility for the various programs would have had to be done on a case-by-case basis. It would have isolated the poor in a system that not only denied them self-determination but also seemed designed to keep them in perpetual poverty. In the end, understandably, the civil rights organizations chose not to support it.

However, civil rights groups were given another opportunity to present their welfare reform proposals when President Jimmy Carter, elected in 1976, announced his welfare reform plan in 1977.

Program for Better Jobs and Income

As usual, welfare reform had been an issue during the 1976 presidential campaign, but Carter was vague about what form his version would take. He merely promised more than incremental change and a replacement of the current system with one that encouraged work and family life and which reflected "both the competence and compassion of the American people."[62]

The primary responsibility for developing a welfare reform plan was given to Joseph Califano, Carter's secretary for Housing, Education, and Welfare. Califano appears to have had a good understanding of the problems of the poor and realized that educating the public about welfare reform was imperative owing to the myths about welfare recipients and the propensity of the public in general to regard welfare recipients as being mainly black, lazy squanderers of money as well as being cheaters. Califano began by pointing out that "90 percent of impoverished Americans either work full time, or are persons no civilized society would require to work. . . . The over-whelming proportion of people who can and should work do so. They stay poor because they do not earn enough money."[63]

Chances for a liberal welfare reform act seemed fairly good. Moynihan, now a newly elected Democratic senator from New York and chair of the new Senate Finance Subcommittee on Public Assistance, was enthusiastic about welfare reform as was James Corman (D, Calif.), chair of the House Ways and Means Subcommittee on Unemployment Compensation and Public Assistance. In addition, Rangel, a member of Corman's committee, worked closely with Corman. Their idea of welfare reform centered on improving the system, including an increase in benefits instead of focusing on the typical concern over cutting costs, which was what "welfare reform" usually meant. However, Carter made it clear that he expected a plan that would cost no more than the present welfare system *and* provide fiscal relief to the states. He thought a major step toward welfare reform could be accomplished by combining cash assistance with jobs programs. Califano and almost everyone with whom he consulted thought it was impossible to reform the welfare system without increased funding, but Carter remained adamant about a zero-cost plan.[64]

The basic plan that emerged consolidated three major programs—AFDC, SSI, and food stamps—into a complicated two-tier public assistance program. The first tier was comprised of the unemployed who were expected to work: one adult from a two-parent family, single parents of older children, and childless individuals and couples. Those in the first tier would be placed in public service employment (PSE). The second tier contained the poor not expected to work: the aged, blind, and disabled, and adults in single-parent families with young children. Although this was not stated, there were actu-ally three tiers since the Comprehensive Employment and Training Act (CETA) program would be continued.[65] CETA workers would earn more than PSE workers, and PSE workers (first tier) would receive a higher income than those not expected to work (second tier). The second-tier income would be below the poverty line. In order not to punish PSE recipi-ents who were unable to find jobs in the private sector, they would be moved to the higher CETA income if, after a certain period of time, the government had not been able to provide a CETA job. The plan offered no fiscal relief to the states, and many would have to furnish supplements to maintain the cur-rent level of the state's welfare grant.[66] Once again, assumptions about the able-bodied unemployed created a complex system that even punished those who were clearly unable to work.

Carter's welfare reform plan, Program for Better Jobs and Income (PBJI), suffered the same fate as Nixon's Family Assistance Plan—it did not pass. It might have passed if voters in California had not voted for Proposition 13 (a revolt against government spending) while PBJI was being considered. The day after the vote in California, PBJI was dead. To Congress, the results of that vote clearly signaled that the public did not want any new government-financed programs for the poor.[67]

Somewhat jaded by this time, the civil rights organizations were less enthusiastic about PBJI than they had been about the original draft of FAP. During the legislative process concerning PBJI, the same issues that had been raised about FAP resurfaced, and once again the civil rights organizations presented their opinions about welfare reform to Congress. They argued, as they had earlier, that it was unnecessary to make welfare recipients work; they wanted to work. The assumption that they had to be forced to work invariably created very complicated punitive systems that did nothing to reform the welfare system and increased administrative costs.

Califano, in an effort to accomplish a zero-cost welfare system, looked for money in other programs which could be used for the welfare reform plan. One source under consideration involved eliminating some federal low-income housing subsidies. The Office of Management and Budget (OMB) supported this plan; it contended that even though it would reduce the average subsidy for each recipient, "the resulting distribution would be far more equitable and would leave the majority of poverty households better off."[68]

The NUL disagreed. Maudine Cooper, deputy director of NUL's Washington Bureau, testifying before the Senate Banking, Housing, and Urban Affairs Committee, said she believed that housing subsidies for the poor were extremely important because they protected the poor from exploitation by the private housing market. Adding a small amount of money to their cash grant would only encourage more exploitation and was highly unlikely to lead to improved living conditions. Cooper thought housing subsidies should be used to improve inadequate housing—as "strategies against housing deterioration, neighborhood decline and city decay." The OMB's proposal symbolized "giving up on cities." It was common practice for landlords of the poor to "organize welfare ghettos, renting only to welfare tenants in a given neighborhood."[69]

Patricia Harris, secretary of the Department of Housing and Urban Development (HUD), was livid about the proposal, and when Carter persisted with this plan, Harris leaked it to the press. White House lines were overwhelmed with calls, but not from any groups representing the poor. The calls came from bankers, contractors, and other industries related to housing. Carter reluctantly backed off.[70] The housing industry's interest in this benefit supported Whitney Young's contention, during an earlier testimony, that government benefits are only stigmatized and called welfare when they go to the poor.

When Rangel testified, he told the committee that he was appearing on behalf of himself and the Welfare Reform Committee, composed of ten members of Congress from the Northeast who were part of the Northeast-Midwest Economic Advancement Coalition. The coalition's main contention was that PBJI did not recognize the shortage of private-sector jobs in the Northeast and would be a fiscal burden to New York. It was unlikely that the economic situation would change in the next two to three years, and people would remain in PSE for too long a period of time. Rangel suggested establishing some kind of an incentive for public- and private-sector employers to fill future job vacancies with workers from PSE.

Rangel said the program also failed to address the necessity of providing job-related benefits (excluding retirement) to those in PSE. As a result, most participants would be restricted to this category but denied the benefits of the CETA employee who was doing the same kind of work. The CETA employee would receive a higher wage and be eligible for the Earned Income Tax Credit,[71] but the PSE worker would not. Rangel thought this was grossly unfair; it made more sense to concentrate on a full employment policy.[72]

Ronald Brown of the NUL supported Rangel when he testified against PBJI. The NUL preferred "job creation through a full employment policy" and thought this, along with national health insurance, "should be the primary approach to preventing and eradicating poverty." A system that was equitable and universal was needed with federal administration, a federal minimum benefit, administrative simplicity (which, Brown said, would be possible without the inclusion of work requirements), an eradication of stigma, and cash rather than in-kind benefits.

The NUL was especially critical of the mandatory work requirement, unnecessary because "only 2 percent of 26 million people even resemble the mythical welfare stereotype: Nonaged, nondisabled males who do not work." Carter's plan was based on the assumption that jobs were available or could easily be created to meet the needs of all individuals who could work. Statistics showed that this had never been the case except perhaps during the Korean conflict and World War II. Brown was in agreement with Califano's statement: "Most of the poor are poor, not because of some personal failing, but because of events they cannot control, . . . not because they won't and don't work, but because when they do work, they do not earn enough money to lift them out of poverty." The NUL believed that the best way to deal with poverty was to "make the necessary reforms in those other systems."[73]

When Rangel testified before Moynihan's committee, he was generally positive toward the welfare reform bill since he, as a member of the Ways and Means Committee, had worked on it. His main concern was with what appeared to be a "slackening of support from the White House as it relates to welfare reform." He told the senators he had learned from the House leader that the president's list of ten priority bills had not included welfare reform. Moynihan was surprised to hear this and commiserated with Rangel because he knew he had devoted a lot of time and effort to revising the bill. Rangel said it appeared that the bill had not even been referred to the standing committee which had jurisdiction. Moynihan said, "Oh my God. Do you mean we are going to lose this again?" (Moynihan was alluding to FAP.) The press was at the hearing and Moynihan hoped it would report this. Rangel and Moynihan agreed that "this was the Congress to do welfare reform."[74]

The NAACP's Clarence Mitchell also testified before the Senate subcommittee and, like Rangel, generally favored the bill but had recommendations for improvement such as raising the minimum benefit level to at least the poverty line. After commenting on how this would probably be too expensive, Moynihan chose to discuss the concerns raised by Rangel, the lack of support for the bill by the administration. He believed the Senate would produce a good bill that would go nowhere if the House lost interest in welfare reform. Mitchell suggested some procedural strategies that would use "a Senate vehicle" to amend a bill in the House and keep it alive. Moynihan and Mitchell agreed that the bill needed to pass.[75]

The Children's Defense Fund (CDF), a national advocacy agency established by Marian Wright Edelman in 1973, submitted a written statement to the same subcommittee, outlining criteria for welfare reform which reinforced the testimony of the civil rights organizations. Existing welfare policies "overlooked the fact that only about 6 percent of *all* families resemble the typical image—two parents, an employed father, mother at home, and two children—and that poor families, like most families, strive hard as they can to attain the best possible life for their children." Also overlooked were the "broad economic and social pressures on families today—like unemployment, inflation and racial discrimination." CDF proposed replacing the "existing patchwork of income maintenance programs" with a federal system that provided a "guaranteed, uniform minimum income" to all needy persons, cash payments that assured "a floor of decency beneath every American child" and which did not base eligibility on family composition. The emphasis on work requirements was "misplaced and harmful to children." It supported a full employment policy whereby public service employment would not be treated as inferior to private or regular public employment and would provide meaningful and not "make work" jobs.[76]

Ronald Brown testified on three bills that were being considered by the Ways and Means Committee.[77] He congratulated Rangel and Corman on their leadership in the area of welfare reform but was critical of PBJI, reminding the committee that on two previous occasions the NUL had appeared before Congress to urge enactment of welfare reform legislation and pleading that "blacks and the poor not be required to bear an unequal share of the burden which has resulted from a poorly functioning economy." Brown said that in 1975, "after years of responding to a variety of proposals, the NUL's board of trustees adopted a basic position on income maintenance." This embodied the belief that the best approach to preventing and eradicating poverty was to place a floor under all incomes with a "universal refundable credit income tax" in combination with a full employment policy and national health insurance. This "ecumenical approach" would bring poverty and unemployment to the forefront as national problems and essentially eliminate the present welfare system. This remained the guidepost by which the NUL evaluated all proposals for welfare reform.[78]

One bill, which proposed block grants to give the states more control over the program, was completely unacceptable. The other two mandated a national minimum for all AFDC recipients and, although Rangel's was the more generous, the NUL thought the amounts in both bills were too low since they were considerably below the poverty line. Although both would significantly improve the AFDC and SSI programs by including two-parent families under AFDC-UP and poor singles and childless couples under SSI, the NUL was disturbed and offended that in "every piece of new legislation the overriding consideration excepting cost is how to control the so-called cheaters." This was unnecessary.[79] Soon after Brown's testimony, PBJI was rejected by Congress.

The civil rights organizations had been "lukewarm" on the bill, and while presenting proposals to improve its policies, they had been pushing much harder for the passage of another bill which, since 1975, had been under consideration by Congress: the Full Employment and Balanced Growth Act. For them, as they had repeatedly stated during testimony on both previous welfare reform bills, a full employment policy was the ideal welfare reform plan.

The Full Employment and Balanced Growth Act of 1978

The Full Employment and Balanced Growth Act evolved during Gerald Ford's administration from the 1974 Equal Opportunity and Full Employment Act introduced by Congressman Augustus Hawkins (D, Calif.). During testimony on the welfare reform bills, the civil rights organizations had repeatedly expressed concerns over the high unemployment rate among African-Americans and had proposed a public works program as a solution to welfare dependency. They did not think the country had a welfare problem; it had an unemployment problem. The public and private sectors could not provide jobs to all who were willing and able to work. The CBC and civil rights groups enthusiastically endorsed Hawkins's bill and mobilized efforts to get it through Congress.

At the NUL's 1974 annual conference, Jordan said its theme, "Full Employment as a National Goal," was selected "because of the conviction that unless there are decent wages for everyone willing and able to work, our nation will continue to be haunted by the specter of a growing number of people for whom there are no useful roles in our society." He hoped the discussion would "broaden understanding of full employment" and that America would recognize it as "an idea whose time has come."[80]

Hawkins, a principal speaker, told conference participants that his bill, like the original 1945 full employment bill, would give "all adult Americans willing and able to work . . . the right to equal opportunities for useful paid employment at fair rates of compensation," adding, "this is the first, the most human, the most fundamental meaning of full employment." Hawkins explained that it was this meaning that was attacked in the 1945 bill and which had resulted in the substitution of the phrase, "maximum employ-

ment production power," for the term "full employment" in the Employment Act of 1946. More recently, "maximum employment production
power" had been interpreted to include economic growth and price stability,
even though these terms were not mentioned in the 1946 act.[81] As a result,
"full employment" had come to mean whatever unemployment rate was
deemed necessary to control inflation, and there was more concern about
controlling inflation than reducing the unemployment rate.

The bill would require the president to issue an annual labor report that
would include the number of people working as well as those not working
or seeking work. Current labor statistics did not include the total supply of
labor because they did not count those who, after searching for work over a
long period of time, had become discouraged and were no longer actively
seeking a job; nor did the statistics include the underemployed. "This has
led," Hawkins said, "to a topsy-turvy percentage gain of defining full employment in terms not of the number and kind of paid jobs but rather some
politically tolerable level of unemployment." This had started with 2 percent
and had now reached 6 to 7 percent. Hawkins's bill would rectify this situation with the creation of a Standby Job Corps in which a job seeker would
have the right to register and be placed in transitional employment until
suitable regular employment became available.[82]

The consistent testimony of the civil rights organizations is evident: they
portrayed the bill in universal terms, believing this would aid its passage;
they consistently admonished congressional committees to recognize a hidden unemployment index which showed that unemployment among
minorities was considerably higher than the BLS indicated; they attempted
to refute criticisms that a full employment policy was too expensive by citing the high costs of unemployment benefits and other related welfare programs; and they criticized the trade-off between inflation and unemployment rates.

The National Committee for Full Employment, an interracial coalition of
more than forty labor, business, government, religious, professional, advocacy, and civic organizations, was formed to pressure for passage of the bill.
Representative of this coalition were its cochairs, Coretta Scott King, president of the Martin Luther King, Jr. Center for Social Change, and Murray H.
Finley, president of the Amalgamated Clothing Workers of America. The
executive directors of the NAACP, NUL, and NCNW were all board members, and of course the CBC cooperated with this group.

Unfortunately, the act suffered the same fate as the 1946 Employment Act—it was symbolic legislation which established goals without providing enforcement mechanisms to reach them. It did not guarantee jobs to all Americans willing and able to work but established "as a national goal the fulfillment of the right to full opportunities for useful paid employment at fair rates of compensation for all individuals able, willing, and seeking work."[83]

Hawkins knew that the passage of an act with real "teeth" in it would be a formidable battle. The same arguments used against the 1946 act would be used against his bill. Full employment was considered costly and inflationary; long-term economic planning was seen as socialistic. Furthermore, if the bill was regarded as one that would primarily help African-Americans, it would be doomed since racial tension around affirmative action was growing. Many whites viewed affirmative action as a zero-sum game and considered that when blacks gained, *they* lost.

The title of the bill, Equal Opportunity and Full Employment, along with the fact that it had been introduced by a black congressman who emphasized high unemployment among blacks, caused some confusion about its purpose; many viewed it as an antidiscriminatory measure. Hawkins was quick to explain that this was not the bill's primary goal. Equal employment opportunity and genuine full employment were interwoven because employment discrimination would be minimized in a full employment economy.[84]

When the civil rights organizations testified in favor of the bill, they recognized that it had to be portrayed in universal terms if it were to pass. Unemployment had to be understood as a national problem, not just a black problem; everyone would benefit from a full employment policy. The bill had the potential to reduce poverty, welfare dependency, and crime; in addition, the organizations believed that racial tension around affirmative action and competition for jobs would be significantly lessened.

The House Education and Labor Committee's Subcommittee on Equal Opportunities (which Hawkins chaired) held its first hearings on the bill in Detroit, at the invitation of Charles Diggs and John Conyers, House Democrats and members of the CBC. Both Diggs and Conyers testified in favor of the bill along with a young woman from the NAACP Youth Council. Diggs began his testimony by saying he felt like "the Captain of the Titanic"; only in Detroit was it possible to understand the "true catastrophes of our present economic problem." Unemployment statistics were "almost beyond belief"; 23 percent of the people in Detroit were unable to find work. In some areas six out of ten workers were out of a job. Much of the progress made by black and other minority workers had eroded; welfare rolls were rising. Hawkins's bill was "vital to the people of Detroit."[85]

John Conyers regarded the bill as "a well-rounded piece of legislation" that was "long overdue." He was gratified that some young people had been scheduled to testify because part-time employment was badly needed by this group, but this problem was seldom addressed.[86] The NAACP Youth Council representative (Julie Chenault) agreed with Conyers. She said that youth heard all the time that a good education was necessary if one were to get a decent paying job, yet many young people needed a job as a means for financing an education. "The situation [looked] absolutely hopeless" to them.[87]

When Hawkins's committee held hearings in Atlanta, Coretta Scott King was the opening witness. She was critical of Washington officials who were more concerned about inflation than high unemployment and who "very calmly assumed that greater numbers of American workers must lose their jobs as front-line soldiers in the battle against inflation." King recognized that the theories behind these assumptions were very complex, but despite these complexities she did not accept the belief that full employment was an impossible goal. The issue of social and economic justice was far too important to be left to economists.[88] The Atlanta NAACP and Urban League also testified in favor of the bill. Donald Webster, representing the NAACP, acknowledged that the bill would benefit everyone, *but* due to racial discrimination, African-Americans would continue to have special needs. He was particularly concerned about the manner in which statistics "would accurately reflect the unemployment rate in a non-discriminatory manner." Since the full employment programs would be implemented whenever the unemployment rate exceeded 3 percent, minorities would be adversely affected when the national rate remained below 3 percent for a long time. For them it would be considerably higher. Statistics should "reflect the unemployment rate in a non-discriminatory manner." The NAACP was also apprehensive because state and local governments and the private sector would have considerable control over the U.S. Full Employment Service and the Job Guarantee Office (to be created by the act). Based on past experiences, this troubled the NAACP, which wanted at least some involvement in the selection of "any committees and councils that might be established" to assure that the act was "implemented in a nondiscriminatory manner" and "in accordance with prescribed labor standards."[89] Lyndon Wade, executive director of the Atlanta UL described the effect of high unemployment on Atlanta's black population, especially housing evictions, and thought the act could resolve many urban problems.[90]

When Ronald Brown of the NUL testified before a subcommittee of the Joint Economic Committee, he told the members that, as a result of a Black Economic Summit the NUL had cosponsored, major black organizations from across the country had made full employment a goal and had issued a strong statement in support of the bill: "One of the measures of any economy or system of government is its ability to provide meaningful jobs in the public and private sector at an equitable and adequate wage for all citizens who are willing and able to work."[91]

Brown expressed his concern about the increase in unemployment among blacks and the Labor Department's use of unemployment statistics that did not count discouraged workers (those who no longer even looked for work). The official rate of 14.2 percent for black workers was probably double that figure, and for these long-term unemployed workers, emergency jobs legislation, such as CETA, was not helpful because it was directed toward recently unemployed persons and failed to recognize or provide adequately for the hardcore unemployed. The league's "most overriding concern" in the establishment of a full employment policy was to stop the government's practice of placing a disproportionate burden of fighting inflation upon minorities and poor people—the groups most in need of government assistance.

Brown said the NUL had gone on record as favoring three procedures to establish a full employment policy: create incentives to make the private sector start hiring again; develop "a revised updated form of WPA type program to put people back to work through a massive public works program to build homes, schools, roads, bridges, and other things, particularly in the inner city"; and initiate "a massive public employment program" which guaranteed "to all workers, a decent job at a decent wage."

Brown ended his testimony by emphasizing the necessity of portraying the bill in universal terms, "to put the problem in national perspective," because even though unemployment in the black community had not fallen below 9 percent for the past ten years, "there has been no great trauma, no

great concern." He believed this inertia was related to the government's failure to recognize that there was still "a good deal of racism . . . in the country." If the situation continued to be perceived as a black problem, there was
little hope of getting the kind of action that was needed. More could be
accomplished by addressing the issue in the context of a national problem,
so "devastating to the entire Nation" that it needed a national solution.
Brown pointed out that thirteen million out of the sixteen million unemployed people were whites who "ought to be outraged" by the inaction of the
administration and Congress.[92]

Hawkins's bill, criticized because it lacked a comprehensive economic
plan to achieve its goal, did not have strong support and remained in subcommittee. To overcome this criticism, another bill, the Balanced Growth
Act, was linked to it. But, in contrast, this bill, introduced in the Senate by
Hubert Humphrey (D, Minn.), met with equally lackluster enthusiasm
because it offered a plan without a clear goal. Consequently, the two bills,
one with a goal and the other with a plan, were combined to create the Full
Employment and Balanced Growth Act of 1976 (also referred to as the
Humphrey-Hawkins Act).

Representing the CBC, Yvonne Burke (D, Calif.) testified before
Hawkins's committee in favor of the revised bill, reminding the committee
that the CBC had supported the bill since its inception and that it had broad
support from diverse groups in the country. The CBC was critical of "the
tendency of our national leadership to look at . . . destructively high rates of
unemployment as *acceptable*." Recently, the administration had expressed
optimism when the overall unemployment rate declined to 7.6 percent, but
had showed little concern over the official unemployment rate of 13.7 percent among blacks. This figure, Burke contended, was actually higher: the
NUL's December 1975 "Quarterly Economic Report on Black Workers" estimated black unemployment to be more than 25 percent—and probably
higher in central city areas. Against the argument that a public works program making the federal government the employer of last resort would be
too costly, Burke countered that the estimated cost of $12 billion for the full
employment programs the bill would establish was far less than the $19 bil-
lion the government had paid out in 1976 for unemployment benefits and
other related welfare programs.[93]

Testifying before the House subcommittee once again and before the
Senate's Labor and Public Welfare Committee,[94] Coretta King reiterated her

criticism of the trade-off between inflation and unemployment. With the unemployment rate among black youth at a staggering 40 percent, many of these young people faced a bleak future that offered almost no possibilities of work; the country ran the risk that at least some would turn to crime "in a desperate quest for a shred of importance and identity." Mrs. King thought the greatest concern should be the "self-respect and self-confidence drained away as enforced idleness keeps people from the sense of usefulness a job provides."[95]

When the NUL's Jordan testified before the Joint Economic Committee (chaired by Humphrey on the occasion of the thirtieth anniversary of the Employment Act of 1946), he reminded the committee that the act had developed out of fear of a renewed depression; now, thirty years later, there was at least partial confirmation of that fear. The nation was experiencing its highest rate of unemployment since the Great Depression (over 8 percent). Furthermore, joblessness was not spread equally; it was concentrated "on those whose opportunities [were] already unequal because of the effects of racial discrimination." Although the overall official unemployment rate for blacks was 12.9 percent, the league believed a more accurate rate was 24.6 percent.[96]

Jordan, like those who had testified earlier, put the bill in a universal perspective by defining it in terms of costs and benefits. Socially, the high cost of unemployment reflected a dangerous divisiveness in society: on economic grounds, it revealed a tremendous waste of human resources; on budgetary grounds, a gross miscalculation of national priorities. "For every million unemployed, it costs the Federal Government some $16 billion in lost taxes and in necessary support payments." Surely it would be wiser to invest in job creation and manpower training that would bring productive jobs to the unemployed.[97]

To illustrate the advantages of investing in such policies, Jordan described NUL's labor education advancement program, funded by the federal government. Since 1967 the NUL had spent $22 million on counseling, training, and helping to find jobs for minority individuals in the construction trade. Jordan said some would call this "social spending" when it should actually be called "an investment," with a return that would be "envied by anyone on Wall Street." The NUL had found jobs for sixteen thousand people, many in nontraditional jobs or in construction jobs once barred to blacks. By 1975 those sixteen thousand workers had earned over $380 million in salaries, and since 1967 the government had received over $90 million back in taxes on these earnings. Here, then, was an effective program that needed to be replicated on a larger scale.[98]

Jimmy Carter, as the 1976 Democratic nominee for president, had remained a member of the National Full Employment Action Committee during his campaign for office, and civil rights organizations tried to get a strong endorsement statement from him. (Coretta King said he had signed on while governor of Georgia, and although he was never active in the organization, at no time had he asked her to remove his name from the list.)[99] Carter avoided endorsing the Humphrey-Hawkins bill until late in his campaign. (This late endorsement was regarded by the CBC as an attempt to appease African-Americans after he had used the term "ethnic purity" while responding to a question about housing discrimination.)[100]

When Carter became president and did not support the bill, the CBC accused him of reneging on his campaign promise when it launched a massive drive promoting passage of the act as its highest priority of the 1978 legislative agenda. The CBC enlisted the help of civil rights organizations: "It is not enough that a few 'leaders' endorse the legislation—what is needed is a groundswell at the grass roots level throughout the country directed at members of Congress." The CBC pointed out that although 53 percent of the black population was in the South, representatives of at least ten southern states had "not yet seen fit to support legislation that affects so many of their constituents." It asked organizations to conduct a letter-writing campaign and to arrange lobbying groups to meet with elected officials during the February recess.[101] Such activities made little difference to the progress of the bill.

When Brown testified again before Hawkins's committee, he assured him that the NUL was in full support of the amended bill but thought that some sections needed to be strengthened. The bill proposed five-year goals that would determine when countercyclical measures, such as a public works program, would be implemented with "every effort . . . made to reduce differences among teenagers, women, minorities." The NUL thought that each of the five-year goals should include "complementary" objectives with a specific strategy to reduce unemployment among these groups.[102] Relying on the overall unemployment rate to implement policies would be extremely unfair in areas where unemployment was considerably higher than the national rate indicated. Statistics clearly showed that "specific targeting was essential" if the administration was "serious about attacking unemployment, particularly in federally defined poverty areas."[103]

The NUL was also troubled with the bill's "old reservoir job concept" because this meant that people "at the lower end of the economic spectrum"—in other words, those who were the least skilled and who had the greatest difficulty finding work in the private sector—would be relegated to the most unattractive projects. Such a policy penalized the jobless for a plight caused by the downturn of the economy, not by them, and trapped them in a punitive program that offered little or no opportunities for getting out, unless they were given special consideration.[104]

When a watered-down version of the bill was passed by the House, the National Committee for Full Employment claimed its "massive grass roots pressure" and "effective coalition lobbying" had paid off.[105] It urged supporters to make an all-out effort to press for passage of the bill at this time because it was unlikely that an opportunity to pass full employment legislation would "come again for many, many years."[106] When Carter finally endorsed the bill, the National Committee noted that "we face the final battle to pass Humphrey-Hawkins." Most important now was to prevent a filibuster and attempts to further weaken the bill in the Senate. Continued grassroots pressure was crucial.[107]

When the act finally passed, NUL's Washington Bureau cited it as one of its 1978 "legislative victories."[108] Hawkins thought the fact that the House and the Senate had been able to come to an agreement and pass the act was an immense achievement.[109] On the positive side, there was at last some official recognition of unemployment as a serious problem. The act acknowledged that "unemployment exposed families to social, psychological, and physiological costs, including disruption of family life, loss of individual dignity and self-respect, and the aggravation of physical and psychological illnesses, alcoholism and drug abuse, crime, and social conflicts."[110] The civil rights organizations could appreciate this language because it gave credence to what they had been saying for many years.

Nevertheless, the act was a very weak version of the original bill. The government was no longer required to provide "last resort" jobs for the unemployed. It "permitted" the president to establish a "reservoir of public employment" but did not mandate any specific trigger for this. Furthermore, a public employment program could not be created until the act had been in operation for two years. When, if ever, it was set up, it had to protect the private sector. The jobs were to be useful, in the lower ranges of pay, and targeted at areas with the worst unemployment problems.[111] This seemed to express the worst fears of the organizations—truly a description of a "reservoir job program" without any special efforts to help those in the program advance to better jobs, as proposed by the NUL.

Essentially, the Full Employment and Balanced Growth Act of 1978 was a law of good intentions that established laudable goals and put forward a declaration of principles, but without any enforcement policies. It did not include the NUL's suggestion regarding specific strategies for reducing unemployment among disadvantaged groups. Instead, "every effort" was to be made "to reduce those differences between the rates of unemployment among youth, women, minorities, . . . and other labor groups." The secretary of labor was to "take such action as practicable to achieve the objective."[112] Wage and price controls would not be used to control inflation. This would be done by monitoring inflation (which could be interpreted as allowing the unemployment rate to increase), and instituting other measures that were dependent on the cooperation of the private-sector economy.[113] The act offered no real immediate relief to the long-term unemployed; thus, many had no alternative but to rely on a punitive welfare system to survive.

To the civil rights organizations, a full employment policy was the personification of welfare reform, and although the Full Employment and Balanced Growth Act had little resemblance to Hawkins's original bill, they regarded its passage as a victory. They felt a shared ownership in the act because it had been introduced by Hawkins, a black congressman and, at least originally, it had included policies that would have made a significant difference to their constituents. Civil rights groups appreciated the act's recognition that many social problems were directly related to structural unemployment rather than to some mistakenly perceived pathology among the poor. They hoped the act's passage would prove to be a harbinger for future legislation to reduce poverty through employment programs. However, this was not to be. With the election of Ronald Reagan in 1980, the country became decidedly more conservative and increasingly less supportive of the civil rights organizations' dual agenda.

TEN

Confronting Conservative Policies: The 1980s

The Republicans and Black Conservatives

On December 12–13, 1980, one month after Ronald Reagan was elected president, a conference of mostly black conservatives was held at the Fairmont Hotel in San Francisco. Sponsored by the Institute for Contemporary Studies, approximately fifty people assembled to talk about specific ideas and policies the incoming presidential administration should consider in dealing with black Americans. The main representative of the incoming administration was Edwin Meese III, already designated as counselor to the president with cabinet rank (and later to serve as attorney general). It was an interracial gathering: conservative economists Milton Friedman and Michael J. Boskin were there and made presentations. Not all the blacks were conservatives or Republicans: former Manhattan Borough President Percy E. Sutton (a Democrat); economist Bernard Anderson; political scientist Martin L. Kilson.

This was, however, distinctly a conference to give voice to what was called new ways of thinking about and approaching social policies affecting black Americans. As such, no one doubted that most of the blacks in attendance were quite pleased with the election of Republican Reagan over Democrat Jimmy Carter. And these were the blacks who could be expected to play significant roles in the new administration. They were not part of the established civil rights groups, at least not in national leadership roles. One, Clarence M. Pendleton, Jr., was, indeed, president of the San Diego Urban League and would be appointed to chair the United States Civil Rights

Commission. Another participant was Clarence Thomas, then aide to Sen. John C. Danforth, and eleven years later to be appointed to the United States Supreme Court.

The tone of the conference was upbeat and more than a little optimistic about what might come from such a gathering. This was the first time a new president had clearly given his stamp of approval to a group of black conservatives in such an open, sympathetic manner. And the conference was widely covered by the media. Black conservatives had voiced their views for years on various issues, though they were usually at odds with the major civil rights leaders. But up to now they had mainly been confined to small conservative forums and were hardly accorded a mass following in the black communities. They had challenged the established civil rights groups on a range of issues including school busing, the "war on poverty" programs, full employment proposals, affirmative action policies, and the role of government in the economy. Now they would be more visible, more vocal, and, they hoped, much more influential.

Edwin Meese promised as much:

> This conference is more than just another event. It is a significant starting point. . . . The fact that people are talking about pluralism is directly at odds with what I saw the other day when I attended a meeting, along with the then president-elect, with some of the people who purport to represent the leadership of the black community. [Reagan had recently met with leaders of the major civil rights organizations.] I am not in any way disagreeing or putting them down, but I think the difference between that meeting and this conference is significant. They were talking about the last ten years. You are talking about the ideas of the next ten years or beyond.[1]

The Fairmont conference proposed very different philosophical and programmatic ideas from those coming from the civil rights groups over the previous five decades. This was the foremost attraction of the Fairmont group to the incoming Reagan administration. Their stated views challenged what they considered to be the hegemony enjoyed by the civil rights groups in discussions of policies pertaining to blacks. They strongly believed that those groups were not as representative of the black masses as was popularly perceived and portrayed in the media. For the moment, it was not important precisely how influential *they* were with the black masses. The fact that 86 percent of the black electorate had voted for Reagan's opponent was not the main point of concern. There was hope that now their views would be given increased access to the highest councils of governance. This new fact alone might provide them a degree of credibility—with both blacks and whites—they had never experienced.

These were some of the black people the new administration hoped would significantly change the racial/social welfare policy debate in the country. The president of the Institute for Contemporary Studies, Glenn Campbell, suggested that the conference even stirred "a national debate . . . on who speaks for blacks, and where future progress may be found."[2]

The black conservatives proceeded to lay out the main points of their disagreement with established civil rights leaders. Foremost was the view that too much reliance was placed on government-supported welfare programs. Such programs mainly created and perpetuated a dependent class. Rent controls and minimum wage laws severely harmed the poor, young, and blacks in particular. Not enough attention was paid to the actual effect such laws had on those supposedly to be helped. Government welfare programs largely created jobs for middle-class bureaucrats and social workers who made a living off of servicing the "underclass." The black conservatives advocated an educational voucher system to permit the poor to send their children to private schools, just as more affluent parents were able to do.[3]

Much more emphasis should be placed on freeing the market economy from too much government regulation and planning. Future associate justice Clarence Thomas told the conference: "Personally, I believe that, as black people beginning the 1980s, we need to look to ourselves for solutions, not forgetting the preclusive practices that have occurred, but definitely putting the primary role, the primary responsibility for the solution to these problems on ourselves."[4]

Time and again during the two-day conference and in subsequent writings from this group and others who shared their views was the conclusion that most black Americans were not well served by the leadership of the old-line civil rights organizations. Those groups, tied to outmoded "liberal nostrums," were not prepared to lead the black masses to the new stage of struggle for self-sufficiency and economic development.[5]

Such ideas, understandably, resonated well with new Reagan officials. The incoming conservative administration could identify with this kind of thinking, especially when it came from black scholars, entrepreneurs, and activists. These presented a welcome relief from the refrain heard for so many years from leaders of the established civil rights organizations.[6]

Thus, fortified with these views from a newly visible force, President Reagan could go before the annual meeting of the NAACP in June 1981, assured that even if *that* particular audience did not agree with him, there were other ideologically compatible blacks who did. The new president accepted the invitation and gave a polite and clear sketch of what that organization and the country could expect from his tenure in office in regard to civil rights and social welfare policies.

"We cannot be tied to the old ways of solving our economic and racial problems," Reagan told the NAACP audience.[7] Such old ways meant relying on the massive federal programs of the 1960s and 1970s. Such programs did not work, "despite [as with education] a massive influx of Federal aid." Such programs failed, and they increased frustration and mistrust. The best approach was to insure "a strong, growing economy without inflation." This was "an absolute moral imperative." Jobs should (and could) be created by and in the private sector, not by the government. The private sector would be able to do this if it were relieved of the burden of high taxes, inflation, and cumbersome regulations. "The Government can provide subsistence, yes, but it seldom moves people up the economic ladder. . . . Free enterprise is a powerful workhorse that can solve many problems of the black community that government alone can no longer solve."[8]

Reagan endorsed the idea of "free enterprise zones" and articulated his support for historically black colleges. He opposed school busing as a means of achieving desegregated schools. He promised that his administration would not tolerate racial discrimination by the government and that there would be no "retreat on the Nation's commitment to equal treatment of all citizens." To be sure, he was proposing budget cuts, he said, but contrary to those who were either ignorant or "practicing, for political reasons, pure demagoguery," these budget savings would help, not harm, the poor in the long run. And this was the case precisely because his fiscal policies were aimed at strengthening the market economy, which would redound to everybody's benefit—the rich and the poor as well as all racial and ethnic groups.[9]

That was it. That was the new president's promise to traditional civil rights forces; the decade was launched. Reagan biographer Lou Cannon reported that the NAACP audience gave Reagan "one of the coolest receptions of his presidency."[10]

Summits, Agendas, and Policy Arguments

Even before Reagan's election, civil rights groups christened the decade with their own "black agenda" conference. More than one thousand black leaders representing over three hundred organizations (national and local) convened in Richmond, Virginia, from February 28 to March 2, 1980 "to adopt a national political, social, economic and international agenda for the decade of the Eighties."[11] The major civil rights groups played prominent roles.[12] The three-day meeting held several workshops—on jobs, inflation, economic policy, housing, urban and rural development, business and economic development, labor markets, education, income maintenance, health, criminal justice, U.S. foreign policy, U.S.–South African relations, African and Caribbean economic development, and voter mobilization as well as on political parties, "using the Census to achieve political and economic objectives," civil rights enforcement and expansion, the Equal Rights Amendment, black youth, and media ownership and management.

With such a large list, clearly only the broadest of statements and recommendations could emanate from the gathering. For the most part, that was precisely the result. Indeed, most of the 119 recommendations were a mix of general policy preferences cumulated over the past several years outlining a set of ideas that were at variance with both black conservatives and a distinctly possible future Reagan administration. The conference's "black agenda" called for an active national governmental role in the economy and strong enforcement of civil rights.

In many instances, the "agenda" did address matters that participants felt should be dealt with by blacks themselves, such as forming local pressure groups "to place greater demands on the political system" and developing stronger black organizational support "for African liberation groups" in South Africa. More reliance on black churches was stressed as a means to broaden mass political support. On crime, "national attention" should be focused on "crime prevention and rehabilitation of the criminal offender particularly while the offender is confined within the penal institution."

Over the coming decade, black conservatives, especially, would condemn the established groups as not concentrating enough on self-help efforts and on what blacks themselves could do to alleviate their own problems. This would apply notably to efforts at instilling a greater sense of moral values and family bonds. Too much emphasis was placed, they would contend, on what the government should do for blacks who perceived themselves as "victims" of racism.[13]

On some matters, however, the Richmond "black agenda" was more specific, particularly when addressing what some federal policies should be. The final recommendations, for example, opposed the death penalty, supported "prenatal care for all women, regardless of financial status," and opposed renewal of the selective service registration and the draft. Unconditional support "for a full employment program which provides jobs at decent wages for all who need and want them" was specifically mentioned in three places in the final report. There was a call for a guaranteed income "within 25% of a decent standard of living as defined by the BLS," as well as for "comprehensive health care services to all Americans, equally, regardless of economic status." These were old issues, of course, which had been rejected as politically unfeasible and economically too costly, but the black organizations had to keep their record of commitment intact. In addition, they opposed the way federal money was being allocated to urban and rural areas: "Greater emphasis should be placed on categorical programs and specific targeting of development programs on the most distressed communities. Entitlement programs like general revenue-sharing should be de-emphasized."[14]

Neither was the conference inhibited in calling for direct aid to black entrepreneurs and contractors: "There should be specific minority set-asides in the National Public Works and Economic Development Act."[15]

The final document clearly sought to combine both the civil rights and social welfare agendas. Both the conference and its final report obviously intended to speak to the encompassing interests of a mass black constituency at all economic levels. At once too comprehensive to be the focus of concerted political action and too general in some instances to serve as a means to mobilize follow-up activity, the report was not a call to single unified action, nor was it meant to be.

This process of holding large meetings, frequently labeled "summits," became a familiar feature during the 1980s. In addition to the annual conventions of the civil rights organizations, other groups came on the scene to articulate essentially the same ideological views regarding social welfare policies—and to hold "summits." Invariably, a laundry list of resolutions covering both civil rights and social welfare matters would be issued and, as often as not, labeled "a Black Agenda." But equally as often, such groups also took pains to emphasize that their recommendations were intended to help *all* Americans, not just blacks.

In the spring of 1984, the NUL and NAACP cosponsored a major conference, "The Black Family Summit," at Fisk University in Nashville, Tennessee, to deal, yet again, with the worsening "crisis" of the black family under the fiscally constraining policies of the Reagan administration. More than 175 representatives from national black organizations—civic, religious, political, and educational—attended the three-day meeting. The issues raised were the same as those addressed at countless other "summits" over the years but this time with the added urgency of how to mount an effective challenge to the current mood and especially to the increased attention being paid in the media to the outspoken black conservatives, some of whom now held high national administrative posts. This was not, to be sure, the first time the groups had had to contend with conservatives in pursuing the dual agenda, but the 1980s differed in significant ways from previous times. Now, with important civil rights laws on the books, and the passage of long-needed social welfare legislation in the 1960s, the Reagan administration was pursuing national policies which, in the eyes of civil rights groups, would not only slow down the process of responsive federal involvement but actually *reverse* that trend. Even the Supreme Court could no longer be viewed as a viable alternative to check conservative tendencies. The Court itself was becoming more conservative, and the appointment of Clarence Thomas in 1991 to fill the vacancy left by Thurgood Marshall during the Bush administration was an added blow to the prospects of the dual agenda. (At the Fairmont conference, Thomas had been one of the strongest critics of the traditional civil rights organizations.) Many in the civil rights groups felt besieged as the prospect loomed that even the gains made thus far could be wiped out. Clearly it was vital for the groups to mount new defensive and counteroffensive strategies on both the civil rights and social welfare fronts.

Yet many of the recommendations of the Fisk conference amounted to little more than extended general statements of good intentions and liberal philosophical leanings. For example, on single-parent black families: "Socialize children of both sexes to understand and appreciate equality in roles and the need for sharing." "Facilitate the involvement of fathers in parenting." "Give equal attention and concern to rearing of responsible sons and daughters." These are hardly controversial prescriptions, nor, given the nature of the problem, were they likely to provide much guidance or real insight into just how to implement such nice-sounding general "charges."

Interestingly, the Fisk conference was preceded two months earlier by a meeting of 755 participants at the fourth annual meeting of the National Policy Institute in Washington, D.C., a gathering cosponsored by relatively new black leadership groups on the national scene. While not precisely "civil rights" organizations per se, they developed out of the electoral (and appointive) political arena, and their membership included Democrats and Republicans. The cosponsors were the Joint Center for Political Studies (a think tank founded in 1970, which became the Joint Center for Political and Economic Studies after 1991), the Congressional Black Caucus, the Judicial Council of the National Bar Association (black judges), the National Association of Black County Officials, the National Black Caucus of Local Elected Officials, the National Black Caucus of State Legislators, the National Caucus of Black School Board Members, and the National Conference of Black Mayors.

The agenda was virtually the same as that dealt with at the Fisk conference only a couple of months later and, indeed, at every other such large summit-type meeting of black leaders throughout the decade. In the 1980s there was the sense of, if not a new, at least a certainly heightened level of "political activity" occurring (namely, convening and attending "summits" on the "crisis" in the black communities). But why were there so many separate meetings, sometimes with overlapping attendance, with virtually the same agendas and reasonably predictable similar recommendations? Several possible answers explain this almost frenetic conference-going throughout the decade.

First, by the 1970s and 1980s many more national (and locally based) African-American groups had come into existence. The several organizations of national and statewide black elected officials offer good examples. Each felt compelled to articulate its position for the record on issues— whether civil rights and race, or social welfare policies and programs—that clearly brought them into focus as distinctive organizations.

Next, big meetings presented a way to attract media attention—as the mass marches had done in the 1960s—with the important-sounding sobriquet of "summit" added to the mix. This implied a high-level, serious-minded meeting of minds "to plot strategy" and to set definitive guidelines for future action. The larger the group, the greater the likelihood of media coverage. Clearly, these various meetings also served to put a stamp of "legitimacy" on "prominent leaders" for the conveners as well as the attendees. This was no minor consideration in a time when so many groups and individuals were vying for the leadership spotlight.

A third reason is evident since almost every "summit" featured presentations from a new cadre of mostly black policy experts and activists, all armed with the latest up-to-the-minute empirical studies. Without question, conference discussions were strong on data and description, weaker on specific proposals, and weaker still on the exact political analyses needed to implement the many proposals. In fact, a careful review of many conference and "summit" reports and documents reveals virtually no attention to the latter subject—except the usual general call for the need "to lobby" and "to mount voter registration and get-out-the-vote" campaigns. In this sense, the meetings, in addition to being much larger, differed strikingly both in tone and substance from the strategy meetings held in earlier decades when NAACP and NUL representatives discussed where and how to get votes in congressional committees for support of particular measures. This sort of information surely was available in the 1980s, but it was not the kind of discussion that would hold the attention of hundreds at a two-day "policy" conference. And the media seemed more interested in short and simple sound-bites than in more intimate but complex political calculations on how to persuade a few reluctant members of Congress to support one's position.

Such "summits" were also held, in all likelihood, because the organizations, so besieged by the conservative mood in the country, felt obliged to state and restate their opposition to that mood as often as possible. This was important, lest the conservative arguments (not to mention policies) be accepted by default.

Neither should one overlook the need to hold such meetings if only to bolster the morale of group members who were constantly being confronted with charges that their organization's leaders were becoming ineffective and irrelevant. Conducting meetings and pronouncing positions, however general, at least showed where one stood on the issues and demonstrated that one had not wavered in long-standing commitments to civil rights and progressive social welfare policies. It would not be too far-fetched to suggest that "mass meetings" in the 1980s replaced the "mass marches" of the 1960s as vehicles of popular political expression and protest.

Civil rights groups of course knew that summits and reports alone were not sufficient to deal with the issues. They continued to operate in the less visible world of congressional hearings, commenting on specific bills and offering alternatives. They were also aware of the subdued reception they were getting from a budget-conscious, deficit-fearing Congress. In 1980, when SCLC representative Raymond Fauntroy testified on national health insurance to support a comprehensive plan put forth by black congressman Ronald Dellums (D, Calif.), he was advised not to call for a complete over-haul of the nation's health system. That, according to Congressman Cecil Heftel (D, Hawaii), was unrealistic. It would be better to focus on how to get "the so-called Medicaid dollars into a better way of serving the poor areas of the country."[16] The country was not interested in changing what it had, so why not work on ways to provide help "particularly to the poor blacks." To advocate for a national health system was living in "euphoria," and the con-gressman concluded: "We know it is legislatively impossible" and that the country was not "ready to abdicate the present system."[17]

This was a congressional response civil rights groups had been hearing for decades. (They heard the same admonition in the 1960s in response to the Freedom Budget.) They were ahead of (or at least out of step with) the times, but they cannot be accused of not having raised the issues. Still, the world of intricate policy-making was far different from the consensual and receptive world of the black leadership summits.

The best way to achieve better results in gaining effective social welfare policies, it appeared, at least in the near term, was for particular groups to focus their activity upon specific issues and then attempt to mobilize sup-port. Such efforts could be seen in the constant flow of testimony before con-gressional committees by civil rights groups. Here, as always, they marshaled their data, allied themselves with other groups where possible, and presented their arguments. Broad generalizations were of little value in such forums. Realizing that the conservative tide had set in both on Capitol Hill and in the White House, civil rights organizations nevertheless pursued their arduous task, supporting and opposing particular legislation, citing achievements and failures of certain programs, all the while fully aware that influencing lawmakers with the power to vote proposals up or down was far more cru-cial than issuing "black agendas" that might, at most, attract ephemeral media attention.

On a more positive note, beginning in the 1970s and continuing into the

1980s there was a marked increase in African-American members of Congress, which greatly enhanced opportunities to introduce bills, hold hearings, and provide forums for civil rights groups to articulate their views. This was a decided change, brought about by the successful utilization of the Voting Rights Act of 1965, which permitted black voters to elect more blacks to Congress. This historic law, along with plans that allowed the boundaries of certain congressional districts to be redrawn, resulted in an increase in membership of African-Americans in Congress from four in 1966 to forty-one in 1994. Therefore, civil rights groups were not without sympathetic friends in Congress— both black and white—albeit not nearly sufficient in number to offset the growing conservative forces in Congress and the country. Notwithstanding this formidable political hurdle, civil rights groups continued to pursue their dual agenda. As could be expected, they never lost an opportunity to press their policy preferences, especially on the perennial issue of employment.

Supporting the main provisions of the Youth Employment Act of 1979, Robert McAlpine of the NUL told a House subcommittee that more efforts should be placed on providing elementary school students, before they became teenagers, with job skills.[18] The NUL was careful to point out that some proposed amendments allocated job-training funds on the basis of *adult* unemployment data. This was unacceptable. What was more relevant was to look at the unemployment rates of minority *youth*; thus, the law would be led to "target" the places of greatest need.

Without question, the NUL most strongly espoused approaches that sought to put the largest amount of money where the need was greatest. This was the case in its support of the Targeted Jobs Tax Credit. This policy, established in 1978, provided tax relief to those employers who hired employees deemed "structurally and chronically unemployed." In the NUL's view, the program had great potential but was hampered by poor coordination between government agencies and potential private-sector employers. The law permitted employers to apply for tax credits retroactively; employers thus gained a subsidy for employees they had already hired. The NUL considered this idea to be inexpedient. "Some employers now benefiting from the tax credits weren't even aware of the program's existence prior to hiring, and then they were allowed to accrue a financial gain without necessarily altering their hiring practices."[19] Unfortunately, at least 80 per cent of the subsidized employees fell into this category, the NUL noted.

The essential component of a successful tax program is the incentive factor that makes hiring from targeted groups desirable. With the retroactive certification, this measure is absent and subject to, we believe, exploitation amounting to incalculable losses in Federal revenues.[20]

The Urban League wanted the retroactive certification process to be rescinded so that "a higher allocation of the subsidies provided under the program . . . [could be] used to stimulate new employment."

The NAACP, in turn, reiterated its adamant opposition to the familiar conservative argument for paying subminimum wages to young workers. According to that argument, new young workers receiving less than the minimum wage would get valuable work experience that would allow them to move up the labor market ladder; at the same time, employers would not be inclined to reduce their workforce in the face of higher wages for workers who more than likely were not worth even the minimum wage. The NAACP opposed any youth minimum wage differential. The organization's position was that youth hired below the minimum wage would, in all probability, *not* receive the "kind of skill and/or training which will prepare them for upward mobility in the workforce." Indeed, most entry-level jobs actually require minimal training and skill. And, unfortunately, the racial component itself could not be overlooked. The NAACP concluded:

A subminimum wage would have a disparate impact on black youth. Black youth, already suffering from racial discrimination in the workforce, would probably have a reduced chance of being hired inasmuch as business and industry is moving to the suburbs. This would be compounded by the fact that the lowered wage would result in decreased purchasing power and a substantially lowered standard of living, which runs counter to the legislative intent of the Fair Labor Standards Act which calls for a minimum wage consistent with a minimum standard of living for all workers. . . . The group with the most to gain from a youth differential is the employer who could make high profits as a result of "cheap labor."[21]

The National Urban League joined in a coalition with eighteen other groups appearing before Congress to support proposals to extend youth employment and demonstration programs (S. 648). These proposals had been made by Sen. Dan Quayle (R, Ind.), chairman of a senate subcommittee pushing the bill (and, later, vice president under George Bush); the NUL indicated its approval of the senator's efforts. Expressing "nervousness," however, about ideas of subminimum wages for youth, the NUL highlighted some results it was getting from government-sponsored youth training programs but warned that the various programs had to be seen as a "package." Some critics attacked particular jobs programs, but the NUL's point was that the entire family ought to be the focus, "not just in terms of a CETA job, but in terms of the food stamps that are available to the family, the housing that is available to the family, the whole need of that individual family."[22]

The NUL was characteristically wary of giving too much power to the states through block grants, as had been started under the Nixon administration in the 1970s.

> To grant States almost total responsibility for planning and implementation at this time would dangerously expose the comprehensive jobs training concept to the vulnerabilities of local voting blocs and political pressures. . . . Therefore, we recommend the maintenance of the present Prime Sponsor system with a strong federal role for oversight and monitoring.[23]

All the programs should be targeted to the "economically disadvantaged," but those groups "with significant barriers to employment" (e.g., the disabled, the homeless, and those with minor criminal records) should "be given priority status after entrance into the program." Moreover, community-based organizations should be "explicitly mandated as eligible service deliverers." All the proposed job-training bills emphasized a "partnership between for-profit and non-profit organizations." Realizing a growing mood in Congress to tie job training more closely to private corporations, the Urban League sounded a note of caution and realism about such an approach: "While we agree with this, we must also point out that many among corporate America, who are friends of the NUL, admit that they are not suited to serve the hardcore structurally unemployed."[24]

In 1982 the Job Training Partnership Act (JTPA) was passed, replacing CETA. JTPA, more in line than CETA with the ideological goals of the Reagan administration, channeled federal funds directly to private businesses rather than through local governments. In 1986 an official of NUL presented Congress with an assessment of that organization's experience with JTPA in twelve localities on the West Coast.[25] One problem was evident. Many trainees needed financial support such as child care in order to participate in the program. The JTPA funds only allowed for reimbursement of transportation. This seriously hampered recruitment of potential program participants.

There was continuing concern over just how helpful the business executives would be who served on the Private Industrial Councils (PICs) that had charge of local JTPA programs. In spite of (or perhaps because of) the NUL's long history of working with the private business sector in providing jobs (which was described at the congressional hearing), the organization could not be optimistic that the participation and interest of top executives would be more than superficial. The NUL knew from experience that better job-hiring results came about only when high-level management decided to become seriously involved. The group's testimony was candid on this point:

> In some communities we find that private-sector leadership is not involved as envisioned. There are very beautiful statements and so on, but their personal involvement is not there. Lower level management personnel serve on the PIC and they are often unable to deliver in terms of job opportunities for persons trained through the programs.[26]

The NUL clearly preferred the federal government to take a more active role in conjunction with such social service programs. But the league recognized that the conservative mood in Washington sought to diminish, not increase, the national government's involvement in favor of private-sector participation. The political climate was not conducive to the ideas or desires of the NUL or any of the other civil rights groups.[27] "The issue is not welfare or compensation, but jobs," one NUL official told Congress in 1984. "For this to occur across the jobs field, Government must become the prime mover of employment initiatives."[28]

At the same time, civil rights groups were sensitive to the politics surrounding various programs (such as job training), which sought to include the less needy . Efforts "targeting" or restricting benefits to only those who needed help the most were frequently thwarted by legislators who insisted that *their* constituents also be allowed to receive benefits, thereby spreading already scarce resources even thinner. As the NUL official told the congressional committee:

> If we look at the programs for youth, the YEDPA [Youth Employment Development Program Act] programs, there are provisions which will allow young people from middle-income America, if you will, to participate in those programs. We have as a part of our political structure decided every program not here virtually ought to provide a little bit for my constituency and your constituency, and so on. . . . The politics have far outweighed [the] goal.[29]

Likewise, civil rights groups fully understood that the more specific the national grants of funds were, the better. That is, "categorical grants" that stipulated fairly precisely just how local and state authorities could spend the money (say, for health, education, housing, or employment) were far more preferable than "block grants," which spread funds over too broad a field. Giving states and localities such unrestricted leeway often meant that the neediest citizens, who of course had little political influence, would be short-changed in allocation decisions. The NAACP clearly spelled out the political consequences:

> The net effect of shifting from categorical grants to smaller block grants in various employment, health and human services, and education programs would very likely be negative for blacks and other minorities. Part of the neg-ative effect could be traced to the known insensitivity of State legislatures and city halls to minority populations at state and local levels, part is due to the inherent nature of those human capital-type programs as compared to phys-ical capital-type programs and the commitment of organized and powerful private interests to the latter.[30]

At least one conservative congressman, Jack Kemp (R, N.Y.), strongly advocated the use of "enterprise zones," a concept not entirely unattractive to civil rights groups and, therefore, not automatically rejected out of hand by them. In fact, the notion had many elements of targeting and potential job creation that they found appealing. Essentially, the idea was to use fed-eral, state, and local tax incentives to lure private businesses to areas of high unemployment and low income. (As such, it was not too dissimilar to the Area Redevelopment Act of the 1960s under the Kennedy administration.) A business that agreed to locate its facilities in such "zones" could be offered tax rebates on payroll and property taxes, or funds to build access roads, or given other possible inducements. Certainly, the inner cities could benefit economically, presuming that companies would employ local residents. Both the NUL and NAACP were receptive to such a proposal. The NUL in fact saw it as a chance to revitalize the inner cities while providing residents with some hope to participate in the process. Enterprise zones had "the potential for helping to do both," and "promising much."[31] But the NUL worried that other tax incentives might compete with this plan by trying to entice corporations to move out of the cities and build new plants in subur-ban areas. The NUL hoped this would not happen and suggested that "incentives . . . should be narrowly targeted to create jobs where they are needed most." This would make tax breaks "for the rehabilitation of aging plants" more likely than for building new ones. Any proposal that made it more attractive *to stay in* or *move to* the inner cities was welcomed, but "we are cognizant of the potential failure of such a proposal should businesses be granted even greater concessions for moving away from the urban area."[32]

As the 1980s proceeded, it became evident that finding ways to cut the budget would dominate much of the country's fiscal policy. And social welfare programs were seriously vulnerable. Not only did civil rights organizations face the task of offering (as they had always done) their own ideas and proposals for *expanding* social welfare programs, now they had to confront the acute challenge of fighting a defensive battle, of trying to stem the forces intent on cutting back or eliminating many of the programs already passed.

Budget Battles

Without question, there was throughout the eight years of the Reagan presidency no love lost between civil rights organizations and that administration. And statements from President Reagan impugning the motivations and veracity of civil rights leaders did nothing to alleviate the mutual hostility. At one point near the end of his second term, Reagan suggested that some leaders continued to emphasize racism and the plight of blacks as a way of maintaining their leadership. He wondered "if they [civil rights leaders] really want what they say they want. Because some of those leaders are doing very well leading organizations based on keeping alive the feeling that they're victims of prejudice."[33] From the beginning of his administration, Reagan had promised to chart a less governmentally involved course regarding social welfare issues, one almost 180 degrees opposite that pursued for decades by civil rights groups.

This intent was reflected in the several budgets the administration presented to Congress each year. There were cuts either in the actual amount of spending or on the growth of spending on many social welfare programs, to the chagrin of civil rights leaders, many of whom consistently testified against those reductions.[34] The Congressional Black Caucus took the lead in defending against the decreased spending by annually offering its own "alternative budget" proposals. And each year the CBC's budgets were ritualistically voted down.[35] Invariably, the CBC called for more social welfare spending and rejected the tax cuts for the wealthiest taxpayers. These items, obviously, reflected the thinking of civil rights groups. The CBC proposed reduced taxes for lower-income workers and favored increasing deductions for those same taxpayers; also, the Earned Income Tax Credit should be increased, and tax incentives for businesses in "targeted areas" of low employment should be passed.

There was substantial interaction between the various members and staffs of the CBC and those of the civil rights organizations. They attended one another's annual conventions as major speakers, participated in each other's workshops, and shared policy statements and political information. Therefore, it was not surprising to see civil rights leaders testifying on the budgets in the same vein as CBC members. The NUL's John Jacob lamented the proposed elimination of such social welfare programs as the Community Services Block Grants, Legal Services, and Urban Development Action Grants. In 1986 he told the House Committee on the Budget, "The single most serious problem facing the black community is employment"—a conclusion the civil rights organizations had been drawing for at least five decades.[36] "But job creation and job-training programs have been destroyed or cut heavily and this proposed [FY 1987] budget continues the national neglect of economic opportunities for the poor." The NUL realized that the new budget law (the Gramm-Rudman-Hollings bill, discussed below) had put limits on congressional expenditures in various ways, but this certainly did not prohibit Congress, if it wished, from raising additional revenues by raising the taxes of the affluent. "Poor people have paid for this economic boom and for tax breaks for the affluent with unemployment, reduced survival programs, and shattered hopes. . . . I urge you to prevent further injustices by rewriting this budget in a way that places the needs of the poor at the top of your priority list."[37]

Responding to the demand from some fiscal conservatives for a constitutional amendment to require a balanced budget, the NAACP testified before a Senate committee in 1984 against the idea. Although the organization recognized that budget deficits should be attacked, it considered this idea to be an ill-advised way to go about it. In addition, the NAACP's representative frankly worried about what such an amendment would mean for poor people:

> The NAACP views this and all constitutional amendments to balance the budget as a threat to the poor because it would endanger Federal funding of social and other programs designed to aid the poor, minorities, and distressed areas of our Nation. These very programs are already under attack and have been drastically reduced in ways that are threatening the very survival of the poor in America. The NAACP is confident that a balanced budget amendment would force further cutbacks in these vital areas.[38]

Throughout the decade, the various civil rights organizations sought to fight the budget cuts by entering into temporary coalitions with other groups. This included joining with Hispanics, low-income housing groups, and rural groups to resist cuts by HUD in funding for the Community Services Block Grant program for housing assistance for "low and moderate income persons."[39]

Similar coalition efforts were made regarding government regulatory reforms.[40] The groups understood the desire to eliminate "unnecessary regulation," but they were also concerned that the process of *de*regulation be given the same tight economic analysis as the process involved in regulatory rulemaking (in other words, there might well be as much harmful economic consequences resulting from *de*regulation as from continued regulation). On another front, the NUL joined with several groups to oppose cuts in funds for education.[41]

A significant feature of the civil rights struggle in the 1980s was the two campaigns for the presidency mounted by the Reverend Jesse Jackson. Bringing his experience of two decades of social activism with the SCLC and Operation PUSH (People United to Serve Humanity, an organization he formed in 1971), Jackson had an established record of leadership and a widely admired capacity to mobilize the masses. Under a new organization, the National Rainbow Coalition, Inc., he sought the Democratic presidential nomination in 1984 and 1988, chalking up impressive results in the primaries, especially among black voters. His platforms reflected all the points being raised by civil rights organizations, which added an electoral political dimension to their lobbying efforts. Jackson's campaigns also brought thousands of newly registered black voters onto the voter rolls and into the voting booth, a calculus not to be overlooked in the important process of politicization and mobilization.[42]

Family Support Act of 1988

Social welfare programs ultimately must come from Congress, passing through a labyrinth of institutional processes and political bargaining. In the mid-to-late 1980s, the issue of welfare reform surfaced yet again. As we have seen with the Family Assistance Plan under Nixon, with the fight for full employment and welfare reform under Carter in the 1970s, and again under Reagan, Congress was prepared to address the issue of public assistance.

No one disagreed with the general proposition that it was better for able-bodied adults to be self-supporting than to be on welfare. And it was generally accepted that "dependency," especially the long-term dependency of the able-bodied, was not a desirable condition or prospect. But attaining a condition of "self-sufficient" independence was one thing; *how* to move out of a welfare situation of poverty and dependency that probably took years in the making was quite another.

When the issue was raised in the late 1960s (see chapters 8 and 9), conservatives insisted on an approach that would require recipients to work (in private or public jobs) as part of their eligibility to receive welfare payments. This meant, of course, requiring mothers with small children to leave home for employment, frequently in low-paying jobs. Civil rights groups generally opposed such proposals, seeing them as punitive and inconsiderate of the needs of the children. The idea calcified among conservatives that welfare somehow presented an attractive alternative for many poor adults either (supposedly) unwilling to work or insufficiently trained to get and hold decent-paying jobs in the labor market. In other words, the lack of a job really became a matter of a deficiency on the part of the recipient, a negative attribute of the individual rather than an inherent and systemic structural economic problem. Any number of such negative attributes—laziness or lack of motivation or drug abuse or sexual promiscuity or educational inadequacy—were singularly or collectively lumped together as the main cause(s) of the growing dependency on welfare.

To many liberals, and certainly to most members in the civil rights organizations, such attitudes simply "blamed the victim" and showed no compassion or understanding for those historically locked into a situation not of their own making and often beyond their control except under extraordinary circumstances; out of a long history of deliberately restricted and economically deprived communities (usually the result of opportunities denied by racism, ignorance, and intolerance), many people born into poverty and welfare were destined to remain there without concerted, "targeted" efforts from the *national* government to help lift them out. Civil rights organizations knew the hard facts of persistent welfare status—the glaring headlines and tabloid stories of multigenerational welfare families with grandmothers only in their late-thirties, the shocking number of unwed teenage mothers, the alarmingly high incidence of drugs and crime. Civil rights groups continued to insist, however, that social welfare policy ought not only to consider the need to end dependency (which was certainly desirable) but also to recognize, admit, and engage the tremendous commitment needed to overcome the vast social and economic problems which had spawned a permanent dependent class. By the late 1980s, of course, these old analytical arguments had hardened into ideology when it came time for Congress to take up the subject again.

On one issue there appeared to be an emerging consensus. Many liberals no longer steadfastly opposed the idea that welfare mothers should be required to work outside the home. Several factors helped contribute to the acceptance of this idea, not the least being that working mothers, both relatively affluent and otherwise, were clearly becoming the norm in American society. In 1987 the Department of Labor reported that 64.7 percent of all women in the United States with children under the age of eighteen worked outside the home, and 52.9 percent of women with children under the age of three did so.[43]

A widespread, if not prevailing, view was voiced by Republican senator William L. Armstrong of Ohio: "People ought to work, because it's unfair to ask other people to support them indefinitely."[44] A liberal supporter of welfare reform, Congressman Thomas J. Downey (D, N.Y.), apparently unaware of the long history of the dual agenda of the civil rights organizations, went so far as to suggest: "We have to give the conservatives their due—they always have emphasized the importance of work."[45]

A similar account of the new receptivity to "work" was reported in an interview with Sen. Daniel P. Moynihan, a major player in the legislative battles over welfare. It was now acceptable, the senator concluded, to talk of mothers in the workforce. The reporter paraphrased Moynihan as saying that "many of those who crusaded against 'workfare' programs in the 1970s now take a different view. They admit that requiring work or training from able-bodied recipients can help reduce welfare dependency."[46] This interpretation, as we shall see, was not entirely accurate regarding the views of some civil rights groups. "Workfare" was *not* the same as work or the need for jobs, which civil rights groups had been championing all along.

To be sure, Moynihan had become the most prominent member of Congress to be associated with the welfare issue in the two and a half decades since his report on the Negro Family (see chapter 7) and the fight for the Family Assistance Plan under Nixon (see chapter 9). His expertise on the subject was now highly respected by his colleagues, and even some liberals who had strongly opposed him in the 1960s no longer automatically rejected his views. In 1987, Eleanor Holmes Norton, former head of the Equal Employment Opportunity Commission under President Carter, explained: "I don't see a lot of people thinking about Moynihan in those terms now. Maybe it's because the issue of welfare has become so urgent and Moynihan has spoken with such relevance in today's terms that people are not harking back 20 years ago to an issue that no longer speaks to these times."[47]

Obviously mindful of the controversy which had swirled around his 1965 report, Moynihan was encouraged by what he saw in the late 1980s as the emergence of three general points of consensus: (1) that able-bodied welfare recipients should be required to work or train for jobs; (2) that government had a responsibility to provide job training and child care for those who worked; and (3) that absent parents should be expected to contribute to child support. He was, of course, bitter that the "opportunity" to achieve these goals had been lost two decades earlier ("We lost a whole generation of people and let something metastasize"),[48] but he was now hopeful that a more receptive atmosphere existed. One important element in regard to welfare reform at this time was the National Governors Association (NGA), led by its newly elected chairman, Gov. Bill Clinton of Arkansas. The NGA wanted welfare reform and made this known to the Reagan administration. The NGA was receptive to a recipient work-requirement provision but worried that such a mandate might be expensive and administratively cumbersome. Job training was seen as the key. "Philosophically, I don't have any problem with some kind of work requirement," Clinton said. "But it's counterproductive to substitute make-work for meaningful training."[49] The governors did not want to get too embroiled in specific details, but they did want the Congress and the president to enact a bill that contained the three basic principles Moynihan had articulated.

Moving to specifics, by far the most liberal proposal (H.R. 1720) came from the House Committee on Education and Labor, and would replace AFDC procedures with a "family support" program. States would be required to set up work, education, and training programs for welfare recipients (with the federal government paying 60 percent of the costs), and welfare benefits would be increased. H.R. 1720 had the initial backing of the top Democratic leaders in the House. Jobs in the private sector would be sought through a program called NETWORK (National Education Training Work), with the emphasis on helping long-term welfare recipients and those most likely to become so. Parents with children aged fifteen and under would not be required to participate unless the *state* government made training and day-care services available. Those states raising benefits (a minimum level of at least 15 percent of the state's median income was required) would be given financial incentives. If welfare recipients went off the welfare rolls, they would not lose their Medicaid coverage for nine months or their day-care support for six months. Importantly, *all* states would have to adopt AFDC-UP. If people worked but still received welfare because of their low pay, the first one hundred dollars of earned income per month and 25 percent of additional income would not be counted in computing benefits. In addition, noncustodial parents would be pursued diligently to make child-support payments. The federal government would provide $600 million for five years for child care.

All these provisions had been worked out over several weeks and months of tedious bargaining with the House committee among those wanting more liberal measures and those favoring less. H.R. 1720 finally proposed a total package of $5.5 billion over a five-year period, down from its original proposed cost of $11.8 billion.

Money, usually a major factor in the consideration of any welfare reform bill, presented an especially acute problem this time because Congress was laboring under the constraints of the Balanced Budget and Emergency Deficit Act of 1985 (the Gramm-Rudman-Hollings bill), which mandated certain target levels for deficit reduction each year. Failure to meet these levels would force automatic across-the-board cuts in several social programs. Thus, the more generous goals of House liberals had to be sacrificed. "There's a shortage of money," Congresswoman Barbara B. Kennelly (D, Conn.) remarked. "It's obvious to the whole world we have to scale back our proposals."[50] Senator Moynihan noted an ironic contrast between the current debate and the one over FAP in the early 1970s, commenting that "in the whole two years I was involved with it [FAP]—I never heard the subject of money raised."[51] (While this may reflect Moynihan's experience in that debate, this is not the way Nixon aide H. R. Haldeman presented Nixon's view on FAP, as pointed out in chapter 9.)

Meanwhile, in the Senate, another liberal bill (S. 514), offered by Sen. Edward M. Kennedy (D, Mass.), was making its way through the process. Known as Jobs for Employable Dependent Individuals (JEDI), the bill, meant to amend the JTPA program, authorized the payment of bonuses to states that successfully placed long-term welfare recipients into private-sector jobs. Essentially, therefore, if a former welfare recipient worked in the private sector for one year, the federal government would pay the state an amount equal to 75 percent of the yearly benefits the federal government *would have* provided the state had the welfare recipient remained on welfare. After two years, a 50 percent bonus would be paid, with 25 percent after three years.

The conservatives, especially the Republicans, taking their cue from the Reagan administration, had very different ideas about how the welfare system should be reformed. They wanted much more leeway given to the states to devise their own welfare programs. The liberal H.R. 1720 relied too heavily on national government control to suit conservative taste, and, above all, it was too expensive. Conservatives thought welfare benefits should not be increased at all and that parents whose children were one year and older should be required to participate in the work-training education program. Likewise, AFDC-UP should remain optional for the states to adopt or not. Liberals wanted carefully defined standards for child care; conservatives wanted these standards left to the states to determine. Sen. Robert Dole (R, Kan.) bluntly stated at one point: "I think there's a willingness [to move welfare legislation], but not if it's going to spend a lot of money."[52]

Congressional conservatives were willing, however, to go beyond Reagan's position and agree to some benefits for those making the transition from welfare to work—that is, they were willing to accept education and training programs that aided that process. Especially appealing to conservatives was the idea of workfare, which was widely accepted to mean "exchanging work for benefits" or "working off" benefits. Senator Dole successfully offered an amendment to a Senate bill (S. 1511) that required one parent in a two-parent welfare family to work at least sixteen hours per week in the Community Work Experience Program (CWEP) at public or nonprofit agencies, or in subsidized jobs.[53] Most legislators, liberals and conservatives alike, readily concluded that if Reagan was not to veto a welfare reform bill, it would *have* to contain a workfare provision.

But this provision proved to be not as attractive to some state governors as had initially been anticipated. First, it would be expensive and the federal government was providing only some of the cost. And then the state would have to set up its own work programs and administer them. There was a question, also, about how useful these workfare activities actually would be in providing work experience. Republican governor Thomas H. Kean of New Jersey believed that the money would be better spent on education and training.[54]

The NUL and the Children's Defense Fund were prominent in advocating the positions of their allies in the civil rights community. They concentrated their arguments on three major points. First, they supported the focus on "jobs" but constantly reiterated that this was *not* the same thing as workfare (which mandated labor). Second, they thought the emphasis should be on helping those *most* in need, no small matter considering the outcry over limited resources. And third, they adamantly opposed any abdication of responsibility and authority over welfare programs by the federal government to the states.

On jobs, the NUL liked the idea of giving financial bonuses to those states most successful in training and actually placing people in "living wage jobs."[55] This clearly did not mean "workfare" and the result was the creation of "viable employment" and "real jobs."[56] But the Children's Defense Fund cautioned against relying on "work experience activities" that could "degenerate into punitive mandatory workfare programs."[57] In addition, Marian Wright Edelman stressed the need to accept the fact that in order to talk about jobs for people, it was equally important to focus on other parts of the problem: child care support, income support, and training. And by all means, she kept insisting, "do not go cheap on child care."[58]

The next important point was that, since funds were limited, these should be directed to those *most* in need. As politically difficult as this would be, it was necessary if welfare reform was to be taken seriously. Edelman testified that "in the absence of adequate resources to serve even a majority of adults on AFDC, the great danger is that states will spread their resources too thinly, relying heavily on short-term low-cost intervention and thereby diluting the effectiveness of welfare employment programs."[59]

Complementing this view was the belief that provisions *requiring* people to work were totally unnecessary. The reality was that there were not enough real jobs for those who needed and would accept them, thus emphasis should be placed on filling this need—creating more real jobs. The heavy emphasis on *mandating* workfare programs seemed, to Edelman, motivated by an intent to punish supposedly irresponsible parents. "It is time for us to move away from punishing children because of the judgments that we choose to make about their parents."[60]

The third point stressed by the groups centered on the role of the federal government in the welfare process. Keenly aware that conservative sentiment wanted to give states wider authority to pursue their own welfare reforms through a system of "waivers" granted by the federal government, the NUL felt apprehensive and alarmed at this trend. One official concluded that this would pave the way "for [the] eventual abandonment of 50 years of responsibility and sensitivity on the part of our Federal Government in the employment area."[61]

After two years of extensive hearings, testimony, congressional debates, and bargaining, Congress passed and President Reagan signed the Family Support Act on October 13, 1988. Typical of the complex political process of the American governmental policy-making system, the final result contained some of the provisions advocated by the civil rights organizations but certainly not all. What had started out as a fairly sweeping and ambitious bill (H.R. 1720) supported by liberals and set to cost $11.8 billion over a five-year phase-in period ended up as a considerably more circumscribed $3.34 billion compromise.

The law required certain welfare recipients to participate in newly established "workfare" programs and also directed states to set up education and training programs in which they had to enroll at least 20 percent of the recipients in their jurisdiction over a seven-year period. The jobs program had to be statewide (unless the state could show that this was unfeasible) and the newly created position of Assistant Secretary of Health and Human Services[62] was set to coordinate this program with the current JTPA. Parents with children under the age of three were exempted, but states could require the participation of both parents if child care was guaranteed. One important concern of civil rights groups—that of targeting—was dealt with: at least 55 percent of a state's funds was pegged to go to long-term recipients or to those (under age twenty-four) who were thought likely to become long-term dependents. In implementing the work program, states had to take into account local job opportunities as well as the supportive needs of recipients. States were also expected to provide the costs for transportation to jobs and any other reasonable work-related expenses. Jobs had to pay at least the minimum wage, and recipients required to work could not be used to displace workers already employed or laid off from their jobs.

Regarding child care, states had some discretion in providing such care, with the understanding that certain basic standards of health and safety had to be maintained, whether in established child care centers or in private homes. Automatic withholding of child support payments from an absent parent's paycheck was allowed unless otherwise waived for "good cause," or if both parents agreed to an alternative arrangement. Specific measures were stipulated to tighten procedures for determining paternity and locating absent parents.

Education and training programs aimed at preparing the recipient for a permanent job had to encompass remedial courses, on-the-job-training, English proficiency, "job-readiness activities," or any combination of these. HHS would oversee state programs in this area.

The absolute cash benefit levels of welfare families were not increased, but the amount of extra money a family received that was not to be counted in determining welfare eligibility was increased from seventy-five dollars per month to ninety dollars. This was coupled with a provision stating that the Earned Income Tax Credit a family received could *not* be counted in determining welfare eligibility. Medicaid benefits were to be protected for at least twelve months for those moving from welfare to low-paying jobs that provided no health benefits.

The Family Support Act further required *all* states, beginning in 1990, to adopt AFDC-UP policies, but those states new to the program were allowed to offer limited cash benefits for up to six months of each succeeding twelve-month period. Medicaid benefits could not be denied even when no cash payments were made. However, states could stipulate up to forty hours per week of workfare participation, and they could withhold payments until after the work was performed.

Not least, in virtually every instance, states had the right to apply for "waivers" from HHS, a first step in substituting their own alternative plan for any given provision. The new law also contained numerous other specific and often intricate provisions covering such topics as demonstration projects, an interstate child-support commission, detailed work-participation requirements, reporting and monitoring procedures, assessment of employment and training plans, financing mechanisms, periodic reevaluations, and modification of the child-care tax credit. Each of these minute details reflected the policy preferences of many of the political interests involved in developing this new welfare reform measure.

As always, there were the usual concerns that both conservatives and liberals insisted on protecting. At one point in the long deliberations, Sen.

William Armstrong (R, Ohio) bluntly spoke about the "workfare" requirement: "The [Reagan] administration wants people to work. They're not hung up on details."[63] Senator Moynihan understood this political imperative all too well when he observed: "We can never seriously raise the question of benefits until we convince the American public that this is first and foremost a work program."[64]

But it was of course the federal budget deficit itself that loomed as a defining factor over the fate of welfare reform. Whether recipients had a viable work program to participate in or not, there was only so much money that could be spent on reforming the welfare system. Conservatives had proposed a $2.8 billion bill, and House Minority Leader Robert H. Michel (R, Ill.) advised that that amount "is frankly at the outer limit of what not only the president would accept, but I think frankly what the American people as well want to accept at this time."[65]

Civil rights organizations knew that the price tag would be high—or at least more than the Congress would be willing to allocate—to keep mandated workfare programs from being more than just punitive and useless busywork which did not lead to better and more valuable working skills. This was their abiding fear. *Requiring* welfare recipients to participate in "workfare" when there were no jobs for them in the regular labor market would be a formidable tool in the hands of conservatives who connived to score easy political points with many of their constituents who saw AFDC-UP recipients as unworthy, parasitic dependents. Indeed, after a certain point, when hard numbers were placed on real needs, one would think that the old refrain about moving people out of welfare and into work and self-sufficiency would no longer be adequate. And yet, in the summer of 1988, a presidential election year, one could expect these same banal generalities to abound. Soon to receive his party's presidential nomination, Vice President George Bush told the NAACP convention that year: "We should seek to keep families together, not split them apart. Move recipients from dependence to independence, off welfare and into the world of work, and involve the private sector."[66]

At the time (and even today), probably few NAACP delegates would have disagreed with those sentiments. But it is also likely that few would have agreed with the vice president on what was required to bring about such results. This was precisely the problem faced by the civil rights organizations:

the issue was not one of ultimate ends but rather of the necessary means to achieve the desired outcome.

From his experiences with the issue of welfare reform and race over the past two decades, Senator Moynihan also keenly understood that there was another intransigent (and more insidious) conceptual hurdle that it was necessary to overcome. In 1987 he told a reporter why he insisted now on focusing the discussion on helping children, not on helping blacks or other minorities. The racial overtones had to be avoided. Whenever welfare issues were couched in racial terms, Moynihan observed, this has "spelled doom for past reform efforts."[67] To civil rights organizations used to pursuing a dual agenda over the past several decades, this old political lesson had long since become a sad truism.

After 1962, each congressional focus on welfare reform had brought further evidence that the mood for change was clearly in a direction opposite that preferred by the civil rights groups. Policymakers increasingly sought ways to reduce benefits and costs, impose stricter eligibility requirements, and give the states greater power to devise their own systems. Exactly how far these sentiments would go became manifest just a few years later in the 1990s.

ELEVEN

"New Democrats"—and More Republicans: The 1990s

Civil rights organizations always understood the volatility of the race issue in American politics. They had been dealing with the problem in regard to the social welfare agenda since the New Deal. They had been advised constantly over the last sixty years to seek ways to mute the race issue in the interest of achieving "larger" socioeconomic goals that would encompass benefits for *all* groups across race and class lines. At the same time, they were aware how difficult such a process was. As often as not, seeking and achieving "universal" goals did not, unfortunately, bring the desired and predicted results, as the evidence in this study has shown. But historical experience did not deter some observers from continuing to urge the political and economic wisdom of this approach. Professor William J. Wilson advised that *"the hidden agenda for liberal policymakers is to improve the life chances of truly disadvantaged groups such as the ghetto underclass by emphasizing programs to which the more advantaged groups of all races and class backgrounds can positively relate."*[1] He also concluded that, with such an approach, programs intending to help the poor "would be considered an offshoot of and indeed secondary to the universal programs."[2]

The "Hidden Agenda" and the 1992 Election

One strategy that led to the 1992 presidential election of Bill Clinton was not lost on many observers of that campaign. Six weeks before the election, one veteran columnist wrote: "No matter how far ahead the polls say he is, Bill Clinton cannot win the presidency unless he wins a lot of electoral votes in the South. I sense that Clinton knows this, which is why he is following a strategy of not embracing black Americans to the point that he provokes the 'Bubbas' of the old slave states [to] vote against him."[3] And another columnist candidly commented: "Democrats are pushing race relations into the background because they do not want Jesse Jackson in the foreground. Republicans don't see political capital in talking about it at all."[4]

The conscious strategy stemmed from two sources: the belief that the "New Democrats" represented by the Clinton-Gore team understood the negative volatility of the race issue in American politics; and, just as important, that the new administration was committed to progressive social welfare policies that would be "universal" as well as "targeted." In the circumstances, and coming on the heels of twelve years of the Reagan and Bush presidencies, this was not an entirely unreasonable expectation. In 1990 the Bush administration had decided there was no need to embark on any new antipoverty measures. As one official put it: "It was fun to think about these things. But for the time being, we concluded that we don't want to do anything new, that we should just make things work better and give states more flexibility to do demonstration projects, as President Reagan proposed."[5]

The 1992 election, then, was seen by civil rights groups as an opportunity to start again. Neither Bush nor Clinton was considered a 1960s-style Lyndon Johnson, but Clinton's social welfare leanings were clearly to be preferred. While both candidates agreed that creating jobs was an important issue, Bush was more inclined to give tax breaks to businesses and investors to achieve economic growth. Clinton still believed in the usefulness of government expenditures on public works and in giving tax breaks mainly where they were most likely to lead to job creation. Civil rights leaders clearly preferred Clinton. The Democrats' campaign booklet, *Putting People First*, talked in terms of "$20 billion Federal investment each year for the next four years, leveraged with state, local, private and pension contributions."[6] It called for "target funding . . . to rebuild" the nation's infrastructure, and for increasing the Earned Income Tax Credit for the working poor; it asserted that "affordable, quality health care will be a right, not a privilege," and that "every American will be guaranteed a basic health benefits package." Moreover, the booklet proposed up to two years of education and training for people on welfare, and to provide child care while they prepared for jobs in the private sector or "through community service."[7] These were certainly ideas that came close to what civil rights organizations had been promoting.

Therefore, they could be reasonably encouraged over the prospect of a Democratic victory. Apparently, the black electorate shared these expectations, giving the Clinton-Gore team 82 percent of its votes.

But some two years before the 1992 presidential campaign even began, the NUL issued a new Marshall Plan for America. Reminiscent of the "Domestic Marshall Plan" introduced thirty years earlier by Whitney Young, the new Marshall Plan also emphasized the need for a "multi-faceted strategic investment program for economic growth." Importantly, it hoped to target resources by "concentrating on areas of greatest need." In the 1990s the Urban League was now careful to point out that the new Plan "is not a 'social program,' but an economic investment program designed to serve overriding national interests."[8] And although the plan may have had its genesis in the 1960s, there were major differences to the original. First, the 1960s plan had been more specific in focusing on the need of black Americans due to years of neglect. Although Young sought to de-emphasize the plan's race-specific compensatory features, his ideas were widely viewed as a program primarily and initially for African-Americans. Indeed, as we saw in chapter 7, debates characterized the plan as proposing "racial preferential treatment" and instituting "reverse discrimination" by favoring blacks. In 1991 the NUL explicitly wanted to avoid such criticism. African-Americans certainly would benefit, but largely because they were a part of those in greatest need. Thus, the NUL now heralded its plan as one meeting the needs of "all" poor people.

Another important difference from the 1960s plan was that now the NUL could elaborate its ideas more fully. The new plan put emphasis on investments (expenditures) in human capital (e.g., education, job training, and job counseling), "targeting those with the most severe barriers to employment,"[9] and on developing the physical infrastructure of the nation. Many new job-creation programs would flow from the latter in repairing and building roads, bridges, mass transit systems, and aviation facilities. Investments would be made to improve water supply and treatment facilities. (The NUL had also suggested these ideas during debates on Carter's welfare reform bill.)

And just how were these investments to be financed?

The National Urban League proposes a base allotment of $50 billion per year, *above* monies normally allocated to human resource and physical infrastructure purposes, be set aside to fund the program over a 10-year period. Thus, we are advocating a total investment of $500 billion dollars.[10]

And, as always with the civil rights groups, the argument was made that "the cost of *not* implementing the program and funding it adequately is too high."[11]

Throughout 1991 and 1992, the NUL pushed its ideas in public speeches, columns, and before Congress. John Jacob outlined the new Domestic Marshall Plan before a Senate committee and urged Congress "to make our Marshall Plan for America a legislative priority."[12] Local affiliates were urged to contact their representatives in support of incorporating the plan into the FY93 federal budget and "for active support for legislation that incorporates the Marshall Plan proposals."[13] A steady stream of such activity came from the NUL's Policy and Government Relations Office in Washington.

Jacob also pushed 1992 presidential candidates to focus on the Marshall Plan in their campaigns.[14] Such proposals would "jump-start local economies and create jobs." Again, minority workers, contractors, and entrepreneurs would benefit but not exclusively; this was not a race-specific proposal. It was one based on socioeconomic needs.

Even before the November 1992 results were in, the NUL began comparing its Domestic Marshall Plan with Clinton's various proposals and, on balance, the assessment was optimistic. Both emphasized "rapid job creation and economic recovery," stressing investment in human resources and "upgrading of physical infrastructure." Both focused on promoting "infrastructure projects as an employment strategy" and concentrating on education and job training. Importantly, however, there were key differences. The NUL stressed "individuals, groups, and communities most in need" while Clinton's proposals were "generally less targeted to [the] disadvantaged, more universalistic, with main emphasis on needs of [the] broad middle-class."[15] Moreover, the NUL called for $500 billion over ten years while Clinton proposed $200 billion over four years (and which included health care reform, government restructuring, and other matters not included in the Domestic Marshall Plan). Thus there were obvious points of disagreement on commitment of funds and length of time. But, under the circumstances, this was far better than what the NUL and other civil rights groups had been facing from the administrations of Ronald Reagan and George Bush.

Optimism heightened with the new president's high-level appointments. He put an astonishing number of African-Americans in his cabinet and in top administrative posts—one of whom was former NUL vice president Ronald Brown, as secretary of commerce. And no one missed the close advisory role of former NUL president Vernon Jordan or the fact that both Hillary Rodham Clinton and the new secretary of health and human services, Donna Shalala, were once board members of the Children's Defense Fund and good friends of Marian Wright Edelman. Given these factors, optimism seemed warranted, even if cautious. The president of the Joint Center for Political and Economic Studies, Eddie N. Williams, warned: "The euphoria of victory must not obscure the fact that the problems for a great many African-Americans are massive and complex. . . . Addressing these problems will require . . . the dedication of significant financial resources at a time when available dollars are scarce."[16]

Precisely how challenging the task would be was demonstrated in the new administration's first effort to deliver on its pledge to seek immediate funds to create jobs for those who were not—in early 1993—benefiting from the economy's recovery from the recent recession. The administration concluded that there was a need for a supplemental appropriation and asked Congress to support what came to be called the economic "stimulus" package.

This would be the first test of the "hidden agenda" strategy. Hopefully, Congress would respond favorably to a proposal that called for "emergency" funds of $16.3 billion as a supplement to the current FY93 budget. The proposal included money for job creation (particularly summer jobs for youth, and infrastructure construction projects), for increased Head Start support, and infant nutrition care. These latter expenditures were described as "investments" in human development. In addition, there would be an extension of the unemployment benefits period due to expire in April 1993. There were proposals to support the small business loans program, as well as funds for research and development work by businesses, colleges, and universities. The administration justified the overall package as one designed to help those who were still unemployed, even though the economy was improving (it was labeled a "jobless recovery"), and as necessary for continued long-term economic growth. These were ideas the civil rights groups certainly favored—emphasis on immediate job creation, helping those most in need (targeting), and at the same time providing for continued support for preschool and children's programs.

Likewise, encompassing these programs in a package that contained benefits for others, namely the better-off nonpoor, would surely invite broader support. The "hidden agenda" was in play. There was no explicit reference to African-Americans; these programs would obviously be cross-racial in application. Summer jobs would be welcome in inner cities where unemployment and crime were rampant, and the proposed $1 billion for the Job Training Partnership Act would be applied to helping "disadvantaged youths."[17]

Ultimately, the administration's original $16.3 billion package failed in the Senate, killed by a Republican filibuster; and only some portions survived— namely, the extension of the unemployment benefits period and some funds for construction projects, summer jobs, and college loans. This was a far cry from the original request to "jump-start" the economy, and the most needy were hardly favored. It was difficult to build political support for those who were at the bottom of the economic ladder, the very people the civil rights groups were most concerned about.

As the original package was going down to defeat in the Senate,[18] Sen. Robert Byrd (D, W.Va.) put his finger on a critical problem. The surviving package would, indeed, provide help for those already covered by social insurance in the labor market (by extending their unemployment benefits), but it would do little for those outside that sphere. He characterized the result: " 'Billions for unemployment, but not one cent for jobs'—that is the battle cry we hear from the other side of the aisle."[19] This was a consequence civil rights groups had predicted for years, and this was precisely the reason they had always argued first for coverage of *all* workers under *social insurance* provisions and for the creation of "real" jobs that would provide stronger economic and political protection for such workers. What was happening with regard to the stimulus package in 1993—that is, exploiting the greater political vulnerability of those left out of tier 1 of social insurance coverage—had been entirely foreseen decades earlier by civil rights groups as a likely consequence in dire economic times, and even under ostensibly favorable circumstances.

Given this history and developing economic circumstances, the "hidden agenda" strategy was rendered increasingly problematic. By failing to take into account the important structural flaws of such a highly differentiated social protection system, efforts to improve the economic well-being of those *most* in need by emphasizing programs for those already better off (and mainly set apart in another segment of the social protection system) became easier said than done.

The early months of the Clinton administration, however, did contain some hopeful achievements on the social welfare front. Even as the "emergency" stimulus package was being severely scaled back, the administration proceeded to promote its own version of "enterprise zones." As noted in the previous chapter, the idea had originally been pushed by conservatives in the early 1980s, with the support (albeit qualified) of most of the civil rights organizations. Indeed, a bill had been passed in 1988 but with little implementation powers.

Now President Clinton wanted to move in the direction of a much more effective program to target economic aid to the most needy geographic areas. Civil rights groups certainly saw this as being beneficial to their constituents, although the "zones" would of course not be exclusively in black areas. The following was proposed: (1) ten areas designated as "Empowerment Zones" (six urban and three rural, with one on an Indian reservation) were to receive their greatest assistance in the form of tax credits on employee wages to all workers in the zones; (2) companies outside the zone which hired residents living in the zones would get tax credits for certain targeted jobs; (3) a 50 percent credit (up to $700) would be allowed on employers' contributions to retirement plans for each employee who worked and lived in the zones; (4) investment tax incentives would be given to zone businesses whose workforce comprised at least 35 percent zone residents; (5) faster depreciation allowances; (6) tax-exempt bonds for zone businesses; and (7) an expanded low-income housing credit would be allowed in zones considered "difficult to develop" (i.e., those with a 30 percent or more poverty rate, according to the latest census). Moreover, an additional one hundred "Enterprise Zones" would also receive assistance (but not as much as the ten Empowerment Zones). Here was a policy, then, decidedly aimed at specifically helping the nation's poorest areas.

There were, of course, ideological disagreements. Conservatives wanted more tax credits and incentives for businesses as well as less federal government intervention at state and local levels; liberals wanted more funds for education and job training for those living in the zones. Nevertheless, the Empowerment-Enterprise Zones idea itself had unusually broad ideological support. The Congressional Black Caucus noted that it was working closely with the NAACP in pushing this and similar progressive economic issues. And while admitting that Empowerment Zones could hardly answer all the problems of the poor, some black leaders observed that the measure at least tried to target those communities most desperate for help. Recognizing the need to show even a modicum of progress to frustrated constituents, Congressman Charles B. Rangel of New York concluded: "That's the reason why we hold on to [Empowerment Zones], . . . not because we feel that it is in any way an answer to the problems of the inner city. It's our only ray of light coming from a long, dark tunnel."[20] Thus, the obvious attraction was twofold: first, these "zone" proposals *targeted* economic resources; second, they at least had reasonably broad political support.

After the normal bargaining in Congress, a bill was passed and signed by President Clinton on August 10, 1993. The president got most of what he asked for, with some modifications—nine (not ten) Empowerment Zones, and ninety-five (not one hundred) enterprise zones. (The zone for the Indian reservation was dropped, but measures dealing with this segment of the population would be considered in the future.) Meanwhile, the new law was to provide $1 billion over the next two years for these zones, and businesses hiring residents of the zones would receive tax credits on wages.

After a little more than a year of the Clinton administration, civil rights groups had every reason to feel less embattled than they had felt for some time in terms of their social welfare agenda. A "family preservation" measure providing funds for family counseling and other services had passed. The Food Stamp program had been revised to allow more families to become eligible, and Food Stamp benefits were raised. A "family and medical leave" bill was enacted which allowed workers to take up to three months without pay to care for a newborn baby or to tend a sick child, spouse, or parent. A national service program passed, permitting young people to work two years in community service for minimum pay in exchange for $4,725 a year, which could be applied to college or school costs for two years. And an increase in the Earned Income Tax Credit, important to low-income wage earners, was enacted as part of the Clinton budget.

While these various programs cost relatively little as far as the overall budget was concerned, in the larger scheme they signaled the possibility that a corner had been turned—not a very sharp turn, perhaps, but a perceptible one. Civil rights groups began to feel that, at least from their perspective, they could look forward to a more enlightened reception to the other items on their social welfare agenda.[21] In addition, the Commerce Department, under former NUL official Ronald Brown, became more active in economic development projects in poor communities. This included pushing for a "competitive community program" which involved loan guarantees and other assistance to local groups and businesses to help poor communities become more economically competitive. This was clearly the sort of targeting civil rights groups had been advocating and the kind of activity, however small, that supporters of the new administration expected and welcomed.[22] But if 1993 presented a ray of light (notwithstanding the setback for the president's economic stimulus package), the glow was soon to dim as issues of universal health care and welfare reform came to the fore yet again.

Health Care Reform: Testing "Universalism"

As early as 1989, during the Bush administration, there had been an ominous indication that socioeconomic class differences might jeopardize efforts to extend health care coverage. Congress had passed a bill in 1988 providing protection for Medicare beneficiaries faced with high medical bills due to catastrophic illness. All thirty-three million people enrolled in Medicare would benefit. A limit (cap) was put on out-of-pocket expenses for hospital care, doctor bills, and prescription drugs. But, and here was the sticking point, this benefit was to be paid for *by the beneficiaries themselves* in two ways: first, there would be increases in the monthly premiums deducted from the Social Security checks of *all* Medicare beneficiaries; in addition, the more affluent (those who paid more than $150 per year in income tax) would be assessed a "supplemental premium" (i.e., a surtax). It was estimated that about 41 percent of Medicare beneficiaries would be required to pay the surtax, meaning that the remaining 59 percent, the poorer beneficiaries, would be spared that financial burden. The higher income elderly, in other words, would be paying for the lower income elderly.[23] Senate Majority Leader George Mitchell (D, Me.) saw this "progressive, income-related financing method [as] a sincere attempt to provide an equitable way to distribute the burden of additional costs of expanded benefits fairly among the elderly population."[24]

The new law also created a commission—chaired by Congressman Claude Pepper (D, Fla.), a long-time advocate of senior citizens' interests—to study two other matters: how to deal with the rising costs of long-term illness for the elderly, and how to provide health care for the estimated thirty-seven million Americans without health insurance. But the law was hardly on the books before strong voices were raised opposing it, voices from highly organized senior citizens' groups whose members would be required to pay the surtax. No one misunderstood the complaint: the better off elderly did not see why *they* should be required to subsidize the less-well-off elderly. Witnesses appearing before the Senate Finance Committee, chaired by Sen. Lloyd Bentsen (D, Texas), threatened retaliation at the polls if the law itself were not repealed (let alone just the surtax). While the Bush administration supported the new law, many liberals in Congress began to back away, urging that costs should be borne by all the taxpayers, not just the more affluent elderly. In addition, some critics noted that many senior citizens did not need the added protection because they already had protection from their own private plans. The Congressional Research Service reported that approximately 23 percent of Medicare beneficiaries were in this category.[25] Thus, although they were far from being a majority of those who benefited, this mobilized force effectively pressured Congress to repeal the law only eighteen months after its passage. The politically powerful persuaded lawmakers that benefits should either be funded by all social security taxpayers or be repealed.

Some legislators concluded after this that the effort to extend catastrophic health care coverage was not worth the hassle, and that what most people really wanted was long-term health care insurance. But they were skeptical of chances to achieve even this—as the Pepper Commission was beginning to find out.

The NUL urged the commission to "adopt a national health insurance plan that provides affordable, quality health care for all citizens, and is reflective of the needs of all unserved and underserved populations."[26] This view seemed to coincide with that of some lobbyists after the repeal of the catastrophic health law. "The old strategy of piecemeal, incremental reform may be coming to an end," said John Rother of the American Association of Retired Persons (AARP).[27]

The experience with the catastrophic-cost law ought to have been sufficient to warn of the difficulties of assuming broad consensus and universal appeal of social welfare programs. But a few years later when the Clinton administration attempted to scrap the piecemeal approach and go for a comprehensive health bill, the same realities emerged in force. What was, indeed, a crisis in health care coverage for some simply did not apply to many others. People would be differentially affected by efforts to achieve universal coverage, and those various specifics could spell the difference between victory and defeat.

What has become more evident than before is that these real socioeconomic differences have been strongly connected to the *two-tier* social security system put into place in the 1930s. As a result of that system and the important benefits it provided to those fortunate enough to come under social insurance coverage, such beneficiaries have been able to gain far greater protection than those late in coming to or (as will be elaborated in the concluding chapter) never involved in that tier. It has now become quite problematic to suppose that, by helping the better-off people in tier 1, then those in the tier 2 category will necessarily benefit. The ensuing struggle over "universal" health care reform in the 103rd Congress (1993–94) offers a good illustration of this.

On September 22, 1993, President Clinton gave the country and Congress his six basic principles for a comprehensive reform of the nation's health care system. He wanted a law that guaranteed universal health care coverage to every American that involved security, simplicity, savings, choice, quality, and responsibility. Among other things, his proposal called for employers to pay 80 percent of the average cost of a health plan, with employees picking up the remaining tab. Special allowances would be made for employers with no more than fifty workers. A series of regional health care "alliances" would serve as purchasing agents for insurance, negotiating with competing health care providers for the best plans for their enrolled participants. Large employers could opt to set up their own "corporate alliance," but in any case the various provider plans had to meet certain basic national standards to be determined by a National Health Board. Poor people would be eligible for federal subsidies in various ways, and in some instances the federal government would pay their employer's share of the health alliance premium. No one would be left uninsured. Everyone would receive a "Health Security Card" that they could carry with them and which would entitle them to a basic package of health care services. The elaborate proposal dealt with, among other matters, "doctor choice," health maintenance organizations (HMOs), and various provisions for financing.

This overall elaborate plan would be regulated by a National Health Board of seven members, nominated by the president and confirmed by the Senate. The Department of Health and Human Services would monitor the various "alliances" and the conduct of the states in enforcing the law. Federal advisory boards composed of health professionals would be utilized to consult on matters of drug prices and quality of care.

The Clinton proposal was a mix of public and private involvement in health care reform, relying heavily on market forces to hold down costs through competition among providers for health alliance business. The comprehensive and complex proposal ran to 1,342 pages. Such an ambitious plan inevitably invited numerous opportunities for opponents and even cautious supporters to pick it apart and propose various options for the various parts, which was exactly what happened throughout the year following its introduction to Congress.

A more liberal proposal was a "single-payer" plan proposed by Congressman Jim McDermott (D, Wash.). Under the single-payer system, the federal government would collect premiums and pay for benefits. States would set up various programs, and everyone would have to be covered. The role of private insurance companies would be minimized.

Other proposals would not require ("mandate") employers to provide health insurance but would make it voluntary. Those persons who purchased insurance would be given a tax deduction for their expenditure. More conservative proposals would not insist on immediate universal coverage but rather would set target dates. Likewise, a distinction was made between universal "coverage" (which Clinton and the single-payers wanted) and universal "access." The latter meant that there should be a variety of plans to choose from, depending on people's needs and their ability to pay. This, obviously, was not the same as *requiring* universal coverage.

In addition, while the Clinton plan authorized a National Health Board to set limits on how much insurance premiums could increase each year, other plans preferred to rely entirely on market competition between the providers. They voiced the perennial fears of too much government power over the essentially private health care industry. (Clinton's plan linked annual premium increases to the inflation rate, which in 1994 was roughly 3 percent.)

Civil rights organizations welcomed this revived and serious attention to establishing a universal health care system. Throughout the years, they had been calling for national health insurance as a major part of their social welfare agenda. At a conference addressing the health care needs of African-Americans convened by the NAACP Legal Defense Fund (a separate entity from the NAACP itself), Johns Hopkins University, and Meharry Medical College, the National Urban League emphasized the connection between employment and private health insurance, noting that "racial barriers to employment can also pose barriers to health insurance coverage."[28] This meant that African-Americans were "less likely to have well-paying jobs with employer-financed comprehensive health insurance." Therefore, government had to be far more involved in seeing that those persons on the fringes of the real labor market were not short-changed in receiving adequate health care coverage. The best way to guarantee this was through an enforceable universal health care plan. As complicated as it was, Clinton's plan (though by no means the "single-payer" plan preferred by the civil rights organizations) was at least moving in a positive direction.

In testifying before the White House Health Care Task Force in 1993, NUL's Robert McAlpine told the group that access to health care was a serious problem "for those of lower social and economic status."[29] The problems of those at the bottom should receive particular, targeted attention. This meant "promoting family-oriented community-based health care" and emphasizing prevention over treatment as well as training minority health care professionals who were more likely to administer to the underserved minority populations. Since for-profit hospitals did not have the best record in providing maximum quality service to the poor, "special" attention should be given to this situation.

As the national debate proceeded, the NUL recognized that universal coverage could probably not be achieved immediately. There were pressures to hold down costs and not to add to the already huge budget deficit. At the same time, the organization concluded: "The phase-in to universal coverage must be put on a firm, expeditious timetable. It must not be held hostage to the materialization of projected cost savings." The organization wanted "prenatal care, birth control, and abortion" included in any package of basic benefits. And, "to the degree possible, funding should be linked to ability to pay." This meant that copayments and deductibles required of poor patients, which could serve as financial barriers, "should be avoided or minimized."[30]

The most coordinated and inclusive effort to participate in the growing health care debate in 1994 was orchestrated by the Congressional Black Caucus. The CBC convened a Legislative Working Forum on Health Care Reform, inviting forty major African-American organizations—civil rights, civic, health care, academic, religious—to participate. Meeting on Capitol Hill in all-day working sessions, various aspects of all the current proposals before Congress were analyzed and recommendations made.

The NAACP and the NAACP Legal Defense Fund were meticulous in dissecting the various proposals, offering substitute draft language for specific provisions in the Clinton plan. The two NAACP organizations focused especially on the inability of poor people to pay for necessary health services. Therefore: "An acceptable health reform bill must fully subsidize premiums for low-income people" earning less than the amount set as the federal poverty level.[31] There were certain medical benefits currently provided to Medicaid patients—such as dental care, eyeglasses, mental health, and substance abuse treatment—that would only be covered in due time under most of the new proposals. "Phasing in benefits such as dental services and mental health and substance abuse services is unacceptable." Thus, the organizations concluded that "the bill should not reduce or eliminate any health services currently required by the Medicaid program for all Medicaid eligible individuals and all benefits should be mandatory upon the effective date of the Act."[32]

The NAACP noted a proposal to "cap" payments to hospitals serving "vulnerable populations"; the cap was set at $800 million per year for only a five-year period. This, likewise, was unacceptable to the NAACP: "This may not be enough money for municipal, not-for-profit, voluntary and traditionally minority hospitals. *The subsidy cap should be eliminated and sufficient funding for such providers guaranteed.*"[33]

The NAACP paid particular attention to proposals relating to performance standards. The proposed National Health Board would create a National Quality Management Council which would develop national measures of quality performance and report annually to Congress. This provision, according to the NAACP, should be enlarged "*to require States* to monitor and enforce health plan compliance with quality performance standards." And no health care plan should be certified by a state unless the standards were met.

Combining concerns for both the social welfare agenda and the civil rights agenda, the NAACP organizations noted that the Clinton plan "would not provide sufficient civil rights protection."[34] States should be required to submit "civil rights compliance plans." Such plans would have to detail "how the proposed alliance areas will impact access to health services for underserved communities and populations, including minority communities, low-income communities, high-risk populations, rural areas and persons with disabilities."[35]

Of major concern was the possibility of "insurance redlining," which consisted of literally or figuratively drawing a red line around certain areas on a map and not doing business within those boundaries. Civil rights groups were keenly aware of a history of such discriminatory practices in mortgage financing and automobile insurance. Companies traditionally circumvented high-risk (frequently minority) areas or charged higher rates. The same practice was likely to occur with health insurance. Civil rights groups wanted to flag this possibility at the outset and suggested: "In order to reduce insurance redlining, states must have an affirmative obligation to create regional alliances areas that are not socio-economically identifiable, racially identifiable, or identifiable in any other way that may reduce the likelihood that health plans will seek to serve them."[36] Each regional health alliance would be required to outline how it would comply with the antidiscrimination provisions.

The experience of civil rights advocates was brought to bear in another way. Sensitive to various subterfuges used over the years to deny black citizens protection on supposed grounds other than race, the organizations were alert to such possibilities in the health alliance proposal. A regional alliance might easily and deliberately fill up its rolls with "desirable" enrollees and then close its doors to the "undesirable" on the basis of "over-capacity." The NAACP sought to amend the Clinton proposal so that

> Each regional alliance shall establish a method for establishing enrollment priorities in the case of a health plan that does not have sufficient capacity to enroll all eligible individuals seeking enrollment [INSERT, "in a manner that will ensure enrollment of traditionally underserved populations, including, but not limited to, those described in the anti-discrimination provisions of this Act"].[37]

Therefore, even with ostensibly "universal" social welfare programs, civil rights groups could not assume that administrative practices would automatically be equitable, and so the best way to ensure this was to make the statutory language as explicit as possible.[38] Years of hard experience had taught civil rights groups not to make naive assumptions in regard to so-called color- or class-blind laws.

Other groups generally voiced similar concerns on basic issues. Jesse Jackson's National Rainbow Coalition, Inc., preferring a single-payer plan, also supported "sin taxes" (taxes on cigarettes and liquor) as one means of raising revenues to support a universal health package, as well as "price controls on both pharmaceutical companies and insurance companies."[39] The National Medical Association (NMA), an organization of African-American doctors, also preferred the single-payer plan.[40] And the NUL wanted to emphasize that a universal plan should base premiums on a family's ability to pay "and not solely on employment status." Otherwise a two-tier system of medical service could develop, with the wealthier receiving better care than lower-income families.[41]

In the 103rd Congress, none of this came to pass. Clinton's ambitious universal health care proposal never came up for a final vote, and there were many analyses to explain this outcome. It was reasonable, one could conclude, to start out thinking that such an issue would surely receive sufficiently broad-based support to ensure passage in some useful form. This was, after all, an issue that touched everyone: it was a universally perceived necessity; it had been on and off the national policy agenda since the New Deal; virtually every American would have an interest in and would benefit from a "universal" approach that promised to deal with extending coverage and containing costs. But this seemingly reasonable presumption also contained the very reasons for the approach's vulnerability, rendering problematic the idea that by helping the middle class, those lower on the socioeconomic scale would also benefit. Such a notion, with its genesis in the social insurance formula instituted in the New Deal, was no longer so clear.

Under the New Deal, there had been a much larger group of people in similar abject need (for instance, only about 15 percent of employees had any private retirement pension plans). Thus, a social insurance/job-related pension system was broadly appealing. As a result of several important New Deal acts, many Americans gained a foothold that provided at least a modicum of security and opportunity for development. They benefited not only from tier 1 benefits but also from the protection provided by organized labor's ability to bargain and negotiate increasingly attractive union contracts for its working-class members. Those persons left out of these important earlier provisions would have a distinct disadvantage in terms of accumulated assets for their families and heirs. The more fortunate ones would be in a position to develop and secure gains that would, in time, have an enormous impact on exactly what constituted "universal" need. Indeed, at one point in the health care debate in 1994, Senator Moynihan bluntly stated that there was in fact no health care crisis, a conclusion hardly resonant with many of the constituents in the civil rights groups, but one that nonetheless more accurately reflected the degree of erosion the concept of "universality" had undergone when applied to certain critical issues such as health care.

To be sure, everyone did feel concerned about coverage and cost, but in 1993 as much as 85 percent of the American population *already had* health insurance coverage *of some sort.* To cover the remaining 15 percent, then, meant making readjustments that could impinge, even if ever so slightly, on programs many people were currently participating in or comfortable with, either through their employers, former employers, union agreements, or various private plans. Under the circumstances, and perhaps understandably, some persons were reluctant to give up certain concrete advantages— in their choice of doctors, in sundry components of the benefit packages, or in affordable premium payments—for an amorphous common universal good (namely, coverage for everyone) that might prove costly and unworkable. In other words, a "universal" health care program clearly threatened to have a *differential impact* on every individual in the public and private labor markets. This threat alarmed many who felt secure in the current system and made the concept of "universality" much less attractive to the general population.

This differentiation, we argue, is traceable to the important social welfare decisions in the New Deal that set up the original two-tier system. Those persons immediately able to move into tier 1 social insurance through job-based status and other protections developed entrenched interests that simply came to be vastly different from the interests and needs of those coming late *or never able to get a foothold in the viable labor market.* It should now be clear that access to and participation in the regular labor market is the key that opens the door for working-class and middle-class Americans. Anything less is peripheral, beside the point; tier 2 status, with all its attendant political and economic disadvantages, is the road that leads nowhere. Recognizing this from the beginning, civil rights groups pushed hard all along for "real" jobs in the regular labor market and warned of a growing gap between those brought into the system and those left out.

The health care debate in the 103rd Congress was accompanied and complicated by several optional plans and considerable mass media advertising appealing to—some might say pandering to—particularistic interests. Whether such representations were accurate or not, they found a wide and receptive audience that was wary enough to know what it had and to speculate if this so-called bold new "universalism" would indeed, on balance, actually be beneficial or not *for them*.[42] In such a heated atmosphere, calls from civil rights groups to target resources *selectively* to those most in need of health care coverage generally fell on deaf ears, whether such calls were couched in socioeconomic arguments emphasizing class differences (as they often were) or in purely race-specific terms.

As more than a few analysts later observed, the general call for fundamental *change* in the health care system failed to arrive at a universal meaning of just what "change" meant. One account of a focus group in the debate noted that "asking people exactly what they meant by radical change, they said: 'If I lose my job, I don't want to lose my coverage. I don't want it to cost so much.'" This same account continued:

> Mr. Clinton's allies continually qualified their support by *expressing concern about specific parts of his plan. Labor unions worried that Mr. Clinton was going to tax some of the benefits they had won in collective bargaining.* Doctors specializing in internal medicine supported much of Mr. Clinton's plan, but objected to the proposed cutbacks in Medicare and to the idea of Federal limits on private health insurance premiums.[43]

Moreover, an advocate of universal insurance stated: "The American people want change as long as it doesn't cost them too much or affect them too much personally."

The White House understood this vexing problem of differential impact only too well. As one assessment pointed out:

> The improvement in the economy—for which voters, curiously enough, seem to give Mr. Clinton little credit—has caused people to be less fearful about losing their jobs, and with them their health insurance. That, some White House officials believe, has taken some of the urgency out of the debate. Public attention has turned to crime and other urban problems.[44]

Another person noted that some rank-and-file union members worried that they might lose the "good coverage they enjoy now." And a communications union official flatly raised the issue about differential impact and the two-tier system when commenting that "we spent several decades getting to the point that telephone companies now pay 100 percent of the health insurance premiums for our members. The Mitchell bill [Sen. George Mitchell had proposed a compromise] *would undermine the progress we've made*."[45]

While such sentiments were obviously troubling to the White House, they were no less so to civil rights organizations trying to pursue a "universal" strategy that sought to bring much-needed help to the neediest—those who had no union or other powerful special interests behind them, or even jobs. Civil rights groups had themselves spent "several decades" at this task, but the political landscape had changed. Their social welfare agenda was now faced with a new reality of the meaning of "universalism." And so the forward-looking Clinton universal health care proposal lingered and died, and attention turned to other issues, including welfare reform.

The Republicans' "Contract with America" (1994) and "Welfare Reform" (1996)

In the November 1994 mid-term elections, a new conservative force took control of both chambers of Congress, put the Clinton administration on the defensive, and promised a new direction in dealing with social welfare issues that was almost 180 degrees from what civil rights groups had been advocating for decades. More emphasis was placed on devolving power to the states in various social welfare programs, and universal health care was off the table. No one, liberal or conservative, talked seriously, if at all, about achieving what civil rights groups had made the virtual mantra of their social welfare agenda, namely, a full employment economy. One of the first issues to occupy the attention of the 104th Congress was renewed attention to welfare reform.

Clinton and the 103rd Congress had made a stab at revising the public assistance program, building on the weakly implemented Family Support Act of 1988. But it soon became apparent that if many recipients were really going to be "required" to work, this would call for far more funds—national, state, and local—than were realistically available. No one wanted to maintain the current welfare system. That old debate was reasonably settled; but to change it so that more people could become self-sufficient meant creating jobs and finding other resources, which led many honest analysts to conclude, sadly, that it might actually be *cheaper* to keep people on welfare than to have them gainfully employed. This was especially so if such employment had to include, as it certainly did, a large public works program and support services (child care, health care, work-related expenses). These issues had been faced most recently with the Family Support Act of 1988.

The Clinton administration quickly faced this reality. As a candidate in 1992, Clinton had promised "to end welfare as we know it." In 1993 and early 1994, four administration proposals emerged: (1) to expand the Earned Income Tax Credit for the working poor, with the goal of raising the incomes of over one million workers above the poverty line; (2) to make a renewed and intensive effort to get child-support payments from absent parents; (3) to require welfare recipients to get training, education, or work experience, and, if necessary, to instigate a workfare plan; and (4), the most innovative proposal, to limit certain welfare recipients who were able to work to only two years on welfare; after that, they would be expected to work (if they could not find a job, the federal government would guarantee them a low-paying public service job or have their wages subsidized in a private-sector job). The debates and congressional hearings proceeded throughout the spring and summer of 1994. The result? Nothing happened. Everyone ultimately understood that such proposals (especially the fourth item) would still end up costing *a lot* of money.[46]

Then came the November Republican victory, and the new, decidedly more conservative congressional majority offered an entirely different agenda. For the first time, the Republicans' "Contract with America" (a House Republican campaign document) paid serious attention to ending the "entitlement" feature of certain tier 2 public assistance programs. Proposals were made to give the states a specific limited amount of money in the form of block grants. The states would then have the responsibility of dealing with their own social welfare problems with "capped" federal funds. If a state exhausted its federal allotment as well as its own resources, it would be under no obligation to provide assistance to those in its jurisdiction still in need. And the federal government would be very lenient in giving the states wide latitude in devising various programs tailored to their particular circumstances.

This clearly flew in the face of every argument that civil rights groups had been making over the past sixty years favoring the national government's involvement in funding, standards of performance, and monitoring of state/local administration. In addition, there was no pretense that the federal government would assume the responsibility to provide adequate resources for job creation if the private sector could not perform this task. And no honest policy analyst, conservative or liberal, dared presume such a possibility.

In 1994 and 1995 the welfare reform debate moved forward. The NUL analyzed the various proposals. Hugh B. Price, the organization's new president, concluded:

> Everyone agrees that work is better than welfare. But that implies investing in the intensive education, job training and job creation programs many poor

people need to become self-sufficient. With 7.6 million people now officially unemployed—and millions more out of the labor force because they haven't been able to find work—where will the five million adults now on welfare find jobs? And without jobs and welfare, how will the nine million children in their families survive?[47]

What was needed were "publicly created jobs doing valued work in communities where there simply aren't enough private jobs available."[48] This was an old argument; but civil rights organizations had no choice but to continue to make it.

On December 27–28, 1994, the seventeen-member Black Leadership Forum (including all the major civil rights groups) met in Washington, D.C., in what can best be described as an atmosphere of ominous siege. They were keenly aware that every argument they had been making for viable approaches to the social welfare agenda would now be seriously challenged by a Congress determined to chart a very different course. On welfare, they issued a statement that called for strengthening families, promoting good parenting, increasing "the capacity for self-support," encouraging and rewarding work, and protecting "the interests of all children."[49] In tone and substance, these sounded similar to the general "summit" statements issued prolifically during the Reagan years of the 1980s. They were also very likely issued for the same reasons—namely, to restate a commitment, notwithstanding the dire circumstances. They were hardly new or even radical goals, but the fact is there was now a much stronger and seemingly more determined conservative force in Congress that would agree with each of these goals, and yet have an entirely different set of policies and ideas on how to achieve them. The problem was not so much in the laudable general ends but, as always, in the details of the *means* to realize them.

Those details surfaced in a final bill signed by President Clinton on August 22, 1996. In virtually every respect it contained all the fears of civil rights organizations. The federal government's sixty-year commitment to AFDC was replaced by capped block grants to the states, leaving the states with considerably more power to structure their separate welfare programs. Mothers with children over age five are required to work within two years of receiving benefits. Those mothers with children under age five are exempt from the work requirement if they are able to prove that affordable child care is not available. States must have 25 percent of adult welfare recipients working at least twenty hours a week by July 1, 1997, and 50 percent in 2002. States that fail to meet these requirements will have their block grants reduced. No family can receive cash benefits for more than five years, but each state can claim an exemption for up to 20 percent of welfare cases determined to have special hardships. Federal funds through Supplemental Security Income for low-income children with disabilities will be gradually cut over a six-year period. Severe restrictions are placed on legal immigrant, noncitizen families. Precisely how "work" is defined (for example, whether job-training, education programs, and job search would count as work) was not spelled out. Nor is it determined how the various states will coordinate their programs and monitor persons who move between state jurisdictions.

When the bill became law, many state officials began pressing the Department of Health and Human Services for answers to specific implementation questions.[50] Neither national nor state officials had answers to the myriad problems posed by this new welfare policy.

President Clinton and other supporters of the bill promised to "fix" the situation beginning with the next congressional session in January 1997. Few, however, were sanguine about the prospects for positive modifications anytime soon. To be sure, efforts would be made, and civil rights organizations, as always, would be engaged in the process. Those groups over the years have been fighting a losing battle over their social welfare agenda. But this does not suggest that they have nothing or little to offer to future debates. In fact, as the problems become even more manifest (as many policy analysts predict if thousands are removed from the social protection rolls), the next few years might well provide an opportunity for civil rights organizations to be taken more seriously *precisely because they have been warning against such dire consequences for so long*. We turn to this matter in the concluding chapter.

TWELVE

Conclusion: The Future

The sixty-year story of the civil rights organizations' dual agenda can be summarized by stressing their three main social welfare policy preferences: federal hegemony, a universal social welfare system, and jobs in the regular workforce. Each of these issues remains relevant to future discussions of race and social welfare policy.

Federal Hegemony: Social Welfare and Affirmative Action

There have long been two agendas working as the driving force behind the actions and concerns of the civil rights organizations. These groups have always focused not only on racial discrimination but also on issues of general socioeconomic concern. The latter approach has probably been obscured because racial discrimination had played such a prominent role in American history. People have automatically assumed that when civil rights organizations spoke and acted, they were doing so only in an effort to combat the perfidious nature of racism in American society. To be sure, this has been a constant concern precisely because racism has been, in various forms, a continuing presence in American society. Thus it has been presumed that civil rights organizations, as interest groups, have been steadfastly acting from that single motive. Even in the face of clear evidence to the contrary, as documented in this study, civil rights groups have been constantly admonished to pay attention to more "universal" matters. The fact that they have been trying to do just that over the past sixty years has been overlooked. Civil rights organizations have thoroughly understood the necessity of keeping a delicate balance between their concern to end racial discrimination (both de jure and de facto) and their equally important concern to bring about viable social welfare policies for *all* Americans. Precisely for this reason, they have had to chart a course that has required them to confront the explosive issue of race in American politics. Perhaps more than anyone, they have understood that race per se has been, and remains, a dangerously divisive aspect of American life. They knew that pointing out instances of discrimination would likely stir up deep-seated animosities. And yet they recognized that the struggle to achieve racial justice *and* economic development had to be pursued on both fronts.

Civil rights organizations have, of course, long preferred the federal administration of social welfare programs because of the frequent absence of adequate and wide-ranging protections against racial discrimination at the state and local levels. The simultaneous push for full *and* fair employment has always relied heavily upon the federal government's more general willingness to protect blacks from employment discrimination.

As this book goes to press, for example, the issues of race and affirmative action continue to be widely debated. To some, this debate can be seen as a "wedge" meant to divide liberal ranks. But, in reality, this so-called wedge has been operating over the last sixty years—indeed, ever since the New Deal itself, World War II, and through the postwar and present modern eras. Nevertheless, it is true, the problem is no less vexing in the 1990s. Liberals know that if affirmative action is defined as meaning "racial quotas," this will drain support for more liberal or progressive social welfare policies. Conservatives, on the other hand, sometimes delight in announcing that they actually *do* favor affirmative action—as long as it is based on economic need rather than race. They (and many liberals) claim that they would be willing to support affirmative action for the poor, but not for any particular race. This is seen as being a more equitable and less racially divisive way to avoid giving unfair and unneeded preference to those blacks who can compete on the basis of individual merit.[1] In this sense, affirmative action is understood not so much as a remedy to alleviate past and present racial discrimination (which it always was, of course) but as a means to help those who really need help because they are poor, not because they are members of an ascriptive group.

Civil rights organizations, which have *never* rejected policies to help all poor people, should take up this offer since this approach has *always* been an important feature of the social welfare agenda. But the appropriate consideration (and perhaps terminology) here should not be on "affirmative action" but rather on "selective-targeted" social welfare programs that provide resources first to those most in need. If the current advocates against race-specific affirmative action are truly serious about helping *all* the poor (and not just the black poor), they will find long-standing allies in the civil rights organizations. But these same organizations also know better than anyone how hard it has been to mobilize support across race lines for such class-specific policies because this has been the focus of their truly difficult struggle for a progressive social welfare agenda for more than sixty years.

The California Civil Rights Initiative, a ballot referendum approved in November 1996 (and perhaps a harbinger of similar initiatives in other states), seeks to abolish affirmative action remedies, with many of its supporters calling instead for solutions favoring economically based policies. They contend that "preferential treatment" should be accorded to all poor people, irrespective of race. This should hardly be a "wedge" issue; to the contrary, it is an opportunity to test the veracity of its proponents. Civil rights organizations can and should point to their social welfare agenda as evidence of a long-standing and principled adherence to this precept. If more authority is going to be granted to the states in this area, then the federal government ought to preserve its power to prescribe certain basic national standards, one of which should be that scarce resources be channeled to those most in need—the "targeting" approach civil rights groups have advocated for decades. No discussion should proceed without acknowledging this critical policy preference.

At the same time, such challenges do not negate the struggle to overcome racial discrimination, a continuing concern of the civil rights agenda. Affirmative action, properly understood *as a remedy against any kind of discrimination*, should always be a principle available and protected at least by the powers of the federal government. Civil rights organizations need not and should not back away from *this* struggle. And neither should any American of good will. If we as a nation can learn to recognize the distinct goals of the two agendas, and the different political realities associated with each struggle, American society will better understand the issues and the policies that are necessary to address them.

To drive the point home, it should be remembered that affirmative action is a useful remedy against past and present *discrimination*; targeted social welfare programs are remedies *across racial lines* to deal with seemingly entrenched problems of economic deprivation and need. These are not mutually exclusive goals, but their formulation has sometimes been difficult to grasp because American society and its leaders have been slow to come to grips with the full meaning and promise of the civil rights groups' social welfare agenda.

The Legacy of the Two-Tier System

When the New Deal launched its modern-day version of the American welfare state, it consciously constructed a two-tier system—social insurance and public assistance. The rationale was clear and well-intended. Tier 1 was designed for those with jobs in the regular labor market who contributed through payroll taxes to their old age insurance and who were eligible for unemployment benefits. They were *beneficiaries*, and civil rights groups struggled to get as many low-paying occupations as possible included in this category for obvious reasons. Tier 2 was for those unable or not expected to work who would be helped through public and private charity. Tier 2 did not require *recipients* to contribute—they hardly could. This was the category of "relief" or "welfare," which no one mistook as equal in status or benefits with tier 1.

To the civil rights organizations, it was clear that as long as people did not come under tier 1 protection and had to rely on tier 2, they would be politically and economically vulnerable. For this reason, the NUL promulgated its motto ("Not alms, but opportunity") in the 1930s, while the NAACP, likewise abhorring public assistance as a "dole," championed "We want work, not relief" during the 1930s and 1940s. There could be no prospects for a viable future without ultimately being a member of tier 1. Achieving such a goal, however, has turned out to be a protracted and tortuous struggle.

Plagued by racial discrimination and other economic disadvantages, African-Americans have continually had to push for job-creation programs that would permit them to earn and contribute to social insurance protection. Civil rights groups have never subscribed to the notion—more prevalent in the 1990s perhaps than at any other time in America's history—that poor people in tier 2 (or out of the system altogether) had to be *required* to work.

To be sure, as time passed, there would be the need to provide additional "targeted" services (education and job training) to prepare people adequately for an ever-changing labor market. But the longer people were locked out (initially by force of de jure racial discrimination in employment, union practices, and lack of decent educational systems in many localities) or left out (through inadequate job-creation programs), the tougher it was to bring them into the legitimate labor market. And the longer society procrastinated, the more difficult the problems of gaining entry into tier 1 became. Then, as the public assistance clientele changed over time (especially for AFDC), voices were heard that branded tier 2 recipients as being unworthy people who were unwilling to help themselves and thus required ever more punitive measures to *force* them out of tier 2. Various welfare reform programs were developed to do just that.

Not true, civil rights groups constantly argued. Provide the jobs, and there will be more than enough applicants eager to take them. But seeing no serious effort made in this direction, the organizations became ever more fearful that the image of the lazy welfare recipient, content to have children promiscuously while remaining dependent on the state, would grow and become conventional wisdom. Along with this fear, they dreaded the predicted and burgeoning consequences of growing crime, out-of-wedlock births, and an unemployed labor force increasingly difficult to train and hire. Their worst fears came to fruition in virtually every respect. Adding insult to injury, conservative opponents who had been reluctant to support viable job-creation programs in the first place now harped about a vast dependent class that really did not want to work.

"Workfare," the mantra of many latter-day politicians, exposes the disingenuousness of its advocates when it is understood that workfare itself is *also* public assistance. Workfare does not put people into regular jobs; they remain on welfare in a "job reservoir" category that civil rights groups early on and long ago recognized as being economically discriminatory. *Requiring* people to participate in such programs simply perpetuates the myth that they are preparing for greater things to come in the labor market—but workfare does not provide the special targeted programs that are needed to prepare people for regular jobs. In fact, these programs serve rather to satisfy a political hunger to "get tough" with "undeserving" and "irresponsible" people who "want something for nothing."

By the mid-1990s some states and localities were developing tier 2 "workfare" programs that revealed what was really happening: welfare recipients would be required to work as a condition for receiving their welfare checks. As stated by Republican governor George Pataki of New York in 1995: "You have community service. . . . You're not hiring someone on Home Relief[2] at $18,000 a year to become a public employee. You are requiring them, week in and week out, to show up for public service work."[3]

This policy has enabled New York City, like other cities across the nation, to substantially "downsize" its public workforce and to rely on workfare to provide services that, in the past, had been essential work performed by city employees. A front page article in the *New York Times* described the effect of the budget squeeze on municipal services: hospitals decreased staff, lessening the quality of care, subway trains ran less often, and parks became dirtier. The article noted that "the cleanliness of city playgrounds had improved" because "welfare recipients [had] been put to work with rakes and brooms," although more sophisticated work, like maintaining playground equipment, had "sharply deteriorated."[4]

Using this "no-wage" labor in the parks has saved the city money, but it is patently unfair to the laid-off city workers and to the welfare recipients who are required to work for their welfare grant. Most tier 2 welfare recipients are required to "work off" a welfare grant which, even with a Food Stamp allowance, is considerably below the poverty line ($7,202 for a single person in 1992). A poignant added irony is that many "welfare-workfare" recipients are themselves victims from the city's "downsized" workforce, former city employees who have exhausted their unemployment benefits. Now, no longer eligible for the benefits attached to "regular" jobs, they are unable to find work in the private-sector labor market that would restore them.

Recognizing the diminishing job pool, the New York City transit workers' union agreed to allow thousands of welfare recipients to clean subways and buses in return for a guarantee that no union workers would be laid off through 1995.[5] The New York Metropolitan Transit Authority (MTA), which over the years has had financial difficulties, had already eliminated two hundred jobs and warned that deep budget cuts would still be needed to avoid layoffs if it was not allowed to use welfare workers. With the workfare/welfare recipients, the MTA promised to provide a "cleaner quality of life to the rider." (Riders had complained that buses and trains were becoming "grimier" as a result of the layoffs.)[6] Thus, workfare recipients will perform duties formerly done by union workers.

City officials have defended their use of workfare by insisting that the jobs are supplementary, not a substitute, and that this will allow the city "to do things that haven't been done before."[7] Yet the city hospitals have dismissed hundreds of workers and are relying on the workfare program to fill essential housekeeping and cafeteria jobs that had been performed by union workers.

In the 1970s the mere suggestion of workfare programs usually brought cries of alarm from unions and others that such programs should not replace regularly employed workers and should at least pay the minimum wage. During the 1990s the unions have been slow to respond to the workfare program, but as "downsizing" and layoffs increase, they are beginning to realize that workfare is a menacing threat to their survival. Union leaders are beginning to map a strategy to fight the workfare system, calling for a moratorium on it or at least a reexamination, and perhaps pushing for state legislation mandating that workfare participants have the same wages, benefits, and protection as others doing the same work.[8] This proposed strategy clearly shows the importance of "real" jobs; workfare is not an acceptable alternative.

Faced with harsh budget deficits, cities saw a way to relieve, in part, their fiscal pressures by filling job vacancies resulting from attrition with people on welfare—in other words, by creating a category of "no-wage" workfare employees. Such workers are expected to perform essential work, *but without receiving any of the benefits of tier 1 jobs.* Clearly, "welfare-workfare" threatens to become a vital element of the labor pool, but one built on the shoulders of the poor. Given the fact of the overall shrinking regular job market, people are more than likely to become trapped in this status and to remain dependent. Thus, policymakers who repeatedly profess to want to "reform" welfare in order to promote self-sufficiency and end dependency may very well be designing programs guaranteed to reach the opposite result—namely, an institutionalized no-wage labor force.

Throughout their history, through their social welfare agenda, civil rights groups have consistently battled to avoid precisely these consequences and to move people into tier 1. They have understood *all along* that people trapped in tier 2 are *not* politically protected and that being denied access to tier 1 results in political impotence, as was clearly witnessed in the stillborn effort to achieve universal health care in 1993 and the desperate leap into the unknown that characterized welfare reform in 1996.

This turn of events will doubtless become more aggravated if American society fails to adopt serious employment programs for those most in need. All the more reason then, as noted above, for civil rights organizations to seize the opportunity so serendipitously offered by opponents of affirmative action to call *once again* for a genuinely honest attempt to enact a set of policies specifically aimed at achieving that goal. As this book has shown, such a move would be entirely consistent with the social welfare agenda established by civil rights groups since the 1930s.

The agonizing lessons of America's two-tiered social security system must not be minimized. The wholesale exclusion of substantial numbers of African-American workers from the viable economic protection afforded by tier 1 (as a result both of their uncovered occupations and the insidious evil of racial discrimination at once officially and tacitly sanctioned) denied them an early foothold in a system that has served most other Americans so well for so long. Not until the 1960s, with the passage of momentous federal civil rights legislation (indeed, to date the crowning achievement of the civil rights agenda), did the *legal* barriers slowly begin to crumble. But by this time, through no fault of their own, African-Americans found themselves struggling against an economy finally starting to run out of steam after the post-World War II boom years. "Full employment" seemed out of reach as a reasonable goal, while the cutoff point for what constituted an "acceptable" unemployment level crept ever higher. The structural imperatives of a constricted labor market became even more detrimental to those on the fringes of the economic mainstream. Thus relegated to the far reaches of economic dependence, many blacks remained shut out from the normal work culture at large and the benefits readily granted to other Americans.

The critical historical factor of America's two-tiered social welfare system and the overwhelming effect this has had on the fate of African-Americans can hardly be overstated. Otherwise astute commentators and observers who tend to mitigate the *historical* consequences of racism on present-day conditions have missed this point precisely because they have not adequately understood (let alone debated) the crucial importance of the dual agenda as part of the ongoing strategy of the civil rights organizations.

The Persistent Need: Real Jobs, Not Workfare

For more than sixty years—time and again, over and over—the linchpin of the civil rights groups' social welfare agenda has been the call for "jobs." No major document, organizational proposal, or appearance to testify before Congress has failed to emphasize this fundamental need. Even more specifically, the social welfare agenda has stressed the need for a "full employment" economy. This has been another central credo ever since the March on Washington Movement in 1941, support for the initial Wagner-Murray-Dingell bill in 1943, the full employment bill of 1945, the March for Jobs and Freedom in 1963, the Freedom Budget in 1966, the Humphrey-Hawkins full employment bill and various other responses to welfare reform in the 1970s, and right up into the 1980s and 1990s. If ending segregation and racial discrimination and also gaining the right to vote were critical to the civil rights agenda, then, without question, the necessity of jobs and the idea of a full employment economy have remained the perennial and consistent focus of the social welfare agenda. But in every instance, and at every turn, adequate job-creation proposals have been rejected on the basis of cost—as supposedly being too expensive, or too inflationary (and thus economically unfeasible). In the 1990s, voices from the left and right, from moderates to conservatives, both Democrats and Republicans, have endorsed the general proposition that "the era of big government is over."[9] Such a view clearly has wide implications for domestic policy and hardly bodes well for any serious undertaking in the foreseeable future concerning the vital need for the creation of regular jobs. Nevertheless, although economic constraints, especially in regard to increasing the budget deficit, will doubtless continue to dominate the overall welfare debate, policymakers should still try to find ways for the poor to get better job training, to learn how to change certain antisocial attitudes and behavior, and to begin exploring various self-help endeavors. While such safe approaches (politically, that is) may be showing signs of becoming stale, at least any serious government effort to address these issues is bound to ease the difficulties of those wanting a job.

Finally, one often-ignored aspect of the problem remains to be discussed. The fact is, economic policymakers *have consistently refused* to accept an employment level that allows all who are able and willing to work at a living wage to do so. Whenever the unemployment rate gets too low and approaches what appears to be a reasonably tight labor market (therefore threatening inflation), the Federal Reserve Board steps in to cool things off. Interest rates are raised, employers cut back, and jobs are lost. There is a point, say these economists, where it becomes detrimental to the society at large to have a "full employment" economy.

According to this view, then, a certain proportion of the able-bodied population is clearly expendable; these workers are *not wanted* and *not needed* in the regular labor market. As civil rights organizations have incessantly pointed out, this has been the case since at least World War II: the most economically disadvantaged Americans in the system (and the ones most immediately affected) are basically at the mercy of a *deliberate* economic slowdown to avoid inflation. Yet politicians almost always leave this extremely pertinent information out of the public debate, preferring to make political hay from the more unscrupulous claim that they are saving the taxpayers money by making welfare recipients work for their welfare grant. But to conduct any welfare reform debate (or, for that matter, to devise any job-training program) without addressing this fact, or by pretending that it does not exist, is at best misleading. Politicians and economists alike should make it clear in the public debate that there are *not* enough real wage jobs to employ all those able and willing to work, and furthermore, that there is *no intention in the market economy for this to be otherwise.* Blaming the less fortunate for being caught in circumstances that are largely beyond their control is neither accurate nor honest.

Such openness in the public discourse seems unlikely to lead to any real changes in current or future fiscal or monetary policies, but it might at least induce more enlightened and less punitive attitudes toward those who sincerely want to work in order to earn a decent living, and who try very hard to do so. Such informed discussion could also go a long way toward eliminating the stereotypical view of "lazy and shiftless" welfare recipients who are simply "looking for handouts." This doesn't mean that we should overlook or minimize the present social or personal causes behind an individual's failure to find work or fit into the general society. But we ought to be candid about the inability of the economy to support a full employment policy, given certain economic ideological preferences, and this fact should certainly be on the table as a part of the social welfare policy debate.

Through the years, civil rights organizations have made (and continue to make) their case for better—that is, just—treatment in good faith. Sorry to say, responses to these arguments have not always been clothed with reciprocal integrity. Policymakers may either give lip service to the organizations' ideas or sometimes oppose them outright, not always for ethical reasons. Others stake out safer ground by continuing to put faith in formulas that work but are easily undermined: that things will improve by creating one training program or another, or by giving a bit more attention to "acceptable" social behavior, or (perhaps the best of the lot) by better utilizing private, family, and community resources. Through such means, they say, those at the bottom can surely move into the American economic mainstream (that is, tier 1) like everybody else. Of course, every cliché has its kernel of truth, and without question, many who play by the rules, stay out of trouble, and study to their highest capacity will doubtless be better off than those who choose deliberately not to do so (assuming they have even been given the *opportunity*). But we must not promise more than we can give by claiming, say, that appropriate behavior will necessarily be rewarded with appropriate results. People in desperate economic straits do not, with good reason, believe this. Civil rights organizations may be championing a cause—full employment—that the economic system will not accommodate. But, as the gap between the haves and the have-nots widens in America, we would be wise to recognize an inherent danger: those who are shut out of an economic system's rewards truly have no stake in that system.

This book set out to correct the impression that civil rights organizations have only or mainly been concerned with "narrower" civil rights issues over larger and more "universal" economic problems. As we have shown, by focusing attention on what civil rights groups have actually been saying and trying to accomplish on these matters ever since the 1930s, such is not the case. For more than six decades, the call has gone out, albeit unsuccessfully so far, for more equitable social welfare policies for *all* the poor in our society. But with that call has come a warning from those same civil rights organizations—that the longer we delay, the worse the problems and divisions in American society will become. Unfortunately, this warning remains unheeded. No future social welfare policy discussions should perpetuate this mistake.

NOTES

ONE   Introduction: A Warning Unheeded

1. Lewis, quoted in Jeffrey L. Katz, "Welfare: After 60 Years, Most Control Is Passing to the States," *Congressional Quarterly* (Aug. 3, 1996): 2196.

2. Edelman, quoted in Francis X. Clines, "Clinton Signs Bill Cutting Welfare, States in New Role," *New York Times*, Aug. 23, 1996, 1. Hillary Rodham Clinton had served on the Board of Directors of the Children's Defense Fund, founded by Edelman.

3. Moynihan, quoted in Jeffrey L. Katz, "Senate Overhaul Plan Provides Road Map for Compromise," *Congressional Quarterly* (Sept. 23, 1995): 2911.

4. Ibid., 2911.

5. Correspondence between Congressman Dow W. Harter and Walter White, Oct. 25 and 26, 1937. NAACP Papers, Group I, C-256, Library of Congress, Manuscript Division, Washington, D.C. (hereafter cited as NAACP Papers).

6. Theda Skocpol, "Targeting Within Universalism: Politically Viable Politics to Combat Poverty in the United States," in Christopher Jencks and Paul E. Peterson, eds., *The Urban Underclass* (Washington, D.C.: Brookings Institution, 1991), 433. (More than fifty years earlier another scholar, Ralph J. Bunche, had made a similar inaccurate observation about civil rights groups during the New Deal when he wrote: "It is typical of Negro organizations that they concern themselves not with the broad social and political implications of such policies as government relief, housing, socialized medicine, unemployment and old-age insurance, wages and hours laws, etc., but only with the purely racial aspects of such policies. They are content to let the white citizens determine the expediency of the major policies, and the form and direction they will assume, while they set themselves up as watch dogs over relatively petty issues, as whether the Negro will get his proper share of the benefits and whether laws, once made, will be fairly administered. They thus demark for the Negro a residual function in the society." Bunche, "The Progress of Organizations Devoted to the Improvement of the Status of the American Negro." *Journal of Negro Education* 8 (July 1939): 539–50.

7. A 1972 amendment to the Social Security Act provided for a cost-of-living adjustment (COLA).

TWO   Coping with the New Deal

1. "From 2 Members to 100,000: A Brief History of the N.A.A.C.P.," Sept. 17, 1925. NAACP Papers, Group I, C-293, Library of Congress, Manuscript Division, Washington, D.C. (hereafter cited as NAACP Papers). Also see Charles Flint Kellog, *NAACP: A History of the National Association for the Advancement of Colored People*, vol. 1, *1903–1920* (Baltimore: Johns Hopkins University Press, 1967), 9–30; Mary White Ovington, *The Walls Came Tumbling Down* (New York: Schocken, 1970), 100–46.

2. Nancy J. Weiss, *The National Urban League, 1910–1949* New York: Oxford University Press, 1974), 16–43. Guichard Parris and Lester Brooks, *Blacks in the City: A History of the National Urban League* (Boston: Little, Brown, 1971), 30–36.

3. T. Arnold Hill, "The Urban League and Negro Labor, Yesterday—Today—Tomorrow," *Opportunity* 13 (Nov. 1935): 340–42, 349.

4. NAACP Annual Report (1932), 7.

5. Press release, Jan. 9, 1933 (NAACP Papers, Group I, A-25).

6. NUL Annual Report, 1933. NUL Papers, ser. 13, box 1, Library of Congress, Manuscript Division, Washington, D.C. (hereafter cited as NUL Papers).

7. Ibid.

8. Ibid.

9. Hazel W. Harrison, "The Status of the American Negro in the New Deal," *Crisis* 40 (Nov. 1933): 256, 262.

10. William E. Leuchtenberg, *Franklin D. Roosevelt and the New Deal* (New York: Harper and Row, Harper Torchbacks, 1963), 64–69; Broadus Mitchell, *Depression Decade* (New York: Holt, Rinehart, and Winston, 1947; rpt., White Plains, N.Y.: M. E. Sharpe, 1975), 239–58.

11. Editorial, "A Critical Period," *Opportunity* 11 (July 1933): 199.

12. Asa Spaulding to T. Arnold Hill, n.d. (NUL Papers, ser. 4, box 1). Asa Spaulding, a wealthy African-American who owned a large insurance company, was on the Board for Industrial Recovery and informed Hill that he had received some "confidential information" from a friend in Hugh Johnson's office (director of the NRA) telling him that domestics were not to be included in the codes. This supports the organizations' belief that the involvement of black administrators was extremely helpful to black workers.

13. Minutes of Board of Directors' Meeting, Sept. 12, 1933 (NAACP Papers, Group I, A-10); "Summary of Work Already Accomplished and Suggested Next Steps in Program for the Joint Committee on National Recovery," confidential memorandum (Group I, C-311); letter to Mary Rumsey from Hill, Aug. 30, 1933 (NUL Papers, ser. 4, box 1); Hill, "Labor," *Opportunity* 12 (Feb. 1934): 58.

14. NAACP Annual Report (1933), 7–8.

15. Minutes of the Board of Directors' Meeting, Sept. 12, 1933 (NAACP Papers, Group I, A-10); Eugene Kinkle Jones, "The Negro in Industry and in Urban Life," *Opportunity* 12 (May 1934): 141–44.

16. Leuchtenberg, *Roosevelt and the New Deal*, 64–69; NAACP Annual Report (1933), 7–8.

17. NAACP Annual Report (1933), 7–8.

18. Ibid., 3–4; Minutes of Eastern Regional Conference, Sept. 23, 1933 (NUL Papers, ser. 4, box 21).

19. Jones, "The Negro in Industry and in Urban Life," 141–44.

20. Press release, Oct. 6, 1934 (NAACP Papers, Group I, ser. C, box 322).

21. Ibid.; Gustav Beck, "The Negro Worker and the NRA," *Crisis* 41 (Sept. 1934): 262–63, 279; Hill, "Labor," *Opportunity* 12 (Feb. 1934): 58; Robert C. Weaver, "A Wage Differential Based on Race," *Crisis* 41 (Aug. 1934): 236–37.

22. Arthur M. Schlesinger, Jr., *The Politics of Upheaval* (Boston: Houghton Mifflin, 1960), 396.

23. Hill, "Labor," *Opportunity* 12 (Feb. 1934): 58.

24. Walter White to Green, telegram, Oct. 5, 1934 (NAACP Papers, Group I, C-143); press release, Oct. 6, 1934 (Group I, C-322); NAACP Annual Report (1934).

25. Green to White, Oct. 8, 1934 (NAACP Papers, Group I, C-143); NAACP Annual Report (1934).

26. Press release, Aug. 19, 1933 (NUL Papers, ser. 5, box 33). Correspondence between Hill and William Kelley, executive secretary of Milwaukee UL, Aug. 13 and 15, Sept. 21, 1934 (ser. 4, box 8); correspondence between Hill and Lloyd Garrison, Labor Relations Board, Aug. 27 and Sept. 18, 1934; letter to Donald Richberg, general counsel of NRA, from John Clark, executive secretary, St. Louis UL, Feb. 12, 1934 (ser. 4, box 1); St. Louis UL 20th Anniversary Summary, 1929–38 (ser. 13, box 27); Jesse Thomas, "Negro Workers and Organized Labor," *Opportunity* 12 (Sept. 1934): 277–78, 288; Thomas, "New Wine in Old Bottles" (Nov. 1934): 344–45, 350.

27. NAACP Annual Report (1934), 13–15; Editorial, "Union Labor Again," *Crisis* 41 (Oct. 1934): 300.

28. Editorial, "Goodbye to General Johnson," *Crisis* 41 (Nov. 1934): 332.

29. Leuchtenberg, *Roosevelt and the New Deal*, 48–51.

30. Raymond Wolters, *Negroes and the Great Depression* (Westport, Conn.: Greenwood, 1970), 41; Louis Wright, "The 26th Year of the NAACP," *Crisis* 43 (Aug. 1936): 244–45.

31. Mitchell, *Depression Decade*, 200–205.

32. Wolters, *Negroes and the Great Depression*, 43–45; NAACP Annual Report (1935).

33. Wolters, ibid., 46–47; NAACP Annual Reports (1935–1937).

34. Leuchtenberg, *Roosevelt and the New Deal*, 53, 174, 187; Mitchell, *Depression Decade*, 328–31; National Resources Planning Board (NRPB), *Security, Work, and Relief Policies* (Washington, D.C.: GPO, 1943), 37–38.

35. John A. Salmond, "The Civilian Conservation Corps and the Negro," *Journal of American History* 52 (June 1965): 75–88.

36. Ibid., 80–88.

37. St. Louis UL Annual Report, 1935 (NUL Papers, ser. 13, box 6); Seattle UL Meeting Community Needs Report, 1938 (box 8); "Survey of the Month," *Opportunity* 13 (Aug. 1935): 254, and (Nov. 1935): 345; Hill, "The Government as

Employer and Philanthropist," *Opportunity* 11 (May 1933): 153; NAACP Annual Report (1935).

38. NRPB, *Security, Work, and Relief Policies*, 32, 46, 66–67; Leuchtenberg, *Roosevelt and the New Deal*, 129; Mitchell, *Depression Decade*, 330.

39. NRPB, *Security, Work, and Relief Policies* 46, 66, 267–68, 271–76, 394–95, 546–47; Leuchtenberg, *Roosevelt and the New Deal*, 187.

40. Leuchtenberg, ibid.

41. Newsletter to Executive Board from P. Joyce, Nov. 20, 1939 (NUL Papers, ser. 12, box 1); St. Paul UL Annual Report, 1939 (ser. 13, box 27); Brooklyn UL Annual Report, 1939 (ser. 13, box 6); Memphis UL Annual Report, 1939 (ser. 13, box 16).

42. St. Louis UL Annual Report, 1939 (NUL Papers, ser. 13, box 26).

43. John B. Kirby, *Black Americans in the Roosevelt Era: Liberalism and Race* (Knoxville: University of Tennessee Press, 1980), 112–13.

44. NRPB, *Security, Work, and Relief Policies*, 187, 271–72; Leuchtenberg, *Roosevelt and the New Deal*, 187; Kirby, *Black Americans*, 112–13.

45. Leuchtenberg, *Roosevelt and the New Deal*, 121–22.

46. NRPB, *Security, Work, and Relief Policies*, 43–44; Mitchell, *Depression Decade*, 316–17.

47. NRPB, ibid., 38.

48. Press release, Nov. 29, 1933 (NUL Papers, ser. 5, box 33).

49. New York UL Annual Report, 1934 (NUL Papers, ser. 13, box 19).

50. Leuchtenberg, *Roosevelt and the New Deal*, 121–23; Mitchell, *Depression Decade*, 316–18.

51. NRPB, *Security, Work, and Relief Policies*, 31–34.

52. Ibid., 41.

53. Telegram to Wagner from White and telegram to White from Wagner, May 26, 1933; letter to Wagner from White, May 29, 1933 (NAACP Papers, Group I, C-257).

54. Letter to the editors of the weekly press, June 3, 1933 (NAACP Papers, Group I, C-257).

55. Press release, Aug. 1933 (NAACP Papers, Group I, C-383).

56. Ibid.

57. Editorial, *Opportunity* 11 (Sept. 1933): 263.

58. Report of Distribution of PWA Jobs, 1934 (NUL Papers, ser. 4, box 7).

59. Hill to Perkins, Apr. 4, 1933 (NUL Library, New York).

60. H. T. Keating to Hill, May 5, 1936 (NUL Papers, ser. 4, box 30).

61. J. S. Jackson to Hill, Oct. 14, 1935 (NUL Papers, ser. 4, box 36).

62. NAACP 26th Annual Report (1935).

63. "Along the N.A.A.C.P. Battlefront," *Crisis* 45 (Sept. 1938): 303.

64. "Along the N.A.A.C.P. Battlefront," *Crisis* 45 (Oct. 1938): 334.

65. Robert C. Weaver, "An Experiment in Negro Labor," *Opportunity* 14 (Oct. 1936): 295.

66. Mark W. Kruman, "Quotas for Blacks: The Public Works Administration and the Black Construction Worker," *Labor History* 16 (Winter 1975): 37–81.

67. Weaver, "An Experiment in Negro Labor," 295.

68. "Housing Projects Create Jobs," Workers' Councils Bulletin No. 9, Apr. 23, 1936 (NUL Papers, ser. 4, box 9), 2.

69. NRPB, *Security, Work, and Relief Policies*, 30.

70. Leuchtenberg, *Roosevelt and the New Deal*, 36–59, 120–21.

71. Editorial, *Opportunity* 12 (Dec. 1934): 360.

72. Press release, Nov. 23, 1934 (NAACP Papers, Group I, C-383).

73. Press release, Dec. 22, 1933 (NAACP Papers, Group I, C-383).

74. "The Urban League in Action: Letters from Mississippi," *Opportunity* 13 (Oct. 1935): 319.

75. "The Urban League in Action," *Opportunity* 13 (Sept. 1935): 287.

76. The NUL's actual executive secretary, Eugene Kinkle Jones, had taken a leave to serve as Advisor for Negro Affairs in the Department of Commerce.

77. Proceedings of Regional Conference, Columbus, Ohio, Sept. 20, 1933 (NUL Papers, ser. 4, box 21); NUL Annual Report, 1933 (ser. 13, box 1).

78. Memorandum on "Experiences of Negroes in Connection with the Program of the NRA"; NUL Annual Report, 1933 (NUL Papers, ser. 4, box 1).

79. Ibid.

80. Cyrus Greene to Hill, Aug. 27, 1934 (NUL Papers, ser. 4, box 27).

81. Industrial Relations Dept. Proposed Program, Fall-Winter 1937–38 (NUL Papers, ser. 4, box 6).

82. Leuchtenberg, *Roosevelt and the New Deal*, 128. A Gallup poll revealed that 60% of those interviewed thought government expenditures for relief and recovery were too great, 31% thought they were "about right," and only 9% thought they were too little. George Gallup, *The Gallop Poll: Public Opinion*, vol. 1, *1935–1948* (New York: Random House, 1971), 1.

83. NRPB, *Security, Work, and Relief Policies*, 38–39, 234–37.

84. Leuchtenberg, *Roosevelt and the New Deal*, 187; NRPB, *Security, Work, and Relief Policies*, 63–67, 101, 129, 246–48, 375.

85. "Along the N.A.A.C.P. Battlefront," *Crisis* 42 (May 1935): 152.

86. Lester B. Granger, "That Work-Relief Bill," *Opportunity* 13 (Mar. 1935): 86.

87. Editorial, "The Wages of Wretchedness," *Opportunity* 13 (June 1935): 167.

88. "Along the N.A.A.C.P. Battlefront," *Crisis* 42 (July 1935): 215; press release, May 21, 1935 (NAACP Papers, Group I, C-383).

89. Alfred E. Smith to White, May 28, 1935 (NAACP Papers, Group I, C-383).

90. Lincoln UL "Informer," Mar. 1936 (NUL Papers, ser. 13, box 14).

91. John Crawford to Hill, Jan. 12, 1936 (NUL Papers, ser. 4, box 31).

92. NUL Annual Report, 1938 (NUL Papers, ser. 13, box 1).

93. NAACP Annual Report (1936), 9.

94. John Clark to Hill, Nov. 17, 1938 (NUL Papers, ser. 4, box 36).

95. Brooklyn UL Annual Report, 1939 (NUL Papers, ser. 13, box 6); Memphis UL Annual Report, 1939 (ser. 13, box 16).

96. "The Editor Says," *Opportunity* 17 (Feb. 1939): 34.

97. "The Editor Says," *Opportunity* 17 (Aug. 1939): 226–27.

98. "The Editor Says," *Opportunity* 17 (Nov. 1939): 322.

99. Editorials, "The Willkie Speeches," *Crisis* 47 (Oct. 1940): 311.

100. NRPB, *Security, Work, and Relief Policies*, 235–38.

101. Edwin Witte, *The Development of the Social Security Act* (Madison: University of Wisconsin Press, 1962), 3–8.

102. Ibid.; Mitchell, *Depression Decade*, 306–13.

103. Hill, "A Statement of Opinion on H.R. 2828," Feb. 1935 (NUL Library, New York); "Survey of the Month," *Opportunity* 13 (Mar. 1935): 93; Wilkins to White, memorandum, Feb. 2, 1935, and press release, Feb. 6, 1935 (both in NAACP Papers, Group I, C-257); Statement of Charles H. Houston, Feb. 9, 1935, Senate Finance Committee, *Economic Security Act*, 74th Cong., 1st sess., 640–47 (NAACP Papers, Group I, C-257).

104. White to Morgenthau, telegram, Feb. 6, 1935; press release, Feb. 6, 1935 (NAACP Papers, Group I, C-257).

105. Edwin Witte to White, Feb. 18, 1935 (NAACP Papers, Group I, C-257).

106. Morgenthau to White, Feb. 15, 1935 (NAACP Papers, Group I, C-257).

107. Witte, *Development of the Social Security Act*, 143–44, 194.

108. Ibid., 54–59, 134.

109. Epstein, cited in memorandum to Imes, Delany, Studin, and Williams from Wilkins, Feb. 26, 1935 (NAACP Papers, Group I, C-257).

110. Ibid. Some months after the act was passed, Epstein wrote an article for *Crisis* in which he gave explanations for the exclusion of agricultural and domestic workers, adding that it might be possible to include domestics later but "the cost of administration in the early years make their immediate inclusion inadvisable" (*Crisis* 42 [Nov. 1935]: 347).

111. Testimony of Charles Houston on S. 1130 before the Senate Finance Committee, 74th Cong., 1st sess., Feb. 9, 1935 (NAACP Papers, Group I, C-257).

112. Ibid.

113. Mitchell, *Depression Decade*, 311.

114. In the testimonies of the NUL and NAACP there is a discrepancy in their estimates of the proportion of the black workforce that would be excluded from coverage under the social insurance programs. Houston estimated this to be at about one half, Hill at about two-thirds.

115. Statement of T. Arnold Hill, Acting Executive Secretary of the NUL, Feb. 8, 1935, House Committee on Labor, *Unemployment, Old Age, and Social Insurance*, 74th Cong., 1st sess., 326–28.

116. "Survey of the Month," *Opportunity* 13 (Mar. 1935): 93.

117. Wilkins to White, memorandum, Feb. 2, 1935 (NAACP Papers, Group I, C-257).

118. Arthur M. Schlesinger, *The Coming of the New Deal* (Boston: Houghton Mifflin, 1959), 295–96. Schlesinger says the Unemployed Councils controlled by the Communist Party persuaded Lundeen to introduce the bill.

119. Weaver to Hill, Feb. 13, 1939 (NUL Papers, ser. 4, box 30).

120. Leuchtenberg, *Roosevelt and the New Deal*, 132.

121. Houston to White, memorandum, Oct. 22, 1937 (NAACP Papers, Group I, C-406).

122. Mitchell, *Depression Decade*, 277–80.

123. Memorandum on S. 2926, "the so-called Wagner bill now in the U.S. Senate," Mar. 23, 1934 (NAACP Papers, Group I, C-257).

124. White to William Hastie, Mar. 28, 1934 (NAACP Papers, Group I, C-257).

125. NAACP Annual Report (1934), 13–15; Editorial, "Union Labor Again," *Crisis* 41 (Oct. 1934): 300; White to Wagner and White to Hastie, Mar. 28, 1934 (NAACP Papers, Group I, C-257).

126. Hastie to White, Mar. 27, 1934; White to Wilkins, memorandum, Mar. 28, 1934 (NAACP Papers, Group I, C-257).

127. Edward F. McGrady to White, Mar. 24, 1934 (NAACP Papers, Group I, C-257).

128. White to McGrady, Mar. 28, 1934 (NAACP Papers, Group I, C-257).

129. NUL, "A Statement of Opinion on Senate Bill S. 2926," Apr. 6, 1934 (NUL Library, New York); press release, May 16, 1934 (NUL Papers, ser. 5, box 33).

130. White to Sen. James Couzens, Apr. 11, 1934; Couzens to White, Apr. 12, 1934 (NAACP Papers, Group I, C-257).

131. "The Reminiscences of Lester B. Granger." Tape recording (interviewer not known), New York City, 1960–61. In the Oral History Collection, Butler Library, Columbia University, New York.

132. Press release, June 19, 1935 (NUL Papers, ser. 5, box 33).

133. Leuchtenberg, *Roosevelt and the New Deal*, 151; Mitchell, *Depression Decade*, 277–79.

134. Memorandum on Proposed Labor Plan, 1934 (NUL Papers, ser. 9, box 3).

135. Granger, "Reminiscences"; Granger, "The Negro—Friend or Foe of Organized Labor?" *Opportunity* 13 (May 1935): 143–44; Horace Cayton and George Mitchell, *Black Workers and the New Unions* (Chapel Hill: University of North Carolina Press, 1939), 203–204.

136. Thomas Webster to Hill, Dec. 1, 1935 (NUL Papers, ser. 4, box 7); Granger to N. B. Allen, Aug. 3, 1937; Granger to Hill, memorandum, May 20, 1938, and Granger to Hill, May 29, 1938 (ser. 4, box 29).

137. George W. Thompson to Hill, Jan. 6, 1936 (NUL Papers, ser. 4, box 21).

138. "Survey of the Month," *Opportunity* 16 (July 1938): 215.

139. White to Leland Hawkins, Sept. 25, 1934; press release, Oct. 5, 1934 (NAACP Papers, Group I, C-413).

140. White to Green, telegram, Oct. 5, 1934 (NAACP Papers, Group I, C-413).

141. Green to White, Oct. 8, 1934 (NAACP Papers, Group I, C-413).

142. Houston to White, memorandum, July 11, 1935 (NAACP Papers, Group I, C-413).

143. Hill to Green, Jan. 31, 1935; Green to Hill, Feb. 7, 1935; John Brophy to Hill, Aug. 1, 1935; Hill to Green, Sept. 30, 1935 (NUL Papers, ser. 4, box 1).

144. NUL, "The Urban League and the AF of L, a Statement on Racial Discrimination," *Opportunity* 13 (July 1935): 249; Reginald Johnson, "Supplementary Memorandum presented at the hearing of the AF of L Committee," July 9, 1935 (NUL Papers, ser. 4, box 9).

145. Houston to White, memorandum, July 11, 1935.

146. Memorandum dictated by Hill, Sept. 24, 1935 (NUL Papers, ser. 4, box 1); NUL, Workers' Bureau Leaflet; Workers' Councils Bulletin No. 5, Sept. 18, 1935 (ser. 4, box 9); Minutes of Steering Committee, Sept. 23, 1935 (ser. 11, box 3).

147. Granger to Hill, memorandum, Oct. 21, 1935 (NUL Papers, ser. 4, box 1).

148. *New York Times*, Oct. 7 and 16, 1935.

149. Editorials, "Some Hope for Negro Labor," *Crisis* 42 (Dec. 1935): 369; Conference Resolutions, "Labor," *Crisis* 42 (Aug. 1935): 250; Granger, "Industrial Unionism and the Negro," *Opportunity* 14 (Jan. 1936): 29–30; Hill, "The Negro and the CIO," *Opportunity* 15 (Aug. 1937): 243–44; Hill, "Labor," *Opportunity* 15 (Jan. 1937): 25, 29.

150. Workers' Councils Bulletin No. 16, "AF of L vs CIO," May 24, 1937 (NUL Papers, ser. 4, box 9).

151. Editorials, "Industrial Unions and the Worker," *Crisis* 43 (Sept. 1936): 273; Conference Resolutions, "Labor Unions," *Crisis* 44 (Aug. 1937): 247.

152. St. Louis Annual Report, 1935 (NUL Papers, ser. 13, box 26); Cleveland UL Annual Report, 1934 (box 8); NUL Annual Report, 1937 (box 1); Report of Meeting of Mayor's Arbitration Committee, Aug. 12 and Nov. 12, 1935 (ser. 4, box 36).

153. Leuchtenberg, *Roosevelt and the New Deal*, 261–63.

154. NAACP Annual Report (1937).

155. White to Green, telegram, Oct. 4, 1937; press release, Oct. 8, 1937 (NAACP Papers, Group I, C-256).

156. White to Green, Dec. 6, 1937 (NAACP Papers, Group I, C-257).

157. Press release, Sept. 24, 1937 (NAACP Papers, Group I, C-256).

158. Form letter to 79 senators and 357 congressmen, Oct. 19, 1937 (NAACP Papers, Group I, C-256).

159. White to Elmer F. Andrews, Oct. 17, 1938 (NAACP Papers, Group I, C-257).

160. Press release, Dec. 10, 1937; "Cost of Living as a Basis for Determining Regional Wage Rates" (n.d., c. 1937) (both from NAACP Papers, Group I, C-257); Editorials, "Differential Opposed in Wage-Hour Bill," *Crisis* 45 (Jan. 1938): 21.

161. Memorandum to executive secretaries from Jones, Apr. 19, 1938 (NUL Papers, ser. 12, box 1).

162. "The Editor Says, the Wages and Hours Bill," *Opportunity* 16 (May 1938): 133.

163. Memorandum to the Board of Directors on the National Negro Congress from Wilkins, Mar. 9, 1934 (NAACP Papers, Group I, A-26).

164. Call for National Negro Congress (n.d., c. 1936) (NAACP Papers, Group I, C-183).

165. White to Davis, Apr. 1, 1938 (NAACP Papers, Group I, C-383).

166. A. Philip Randolph, "A. Philip Randolph Tells . . . Why I Would Not Stand for Reelection as President of the National Negro Congress," *American Federationist* (July 1940): 24–25.

167. Church Leaders in Opposition to the Program of the NNC (n.d., c. 1937) (NAACP Papers, Group I, C-383).

168. White to Houston and Marshall, memorandum, June 9, 1938 (NAACP Papers, Group I, C-257).

169. Address scheduled for delivery by William T. McKnight, assistant attorney, Wage and Hours Division, U.S. Department of Labor before the Thirty-first Annual Conference of the NAACP, June 19, 1940 (NAACP Papers, Group II, A-25).

170. Ibid.

171. "The Editor Says," *Opportunity* 16 (Nov. 1938): 322.

172. Press release, Aug. 8, 1939 (NAACP Papers, Group I, C-257).

173. "The Editor Says," *Opportunity* 16 (July 16, 1938): 196–97.

174. Press release, Oct. 13, 1939 (NAACP Papers, Group I, C-257).

175. NAACP Annual Report (1939).

THREE   Fighting for Fair and Full Employment

1. Merl E. Reed, *Seedtime for the Modern Civil Rights Movement: The President's Committee on Fair Employment Practice, 1941–1946* (Baton Rouge: Louisiana State University, 1991), 41.

2. Editorials, "National Defense and Negroes," *Crisis* 46 (Feb. 1939): 49.

3. "A Summary of Activities of the NUL, October, 1940-to-October, 1941." NUL Papers, ser. 1, box 2, Library of Congress, Manuscript Division, Washington, D.C. (hereafter cited as NUL Papers).

4. "Along the N.A.A.C.P. Battlefront," *Crisis* 48 (Jan. 1941): 21.

5. "A Summary of the Activities of the NUL, October, 1940-to-October, 1941."

6. NAACP Annual Report (1940), 7–8; "Along the N.A.A.C.P. Battlefront," *Crisis* 47 (Sept. 1940): 324.

7. Elmer Carter, "The Editor Says," *Opportunity* 19 (May 1941): 130.

8. NAACP Annual Report (1941), 29.

9. Ibid.

10. NAACP Annual Report (1941); Carter, "The Editor Says," *Opportunity* 19 (Jan. 1941): 2–3.

11. "Along the N.A.A.C.P. Battlefront," *Crisis* 47 (Dec. 1940): 390–93.

12. Reed, *Seedtime*, 176.

13. Carter, "The Editor Says," *Opportunity* 19 (May 1941): 130; Lester B. Granger, "The President, the Negro, and Defense," *Opportunity* 19 (July 1941): 204.

14. Editorials, "A Word from OPM," *Crisis* (May 1941): 151.

15. Carter, "The Editor Says," *Opportunity* 19 (July 1941): 195.

16. "Along the N.A.A.C.P. Battlefront," *Crisis* 48 (May 1941): 165.

17. Bettye Collier-Thomas, "N.C.N.W. 1935–1980" (Washington, D.C.: NCNW, 1981), 1–4.

18. "Affiliated Organizations and Metropolitan Councils, 1944," in the Records of the National Council of Negro Women, Bethune Museum and Archives, Washington, D.C., ser. 2, box 2, folder 23 (hereafter cited as NCNW Papers).

19. A. Philip Randolph, "Employment in Defense Industries," address delivered before the 32nd Annual Conference of the NAACP in Houston, Texas, June 25, 1941. NAACP Papers, Group II, A-27, Library of Congress, Manuscript Division, Washington, D.C. (hereafter cited as NAACP Papers).

20. Herbert Garfinkel, *When Negroes March* (Glencoe, Ill.: Free Press, 1959), 37–39; Granger, "The President, the Negro, and Defense," 204–207, 220–21.

21. Editorial, "Administration Pressure Brought on March to D.C.," *Crisis* 48 (July 1941): 230.

22. NAACP Annual Report (1941), 3–4.

23. Garfinkel, *When Negroes March*, 57–61; Jervis Anderson, *A. Philip Randolph: A Biographical Portrait* (New York: Harcourt Brace Jovanovich, 1973), 252.

24. Carter, "The Editor Says," *Opportunity* 19 (July 1941): 194.

25. Ibid.; Anderson, *A. Philip Randolph*, 258.

26. Conference Resolutions, "President's Executive Order," *Crisis* 48 (Sept. 1941): 296.

27. NAACP Annual Report (1942), 5.

28. Conference Resolutions, "President's Executive Order," *Crisis* 48 (Sept. 1941): 296.

29. Granger, "The President, the Negro, and Defense," 204–207, 220–21.

30. Editorials, "Defense Jobs," *Crisis* 48 (Aug. 1941): 247.

31. "Report of Commission on Economics and Employment—NCNW," Oct. 17, 1941 (NCNW Papers, ser. 2, box 1, folder 10).

32. Louis C. Kesselman, *The Social Politics of FEPC: A Study in Reform Pressure Movements* (Chapel Hill: University of North Carolina Press, 1948), 15–16; FEPC, Division of Review and Analysis, "The President's Committee on Fair Employment Practice: Its Beginning and Growth and How It Operates" (Mar. 1944), 1 (NAACP Papers, Washington Bureau, box 69).

33. Reed, *Seedtime*, 30.

34. "Along the N.A.A.C.P. Battlefront," *Crisis* 48 (Sept. 1941): 291; Reed, *Seedtime*, 22–23.

35. Reed, *Seedtime*, 24–27.

36. Editorials, "Progress," *Crisis* 48 (Nov. 1941): 343.

37. Resolutions of the 33rd Annual Conference of the NAACP, July 14–19, 1942 (NAACP Papers, Group II, A-38).

38. Edward S. Lewis, "An Evaluation of the Fair Employment Practice Committee," *Opportunity* 20 (May 1942): 135–36.

39. Editorials, "Vicious Circle—Still," *Crisis* 48 (Oct. 1941): 311.

40. Editorials, "Get Training!" *Crisis* 48 (Oct. 1941): 311.

41. Statement of the NAACP submitted to the Sub-Committee on Senate Resolution 291, introduced by Sen. Claude Pepper (D, Fla.), providing for a full investigation of the manpower resources of the nation and the most advantageous use thereof in the War Effort, Nov. 28, 1942 (NAACP Papers, Group II, A-62).

42. Reed, *Seedtime*, 72–75.

43. Ibid., 72.

44. NAACP Annual Report (1943); Resolutions of the 33rd Annual Conference of the NAACP, July 14–19, 1942 (NAACP Papers, Group II, A-38).

45. Kesselman, *Social Politics of FEPC*, 22–23.

46. Ibid., 19.

47. NAACP Annual Report (1942), 5–6.

48. Granger to McNutt, Sept. 29, 1942; Dickerson to Granger, Oct. 8, 1942; White to McNutt, Oct. 13, 1942; White to Granger, Oct. 15, 1942; McNutt to Granger, n.d., c. 1942 (all in NUL Papers, ser. I, box 16).

49. Reed, *Seedtime*, 77–84.

50. NAACP Annual Report (1943), 19–20.

51. William H. Baldwin to McNutt and Baldwin to Roosevelt, Jan. 13, 1943 (NUL Papers, ser. 1, box 16).

52. Reed, *Seedtime*, 77–116.

53. FEPC, "The President's Committee on Fair Employment Practice," 6.

54. Granger to Roosevelt, June 4, 1943 (NUL Papers, ser. 1, Group 16).

55. Reed, *Seedtime*, 112.

56. FEPC, "The President's Committee on Fair Employment Practice," 3.

57. NAACP Annual Report (1943), 21.

58. Reed, *Seedtime*, 143.

59. Ibid., 346–47.

60. Ibid., 161–62.

61. Memorandum from Granger to all NUL departments, Oct. 12, 1943 (NUL Papers, ser. 1, box 16).

62. Memorandum from the NUL's Industrial Relations Dept. to the executive and industrial secretaries of affiliated organizations, n.d. (NUL Papers, ser. 3, box 461).

63. NUL Annual Meeting, February 16, 1944 (NUL Papers, ser. 11, box 4).

64. Report of Executive Secretary, February 18, 1943 (NUL Papers, ser. 11, box 4).

65. Minutes of the Executive Board, Sept. 14, 1943 (NUL Papers, ser. 11, box 5); "Summary of Activities for 1946" (NUL Papers, Southern Regional Office Papers, box A-80).

66. Anna Hedgeman to White, May 29, 1944 (NAACP Papers, Group II, A-259); Reed, *Seedtime*, 156–61.

67. "Issues Relating to the Future of FEPC," n.d. (NAACP Papers, Washington Bureau, box 69).

68. Speeches in the House by Hon. John S. Gibson of Georgia (Apr. 14, 1944), Hon. John C. Rankin of Mississippi and Hon. Sam Hobbs of Alabama (May 26, 1944), Hon. O. C. Fisher of Texas (June 20, 1944). A. Philip Randolph Papers, FEPC, box 21, Library of Congress, Manuscript Division (hereafter, Randolph Papers).

69. Reed, *Seedtime*, 161.

70. Ibid., 148.

71. National Council for a Permanent FEPC, "Summary of the scope and limitations of the bill for a permanent FEPC (Senate, S. 2048; House, H.R. 3986–4004–4005) as compared with present FEPC," Oct. 16, 1944 (NCNW Papers, ser. 5, box 4, folder 209).

72. Statement of Walter White, June 13, 1944, House Committee on Labor, *H.R. 3986, H.R. 4004, and H.R. 4005 to Prohibit Discrimination in Employment* (pt. 1), 78th Cong., 2d sess., 163–70.

73. Statement of Reginald A. Johnson, Field Secretary, NUL, June 15, 1944, House Committee on Labor, *H.R. 3986, H.R. 4004, and H.R. 4005* (pt. 1), 78th Cong., 2d sess., 218–24.

74. Mary McLeod Bethune Testimony, n.d., c. 1944 (NCNW Papers, ser. 5, box 12, folder 209).

75. Reed, *Seedtime*, 164–65.

76. National Council for a Permanent FEPC, "Flash," vol. 1, no. 3 (Sept. 20, 1944) (NAACP Papers, Group II, A-259).

77. Ibid.; National Council for a Permanent FEPC flyer, "Let's Work Together," n.d. (NAACP Papers, Group II, A-259).

78. Reed, *Seedtime*, 167.

79. Annual Report of the Washington Bureau of the NAACP, 1945 (NAACP Papers, Group II, box A-59); Minutes of National Council for a Permanent FEPC executive committee meeting, Mar. 15, 1945 (Randolph Papers, box 21).

80. Perry to White, memorandum, Nov. 20, 1945 (NAACP Papers, Group II, A-262).

81. White to Perry, Nov. 23, 1945 (NAACP Papers, Group II, A-262).

82. Randolph Papers, box 21.

83. Washington Bureau press release, Nov. 15, 1945 (NAACP Papers, Group II, A-114).

84. Report of the NAACP Washington Bureau for the month of February 1946 (NAACP Papers, Group II, A-664).

85. Perry to White, memorandum, Apr. 24, 1946 (NAACP Papers, Group II, A-664).

86. Ibid.

87. Minutes of the Meeting of the Board of Directors, Dec. 10, 1945 (NAACP Papers, Group I, A-5).

88. Reed, *Seedtime*, 333–37.

89. *Congressional Record*, June 24, 1945, 7147 (as found in NCNW Papers, ser. 5, box 12, folder 210); Hedgeman to Bethune, telegram, July 3, 1945 (NCNW Papers, ibid.).

90. "Summary and Conclusions from the Final Report of the Fair Employment Practice Committee," June 28, 1946 (NAACP Papers, Washington Bureau, box 69).

91. Opening Statement of Clarence Mitchell, Labor Secretary, at the NAACP Conference, June 28, 1946 (NAACP Papers, Group II, A-34).

92. Ibid.

93. Resolutions adopted by the 37th Annual Conference of the NAACP, June 29, 1946 (NAACP Papers, Group II, A-34); Resolutions adopted by the 38th Annual Conference, June 28, 1947 (Group II, A-37).

94. Meeting with Labor Secretary Lewis W. Schwellenbach, Sept. 11, 1946 (NAACP Papers, Group II, A-118).

95. Mitchell to White, memorandum, Oct. 3, 1946 (NAACP Papers, Group II, A-118).

96. Memorandum from Louis T. Wright to all national board members, branch, and youth council presidents, Aug. 25, 1948 (NAACP Washington Bureau Papers, box 69).

97. Ibid.

98. Ibid.

99. NAACP Annual Report (1948), 53–54.

100. NAACP Legislative Program, 1949 (NAACP Papers, Group II, A-193).

101. NAACP Annual Report (1949), 14–15; Wilkins to Clarence Mitchell, memorandum, May 12, 1950 (NAACP Papers, Group II, A-45).

102. NAACP Annual Report (1950), 17.

103. Draft of White testimony for FEPC hearings, Apr. 9, 1952 (NAACP Papers, Group II, A-259).

104. NAACP Washington Bureau newsletter, Oct. 3, 1952 (NAACP Papers, Washington Bureau, box 143).

105. Reed, *Seedtime*, 339.

106. Granger, "Editorial," *Opportunity* 24 (Winter 1945): 2.

107. Reginald Johnson, "In-Migration and the Negro Worker," *Opportunity* 23 (Spring 1945): 102–103; Minutes of the Meeting of the Board of Directors, June 11, 1945 (NAACP Papers, Group II, A-111).

108. Stephen Kemp Bailey, *Congress Makes a Law* (New York: Vintage, 1964), 9–10; *Congressional Record*, Jan. 22, 1945 (as found in NAACP Papers, Group II, A-111).

109. Minutes of the Meeting of the Board of Directors, June 11, 1945; press release, June 14, 1945 (both in NAACP Papers, Group II, A-111).

110. Perry to White, memorandum, July 10, 1945 (NAACP Papers, Group II, A-111).

111. Letters from White to James E. Murray, Joseph C. O'Mahoney, and Elbert Thomas, June 19, 1945, and Murray to White, June 21, 1945 (NAACP Papers, Group II, A-111).

112. George E. Outland to White, July 16, 1945 (NAACP Papers, Group II, A-111).

113. Report on meeting of national organizations on Full Employment bill, Thursday, July 25, 1945 (NAACP Papers, Group II, A-111); Bailey, *Congress Makes a Law*, 85–88.

114. Statement of Julius Thomas, Aug. 27, 1945, House Committee on Expenditures in Executive Departments, *H.R. 2202, Full Employment Act of 1945* (pt. 4), 79th Cong., 1st sess., 1150–56.

115. Ibid.

116. Statement of Walter White before the Senate Banking and Currency Committee on S. 380, Aug. 29, 1945 (NAACP Papers, Group II, A-111).

117. Ibid.

118. Ibid.

119. Press release, Aug. 30, 1945 (NAACP Papers, Group II, A-111).

120. Morris Llewlyn Cooke to White, Sept. 1, 1945 and White to Cooke, Sept. 7, 1945; Resolution of full employment from national organizations, Sept. 12, 1945 (all in NAACP Papers, Group II, A-111).

121. Press release, Sept. 13, 1945 (NAACP Papers, Group II, A-111).

122. Press release, Sept. 19, 1945 (NAACP Papers, Group II, A-111).

123. Telegram from White to J. W. Fulbright and E. P. Carville, Sept. 10, 1945 (NAACP Papers, Group II, A-111).

124. Telegram from White to Senators Arthur Capper, Leverett Saltonstall, David I. Walsh, Homer Ferguson, Arthur H. Vandenberg, Joseph H. Ball, Alexander H. Smith, Harold H. Burton, and Guy Cordon, Sept. 25, 1945 (NAACP Papers, Group II, A-111).

125. Madison S. Jones to White, memorandum, Dec. 10, 1945 (NAACP Papers, Group II, A-111).

126. Bailey, *Congress Makes a Law*, 92–96.

127. Ibid., 127–49.

128. Ibid., 179–87.

FOUR   Pursuing Social Security

1. Statement of Senator Wagner, Feb. 28, 1939. NAACP Papers, Group I, C-257, Library of Congress, Manuscript Division, Washington, D.C. (hereafter cited as NAACP Papers).

2. Ibid.

3. Memorandum from White to Arthur Springarn, Charles Houston, Thurgood Marshall, and Louis Wright, Mar. 7, 1939 (NAACP Papers, Group I, C-257).

4. NAACP Resolutions, July 1, 1939 (NAACP Papers, Group II, A-24).

5. Press release, Apr. 14, 1939 (NAACP Papers, Group I, C-257).

6. Press release, Apr. 28, 1939 (NAACP Papers, Group I, C-257).

7. Memorandum from Marshall (no recipient indicated), May 9, 1939 (NAACP Papers, Group I, C-257).

8. Press release, May 12, 1939 (NAACP Papers, Group I, C-257).

9. Ibid.; Marshall to CTF (identification not known), memorandum communicated from Washington by telephone, May 12, 1939 (NAACP Papers, Group I, C-257).

10. Marshall to White, letter, May 13, 1939 (NAACP Papers, Group I, C-257).

11. Frances H. Williams to Philip Levy (NAACP), letter, Nov. 27, 1939 (NAACP Papers, Group I, C-257).

12. Draft of letter dictated by Houston for White's signature, Nov. 25, 1939 (NAACP Papers, Group I, C-257).

13. Resolutions adopted by the 31st Annual Conference of the NAACP, June 22, 1940 (NAACP Papers, Group II, A-24).

14. National Lawyers Guild, "The New Wagner-Murray-Dingell Social Security Bill," *Lawyers Guild Review* 3, no. 6 (n.d.): 1–27; reprinted by the National Committee on Social Legislation, National Lawyers Guild, Jan. 15, 1944 (NAACP Papers, Group II, A-521).

15. Leslie Perry to White, letter, Dec. 6, 1943 (NAACP Papers, Group II, A-521).

16. Ibid.

17. Perry to Roy Wilkins, letter, Feb. 11, 1944 (NAACP Papers, Group II, A-521).

18. "Negro Physicians and the Wagner Bill," n.d. (NAACP Papers, Group II, A-521).

19. Press release, Jan. 9, 1944 (NAACP Papers, Group II, A-521); NAACP, *Better Social Security* (pamphlet, n.d.) (Group II, A-17).

20. President Truman to the Congress of the United States, Nov. 19, 1945 (NAACP Papers, Group II, A-117).

21. Ibid.

22. Ibid.

23. Statement of Sen. Robert F. Wagner of New York when introducing the "National Health Act of 1945" on the Senate floor, Nov. 19, 1945 (NAACP Papers, Group II, A-115).

24. Ibid.

25. Ibid.

26. Statement of Dr. W. Montague Cobb in support of the National Health Act, S. 1606, on behalf of the NAACP, Apr. 16, 1946 (NAACP Papers, Group II, A-664).

27. Ibid.

28. Ibid.

29. Resolution adopted by the NAACP, June 29, 1946 (NAACP Papers, Group II, A-34).

30. Murray to Perry, letter, May 3, 1947 (NAACP Papers, Group II, A-664).

31. Perry to Wilkins, memorandum, May 22, 1947 (NAACP Papers, Group II, A-114).

32. Press release from Committee for the Nation's Health, May 22, 1947 (NAACP Papers, Group II, A-114).

33. Statement of Dr. W. Montague Cobb, representing the NAACP before a subcommittee of the Senate Committee on Labor and Public Welfare, July 3, 1947 (NAACP Papers, Group II, A-114).

34. Ibid.

35. Ibid.

36. Committee for the Nation's Health, Inc., Legislative Letter No. 5, Aug. 4, 1947 (NAACP Papers, Group II, A-114).

37. National Lawyers Guild, "The New Wagner-Murray-Dingell Social Security Bill."

38. Perry to Wilkins, memorandum, Nov. 28, 1944 (NAACP Papers, Group II, A-114).

39. Social Security Board, "Facing Forward to Peace, Recommendation from the Tenth Annual Report," *Social Security Bulletin* (Dec. 1945): 1.

40. Ibid., 2.

41. Night letter from White to congressmen, Sept. 17, 1945 (NAACP Papers, Group II, A-114).

42. NAACP Washington Bureau Annual Report, Dec. 31, 1945 (NAACP Papers, Group II, A-59).

43. NCNW, "Action Letter," Mar. 8, 1946, in the Records of the National Council of Negro Women, Bethune Museum and Archives, Washington, D.C., ser. 5, box 11, folder 195 (hereafter cited as NCNW Papers).

44. Statement of Mary McLeod Bethune before the House Ways and Means Committee, Mar. 13, 1946 (NCNW Papers, ser. 5, box 11, folder 195).

45. Resolutions adopted at the 37th Annual Conference of the NAACP, June 26, 1946 (NAACP Papers, Group II, A-34); Resolutions passed at the 11th Annual Convention of the NCNW, Nov. 11–15, 1946 (NCNW Papers, ser. 2, box 2, folder 28).

46. Report of Resolutions Committee, June 28, 1947 (NAACP Papers, Group II, A-37).

47. Martha Derthick, *Policymaking for Social Security* (Washington, D.C.: Brookings Institute, 1979), 430.

48. Testimony of Clarence Mitchell before the House Ways and Means Committee on Revision of Title II of the Social Security Act, Apr. 21, 1949 (NAACP Papers, Group II, A-251).

49. Ibid.

50. Ibid.; NAACP Labor Department press release, Apr. 22, 1949 (NAACP Papers, Group II, A-521).

51. Testimony of Clarence Mitchell, Mar. 15, 1950, Senate Finance Committee, *H.R. 6000, Social Security Revision* (pt. 3), 81st Cong., 2d sess., 1,928–32.

52. NAACP Annual Report (1949); proposed resolutions for the 40th Annual Conference (NAACP Papers, Group II, A-42).

53. NAACP draft of pamphlet, "The New Social Security Benefits"; Minutes of Committee on Branches, Oct. 6, 1950; Gloster Current to Alfred Lewis, letter, Oct. 19, 1950 (all in NAACP Papers, Group II, A-521).

54. Henry Lee Moon to Jim Boyack, letter, Sept. 27, 1951 (NAACP Papers, Group II, A-521).

55. "Will Multiply Jobless Negroes," *News and Courier*, Nov. 4, 1950 (press clipping, city not identified; NAACP Papers, Group II, A-521).

56. Current to Alfred Lewis, memorandum, Oct. 16, 1950; Lewis to Current, letter, Oct. 19, 1950 (both in NAACP Papers, Group II, A-54).

57. A. Maceo Smith to Marshall, letter, Sept. 5, 1951 (NAACP Papers, Group II, A-521).

58. Ibid.; Newsletter, Southwest Region NAACP, Aug. 31, 1951 (NAACP Papers, Group II, A-521).

59. Memorandum from Wilkins to editors, n.d., c. 1950 (NAACP Papers, Group II, A-54).

60. L. P. Chambers to the NAACP, letter, Oct. 3, 1951; Constance Motley to Chambers, memorandum, Oct. 15, 1951; Current to Alfred Lewis, letter, Oct. 19, 1950 (all in NAACP Papers, Group II, A-521).

61. NAACP Annual Report (1950).

62. Resolutions made at the 1951 Annual Conference (NAACP Papers, Group II, A-48).

FIVE   Opposing "Liberal" Policies: The 1950s

1. Minutes of Meeting of Board Committee on Legislation, Dec. 14, 1948. NAACP Papers, Group II, A-135, Library of Congress, Manuscript Division, Washington, D.C. (hereafter cited as NAACP Papers).

2. Minutes of the Meeting of the Board of Directors, Jan. 3, 1949, New York City (NAACP Papers. Group II, A-135).

3. Perry to White, memorandum, Dec. 8, 1948 (NAACP Papers, Group II, A-135). White sent Perry's memo to Roy Wilkins for his reaction. Wilkins added handwritten comments saying he would "go along with Leslie on main points. *BUT* what do we do on Fed Aid to Education?"

4. Wilkins to Perry, letter, Apr. 25, 1945 (NAACP Papers, Group II, H-2). Wilkins informed Perry that the ACLU wanted to know the NAACP's position "to guide them in the position they should take. He said he did not want to be in opposition to 'their colored friends,' but he thought the question of principle an important one."

5. From Legislative Program adopted at the NAACP's 38th Annual Meeting, held January 6, 1947, New York City (emphasis added). On other matters explicitly relating to the social welfare agenda, the statement included: "A bill to broaden the Social Security Act so as to include domestics and agricultural workers"; "A minimum wage bill providing a floor of 75 cents an hour for employees producing goods for interstate commerce"; "A bill, either the Wagner-Murray-Dingell bill as introduced in the 79th Congress, or an adequate

variation thereof"; and "Maintenance of rent controls" (NAACP Papers. Group II, A-112).

6. Perry to Wilkins, Apr. 28, 1947 (NAACP Papers, Group II, A-664).

7. Statement of Perry before the Senate Subcommittee on Education in Support of Federal Aid to Education, S. 472, Apr. 25, 1947 (NAACP Papers, Group II, A-664). The NAACP believed that the U.S. Commission on Education (and not a state official) should have the primary authority to oversee nondiscrimination, and elaborate procedures were recommended for auditing the expenditures of funds and otherwise monitoring the activities of local and state educational officials.

8. Ibid. (p. 4 of NAACP document).

9. Resolution adopted by the 38th Annual Conference of the NAACP, Washington, D.C., June 28, 1947 (NAACP Papers, Group II, A-34). At this meeting Truman became the first president to speak before an NAACP Conference. His forceful declarations in favor of civil rights were heartily welcomed by the group. Truman said: "We can no longer afford the luxury of a leisurely attack upon prejudice and discrimination. . . . We cannot, any longer await the growth of a will to action in the slowest state or the most backward community. Our national government must show the way." See Donald R. McCoy and Richard T. Ruetten, *Quest and Response: Minority Rights and the Truman Administration* (Lawrence: University Press of Kansas. 1973), 74.

10. *Shelley v. Kraemer*, 334 U.S. 1 (1948). The Court ruled: "We hold that in granting judicial enforcement of the restrictive agreements in these areas, the States have denied petitioners the equal protection of the laws and that, therefore, the action of the state courts cannot stand."

11. Resolution adopted by the 39th Annual Conference of the NAACP. Kansas City, Mo., June 26, 1948; emphasis added (NAACP Papers. Group II, A-34).

12. S. 712 was a bill to amend the National Housing Act to provide direct loans and incentives to private builders for the construction of homes for persons whose incomes were in excess of that required for eligibility for public housing.

13. Statement of Perry before the Senate Banking and Currency Subcommittee on S. 138 and S. 712, bills to provide a comprehensive housing program, Feb. 16, 1949 (NAACP Papers, Group II, A-114).

14. Ibid. The NAACP also wanted the proposed slum clearance bill "to give preference" in the selection of tenants for the new housing "to families displaced therefrom because of clearance and redevelopment activity."

15. Perry to White, Wilkins, and Marshall, Apr. 28, 1949 (NAACP Papers, Group II, A-114).

16. Draft of letter to branches on public housing program, Sept. 26, 1949, prepared by Henry Lee Moon (NAACP Papers, Group II, A-114).

17. Franklin Horne to Clarence Mitchell, letter, Sept. 16, 1949 (NAACP Washington Bureau Papers, box 91). Section 223(K) of the provision read:

223. Labor

(K) Nondiscrimination. The Local Authority will require that there shall be no discrimination by reason of race, creed, color, national origin or political affiliations against any employee or applicant for employment qualified by training and experience for work in the construction of projects. In order to give effect to this requirement, insofar as it may affect Negro employees on construction, the Local Authority shall insert in all construction contracts a provision that payment to Negro skilled and unskilled labor of stipulated percentages of the amount paid under the contract for such labor shall be considered prima facie evidence that the contractor has not discriminated against Negro labor. The amounts of the stipulated percentages are to be based upon the number of Negro skilled and unskilled laborers employed in construction work in the locality of the project, as reflected by the latest Federal Census.

18. Memorandum from Perry to NAACP branches (Subject: Federal Public Housing and Slum Clearance), Nov. 4, 1949 (NAACP Papers, Group II, A-114). (Later, popular discussion of the "Urban Renewal" program would be described as "Negro Removal" because, in many cities, what the NAACP had warned against was precisely what happened, leading to the development of more concentrated slums.)

19. Fund-raising, always a concern, was discussed: foundations would be pursued; support from labor unions would be sought. Eddie Cantor, the entertainer, would be asked to give a benefit performance, Oscar Hammerstein to set up a benefit performance of *South Pacific* at $60 a seat.

20. Minutes of the Meeting of the Board of Directors, May 9, 1949, New York City (NAACP Papers, Group II, A-135). The resolutions of the 1949 annual convention also contained the following language on health: "The Association endorses in principle the National Health Program proposed by S. 1679, H.R. 4312 and H.R. 4313. However, none of these bills contains adequate provision against segregation in health facilities and medical schools. No health program for the American people can adequately meet the serious health needs of the Negroes unless it assures that the program will be administered entirely without segregation or discrimination because of race, creed, color or national origin. The Association will support such a program only if amendments are made to provide against such basic evil." Resolutions adopted by the 40th Annual Convention of the NAACP, Los Angeles, July 16, 1949 (NAACP Papers, Group II, A-38).

21. See William E. Juhnke, "President Truman's Committee on Civil Rights: The Interaction of Politics, Protest, and Presidential Advisory Commission." *Presidential Studies Quarterly* 19, no. 3 (Summer 1989): 593–610 (quotation at 594).

22. The members of the PCCR were: Charles E. Wilson, president of General Electric (chairman); Charles Luckman, president of Lever Brothers; James Carey, secretary-treasurer of the CIO; Boris Shiskin, economist for the AFL; John Dickey, president of Dartmouth College; Frank P. Graham, president of the University of North Carolina; Dorothy M. Tilly, philanthropist, Atlanta, Ga.; Sadie Alexander, attorney, Philadelphia (African-American); Channing Tobias, officer, YMCA, and Phelps Stokes Fund (African-American); Morris L. Ernst, attorney, New York; Francis P. Matthews, corporate attorney, Omaha, Neb.; Franklin D. Roosevelt, Jr., attorney; Frank J. Haas, Catholic bishop, Mich.; Henry Knox Sherrill, Episcopal bishop, Mass.; Roland B. Gittelsohn, rabbi, New York.

23. Robert Carr, *Federal Protection of Civil Rights: Quest for a Sword* (Ithaca, N.Y.: Cornell University Press, 1947).

24. White to NAACP Branch Officers, "Re: *President's Committee on Civil Rights*," Jan. 14, 1947 (NAACP Papers, Group II, A-481). National officers Robert L. Carter, Donald Jones, and Hubert Delany had suggested slightly different language on this point: "The appointment of this committee was partially a result of NAACP's demands on the Federal Government to investigate the rise of lynchings in America and to take action to stop flagrant denials of civil rights." Walter White changed this (with Thurgood Marshall doing the memorandum) to the wording cited. In both drafts, civil rights violations were the main focus.

25. Perry to White, letter, Jan. 15, 1947 (NAACP Papers, Group II, A-481).

26. Ibid.

27. Robert L. Carter to White, letter, Mar. 12, 1947 (NAACP Papers, Group II, A-481). Clarence Mitchell, then the NAACP's labor secretary, stressed the need for an FEPC law; Mitchell to White, letter, Apr. 14, 1947 (NAACP Papers, Group II, A-181).

28. Juhnke, "President Truman's Committee," 601.

29. President's Committee on Civil Rights, *To Secure These Rights* (Washington, D.C.: GPO, 1947). Professor Juhnke's article (see n. 21, above) is an excellent account of the internal deliberations of the PCCR.

30. Eight years later, Walter White described the PCCR's report as one of the "eight great epochs of the history of the Negro in America." Remarks by White at the Annual Meeting of the NAACP, Jan. 3, 1955 (NAACP Papers, Group II, A-267).

31. Letter from Dean Charles H. Thompson, Howard University, to White, Jan. 7, 1948 (NAACP Papers, Group II, H-2). By "two distinguished committees" Dean Thompson was referring to another report from a different group, the Commission on Higher Education, which he said had "recommended no federal money be paid any state that insisted upon segregation."

32. Ibid.

33. "Negroes' Stake in Housing Legislation," NCNW newsletter, Apr. 12, 1949, Washington, D.C. (NAACP Papers, Group II, A-114).

34. Smith to Donald Jones, Office of Director of Branches, letter, Apr. 27, 1949 (NAACP Papers, Group II, A-114).

35. Perry to Marshall, letter, Apr. 22, 1949 (NAACP Papers, Group II, A-114).

36. Ibid. Another NAACP staff member, however, disagreed with this concession: "As to the second proposal, in my opinion, it is absolutely meaningless. I gather it is intended to prevent race restrictive covenants in deeds and leases on property acquired through the power of eminent domain. It would appear to be the assumption of the framers of this clause that a race restrictive covenant is 'contrary to law.' A more conservative reading of the opinion of Mr. Justice Vinson would lead us to the conclusion that the insertion of a restrictive covenant is not against the law, the covenant being simply unenforceable." "MWP" to Perry, letter, May 12, 1949 (ibid.)

37. Charles Abrams to Mitchell, letter, July 21, 1955 (NAACP Washington Bureau Papers, box 91).

38. Mitchell to Abrams, letter, July 29, 1955 (NAACP Washington Bureau Papers, box 91). In this "Dear Charlie" letter, Mitchell felt compelled to admonish his friend on his use of the term "rider," as well as his logic. He wrote: "First, you brand our amendment as a rider. In Washington, and elsewhere, a rider is something not germane to a bill. Here the term is used to place supporters of a good cause on the defensive. It is like the 'do you want your daughter to marry a Negro' type of reasoning. . . . Third, you mention that the House Select Committee on Lobbying Activities revealed that the 'anti-discrimination rider was conceived as a ruse by the real estate lobby.' This is like calling Roosevelt a communist because our government had a meeting at Yalta."

39. Randolph to Abraham Multer (D, N.Y.), House Banking and Currency Committee, Washington, D.C., June 27, 1955 (NAACP Washington Bureau Papers, box 91).

40. Mitchell to Paul H. Douglas, letter, June 27, 1955 (NAACP Washington Bureau Papers, box 91).

41. Charles V. Hamilton, *Adam Clayton Powell, Jr.: The Political Biography of an American Dilemma* (New York: Athenaeum, 1991), ch. 10.

42. Wilkins to Mitchell, letter, Apr. 5, 1950 (NAACP Washington Bureau Papers, box 70).

43. Mitchell, quoted in letter from Wilkins to Edward M. Turner, president of Michigan State Conference of NAACP Branches, Feb. 23, 1955 (NAACP Washington Bureau Papers, box 70).

44. Ibid. Mitchell was responding to Sen. Patrick McNamara (D, Mich.), who had stated that "we in Michigan feel as strongly as anybody in the country about the segregation problem, because we never had it." Senator McNamara believed that the amendment would "kill [federal assistance] for the whole country, your people in the North as well as your people in the South." Mitchell reminded the Michigan senator that even his state was not above reproach, citing Benton Harbor and Pontiac "where local school boards either have built or plan to build schools in such locations as to make them segregated schools." This reminder signaled an issue—de facto segregation in the North—that would be a major item of the civil rights agenda in the decades to come.

45. Marshall to Mitchell, memorandum, Jan. 24, 1956 (NAACP Washington Bureau Papers, box 71).

46. Press release, "News from the National Education Association," including statement of Evelyn A. Casey, teacher and chairman of the Legislative Commission of the NEA, Jan. 25, 1956 (NAACP Washington Bureau Papers, box 71).

47. Ibid.

48. Arthur J. Goldberg to George Meany, letter, Jan. 16, 1956 (NAACP Washington Bureau Papers, box 71).

49. Press release, "News from the UAW-CIO," Jan. 26, 1956 (NAACP Washington Bureau Papers, box 71).

50. Ibid.

51. Herold C. Hunt, Under Secretary, HEW, to Mitchell, letter, Dec. 20, 1955 (NAACP Washington Bureau Papers, box 86).

52. In April 1956 Roy Wilkins noted this fact and urged the NAACP's branches to step up their campaign in light of three developments: an announcement by

the White House that the president would not withhold funds; a "Southern Manifesto" issued by one hundred southern congressmen and senators calling the Supreme Court's decision "illegal" and pledging to oppose it; and news that "a mob at the University of Alabama stoned Autherine Lucy and drove her from the campus February 6. This action was praised officially in a resolution passed by the Alabama legislation." Wilkins to NAACP Branch Officers, letter, Apr. 24, 1956 (NAACP Washington Bureau Papers, box 71).

Congressman Abraham J. Multer had written Clarence Mitchell earlier, observing that the executive branch had the power to withhold aid from a segregated school district. He felt that a legislative amendment would jeopardize federal aid to education to those states that did not deserve to be hurt. Multer to Mitchell, Feb. 15, 1956 (NAACP Washington Bureau Papers, box 71).

53. Bruce B. Johnson to Adam Clayton Powell, Jr., Jan. 15, 1956 (NAACP Washington Bureau Papers, box 157). Powell sent the letter to Clarence Mitchell with the handwritten notation at the top: "Mitchell, what do you think?" Mitchell's reaction was predictable; the NAACP was not buying. Another writer, the executive secretary of the Federation of Churches of Rochester and Vicinity, and a minister, wrote to Powell that the Supreme Court had given "us a pattern for desegregation." The Supreme Court, in other words, had already laid out a timely path and procedure for desegregation. Powell also sent this letter to Mitchell, but with another handwritten notation: "Mitchell, this man is crazy!" Rev. Hugh Chamberlin Burr to Powell, May 11, 1956 (NAACP Washington Bureau Papers, box 151).

54. Telegram from Theodore E. Brown to several senators, Mar. 4, 1955 (NAACP Washington Bureau Papers, box 70).

55. Six-page, single-spaced memorandum from Phineas Indritz to AVC Officers, Jan. 31, 1956 (NAACP Washington Bureau Papers, box 71).

56. Wilkins to Faith Rich, telegram, May 12, 1955 (NAACP Washington Bureau Papers, box 70). Senator Douglas had advised his Illinois constituents that the Supreme Court's 1954 decision was the law of the land, and now "we are in a stronger position than in the housing debate of 1949." Douglas to "Dear Friend," Mar. 11, 1955 (NAACP Papers, Group II, A-267).

57. Wilkins to Illinois NAACP Branch Presidents, Mar. 4, 1955; note from Wilkins to Mitchell, Mar. 4, 1955 (both in NAACP Washington Bureau Papers, box 70).

58. Notes of meeting with Sen. Gordon Allott (unsigned), Apr. 14, 1955 (NAACP Washington Bureau Papers, box 70). The notes also indicate that this was the position of Sen. Irving Ives (R, N.Y.). The NAACP carefully explained that it was a nonpartisan organization that sought support from both major parties "in favor of civil rights."

59. Remarks by Rep. Stewart L. Udall on "Introducing [the] Federal Aid Bill to Implement the School Integration Decision of the United States Supreme Court," House of Representatives, June 14, 1955 (NAACP Papers, Group II, A-267).

60. Udall to Mitchell, July 1, 1955 (NAACP Washington Bureau Papers, box 71).

61. Mitchell to Udall, July 7, 1955 (NAACP Papers, Group II, A-267).

62. Memorandum on the Powell Amendment, undated but signed Alfred Baker Lewis (NAACP Washington Bureau Papers, box 71).

63. Lewis calculated that if the thirty-five ADA student members who voted for the amendment were not counted, and "only the votes from adults" were counted, then very likely even the liberal ADA would have not have supported the amendment.

64. See n. 62, above. Interestingly, Lewis had written an earlier letter (undated) to newspapers supporting the NAACP's efforts in this tactic.

65. J. H. White, president, Mississippi Vocational College, to Congressman Powell, telegram, July 6, 1956 (NAACP Washington Bureau Papers, box 71).

66. Mitchell to J. H. White, letter, July 10, 1956 (NAACP Washington Bureau Papers, box 71).

SIX   Confronting an Ally: Organized Labor

1. Wilkins, quoted in Ray Marshall, *The Negro and Organized Labor* (New York: Wiley, 1965), 75.

2. Proposed Resolutions, June 8, 1949. NAACP Papers, Group II, A- 42, Library of Congress, Manuscript Division, Washington, D.C. (hereafter cited as NAACP Papers).

3. Ibid.

4. Statement of Clarence Mitchell before the Senate Subcommittee on Labor and Public Welfare on Amendments to the Fair Labor Standards Act, May 11, 1955 (NAACP Washington Bureau Papers, box 133).

5. Wilbur H. Baldinger to Mitchell, letter, Apr. 27, 1955 (NAACP Washington Bureau Papers, box 133).

6. Letter from Mitchell to the Minimum Wage and Industrial Safety Board of the District of Columbia, May 15, 1951 (NAACP Washington Bureau Papers, box 133). In this same year the NAACP endorsed the Brannan Farm Price Support Plan for farmers.

7. Report from Hill to the Honorable Averell Harriman (then governor of New York) on Migratory Farm Labor in the State of New York, Aug. 14, 1958 (NAACP Washington Bureau Papers, box 143).

8. Cited in the Statement of Joseph C. Waddy (accompanied by Clarence Mitchell) on S. 3295 to Amend the Railway Labor Act before a Subcommittee of the Senate Labor and Education Committee, May 15, 1950 (NAACP Washington Bureau Papers, box 160).

9. Ibid.

10. Since Waddy was also general counsel for the International Association of Railway Employees, the Association of Colored Railroad Trainmen and Locomotive Firemen, and the Colored Trainmen of America, the NAACP had asked him to speak on its behalf.

11. Statement of Joseph C. Waddy on S. 3295, May 15, 1950.

12. Letter from George E. Brown to Walter White, Aug. 24, 1950 (NAACP Washington Bureau Papers, box 160).

13. White to Brown, Aug. 31, 1950 (ibid). In reporting this exchange of letters to the NAACP's Board of Directors, White stated: "We also suggested that a great deal of time would be saved in the future if those interested in legislation of this kind would see that it contained appropriate language when it is first drawn up." The NAACP was supported by the United Transport Service Employees (CIO) in testimony (undated) before the House Committee on Interstate and Foreign Commerce given by George L. P. Weaver (NAACP Washington Bureau Papers, box 160).

14. Editorial, *Crisis* 63 (Jan. 1956): 35.

15. Report by Hill to the Annual Meeting of the NCAAP, Jan. 3, 1960, New York City. Cited in Philip S. Foner, Ronald L. Lewis, and Robert Crosnyek, eds., *The Black Worker Since the AFL-CIO Merger, 1955–1980* (Philadelphia: Temple University Press. 1984), 162–69.

16. See Marshall, *The Negro and Organized Labor;* Herbert R. Northrup and Richard L. Rowan, eds., *The Negro and Employment Opportunity* (Ann Arbor: University of Michigan, Bureau of Industrial Relations, 1965); Foner, Lewis, and Crosnyek, eds., *The Black Worker Since the AFL-CIO Merger.*

17. The other was Willard Townsend, president of the CIO's United Transport Service Employees and a board member of the National Urban League (NUL).

18. See Jervis Anderson, *A. Philip Randolph: A Biographical Portrait* (New York: Harcourt Brace Jovanovich, 1973), quote at 302.

19. Anderson, *A. Philip Randolph*, 303–305.

20. Ibid., 71.

21. "Memorandum on Civil Rights in the AFL-CIO," submitted by Randolph at the AFL-CIO's Executive Council meeting at Unity House, Pa. (June 25–30, 1961), A. Philip Randolph Papers, FEPC, box 23, Library of Congress, Manuscript Division (hereafter, Randolph Papers).

22. "Memorandum on Civil Rights in the AFL-CIO."

23. Ibid.

24. AFL-CIO press release, Oct. 13, 1961. Cited in Foner, Lewis, and Crosnyek, eds., *The Black Worker Since the AFL-CIO Merger*, 131–33.

25. Editorial, *Crisis* 68 (Nov. 1961): 566.

26. Ibid.

27. Randolph suggested the following Negroes: Roy Wilkins, NAACP; Martin Luther King, Jr., SCLC; Lester Granger, NUL; James Farmer, CORE; Bishop S. L. Green, African Methodist Episcopal Church; Rev. Gardiner Taylor, Brooklyn, and a member of New York City's Board of Education; Dr. James Nabrit, president of Howard University; and John Sengstacke, president, National Newspaper Publishers Association.

28. The suggested Negro trade unionists for this meeting were: Horace Sheffield, United Automobile Workers, Detroit; Jack Kemp, Building Service Employees, Chicago; Joseph Beavers, Hotel and Restaurant Employees, Washington, D.C.; Eugene Frazier, United Transport Service Employees, Chicago; David Alston, International Longshoremen's Association, Norfolk; Milton P. Webster, BSCP, Chicago; John Thornton, United Steelworkers Union, Wash-

ington, D.C.; Russell Lasley, Packinghouse Workers, Chicago; and Leroy Ford, Laborers Union, Washington, D.C.

29. Randolph, memorandum, "Widening Gulf Between Leaders of Negro and Labor Communities"; attached to June 1961 memorandum, "Memorandum on Civil Rights in the AFL-CIO" (Randolph Papers, box 23).

30. Document in possession of the authors.

31. Randolph, memorandum, "Re: New York NALC Newsletter, May-June, 1962," May 28, 1962 (Randolph Papers, box 29).

32. "Re: New York NALC Newsletter, May-June, 1962."

33. Ibid.

34. Ibid.

35. He also listed banning nuclear testing by "international agreement among the nuclear powers."

SEVEN   Cautious Optimism: The 1960s

1. Parren Mitchell, quoted in the National Urban League's *State of Black America, 1984* (New York: NUL, Jan. 19, 1984), i.

2. Memorandum prepared by Bayard Rustin, Feb. 1963 (emphasis in the original). CORE Papers, Wisconsin State Historical Society, Madison, MS 14, box 7, folder 8 (hereafter cited as CORE Papers).

3. A. Philip Randolph to James Farmer, letter, Mar. 26, 1963 (CORE Papers, MS 14. box 7, folder 8).

4. Ibid.

5. Farmer to Randolph, letter, Apr. 1, 1963 (CORE Papers, MS 14, box 7, folder 8). Some years later in an oral history interview, Rustin amusingly noted that Randolph refused to raise money, leaving that to others like Rustin. Oral History of Bayard Rustin, June 17, 1969, Lyndon Baines Johnson Library, University of Texas, Austin, AC 74–65.

6. Rustin Oral History, ibid.

7. The NAACP had refused to accept Rustin as chairman of the march, insisting that Randolph take that role. (They had concerns about certain controversial political ideas of Rustin's as well as about his questionable moral past.) Randolph assented only if he could have Rustin as his deputy, which obviously meant that Rustin would remain in charge of the details of the operation.

8. The AFL-CIO's Executive Council endorsed the "principles" of the march but chose not to participate as a sponsor. It had no objection to individual unions participating, and Walter Reuther of the UAW was a main sponsor and one of the featured speakers.

9. *March on Washington for Jobs and Freedom—August 28, 1963*, Organizing Manual No. 1, National Office, March on Washington for Jobs and Freedom, 170 West 130th Street, New York, N.Y. (n.d.).

10. Participants were "strongly advised" not to bring children under fourteen. If a Senate filibuster began before August 28, the National Office planned to send daily waves of approximately one thousand people to Washington to protest the filibuster. If a filibuster began after that date, waves of two thousand per day would be sent.

11. Testimony of A. Philip Randolph before the House Committee on Employment and Manpower, July 25, 1963. A. Philip Randolph Papers, FEPC, box 36, Library of Congress, Manuscript Division (hereafter, Randolph Papers).

12. Ibid. Randolph was referring to the protests in Birmingham, Alabama, in March and April 1963.

13. Ibid.

14. Speech by Randolph at the March on Washington for Jobs and Freedom, Aug. 28, 1963. From *Speeches by the Leaders*, printed as a public service by the National Association for the Advancement of Colored People (Washington, D.C.: NAACP, n.d.).

15. Young, speech, "The Social Revolution: Challenge to the Nation," at the 1963 National Conference of the Urban League, New York (Whitney M. Young Papers, Columbia University, New York).

16. August Meier, Elliott Rudwick, and Francis Broderick, eds., *Black Protest Thought in the Twentieth Century*, 2d ed. (New York: Bobbs-Merrill, 1971), 323.

17. "A Memorandum to the President of the United States," National Urban League, Henry Steeger, president, and Whitney M. Young, Jr., executive director, Jan. 23, 1962. NUL Papers, ser. 1, box 55, Library of Congress, Manuscript Division, Washington, D.C. (hereafter cited as NUL Papers).

18. Nancy J. Weiss, *Whitney M. Young, Jr., and the Struggle for Civil Rights* (Princeton: Princeton University Press, 1989), 144.

19. Whitney M. Young, Jr., *To Be Equal* (New York: McGraw-Hill, 1964). See ch. 39.

20. Young, *To Be Equal*, ch. 39.

21. Whitney M. Young, Jr., "The Role of the Middle-Class Negro," *Ebony* 18, no. 11 (Sept. 1963): 66–71.

22. Young, *To Be Equal*.

23. See Stephen J. Herzog, ed., *Minority Group Politics: A Reader* (New York: Holt, Rinehart, and Winston, 1971), 269.

24. Memorandum from Young to Executive Directors, Urban League Affiliates, June 7, 1963 (NUL Papers, Part III, box 476). Of course, given the confederate structure of the NUL, each affiliate would have to consult its own local board and consider particular local conditions in deciding the nature of its specific involvement. There was no certainty that all the affiliates were of one mind on this new call to activism.

25. Minutes of the Meeting of NUL Board of Trustees, May 21, 1953 (NUL Papers, ser. 11, box 4). See also Minutes of the Meeting of NUL Board, Dec. 15, 1953 (NUL Papers, ibid.).

26. Memorandum from Young to Executive Directors, Urban League Affiliates, June 7, 1963.

27. Testimony of Young prepared for the National Advisory Commission on Civil Disorders, Oct. 1967. LBJ Papers, Lyndon Baines Johnson Library (LBJL), Executive SP/JL, box 48, University of Texas, Austin (hereafter, LBJ Papers).

28. Daniel Bell, "Plea for a 'New Phase in Negro Leadership,'" *New York Times Magazine*, May 31, 1964, 29.

29. Kyle Haselden, "Should There Be Compensation for Negroes? No," *New York Times Magazine*, Oct. 8, 1963, 43.

30. Ibid.

31. CORE's James Farmer agreed that even if legal barriers to racial discrimination were removed, "the Negro would still have an enormous job of 'catching up' to do." He believed that "compensatory programs" in education, employment, and child care "should receive top priority." Memorandum from Farmer to the Taconic Foundation, Apr. 12, 1963. Roy Wilkins Papers, box 32, Library of Congress, Manuscript Division, Washington, D.C.

32. Statement by Randolph at New York Branch NAACP Action Workshop, Salem Methodist Church, New York City, June 13, 1964 (Randolph Papers, box 36).

33. Memorandum and attached Draft (Chapter One, "The Economics of Equality") to Publications Committee (League for Industrial Democracy) from Vera Rony, Dec. 18, 1963.

34. Ibid.

35. Lyndon B. Johnson, Commencement Address delivered at Howard University, Washington, D.C., June 4, 1965.

36. Personal statement by Whitney M. Young, Jr., to the Lyndon Baines Johnson Library, June 18, 1969 (Gift by Mrs. Whitney Young, Nov. 11, 1972). Certainly the same metaphors used by Johnson had appeared a number of times previously in Young's speeches and writings. They were all pointing to the need to do something "special" for those who had been historically discriminated against. (Whitney Young died in Lagos, Nigeria, of drowning on March 11, 1971, while attending a conference on relations between Africa and the United States.)

37. Daniel Patrick Moynihan, *The Negro Family: The Case for National Action* (Washington, D.C., Office of Policy Planning and Research, U.S. Department of Labor, Mar. 1965), 5.

38. Lee Rainwater and William L. Yancey, *The Moynihan Report and the Politics of Controversy: The Negro Family and the Case for National Action* (Cambridge: MIT Press, 1967).

39. This, of course, was a clever allusion to President Truman's 1947 Committee on Civil Rights' report, *To Secure These Rights.*

40. Address by King delivered at Abbott House, Westchester County, New York, Oct. 29, 1965. Cited in Rainwater and Yancey, *The Moynihan Report*, 402–409.

41. Farmer, quoted in Rainwater and Yancey, *The Moynihan Report*, 410.

42. Young, quoted in ibid., 414.

43. Rustin, quoted in ibid., 421.

44. Carter, quoted in ibid., 201.

45. William Julius Wilson, *The Truly Disadvantaged: The Inner City, the Underclass, and Public Policy* (Chicago: University of Chicago Press, 1987), 21. See also Thomas B. Byrne Edsall and Mary D. Edsall, *Chain Reaction* (New York: Norton, 1991).

46. Ronald B. Mincy, "The Underclass: Concept, Controversy, and Evidence," in Sheldon H. Danziger, Gary D. Sandefur, and Daniel H. Weinberg, eds., *Confronting Poverty*, 109–46 (New York: Russell Sage Foundation. 1994), quotation at 111.

47. Carter, quoted in Rainwater and Yancey. *The Moynihan Report*, 201.

48. Lee White to President Johnson, memorandum, "Notes for Meeting with Whitney Young and A. Philip Randolph," Aug. 10, 1965 (LBJ Papers, LBJL, Ex Hu 2, box 3). Lee White stated that Bayard Rustin had been "extremely helpful" in a planning session.

49. See memorandum from James Farmer and George Wiley to Morris Abram and William T. Coleman, Jr., Oct. 21, 1965 (George Wiley Papers, Wisconsin State Historical Society, University of Wisconsin, Madison, MS 324, box 6, folder 9); "Background Paper, White House Planning Conference," by Bayard Rustin, Nov. 1965 (Randolph Papers); Whitney Young to Lee White, Special Assistant to the President, memorandum, Aug. 25, 1965 (NUL Papers, Part III, box 314).

50. "Preliminary Report on the Family: Resources for Change," White House Conference "To Fulfill These Rights," Nov. 1965 (George Wiley Papers, WSHS, MS 324, box 6, folder 10).

51. "Preliminary Report on the Family," 15.

52. Ibid., 5.

53. Ibid., 272.

54. SNCC issued a press release giving its reasons for not attending: the president was not serious in dealing with the root causes of black oppression; the earlier emphasis on the Negro family was an attempt to shift "the burden of the problem" onto blacks; civil rights violations continued unabated in the South with no national executive intervention; the conference was a foil to buttress the president's loss of prestige over the Vietnam War.

And, beginning to indicate a shift in the organization's ideology toward "Black Power," the press release concluded: "We . . . call upon all black Americans to begin building independent political, economic, and cultural institutions that they will control and use as instruments of social change in the country." Press release, SNCC, Atlanta, Ga., May 23, 1966 (NAACP Papers, Group IV, box A-90, Library of Congress, Manuscript Division, Washington, D.C.).

55. Rainwater and Yancey, *The Moynihan Report*, 284.

EIGHT   Pursuing a Liberal Social Welfare Agenda

1. Statement by A. Philip Randolph at the White House Conference, Nov. 18, 1965.

2. Randolph to all solicited signatories, July 11, 1966. A. Philip Randolph Papers, FEPC, box 23, Library of Congress, Manuscript Division, Washington, D.C.

3. Ibid.

4. A *"Freedom Budget" for All Americans: Budgeting Our Resources, 1965–1975, to Achieve "Freedom from Want"* (New York: A. Philip Randolph Institute, Oct. 1966), 9–10 (emphasis in the original).

5. *"Freedom Budget,"* 14.

6. See " 'New Politics' Spokesmen Denounce Freedom Budget and Eastern 'Liberal Establishment,'" *New America* 6, no. 3 (Nov. 18, 1966).

7. *"Freedom Budget,"* 19–20.

8. Clifford L. Alexander, Jr., to Harry McPherson, Jr., memorandum, Oct. 3, 1966. LBJ Papers, Lyndon Baines Johnson Library (LBJL), PR 8–2, box 246, University of Texas, Austin (hereafter, LBJ Papers).

9. Ibid.

10. Wilkins, quoted in *Mittletown (Conn.) Press*, Oct. 27, 1966.

11. Whitney M. Young, Jr., "To Be Equal: The Freedom Budget" (column), *Chicago Defender*, Dec. 3, 1966.

12. Cited in the *St. Louis Post-Dispatch*, Oct. 31, 1966, B2.

13. Quoted in Paul Feldman, "Join Freedom Budget Campaign," *New America* 6, no. 3 (Oct. 31, 1966).

14. T. R. Bassett, "Winston Report to CP Stresses Labor's Role in Negro Struggle," *The Worker*, Dec. 13, 1966. The article indicated that the chairman's comments were received with "prolonged applause."

15. Editorial, "As to the 'Freedom Budget,'" *St. Louis Post-Dispatch*, Oct. 31, 1966.

16. Editorial, "The Freedom Budget." *Washington Post*, Oct. 28, 1966. The *Wall Street Journal* took issue with the call for spending more money, pointing out that there were already numerous scandals and much mismanagement of funds in the antipoverty programs. In addition, guaranteeing an income could "destroy the will or incentive" of many people to seek self-supporting roles "in normal society." Editorial, "A Poverty of Thought," *Wall Street Journal*, Nov. 1, 1966.

17. Bruce Biossat, "Full-Employment Plan," *Washington Daily News*, Sept. 26, 1966.

18. Testimony of Dr. Arthur C. Logan, May 8, 1967, Subcommittee on Employment, Manpower, and Poverty of the Senate Committee on Labor and Public Welfare, *Examination of the War on Poverty* (pt. 6), New York City, 90th Cong., 1st sess., 1769–80 (quotation at 1774).

19. An informative summary of this policy development may be found in Wilbur J. Cohen and Robert M. Ball, "The Public Welfare Amendments of 1962," *Public Welfare* 20, no. 4 (1962): 191–233. See also Clarke A. Chambers, "Special Service and Social Reform: A Historical Essay," *Social Service Review* 37 (Mar. 1963): 76–90; Henry Cohen, "Poverty and Welfare: A Review Essay," *Political Science Quarterly* 87 (Dec. 1972): 631–52; and Charles E. Gilbert, "Policy-making in Public Welfare: The 1962 Amendments," *Political Science Quarterly* 81 (June 1966): 196–224.

20. Memorandum from Jeweldean Jones to Urban League Staff; Subject: Pending Health and Welfare Legislation, May 14, 1962. NUL Papers, Part II, ser. 4, box 4, Library of Congress, Manuscript Division, Washington, D.C. (hereafter cited as NUL Papers).

21. The city of Newburgh, New York, provides an example of such a case and was much in the news at the time, accusing welfare seekers of migrating to the state in search of more generous welfare benefits.

22. Memorandum from Jones to Urban League Staff, May 14, 1962.

23. Joseph A. Califano, Jr., *The Triumph and Tragedy of Lyndon Johnson: The White House Years* (New York: Simon and Schuster, 1990), 149.

24. "Resolution of National Urban League: Medical Care for the Aged Through Social Security," released on June 13, 1962 (NUL Papers, Part II, ser. 4. box 14).

25. "Joint Statement on Health Care for the Aged" for the House Ways and Means Committee, Nov. 5, 1963 (NUL Papers, Part II, ser. 4. box 14). In communicating its support to the NASW, the NUL advised that, in addition to signing the petition, it was seeking an opportunity to appear before the congressional committee itself. Letter from Cernoria D. Johnson to Elizabeth Wickenden, Nov. 5, 1963 (NUL Papers, Part II, ser. 4. box 14).

26. NAACP press release: "For Medical Care Bill," May 6, 1965. NAACP Papers, Group III, A-147, Library of Congress, Manuscript Division, Washington, D.C..

27. Ibid.

28. Resolution adopted by the Board of Trustees, Miami Beach, Florida, Aug. 2, 1965 (NUL Papers, Part II, ser. 4, box 14).

29. Attending the meeting were President Johnson; Vice President Hubert Humphrey; Ramsey Clark; John Doar; John W. Gardiner; Nicholas deB. Katzenbach; Louis Martin; Stephen N. Shulman; Robert C. Weaver; Roger Wilkins; Joseph Califano; Harry McPherson; Jim Gaither; Larry O'Brien; Clifford Alexander; Andrew J. Biemiller; Dorothy I. Height; Father Theodore M. Hesburgh; Barbara Jordan; Clarence Mitchell; Archbishop Patrick O'Boyle; Roy Wilkins; Whitney Young; and Rev. Walter Fauntroy. Martin Luther King was returning from Jamaica where he had been working on his book. There is no reliable record explaining the absence of Randolph and Rustin.

30. All quotes from this meeting are taken from "Memorandum for the President Summarizing the Meeting on February 13, 1967," from James G. Gaither to Marvin Watson, Feb. 15, 1967 (LBJ Papers, LBJL, Executive HU 2).

31. There are several accounts, not always in agreement, of the origin and development of the "war on poverty." See James L. Sundquist, *Politics and Poverty: The Eisenhower, Kennedy, and Johnson Years* (Washington, D.C.: Brookings Institution, 1968); Daniel Patrick Moynihan, *Maximum Feasible Misunderstanding* (New York: Free Press, 1969); Peter Maris and Martin Rein, *Dilemmas of Social Reform: Poverty and Community Action in the United States* (New York: Atherton, 1967); Francis Fox Piven and Richard A. Cloward, *Regulating the Poor: The Functions of Public Welfare* (New York: Pantheon, 1971); John Donovan, *The Politics of Poverty* (Washington, D.C.: University Press of America, 1980); and Jill Quadagno, *The Color of Poverty: How Racism Undermined the War on Poverty* (New York: Oxford University Press, 1994).

32. Transcript of discussions at the Florence Heller School for Advanced Studies in Social Welfare at Brandeis University on June 16–17, 1973, as part of the Conference on "The Federal Government and Urban Poverty," cosponsored by the John F. Kennedy Library and Brandeis University (unpublished transcripts).

33. Ibid., 162–63.

34. Judith Russell, "The Other War on Poverty: The Importance of Ideas in Public Policy-Making," Ph.D diss., Columbia University, 1992.

35. Political scientist James Sundquist noted the exceptional nature of this legislative innovation: "One can search the hearings and debates in their entirety and find no reference to the language—which became so controversial later—

regarding the participation of the poor in community action. The whole novel concept . . . was left to the Office of Economic Opportunity in an exceptionally broad grant of discretion." Sundquist, *Politics and Poverty*, 151.

36. Whitney Young spelled out this dilemma to a House committee in the spring of 1967. The antipoverty programs, he said, "need more money. . . . But we have to put some of that money into the hands of the existing Negro leadership who are the first persons to turn to in the event of a riot, and they turn to us if there is tension and they say to us, 'Why don't you somehow get these people to act right?' Well, you can't get them to act right if they are hungry, all we have to say to them is to relax, that we made a lot of progress, that we just got a Cabinet officer. This does not do anything about that hungry stomach." Testimony of Whitney M. Young, Jr., July 12, 1967, House Committee on Education and Labor, *Economic Opportunity Act Amendments of 1967* (pt. 3), 90th Cong., 1st sess., 2241–2319 (quotation at 2282).

In the summer of 1967, at the height of mass riots in Newark, Detroit, and many other cities, Young was featured on the cover of *Time* magazine. Noting the helpless position of established civil rights leaders in such explosive, volatile situations, the caption over Young's picture quoted him: "You've got to give us some victories" (*Time*, Aug. 11, 1967).

37. *Washington Post*, Jan. 16, 1967, 4A.

38. Testimony of Whitney M. Young, Jr., June 8, 1967, Subcommittee on Employment, Manpower, and Poverty of the Senate Committee on Labor and Public Welfare, *Examination of the War on Poverty* (pt. 7), on S. 1545, 90th Cong., 1st sess., 2195–2255 (quotation at 2195).

39. Joseph Califano to the President, memorandum, Mar. 16, 1966 (LBJ Papers, LBJL, Executive Hu/MC; File Name: Whitney M. Young, Jr., folder). The civil rights and labor leaders at the meeting were Martin Luther King, Jr., Roy Wilkins, Whitney Young, Floyd McKissick, John Lewis, Dorothy Height, A. Philip Randolph, Joseph Rauh, Andrew Biemiller, Clarence Mitchell, and Dave Brody.

40. Joseph Califano to the President, memorandum, Dec. 4, 1968 (LBJ Papers, LBJL, Executive WE 8, box 22).

41. The confederation listed as its members the Polish National Union of America; French, French-Canadian, and Belgian Ethnic Groups; National Slovak Society; Greek Order of Ahepa; Lithuanian R.C. Alliance of America; Supreme Venerable Order Sons of Italy of America; Czechoslovak Society of America; Hungarian Reformed Federation of America; Federation of American Citizens of German Descent in U.S.A.; Russian Immigrants Representative Association; Ukrainian National Aid Association of America.

42. Letter from Paul M. Deac, executive vice president, National Confederation of American Ethnic Groups, to Mr. Lee C. White, assistant special counsel to the president, Dec. 6, 1965 (LBJ Papers, LBJL, WE 9, box 38).

43. Ibid.

44. Roy Wilkins and Clarence Mitchell told a Senate subcommittee that unemployment and underemployment, restricted housing, poor health, and a weak educational system fostered an environment where "crime, drug addiction and immorality flourish." Recognizing that some conditions took time to rem-

edy, "We believe some effort should be made, through increased public works programs, to provide employment for all who are ready, willing and able to engage in useful occupations." Testimony of Roy Wilkins and Clarence Mitchell before Senate Subcommittee on Executive Reorganization, Nov. 30, 1966 (LBJ Papers, LBJL, EX FG 431, box 341).

45. Testimony of Wilfred Ussery, National Chairman, National Council of the Congress of Racial Equality, July 17, 1967, House Committee on Education and Labor, *Economic Opportunity Act Amendments of 1967* (pt. 3), on H.R. 8311, 90th Cong., 1st sess., 2198–2205 (quotation at 2204).

46. Ibid.

47. Whitney Young to President Johnson, letter, Aug. 11, 1967 (LBJ Papers, LBJL, General LE/WE 6, box 166).

48. Testimony of Whitney M. Young, Jr., Sept. 22, 1967, Senate Finance Committee, *Social Security Amendments of 1967* (pt. 3), on H.R. 12080, 90th Cong., 1st sess. (NUL Papers, Part III, box 314). All quotes in this paragraph are from Young's statements during these hearings.

49. Testimony of Dr. George A. Wiley, Sept. 22, 1967, Senate Finance Committee, *Social Security Amendments of 1967* (pt. 3), on H.R. 12080, 90th Cong., 1st sess., 1921–23 (quotation at 1921). All quotes in this paragraph are from Wiley's statements or congressional responses during these hearings.

50. Testimony of Dorothy Height, June 9, 1967, Subcommittee on Employment, Manpower, and Poverty of the Senate Committee on Labor and Public Welfare, *Examination of the War on Poverty* (pt. 8), on S. 1545, 90th Cong., 1st sess., 2555–59 (quotation at 2556).

51. "The War on Poverty—Do We Care? (or) What War on Poverty?" Citizens Crusade Against Poverty, Feb. 19, 1968 (LBJ Papers, LBJL, Executive W E 9, box 31).

52. Ibid.

53. Note from President Johnson to Joseph Califano, Mar. 3, 1968; attached to memorandum from Marvin Watson to the President, Feb. 27, 1968, along with the statement ("The War on Poverty") by the Citizens' Crusade Against Poverty (LBJ Papers, LBJL, Executive W E 9, box 31).

54. Jack Greenberg, *Crusaders in the Courts* (New York: Basic Books, 1994), 430–33.

55. Sen. John J. Williams (R, Del.) pinpointed this fact further by calling for a ceiling to be placed on such subsidies. He entered into the *Congressional Record* a list of cash payments to farmers in 1967 that exceeded $25,000. Five farm operatives were paid over $1 million each; 15 were paid between $50,000 and $1 million each; 388 were paid between $50,000 and $100,000 each. There were 4,881 farm owners paid between $25,000 and $50,000 each. He concluded: "It should be emphasized that the payments are not for food produced or for services rendered but rather they are payments not to cultivate the land." Statement in the Senate by Sen. John J. Williams, released May 23, 1968. Martin Luther King Library and Archives (hereafter, MLKLA), Martin Luther King, Jr. Center for Social Change, Atlanta, Georgia (ser. E, folder 8, box 177).

56. The Reverend Jesse Jackson, a young SCLC staffer, was designated "Mayor" of the "city."

57. Telegram from Rev. Ralph Abernathy, president, Southern Christian Leadership Conference, and Dr. Frank Reisman, director, New Careers Development Center, to Clarence Mitchell, n.d. (LBJ Papers, LBJL, Executive LE/HU 2, box 66).

58. Telegram from Clarence Mitchell, advising of his response to Abernathy's invitation, to Dr. John Morsell (chief assistant to Roy Wilkins), Apr. 21, 1968 (LBJ Papers, LBJL, Executive LE/HU 2, box 66).

59. Barefoot Sanders to the President, memorandum, Apr. 29, 1968 (LBJ Papers, LBJL, Executive LE/HU 2, box 66).

60. The cabinet departments were Agriculture, State, Justice, Labor, Housing and Urban Development, Interior, and Commerce. OEO was also visited. The congressional leaders were senators Mike Mansfield, Everett Dirksen, Russell Long, and Thomas Kuchel. House leaders were John McCormack, Gerald Ford, and Carl Albert.

61. "Statements of Demands for Rights of the Poor presented to Agencies of the U.S. Government by the Poor People's Campaign and Its Committee of 100," Apr. 29–30 and May 1, 1968, 14 (emphasis in the original) (MLKLA, ser. E, III, box 177). A senate subcommittee was asked: "The Concentrated Employment Program which the Labor Department predicted would produce 150,000 jobs by January 1968 produced only 8,000 jobs. Why? What went wrong? Can it be that we are still trying the same old approaches and the same people to try to solve the problems of the poor? We cannot answer these questions. We can only say that we need those thousands of still uncreated jobs. We need them badly. We need them now." And even if the predicted figure was reached, that would still be insufficient: "We need a minimum of one million jobs in the public and private sector this year and another million jobs over the next four years" (ibid, 21–22).

62. "Answer of Poor People's Campaign to the Department of Labor Response" (report), June 13, 1968, 2–3 (MLKLA, ser. E, VIII, box 177). PPC leaders and their followers were learning the political facts of life very bluntly. While Willard Wirtz could, in 1963–64, argue forcefully in deliberations of the administration's inner councils for massive public service jobs as a major emphasis of the antipoverty programs, this latitude was not available to him just four years later, when he had to conform to the administration's line in testifying before Congress.

63. "Report of Meeting with OEO Officials," submitted by Lenneal J. Henderson, May 14, 1968 (MLKLA, ser. E, VIII, box 179).

64. "Critical Action Bulletin," no. 1, June 12, 1968 (MLKLA, ser. E, VIII, box 178).

65. Press release, "Poor People's Campaign Continues—Our Gains So Far," n.d. but circa July 1968 (MLKLA, ser. E, VIII, box 179).

66. SCLC press release, "SCLC Calls Boycott of 'Unholy Ground' in 40 Cities," July 2, 1968* (MLKLA, ser. E, VIII, box 179).

NINE   Welfare Reform and Full Employment: The 1970s

1. ADC was changed to AFDC in 1950 when the caretaker of the child was included in the grant; prior to 1950, benefits had gone only to the children in one-parent households.

2. Daniel P. Moynihan, *The Politics of a Guaranteed Income* (New York: Random House, 1973), 81–83.

3. Blanche B. Coll, *Perspectives in Public Welfare: A History* (Washington, D.C.: U.S. Department of Health, Education, and Welfare; GPO, 1971), 76–80.

4. Richard Nixon, quoted in Vincent J. Burke and Vee Burke, *Nixon's Good Deed: Welfare Reform* (New York: Columbia University Press, 1974), 110 (emphasis in original).

5. Nancy J. Weiss, *Whitney M. Young, Jr., and the Struggle for Civil Rights* (Princeton: Princeton University Press, 1989), 191.

6. Roy Wilkins with Tom Mathews, *Standing Fast: The Autobiography of Roy Wilkins* (New York: Viking, 1982), 339.

7. H. R. Haldeman, *The Haldeman Diaries: Inside the Nixon White House* (New York: Putnam's, 1994), 53.

8. Burke and Burke, *Nixon's Good Deed*, 40.

9. Moynihan, *The Politics of a Guaranteed Income*, 50–51.

10. Ibid., 50.

11. Ibid., 10–11.

12. Burke and Burke, *Nixon's Good Deed*, 48–61.

13. Ibid., 138–44.

14. Ibid., 96.

15. "Summary of National Welfare Rights Organization's Achievements, Prepared for Mrs. Martin Luther King, Jr.," n.d. (George Wiley Papers, Wisconsin State Historical Society, University of Wisconsin, Madison, box 24, folder 4).

16. Testimony of George Wiley for the NWRO before the Fiscal Policies Subcommittee of the Joint Economic Committee, June 12, 1968 (George Wiley Papers, WSHS, box 2, folder 4).

17. "NWRO Proposals for a Guaranteed Income," June 11, 1969 (George Wiley Papers, box 22, folder 4).

18. NWRO press release, June 10, 1969 (George Wiley Papers, WSHS, box 22, folder 4).

19. Moynihan, *The Politics of a Guaranteed Income*, 236–37.

20. "Eyes Only" memorandum from Spiro Agnew to the President, May 16, 1969, Nixon Project. (This material may now be found in the Nixon Papers, Nixon Library, Whittier, California. At the time the papers were collected, the indexing of the papers had not been done and were known as the Nixon Project.)

21. Haldeman, *The Haldeman Diaries*, 55.

22. WIN, created in 1967, emphasized work incentives to reduce welfare rolls. AFDC mothers were permitted to work and keep part of their earnings with no reduction in the amount they received from public assistance. Before WIN, all of the mother's earnings were subtracted from the AFDC grant. The WIN program also encouraged the development of day-care centers and job-training programs.

23. Statement of George Wiley for the NWRO, Oct. 27, 1969, House Ways and Means Committee, *Social Security and Welfare Proposals* (pt. 3), 91st Cong., 1st sess., 1013–39 (also in George Wiley Papers, WSHS, box 17, folder 3).

24. Ibid.

25. Ibid.

26. Statement of Clarence Mitchell, Oct. 23, 1969, House Ways and Means Committee, *Social Security and Welfare Proposals* (pt. 3), 91st Cong., 1st sess., 833–37.

27. Testimony of Whitney Young, Nov. 3, 1969, House Ways and Means Committee, *Social Security and Welfare Proposals* (pt. 5), ibid., 1536–63.

28. Statement of Jewell Shepperd on behalf of Dorothy Height, Nov. 7, 1969, House Ways and Means Committee, *Social Security and Welfare Proposals* (pt. 6), ibid., 1940–43.

29. Ibid.

30. Statement of Hon. John Conyers, Jr., Nov. 13, 1969, House Ways and Means Committee, *Social Security and Welfare Proposals* (pt. 7), 91st Cong., 1st sess., 2329–36.

31. Ken Cole to Ehrlichman and Moynihan, memorandum, Sept. 9, 1969. Daniel P. Moynihan Papers, box 275, Manuscript Division, Library of Congress, Washington, D.C. (hereafter, Moynihan Papers).

32. Moynihan to the President, draft memorandum, n.d (Moynihan Papers, box 275).

33. Moynihan to Ken Cole, memorandum, Sept. 17, 1969 (Moynihan Papers, box 275).

34. *Congressional Quarterly Weekly Report* 28 (Mar. 6, 1970): 702–705.

35. Art to Moynihan, memorandum, May 4, 1970 (Moynihan Papers, box 277).

36. Letter to the Editor, *New York Times*, Apr. 21, 1970 (George Wiley Papers, WSHS, box 17, folder 4).

37. Statement of Whitney Young, Aug. 31, 1970, Senate Finance Committee, *Family Assistance Act of 1970*, 91st Cong., 1st sess., 1748–65.

38. Ibid.

39. George Wiley to Welfare Rights Leaders and Friends, memorandum, c. Sept. 1970 (George Wiley Papers, WSHS, box 17, folder 4).

40. Leonard Garment to Bishop G. Spottswood, June 30, 1970 (Moynihan Papers, box 408).

41. Bishop Stephen G. Spottswood to Leonard Garment, telegram, July 1, 1970 (Moynihan Papers, box 408).

42. Moynihan to Nixon, memorandum, June 30, 1970 (Moynihan Papers, box 275).

43. Radio TV Reports, Inc., "Dr. Daniel Patrick Moynihan Interviewed," July 24, 1970 (Nixon Project).

44. Statement of Whitney Young, Aug. 31, 1970, Senate Finance Committee, *Family Assistance Act of 1970*, 1748–65.

45. Daniel P. Moynihan to Whitney Young, letter, Aug. 31, 1970 (Moynihan Papers, box 277).

46. "Welfare Assistance," NAACP Annual Report (1970), 13.

47. Statement of Clarence Mitchell, Sept. 10, 1970, Senate Finance Committee, *Family Assistance Act of 1970*, 91st Cong., 1st sess., 2095–2102.

48. "NWRO Minimum Requirements for Improving the Family Assistance Plan," Nov. 10, 1970. NUL Papers, ser. 3, box 314, Library of Congress, Manuscript Division, Washington, D.C. (hereafter cited as NUL Papers).

49. Statement of the NUL (by Jeweldean Jones Londa) on Welfare Reform Legislation, Nov. 19, 1970 (NUL Papers, ser. 3, box 314).

50. Burke and Burke, *Nixon's Good Deed*, 161–62.

51. Laurance E. Lynn, Jr., and David deF. Whitman, *The President as Policymaker: Jimmy Carter and Welfare Reform* (Philadelphia: Temple University Press, 1981), 19.

52. Paul Ruffins, "The Black Caucus: 20 Years of Achievement," *Focus: The Monthly Magazine of the Joint Center for Political and Economic Studies* 18 (Sept. 1990): 3–4.

53. "The NWRO Bill," *Congressional Record*, 92nd Cong., 1st sess., 1971, 117, pt. 6:7916.

54. Haldeman, *The Haldeman Diaries*, 181.

55. Alexander Butterfield to Ehrlichman, memorandum, July 11, 1971 (Nixon Project); Moynihan, *The Politics of a Guaranteed Income*, 371.

56. Moynihan, *The Politics of a Guaranteed Income*, 371.

57. NWRO criticism of H.R. 1, n.d. (c. 1971) (George Wiley Papers, WSHS, box 17, folder 3).

58. George Wiley to Members of the Senate, memorandum, Dec. 4, 1970 (George Wiley Papers, WSHS, box 17, folder 4); National Urban Coalition, "Goals and Strategies for Federal Income Support Programs," Aug. 1971 (George Wiley Papers, WSHS, box 20, folder 10); NWRO, "Ways and Means Welfare Bill, H.R. 1: The Gaps in F.A.P.," May 14, 1971, in the Records of the National Council of Negro Women, Bethune Museum and Archives, Washington, D.C., ser. 29, box 9.

59. Statement by Vernon E. Jordan, Jr., on the Social Security Amendments of 1971, H.R. 1, before the Senate Finance Committee, Feb. 3, 1972 (NUL Papers, ser. 3, box 314).

60. Another holdover from FAP was the National Health Insurance Act, which was proposed to solve the "notch effect" problem. The "notch effect" refers to a sudden loss of benefits when a recipient's income comes in just above or just below a cutoff point. In the case of FAP, a family could abruptly lose Medicaid when the head of household's income from work rose above the maximum income allowable for Medicaid eligibility.

61. "NAACP 64th Annual Convention Resolutions," July 2–July 6, 1973, *Crisis* 81 (Apr. 1974): 5.

62. Joseph Califano, Jr., *Governing America: An Insider's Report from the White House and the Cabinet* (New York: Simon and Schuster, 1981), 321.

63. Califano, *Governing America*, 327.

64. Ibid., 322.

65. The 1973 CETA was a special revenue-sharing program enacted during the Nixon administration to consolidate many job-training programs created during the 1960s. State and local organizations contracted with public and nonprofit institutions to provide jobs and training. Thousands of subsidized jobs were created through this act. Eligibility was based on attributed need—one only had to be unemployed to obtain a CETA job. Most of the jobs required some degree of skill, making the program especially helpful to white-collar workers.

66. Califano, *Governing America*, 320–66.

67. Ibid., 362.

68. Ibid., 331.

69. Statement of Maudine Cooper, Aug. 8, 1977, Subcommittee on Housing and Urban Affairs of the Senate Banking and Currency Committee, *Welfare Reform and Housing Proposals*, 95th Cong., 1st sess., 38–40.

70. Califano, *Governing America*, 330–31.

71. EITC was enacted in 1975 to provide tax relief to working poor taxpayers with children.

72. Statement of Hon. Charles Rangel, Sept. 30, 1977, Joint Committee of the House Welfare Reform Subcommittee of the Committee on Agriculture, the Committee on Education and Labor, and the Committee on Ways and Means, *Administration's Welfare Reform Proposal* (pt. 2), 95th Cong., 1st sess., 753–64.

73. Statement of Ronald H. Brown, Oct. 21, 1977, the Task Force on Distributive Impacts of Budget and Economic Policies of the House Committee on the Budget, *President Carter's Welfare Reform Proposals*, 95th Cong., 1st sess., 125–35. Maudine Cooper testified in place of Brown, Oct. 31, 1977, reiterating Brown's statement, Joint Committee of the House Welfare Reform Subcommittee of the Committee on Agriculture, the Committee on Education and Labor, and the Committee on Ways and Means, *Administration's Welfare Reform Proposal* (pt. 3), 95th Cong., 1st sess., 1680–86.

74. Statement of Hon. Charles B. Rangel, May 4, 1978, Subcommittee on Public Assistance of the Senate Finance Committee, *Welfare Reform Proposals* (pt. 5), 95th Cong., 2d sess., 1228–33.

75. Statement of Clarence Mitchell, May 4, 1978, Subcommittee on Public Assistance of the Senate Finance Committee, *Welfare Reform Proposals* (pt. 5), ibid., 1249–55.

76. Communications statement received from the Children's Defense Fund, n.d. Subcommittee on Public Assistance of the Senate Finance Committee, *Welfare Reform Proposals* (pt. 5), ibid., 1317–28.

77. Rangel jokingly told the committee that since he had occasionally been Brown's babysitter when he was growing up in New York, he was certain that Brown's testimony would "be for the family concept which we are so concerned with." Brown replied, "Mr. Rangel has blown my image." This relationship illustrates the informal and expanded access the civil rights organizations had to the legislative process through the Congressional Black Caucus.

78. Statement of Ronald Brown, June 27, 1979, Subcommittee on Public Assistance and Unemployment Compensation of the House Ways and Means Committee, *Welfare Reform Proposals* (pt. 1), 96th Cong., 1st sess., 363–69.

79. Ibid.

80. NUL, *"Full Employment as a National Goal": Proceedings of the 64th NUL Conference, July 28–31, 1974* (New York: NUL, 1974).

81. Ibid., 39–40.

82. Ibid., 40–42.

83. Public Law 523, Oct. 27, 1978, 95th Cong., 2d sess., Full Employment and Balanced Growth Act (H.R. 50), *U.S. Statutes* 92, pt. 2 (Washington, D.C.: GPO, 1979): 1887–1908.

84. Hawkins, letter to the editor, *New York Times*, Oct. 10, 1975.

85. Statement of Hon. Charles C. Diggs, Mar. 24, 1975, Subcommittee on Equal Opportunities of the House Education and Labor Committee, *Equal Opportunity and Full Employment Act* (pt. 3), 94th Cong., 1st sess., 14–24.

86. Statement of the Hon. John Conyers, Jr., Mar. 24, 1975, ibid., 24–37.

87. Statement of Julie Chenault, NAACP Youth Council, Mar. 24, 1975, ibid., 118–19.

88. Testimony of Coretta Scott King, Apr. 4, 1975, ibid., 253–60.

89. Testimony of Donald Webster on behalf of the Atlanta Branch of the NAACP, Apr. 4, 1975, ibid., 290–304.

90. Statement of Lyndon Wade, Executive Director, Atlanta Urban League, Apr. 4, 1975, ibid., 300—308.

91. Statement of Ronald H. Brown, July 7, 1975, Subcommittee on Economic Growth of the Joint Economic Committee, *Employment Problems of Women, Minorities, and Youth*, 94th Cong., 1st sess., 36–42.

92. Ibid.

93. CBC press release, "Testimony of Congresswoman Yvonne Burke," Mar. 16, 1976. Leadership Conference on Civil Rights Papers (LCCR Papers, box K36, folder 2), Library of Congress, Manuscript Division, Washington, D.C. (hereafter cited as LCCR Papers).

94. National Committee for Full Employment Newsletter, May 24, 1976 (papers in possession of authors).

95. Statement of Coretta Scott King, Mar. 15, 1976, Subcommittee on Equal Opportunities of the House Committee on Education and Welfare, *Equal Opportunities and Full Employment* (pt. 5), 94th Cong., 2d sess., 224–26.

96. Speech by Vernon E. Jordan, Jr., Executive Director, NUL, Mar. 18, 1976, Joint Economic Committee, *Thirtieth Anniversary of the Employment Act of 1946*, 94th Cong., 2d sess., 12–19.

97. Ibid.

98. Ibid.

99. "Religious, Labor, Rights Units Join in Full Employment Drive," *Washington Post*, Sept. 9, 1977.

100. "Costs of Jobs Bill," *Washington Post*, Nov. 15, 1977.

101. Walter E. Fauntroy to Yvonne Price, Executive Assistant, NAACP, January 20, 1978; William L. Clay to "Dear Braintrust Member," Feb. 17, 1978; and Parren J. Mitchell to "Dear Supporter," Feb. 15, 1978 (all in LCCR Papers, box K36, folder 8).

102. Statement of Ronald H. Brown, Jan. 26, 1978, Subcommittee on Employment Opportunities of the House Committee on Education and Labor, *Full Employment and Balanced Growth Act* (pt. 2), 95th Cong., 2d sess., 11–16.

103. Ibid.

104. Ibid.

105. *Full Employment Action News*, Mar. 1978 (LCCR Papers, box K36, folder 8).

106. John Carr to "Full Employment Supporters," memorandum, Apr. 18, 1978 (LCCR Papers, box K36, folder 8).

107. John Carr to "Key Full Employment Contacts," memorandum, Aug. 21, 1978; Full Employment Action Council form letter, Aug. 30, 1978,; *Full Employment Action News*, Aug. 1978 (LCCR Papers, box K36, folder 8).

108. NUL Washington Bureau, *Congressional Digest* 5, no. 6 (Dec. 1978): 1–4.

109. Congressman Augustus F. Hawkins, "Statement on House of Representative Passage of Full Employment and Balanced Growth Act of 1978," Oct. 15, 1978 (papers in possession of authors).

110. Public Law 95, Oct. 27, 1978, 95th Cong., 2d sess., Full Employment and Balanced Growth Act (H.R. 50), *U.S. Statutes* 92, pt. 2 (Washington, D.C.: GPO, 1979): 1887–1908.

111. "Humphrey-Hawkins Full Employment Bill," *Congressional Quarterly Almanac* (Washington, D.C.: Congressional Quarterly, Inc., 1979): 272–79.

112. Ibid.

113. Full Employment Action Council, "A Summary of the Full Employment and Balanced Growth Act," n.d. (papers in possession of authors).

TEN   Confronting Conservative Policies: The 1980s

1. Remarks of Edwin Meese III in *The Fairmont Papers: Black Alternatives Conference* (San Francisco: Institute for Contemporary Studies, Dec. 1980), 159–60.

2. *The Fairmont Papers*, xii.

3. Ibid., 8.

4. Ibid., 83.

5. See Thomas Sowell, *Civil Rights: Rhetoric or Reality?* (New York: Quill, 1984); Sowell, *The Economics and Politics of Race* (New York: Quill, 1983); Walter Williams, *The State Against Blacks* (New York: McGraw-Hill. 1982); Robert L. Woodson, *On the Road to Economic Freedom* (Washington, D.C.: Regnery-Gateway, 1987).

6. In the 1980 presidential election, two prominent former associates of Dr. Martin Luther King, Jr., Ralph Abernathy and Hosea Williams, had endorsed Reagan over Carter.

7. Remarks by President Ronald Reagan at the NAACP's 72nd Annual Convention in Denver, Colo.. June 29, 1981. *Weekly Compilation of Presidential Documents* 17 (Washington, D.C.: Office of Federal Register, National Archives and Record Service, General Services Administration, 1981). 699–705.

8. *Weekly Compilation of Presidential Documents* 17:704.

9. Ibid.

10. Lou Cannon, *President Reagan: The Role of a Lifetime* (New York: Simon and Schuster. 1991). 520.

11. *The National Black Agenda for the '80s* (Washington, D.C.: Joint Center For Political Studies, Mar. 1980).

12. Reflective of the broadened political leadership base occurring in the black communities, the conveners were the National Council of Negro Women, National Conference of Black Mayors, the Black Leadership Forum, the National Black Caucus of Local Elected Officials, the National Black Leadership Roundtable, the National Black Caucus of State Legislators, and the Congressional Black Caucus. The NAACP, NUL, Jesse Jackson's "Operation PUSH," the Southern Christian Leadership Conference, the Martin Luther King, Jr. Center for Social Change, and the Joint Center for Political Studies as

well as several prominent black state and local officials took active roles in the meeting.

13. Shelby Steele, *The Content of Our Character* (New York: St. Martin's. 1990).

14. *National Black Agenda for the '80s.*

15. Ibid.

16. Testimony of Raymond Fauntroy, Executive Director, Main Branch, SCLC, Apr. 11, 1980, Subcommittee on Health of the House Ways and Means Committee, *National Health Insurance* (pt. 3), Miami, Fla., 96th Cong., 2d sess., 110–16.

17. Ibid.

18. Testimony of Robert McAlpine, Mar. 13, 1980, Subcommittee on Employment Opportunities of the House Education and Labor Committee, *Youth Employment Act*, 96th Cong., 2d sess., 255–75.

19. Testimony of Maudine Cooper, Deputy Director for NUL's Washington Bureau, Apr. 3, 1981, Subcommittee on Economic Growth, Employment, and Revenue Sharing of the Senate Finance Committee, *Targeted Jobs Tax Credit*, 97th Cong., 1st sess., 46–83.

20. Ibid.

21. Testimony of Althea T. L. Simmons, Director, Washington Bureau, NAACP, Mar. 25, 1981, Subcommittee on Labor of the Senate Committee on Labor and Human Resources, *Youth Opportunity Wage Act of 1981* (on S. 348), 97th Cong., 1st sess., 337–92.

22. Testimony of Maudine R. Cooper, Mar. 18, 1981, Subcommittee on Employment and Productivity of the Senate Finance Committee, *Youth Employment Demonstration Amendments of 1981 (S. 648)*, 97th Cong., 1st sess., 35–46. The other organizations were the National Child Labor Committee, the Opportunities Industrialization Centers (OICs) of America (founded in the early 1960s by the Reverend Leon Sullivan in Philadelphia), the National Puerto Rican Forum, Camp Fire, Inc., United Neighborhood Centers, New York City Mission Society, the National Institute for Work and Learning, Jobs for Youth, the Vocational Foundation, Inc., the National Youth Work Alliance, Girls Clubs of America, Rural New York Farmworkers' Opportunities, Inc., 70001 Ltd., OK–New York, the National Council of La Raza, Youthwork, Inc., the Center for Community Change, and the Fortune Society.

23. Maudine R. Cooper, ibid. The "Prime Sponsor" was a planning council in each service delivery area, whose members were appointed by the chief elected official of the area. The NUL proposed that the council "should include no more than 50 per cent representation from business and industry, at least 15 per cent from community based organizations and representatives of labor, education, veterans and handicapped organizations, the eligible population, and public assistance agencies."

24. Maudine R. Cooper, ibid.

25. Testimony of Ernest Cooper, Regional Director of NUL, Sept. 5, 1986, Subcommittee on Employment Opportunities of the House Education and Labor Committee, *Success of Public/Private Ventures in Employment and Training*, 99th Cong., 2d sess., 44–68. Senator Quayle called this bill his "most comprehensive legislative achievement in the Senate" and "one of the most

important" pieces of domestic legislation during the Reagan years. See Dan Quayle, *Standing Firm* (New York: HarperCollins, 1994), 15, 51.

26. Ernest Cooper, Sept. 5, 1986, ibid. The NUL was perfectly aware—but did not mention—that corporations often assigned their less productive senior executives (those close to retirement or urged to retire, or those with personal problems that made them expendable as far as the profit-making purposes of the company were concerned) to fulfill the company's lip-service to "social responsibility." Such service rarely received top priority in the "bottom line" calculations of many cost-conscious CEOs. On the other hand, any valuable executive who did take time to serve well on the local PIC could eventually find his or her place in the corporation quickly threatened or even usurped by another official on the rise. However, such considerations were seldom voiced in the public, theoretical discourse regarding the actual benefits to be derived from private-sector involvement in social welfare matters.

27. In its annual report, *The State of Black America: 1986* (New York: NUL, Jan. 23, 1986), after calling for a full employment policy, the NUL further urged that a "Universal Employment and Training System should be established that would guarantee the unemployed productive work and the skills training necessary to obtain and hold a job. Such a system would be a joint public-private effort that would include rebuilding the decaying infrastructure of the nation such as its roads, bridges, rail systems and ports, as well as improving public services. . . . The Job Training Partnership Act should be modified so as to become more effective through the provision of increased funding, better monitoring to ensure compliance with program targeting, *and mandated participation of community based organizations*" (178–79; emphasis added).

28. Testimony of Dr. Douglas G. Glasgow, Vice President for Washington Operations, NUL, Mar. 1, 1984, Subcommittee on Domestic Monetary Policy of the House Committee on Banking, Finance, and Urban Affairs, *Building and Sustaining the Economic Recovery: Credit Conditions, Employment, and Economic Prospects* (pt. 8: *The National Perspective*), 98th Cong., 2d sess., 10–187.

29. Ibid.

30. Testimony of Althea T. L. Simmons, Jan. 30, 1981, Senate Appropriations Committee, *Economic Overview FY82, Special Budget Hearings* (pt. 7), 97th Cong., 1st sess., 481–577.

31. Testimony of Maudine Cooper, July 16, 1981, Subcommittee on Savings, Pensions, and Investment Policy of the Senate Finance Committee, *Urban Enterprise Zones* (on S. 1310), 97th Cong., 1st sess., 67–79.

32. Ibid.

33. *New York Times*, Jan. 14, 1989, 8. Civil rights leaders appeared to take some comfort in the fact that the president at least was ending his two terms. "I think that Mr. Reagan is going out of office the same way he came in, fantasizing about civil rights problems," Mary Francis Berry of the U.S. Civil Rights Commission said (ibid). "He seems to have learned nothing from the eight years of his presidency."

34. Some programs (e.g., for child nutrition and subsidies for mass transit) suffered reduced appropriations. Others, for instance public service jobs provided by CETA, were eliminated altogether.

35. In 1987 Congressman David E. Price (D, N.C.) noted that the CBC budget received fifty-six votes in the House. It seldom got much higher than that. See David E. Price, *The Congressional Experience: A View from the Hill* (Boulder, Colo.: Westview, 1992), 91.

36. Testimony of John E. Jacob, Feb. 21, 1986, House Budget Committee, *Impact of the President's 1987 Budget* (pt. 1), 99th Cong., 2d sess., 525–69. Jacob appeared with Benjamin Hooks, executive director of the NAACP.

37. Ibid.

38. Testimony of Althea T. L. Simmons, Mar. 6, 1984, Subcommittee on the Constitution of the Senate Judiciary Committee to consider S.J. Res. 5, *Proposed Balanced Budget/Tax Limitation Constitutional Amendment*, 98th Cong., 2d sess., 181–99. Simmons also reminded the committee of the NAACP's understandably long history of respect for the Constitution as a document that guaranteed "fundamental rights and freedom" and provided a structure and process for governance. "The Constitution should not embody a specific budgetary approach which might be popular today but prove inappropriate in later years" (quotations at 185).

39. Letter to the Honorable Henry Gonzales (D, Tex.), dated Oct. 27, 1981, and signed by the National Urban League, National Low-Income Housing Coalition, Working Group for Community Development Reform, Legal Services Community Development Task Force, National Housing Law Project, the Center for Community Change, National Rural Housing Coalition, Rural America, the California Rural Housing Coalition, the Georgia Housing Coalition, New York State Housing Coalition, Pennsylvania Rural Housing Coalition, and the Vermont Fair Housing Coalition. NUL Washington Operation Papers, Part II, box 9, Library of Congress, Manuscript Division, Washington, D.C.

40. A letter to the Honorable Peter Rodino (D, N.J.) from the National Resources Defense Council, Inc., was also signed by the National Urban League, NAACP Legal Defense Fund, American Lung Association, Congress Watch, Consumers Union, Defenders of Wildlife, Environmental Defense Fund, Environmental Policy Center, the Institute for Public Representation, League of United Latin American Citizens, National Audubon Society, National Consumers League, National Legal Aid and Defenders Association, National Wildlife Federation, United Steel Workers of America, and the Urban Environment Conference.

41. Kent Carter to Maudine Cooper, memorandum, Jan. 11, 1982 (NUL Papers, Washington Operation, Part II, box 10). The coalition consisted of the National Urban League, the National Education Association, Lawyers Committee for Civil Rights, National Committee for Citizens in Education, League of United Latin American Citizens, American Association of School Administrators, and the American Federation of Teachers.

42. See Lucius J. Barker and Ronald W. Walters, eds., *Jesse Jackson's 1984 Presidential Campaign: Challenge and Change in American Politics* (Chicago: University of Illinois Press, 1989); Lucius J. Barker, *Our Time Has Come: A Delegate's Diary of Jesse Jackson's 1984 Presidential Campaign* (Chicago: University of Illinois Press, 1988); Penn Kimball, *"Keep Hope Alive!" Super Tuesday and Jesse Jackson's 1988 Campaign for the Presidency* (Washington, D.C.:

Joint Center for Political and Economic Studies Press, 1992); Katherine Tate, *From Protest to Politics: The New Black Voters in American Elections* (Cambridge: Harvard University Press, 1993); Ronald W. Walters, *Black Presidential Politics in America: A Strategic Approach* (Albany: State University of New York Press, 1988).

43. Cited in Patrick L. Knudsen, "House Leaders Still Pressing Welfare Revision," *Congressional Quarterly Weekly Report* 45 (Nov. 14, 1987): 2805–2808 (at 2805).

44. Senator Armstrong, quoted in the *Congressional Quarterly Weekly Report* 46, no. 25 (June 18, 1988): 648.

45. Representative Downey, quoted in the *Congressional Quarterly Weekly Report* 45 (Nov. 14, 1987): 2805.

46. Julie Rovner, "Daniel Patrick Moynihan: Making Welfare Work," *Congressional Quarterly Weekly Report* 45 (Mar. 21, 1987): 507.

47. Eleanor Holmes Norton, quoted in Rovner, "Daniel Patrick Moynihan," *Congressional Quarterly Weekly Report* 45 (Mar. 21, 1987): 507. Holmes, a signer of the Freedom Budget in 1966, would be elected to Congress in 1990 as a Delegate for the District of Columbia.

48. Moynihan, quoted in Rovner, "Daniel Patrick Moynihan," 506.

49. Clinton, quoted in Julie Rovner, "Difficult Conference Likely on Welfare Bill," *Congressional Quarterly Weekly Report* 46, no. 26 (June 25, 1988): 1764.

50. Kennelly, quoted in Mark Willen, "Cost of Democratic Plan Cut in Half: Modified Welfare Reform Bill OK'd by House Subcommittee," *Congressional Quarterly Weekly Report* 45, no. 15 (Apr. 11, 1987): 682.

51. Moynihan, quoted in Rovner, "Daniel Patrick Moynihan," 506.

52. Dole, quoted in Julie Rovner, "Dole Not Ready to Join Moynihan on Welfare," *Congressional Quarterly Weekly Report* 45, no. 30 (July 25, 1987): 1674.

53. Julie Rovner, "Deep Schisms Still Imperil Welfare Overhaul," *Congressional Quarterly Weekly Report* 46, no. 25 (June 18, 1988): 1648.

54. Ibid., 1650.

55. Testimony of John E. Jacob, Feb. 3, 1987, Senate Committee on Labor and Human Resources, *Work and Welfare* (on H.R. 1720), 100th Cong., 1st sess., 111–81, 222–26.

56. Testimony of Dr. Douglas G. Glasgow, Apr. 29, 1987, House Committee on Education and Labor, *Welfare Reform: H.R. 30, Fair Work Opportunities Act of 1987, and H.R. 1720, Family Welfare Reform Act of 1987*, 100th Cong., 1st sess., 63–166.

57. Testimony of Marian Wright Edelman, Apr. 29, 1987, House Committee on Education and Labor, *Welfare Reform*, ibid.

58. Ibid.

59. Testimony of Marian Wright Edelman, Apr. 1, 1987, Subcommittee on Public Assistance and Unemployment Compensation of the House Ways and Means Committee, *Family Welfare Reform Act*, 100th Cong., 1st sess., 301–53.

60. Ibid.

61. Testimony of Dr. Douglas G. Glasgow, Apr. 29, 1987, House Committee on Education and Labor, *Welfare Reform*, 100th Cong., 1st sess., 63–166.

62. In 1978, Health and Human Services (HHS) became a new department, replacing HEW. Education was made into a separate department.

63. Senator Armstrong, quoted in Rovner, "Difficult Conference Likely on Welfare Bill," 1764.

64. Ibid.

65. Representative Michel, quoted in Julie Rovner, "Southern Democrats Bolt: House Orders Its Conferees to Slash Cost of Welfare Bill," *Congressional Quarterly Weekly Report* 46, no. 28 (July 9, 1988): 1916.

66. Bush, quoted in Julie Rovner, "Bush's Endorsement Is Added Bonus: Welfare Conference Begins, Buoyed by Bentsen's Selection," *Congressional Quarterly Weekly Report* 46, no. 28 (July 16, 1988): 1981.

67. Senator Moynihan, quoted in Julie Rovner, "Daniel Patrick Moynihan," *Congressional Quarterly Weekly Report* 45 (Mar. 21, 1987): 503.

ELEVEN   "New Democrats"—and More Republicans: The 1990s

1. William Julius Wilson, *The Truly Disadvantaged: The Inner City, the Underclass, and Public Policy* (Chicago: University of Chicago Press, 1987), 154–55. In a later book Professor Wilson offered solutions that mirrored in virtually every respect the policies civil rights groups had been proposing for decades. Unfortunately, he did not acknowledge this important component and experience of the social welfare agenda of such groups. See his *When Work Disappears: The World of the New Urban Poor* (New York: Knopf, 1996), especially chapter 8, "A Broader Vision: Social Policy Options in Cross-National Perspective."

2. Wilson, *The Truly Disadvantaged*, 154–55.

3. Carl Rowan, "If Clinton, Blacks Can 'Cool it' for a Little Longer . . . ," *Daily News of Virgin Islands*, Sept. 24, 1992, 12.

4. A. M. Rosenthal, *New York Times*, Oct. 30, 1992, A-31.

5. Robert Pear, "Administration Rejects Proposal for New Anti-Poverty Programs," *New York Times*, July 6, 1990, 1 (quote on p. 12).

6. Bill Clinton, *Putting People First: A National Economic Strategy for America* (Little Rock, Ark.: Clinton for President Committee, 1992), 6–20.

7. Ibid.

8. National Urban League, *Planning to Win: A Marshall Plan for America* (New York: NUL, July 1991), 32.

9. NUL, *Planning to Win*, 36.

10. Ibid., 48. Interestingly, the 1966 Freedom Budget had called for $185 billion over a ten-year period.

11. NUL, *Planning to Win*, 48.

12. Testimony of John Jacob, Jan. 30, 1992, Senate Banking and Urban Affairs Committee, *Economic Conditions of Our Nation's Cities*, 102d Cong., 2d sess., 44–53, 74–152.

13. "Action Alert I: Urban League Affiliate Legislative Advocacy Guide for Implementing the National Urban League's Marshall Plan for America," Jan. 1992. (A sample letter was also circulated.)

14. John E. Jacob, "To Be Equal: Campaign Should Focus on Marshall Plan for America," *Westchester County Press*, Oct. 8, 1992.

15. Documents in possession of the authors, prepared by the NUL's Policy and Government Relations Office, Washington, D.C., Nov. 17, 1992.

16. Eddie N. Williams, "The Clinton Agenda Meets Black Expectations," *Focus* 21, no. 1 (Jan. 1993): 2. Williams added: "It is unlikely that the Clinton administration will fully succeed in meeting all of its own expectations, nor those of black Americans. Despite the administration's best intentions, benefits to black Americans will not flow easily" (ibid.).

17. Jon Healey, "Some Projects Could Wither as Stimulus Bill Languishes," *Congressional Quarterly Weekly Report* 51 (Apr. 17, 1993): 949, 951.

18. The House had passed the original bill on March 19, 1993.

19. Jon Healey, "Democrats Look to Salvage Part of Stimulus Plan," *Congressional Quarterly Weekly Report* 51 (Apr. 24, 1993): 1001–1004 (quotation at 1004).

20. Representative Rangel, quoted in Kitty Cunningham, "Black Caucus Flexes Muscle on Budget—and More," *Congressional Quarterly Weekly Report* 51 (July 3, 1993): 1711–1715 (quotation at 1712).

21. A major dispute did develop, however, regarding the civil rights agenda when the president attempted to appoint Lani Guinier, a black law professor, to the high-level post of head of the Civil Rights Division in the Department of Justice. As a former attorney for the NAACP Legal Defense Fund, she had written a number of professional articles on civil rights. Civil rights organizations, understandably, hailed the nomination. Eventually, however, her views on minority voting rights and means to effect greater protection for black groups previously denied access to the ballot and effective representation, gained widespread attention. Her detractors represented her as favoring racial quotas and demanding other "radical" remedies for blacks. Under pressure from the Senate, Clinton withdrew her nomination, stating that after reading her published work, he concluded he did not agree with many of her ideas in that particular area of civil rights. As might be expected, this action did not endear him to his civil rights supporters. Later he appointed another black, Deval Patrick, who, incidentally, had served with Guinier in the NAACP Legal Defense Fund. Because of its substantive nature, this subsequent appointment did manage to take some of the bitterness out of the Guinier episode.

22. "U.S. Investment Plan to Target Poor Areas," *Washington Post*, July 12, 1994, C1.

23. The surtax was set at $22.50 per $150 of tax liability, with a cap of $800 per person (this could rise to $1,050 in 1993). The monthly premium increased by four dollars.

24. Senator Mitchell, quoted in Julie Rovner, "Authors Defend Catastrophic Insurance Law," *Congressional Quarterly Weekly Report* 47 (Jan. 14, 1989): 86.

25. Julie Rovner, "The Catastrophic-Costs Law: A Massive Miscalculation," *Congressional Quarterly Weekly Report* 47 (Oct. 14, 1989): 2712–2715. This account also indicates that about 3.3 million beneficiaries had protection fully paid for by their former employers.

26. "National Urban League Recommendations for Closing the Gap in Health Status of African Americans—For Consideration by the Pepper Commission" (Feb. 21, 1990). Unpublished document in the files of the NUL's Policy and Government Relations Office, Washington, D.C. (copy in possession of the authors).

27. Rother, quoted in Rovner, "The Catastrophic-Costs Law," 2715.

28. National Urban League Statement, "An African-American Health Care Agenda: Strategies for Reforming an Unjust System." Opening Ceremony, Baltimore, Md., Oct. 31, 1991.

29. Statement by Robert McAlpine at the White House Health Care Task Force Public Hearing on Health Care Reform, Washington, D.C., Mar. 29, 1993.

30. Policy and Government Relations Office, National Urban League, "Special Briefing on Key Legislative Issues," *Congressional Digest* 2 (July, 1993).

31. Memorandum, "Key Issues for African-Americans in Health Care," sent to "Interested Parties," from the NAACP and the NAACP Legal Defense and Educational Fund, Inc., Feb. 2, 1994.

32. "Key Issues for African-Americans in Health Care" (memorandum).

33. Ibid.; emphasis in original.

34. Memorandum, "Proposed Civil Rights Amendments to the Health Security Act of 1993,' sent to "Interested Persons," from the NAACP and the NAACP Legal Defense and Educational Fund, Inc., Feb. 2, 1994.

35. "Proposed Civil Rights Amendments to the Health Security Act of 1993" (memorandum).

36. Ibid. The NAACP and NAACP-LDF suggested the following amended language: "Each alliance area shall encompass a population large enough to ensure that the alliance [INSERT, 'is demographically diverse and'] has adequate market share to negotiate effectively with health plans providing the comprehensive benefit package to eligible individuals who reside in the area" (brackets in original).

37. "Proposed Civil Rights Amendments to the Health Security Act of 1993" (memorandum; brackets in original).

38. This meticulous attention to detailed language in the 1990s is reminiscent of the same process civil rights groups pursued in the 1940s in proposing amended language that sought to "ensure safeguards" against blacks being discriminated against in the distribution of federal funds. (See, for example, ch. 5, n. 17.)

39. "Statement of the National Rainbow Coalition," submitted to the CBC's Legislative Summit on Health Care Reform, Mar., 1994 (unpublished).

40. The NMA further recommended allowing "for additional support services in the comprehensive benefit package for low-income persons with special health needs." The NMA also advocated "a realistic sliding scale for premiums and co-payments for individuals above the poverty level," and reduced copayments of low-income consumers who chose nonnetwork providers. (This last point was probably in anticipation that black doctors with low-income patients would likely be less able to join HMOs or otherwise become affiliated with more organized health care provider groups.) "Statement to the CBC Health Care Forum" by Dr. Walter L. Faggett, representing the National Medical Association, Mar. 1994 (unpublished).

41. "Statement of the NUL," submitted to the CBC's Legislative Summit on Health Care Reform, Mar. 1994 (unpublished). The NUL also supported a provision prohibiting insurers from denying health care coverage on the basis of preexisting medical conditions. Robert McAlpine to Congressman Alan Wheat, letter, June 10, 1994, NUL Files, NUL Washington Office, Washington, D.C.

42. See Lawrence R. Jacobs and Robert Y. Shapiro, "Don't Blame the Public for Failed Health Care Reform," *Journal of Health Politics, Policy, and Law* 20, no. 2 (Summer 1995): 410–23. See also Alissa J. Rubin, "Health, Overall Issue Unlikely to Rest in Peace," *Congressional Quarterly Weekly Report* 52 (Oct. 1, 1994): 2797–2801.

43. "For Health Care, Time Was a Killer," *New York Times*, Aug. 29, 1994, A12 (emphasis added).

44. R. W. Apple, Jr., "The Odds on Health Care: Going from a Good Bet to (Maybe) Even Money," *New York Times*, Aug. 14, 1994, 16.

45. Ibid. (emphasis added).

46. A useful assessment of the Clinton administration's welfare reform proposals may be found in *Focus* 16, no. 2 (Winter 1994–95), a special issue from the University of Wisconsin-Madison Institute for Research on Poverty. See especially Robert H. Haveman and John Karl Scholz, "The Clinton Welfare Reform Plan: Will It End Poverty as We Know It?" 1–9.

47. Hugh B. Price, "To Be Equal: Welfare Reform May Harm the Poor," *Westchester County Press*, Dec. 15, 1994, 12.

48. Ibid.

49. Statement of the Black Leadership Forum, "Public Policy and the 104th Congress," Dec. 28, 1994 (Washington, D.C., unpublished).

50. Peter T. Kilborn, "With Welfare Overhaul Now Law, States Grapple with the Consequences," *New York Times*, Aug. 23, 1996, A22. One Iowa official was quoted as saying: "I don't think anyone out there has the whole bill figured out yet. I think there's a lot of anxiety."

TWELVE   Conclusion: The Future

1. Harry V. Jaffa, "The Party of Lincoln vs. the Party of Bureaucrats," *Wall Street Journal*, Sept. 12, 1996, A14. Jaffa argues for such a race-neutral approach based on socioeconomic class: "Affirmative action, rightly understood, would justify a wide variety of outreach programs for those whose lives have been stultified by poverty, broken families, bad schools, and neighborhoods filled with drugs, crime and gangs. One can heartily commend a program for tutoring young blacks, or young whites, who had never had a genuine teacher in a real class-room." Interestingly, Jaffa states that as a speech writer for conservative presidential candidate Sen. Barry Goldwater in 1964, he argued against Lyndon Johnson's candidacy on the grounds that Johnson would "start vast new federal programs" for fear such programs would "create a new class of dependents upon the Democratic Party." Our argument is that those programs are needed now more than ever, and Mr. Jaffa's call—in 1996—for such "outreach" is somewhat disingenuous in the face of the thirty-year lapse.

2. "Home relief," a state and local program (with no federal involvement) for poor but able-bodied adults with no children, is usually referred to as "general relief" in most other states and localities.

3. "Pataki on the Record: Excerpts from a Talk on Campaign Issues," *New York Times*, Oct. 10, 1994, B4.

4. Alan Finder, "How New Yorkers Feel Budget Squeeze," *New York Times*, Nov. 3, 1995, A1.

5. Richard Pérez-Peña, "Transit Union Agrees to Allow Workfare Plan," *New York Times*, Sept. 19, 1996, A1.

6. Ibid., B5.

7. Steven Greenhouse, "New York Union Leader Urges Halt to Broadening Workfare," *New York Times*, Sept. 23, 1996, A1, B5.

8. Ibid., B5.

9. President Clinton used this phrase in his January 1996 State of the Union address to Congress.

Index

41; on geographic wage differentials, 39

organized labor movement, 109–21, 264; and control of Works Progress Administration (WPA) projects, 25–26; and education legislation, 103–104; and Fair Labor Standards Act, 37; and Family Assistance Plan, 178–79; and hiring decisions for Public Works Administration (PWA), 18; racial tension in, 114; and wage rates, 12–13. *See also* labor unions

Outland, George E., 67, 281*n*112
Ovington, Mary White, 270*n*1

Paris, Guichard, 270*n*2
Patrick, Deval, 312*n*21
Pear, Robert, 311*n*5
Pendleton, Clarence M., Jr., 208
People United to Serve Humanity (PUSH), 225
Pepper, Claude, 244–45, 278*n*41
Pérez-Peña, Richard, 315*nn*5–6
Perkins, Frances, 9, 23, 272*n*59
Perry, Leslie, 59–60, 67, 69, 80, 81, 101, 280*nn*80–81&85–86, 281*n*110, 282*nn*15–17, 283*nn*30–31&38, 284*nn*3–4, 285*nn*6–8&13–15, 286*n*18, 287*nn*25–26&35–36; and housing legislation, 94; and President's Committee on Civil Rights (PCCR), 98; and Social Security Act amendments, 76; and social welfare legislation, 91, 92
Peterson, Paul E., 269*n*6
Piven, Francis Fox, 297*n*31
Plessy v. Ferguson. See Supreme Court decisions
Poor People's Campaign (PPC), 168–74

Powell, Adam Clayton, Jr., 102, 104, 107, 289*n*53
Powell Amendment, 102–103, 107, 131
President's Committee on Civil Rights (PCCR), 63, 96–99, 108
Price, David E., 309*n*35
Price, Hugh B., 255, 314*nn*47–48
Private Industrial Councils (PIC), 220
private sector: discrimination in, 50–51, 56–57; and economic development, 143–44; and jobs, 221; vs. public works wages, 23–25; and right to employment, 70
Program for Better Jobs and Income (PBJI), 175, 194, 195, 197
public assistance, 67, 142, 156, 254; vs. full employment policy, 175; two tiers of, 193, 261–65; vs. unemployment insurance, 87–88
Public Health Service, 73
public health services, 27
public service employment (PSE), 189, 193, 195
Public Works Administration (PWA), 16–20
public works programs, 26–27, 126, 198

Quadagno, Jill, 297*n*31
Quayle, Dan, 219, 307–308*n*25

racial discrimination. *See* discrimination
Railway Labor Act, 112–13
Rainwater, Lee, 136, 141, 294*nn*38&40–41, 295*nn*47&55
Randolph, A. Philip, 35, 39, 40, 54, 55, 101, 140, 147, 156, 166, 276*n*66, 277*n*19, 288*n*39, 291*n*21, 291*n*27, 292*nn*3–5&7&21&27&29, 295*nn*1–3, 298*n*39; and labor movement,